.

This book explores popular support for the Church of England during a critical period, from the Stuart Restoration to the mid-eighteenth century, when Churchmen perceived themselves to be under attack from all sides.

In many provincial parishes, the clergy also found themselves in dispute with their congregations. These incidents of dispute are the focus of a series of detailed case studies, drawn from the diocese of Salisbury, which help to bring the religion of the ordinary people to life, while placing local tensions in their broader national context. The period 1660–1740 provides important clues to the long-term decline in the popularity of the Church. Paradoxically, conflicts revealed not anticlericalism but a widely shared social consensus supporting the Anglican liturgy and clergy: the early eighteenth century witnessed a revival. Nevertheless, a defensive clergy turned inwards and proved too inflexible to respond to lay wishes for fuller participation in worship.

DONALD A. SPAETH is Lecturer in Historical Computing, University of Glasgow

Cambridge Studies in Early Modern British History

Series editors

ANTHONY FLETCHER
Professor of History, University of Essex

JOHN GUY
Professor of Modern History, University of St Andrews

JOHN MORRILL
*Professor of British and Irish History, University of Cambridge, and Vice Master
of Selwyn College*

This is a series of monographs and studies covering many aspects of the history of the
British Isles between the late fifteenth century and early eighteenth century. It includes
the work of established scholars and pioneering work by a new generation of scholars.
It includes both reviews and revisions of major topics and books which open up new
historical terrain or which reveal startling new perspectives on familiar subjects. All the
volumes set detailed research into broader perspectives and the books are intended for
the use of students as well as of their teachers.

For a list of titles in the series, see end of book

THE CHURCH IN AN AGE OF DANGER

Parsons and Parishioners, 1660–1740

DONALD A. SPAETH

CAMBRIDGE
UNIVERSITY PRESS

PUBLISHED BY THE PRESS SYNDICATE OF THE UNIVERSITY OF CAMBRIDGE
The Pitt Building, Trumpington Street, Cambridge, United Kingdom

CAMBRIDGE UNIVERSITY PRESS
The Edinburgh Building, Cambridge CB2 2RU, UK   http://www.cup.cam.ac.uk
40 West 20th Street, New York, NY 10011-4211, USA   http://www.cup.org
10 Stamford Road, Oakleigh, Melbourne 3166, Australia
Ruiz de Alarcón 13, 28014 Madrid, Spain

First published 2000

Printed in the United Kingdom at the University Press, Cambridge

Typeface Monotype Sabon 10/12pt.   *System* QuarkXPress™   [SE]

A catalogue record for this book is available from the British Library

ISBN 0 521 35313 0 hardback

For Tam and Ellen

CONTENTS

TABLES

ACKNOWLEDGEMENTS

This book has been many years in gestation. My work for ten years in academic computing, while rewarding, left me with regrettably little time for research and writing on early modern England. The book had its origins as a Brown University Ph.D. thesis. In considering how best to turn the thesis into a book, I came to conclusion that it was necessary to do more to place the incidents of lay–clerical conflict under review in context. Rather than stitching together a number of scattered incidents on various themes, it seemed worth while investigating whether it was possible to cast light on popular behaviour and belief through a number of in-depth case studies. This ambitious programme involved returning to the archives, in particular to mine the rich sources for Exchequer and Chancery in the Public Record Office. A local approach carries with it the dangers of parochialism, so it is perhaps paradoxical that these case studies have led me to look (from a different angle) at some of the political and religious issues that have tended to occupy historians of this period, providing an inkling of the complex relationship between Westminster and the provinces.

I have benefited greatly from the wealth of scholarship published by historians in recent years on religion under the later Stuarts and the Hanoverians, transforming what was a quiet backwater into one of the most exciting periods in English history. In researching and writing this book I have incurred many debts. While I was still an undergraduate, Michael MacDonald awakened my interest in the beliefs of the common people by introducing me to English social history, and in particular to the work of Margaret Spufford. I was fortunate to be supervised as a Ph.D. student at Brown University by David Underdown, to whose gentle guidance, enthusiasm for popular culture, and love of the West Country I owe much. Tony Molho helped me to obtain a Beneficial Foundation Travel Scholarship from Brown, and my grandparents, Rex and Gertrude Arragon, also supported my research financially. I am grateful to the archives listed in the bibliography for permission to use their material and to the archivists for their advice and assistance. Particular thanks are due to the staff of the Wiltshire Record Office, who always cheerfully dropped whatever they were doing in order to help me, and sometimes gave me access to materials and catalogues not available to the general public. The staff of the British Museum's Department of Prints and Drawings kindly tracked down the print which appears on the dust jacket. I am indebted to those scholars who have allowed me to consult and cite their unpublished theses. An earlier version of chapter 8 appeared in *Parish, Church and People* (1988), edited by Susan Wright, and I am grateful to Hutchinson for permission to reuse this material. I also owe thanks to Jane Freeman, Lionel Glassey, Stephen Hobbs, and Kenneth and Helen Rogers for allowing me to refer to sources they were editing or for access to their own notes and transcripts. Research leave for two terms in 1998 granted by the Arts Faculty of the University of Glasgow enabled me to break the back of writing the book; the Department of History has provided a supportive and friendly scholarly environment in which to work, and my colleagues have given an intelligent hearing in seminars to early versions of several chapters. Jonathan Barry, Sam Cohn, Eric Evans, Lionel Glassey, Colin Kidd, Thomas Munck, Bob Shoemaker and David Underdown have read the whole or part of the book in draft, and I am grateful to them for their insights, suggestions and corrections, although naturally I am responsible for any errors that remain. I would also like to thank Ian Green, Martin Ingram and the editors of the series, Anthony Fletcher, John Guy and John Morrill, for their encouragement and patience. The friendship and hospitality of Jonathan Rumens and Susan Thompson on my return expeditions to Trowbridge have been much appreciated. My parents have always encouraged me in my academic career, and their interest in my progress has helped me to pursue this project to completion. I owe most of all to my wife Tam and my daughter Ellen, without whose support and understanding this book would have been neither possible nor worth while, and it is to them that it is dedicated.

ABBREVIATIONS

Alumni Cantabrigiensis	J. Venn and J. A. Venn, *Alumni Cantabrigiensis, Part I* (Cambridge, 1922–54)
Alumni Oxoniensis	J. Foster, *Alumni Oxoniensis, Part I* (Oxford and London, 1888–91)
BL	British Library
Burnet, *Pastoral Care*	*A Discourse of the Pastoral Care* (London, 1692)
CSPD	*Calendar of State Papers Domestic*
DNB	*Dictionary of National Biography* (London, 1899)
Foxcroft	H. C. Foxcroft, ed., *A Supplement to Burnet's History of My Own Time* (Oxford, 1902)
Matthews, *Calamy Revised*	A. G. Matthews, *Calamy Revised: Being a Revision of Edmund Calamy's Account of the Ministers and others Ejected and Silenced, 1660–2* (Oxford, 1934)
Matthews, *Walker Revised*	A. G. Matthews, *Walker Revised: Being a Revision of John Walker's Sufferings of the Clergy during the Grand Rebellion* (Oxford, 1948)
PRO	Public Record Office
Turner, *Original Records*	G. L. Turner, ed., *Original Records of Early Nonconformity* (London, 1911), vol. I
VCH *Wilts.*	The Victoria History of the Counties of England, *A History of Wiltshire*
WAM	*Wiltshire Archaeological Magazine*
Whiteman, *Compton Census*	Anne Whiteman, ed., *The Compton Census of 1676: A Critical Edition* (London, 1986)
WRO	Wiltshire Record Office

Most of the references to sources in the Wiltshire Record Office are in the form D1/39/1 or 1232/10. In the former case, the WRO has been omitted to save space; in the latter, WRO has been included, since the numbers on their own may be ambiguous.

In the text dates are given in Old Style but the year is taken to begin on 1 January. Quotations are given in their original spelling and punctuation.

Case studies and towns mentioned in the text.
(Wokingham, which was partly in Berkshire, is not shown in the correct position.)

—————————————⫸ 1 ⫷—————————————

Introduction

I am always very well pleased with a Country Sunday.

This book will consider the practice and social context of established religion in late seventeenth- and early eighteenth-century England. In its detailed description of worship in the parish of Sir Roger de Coverley, *The Spectator* provides one picture of the manner in which the social relations between the elites, the clergy and the people were expressed through religion. The fictional Tory squire took pains to encourage his villagers and tenants to worship in the parish church in a suitably decent and conformable manner. Sir Roger gave each member of the congregation a Prayer Book and a hassock so that they could kneel and join in the responses. He railed the altar and had religious texts written on the walls, encouraged psalmody, rewarded with a Bible those children who performed their catechism well, and provided the parson with a supply of printed sermons to read in church. Sir Roger also took care to keep the congregation in good order, interrupting the service to chide malefactors, and standing up during prayers to check that his tenants were all present. In his support for the liturgy and scripture, for seemly worship and the edification of the catechism, Sir Roger de Coverley represented one ideal of worship within the eighteenth-century Church of England.[1]

Coverley parish exemplifies the dependency, or social control, thesis, according to which the landed elites and the clergy were united in an alliance which was to their mutual interest. In return for the Church's support of the social and political establishment, the landed gentry defended the worship and privileges of the Church of England. This interpretation, which informs the work of historians as far apart ideologically as E. P. Thompson and J. C. D. Clark, remains the orthodox view of the relations between church and society in eighteenth-century England.[2] Religion is thought to have been generally under the control of the

---

[1] *The Spectator*, no. 112, 9 July 1711.
[2] H. J. Perkin, *The Origins of Modern English Society, 1780–1880* (London, 1969), pp. 33–7; A. D. Gilbert, *Religion and Society in Industrial England: Church, Chapel and Social Change, 1740–1914* (London, 1976), pp. 13–14, 97–110; J. Rule, *Albion's People: English Society, 1714–1815*

1

squire. Thompson describes the Church as one link (albeit a weak one) in the chains which bound the common people. Since, in his view, the cultural relationship between patricians and plebeians was based upon a fundamental antagonism, anticlericalism represented a form of social protest.[3] Clark gives the Established Church a far greater role in the 'confessional state' in which the Church was at the very least an equal partner with the Crown and the aristocracy. The ideological underpinnings provided by the Anglican Church, he argues, were crucial to the continued dominance of the landed aristocracy and gentry throughout the eighteenth century.[4]

The dependency thesis fuses two dichotomies which historians have developed in order to help them understand the social significance of culture in early modern England: one between popular and elite culture, and another between popular and official religion. Although parallel, these dichotomies are nevertheless distinct.[5] Proponents of the binary model of popular and elite culture argue that the two became increasingly polarised during the early modern period.[6] The elites not only withdrew from popular culture but they also sought to suppress its rituals and festivals. The seventeenth-century campaign of the godly against the recreations and good fellowship of their neighbours was one aspect of this cultural war.[7] The two-tiered model has been the subject of extensive criticism on at least two grounds.[8] First, the division of society into only two categories – elite and people – oversimplifies the complexities of the structure of society and raises questions about how each should be defined. E. P. Thompson's elite is different from that of Keith Wrightson, for example. One corrective has been the suggestion that the middling sort, including tradesmen

footnote 2 (*cont.*)

(London, 1992), pp. 35–6. Some authors are vague about which part of the eighteenth century they are describing. Cf. G. F. A. Best, *Temporal Pillars: Queen Anne's Bounty, the Ecclesiastical Commissioners, and the Church of England* (Cambridge, 1964), p. 77, who dates the height of the alliance between squire and parson from *c.* 1780 to 1832.

[3] E. P. Thompson, 'Patrician society, plebeian culture', *Journal of Social History* 7 (Summer 1974): 382–405.

[4] J. C. D. Clark, *English Society 1688-1832: Ideology, Social Structure and Political Practice during the Ancient Regime* (Cambridge, 1985).

[5] For a discussion of the meanings of popular religion, see M. Venard, 'Popular religion in the eighteenth century', in W. J. Callahan and D. Higgs, eds. *Church and Society in Catholic Europe of the Eighteenth Century* (Cambridge, 1979), pp. 138–54, esp. 138–9.

[6] P. Burke, *Popular Culture in Early Modern Europe* (New York, 1978).

[7] K. Wrightson and David Levine, *Poverty and Piety in an English Village: Terling, 1525–1700* (London, 1979); K. Wrightson, *English Society 1580–1680* (London, 1980); D. E. Underdown, *Revel, Riot, and Rebellion: Popular Politics and Culture in England 1603–1660* (Oxford, 1985), ch. 3. Cf. M. Spufford, 'Puritanism and social control?', in A. J. Fletcher and J. Stevenson, eds., *Order and Disorder in Early Modern England* (Cambridge, 1985), pp. 41–57.

[8] B. Reay, *Popular Cultures in England 1550–1750* (London, 1998), esp. ch. 7; T. Harris, ed., *Popular Culture in England, c. 1500–1850* (London, 1995), ch. 1. Martin Ingram was one of the earliest critics of the Wrightson–Levine thesis. 'Religion, communities and moral discipline in late sixteenth- and early seventeenth-century England: case studies', in K. von Greyerz, ed., *Religion and Society in Early Modern Europe 1500–1850* (London, 1984), pp. 177–91.

and substantial farmers, should be regarded as a separate category. This has the advantage of recognising the significant role that the middling sort played in local administration and prosecution. Yet it does little to remedy the second objection to the model, its emphasis upon cultural conflict rather than consensus. Critics have instead emphasised the extent to which different groups in society shared cultural phenomena and redefined them in their own terms. Rather than debating the validity of the two-tiered model, it seems more productive to explore cultural interactions between the people and the elite.[9] As we shall see, religion was also a focus of negotiation between different social groups and cannot be viewed merely in terms of polarisation or the enforcement of elite hegemony.

The dichotomy between popular and official religion has been more persistent.[10] A recent synthesis, while recognising the range of religious views, has restated this opposition by describing the religion of the majority of the population in terms of Pelagianism and folklorised Christianity.[11] Historians have found it difficult to believe that the Church of England could have exemplified popular religion, a view which the debate over the popularity of the sixteenth-century Reformation has appeared to validate. Revisionists have argued that Protestantism led to the dissociation of the people from official religion, so that a popular religion informed by residual elements of Catholicism existed outside the Church.[12] Yet this interpretation can be questioned on several counts. First, it views lay religious practice through the eyes of contemporary critics, including both evangelical Protestants and other clergy, and therefore accepts their post-Reformation value judgements. Each imposed a Manichaean framework upon the world, praising those who conformed to their own high standards of behaviour, while condemning everyone else. Indeed, this binary opposition between sheep and goats, elect and reprobate, is fundamental to Christianity.[13] The puritans merely took the dichotomy to extremes in their belief that it might be possible to identify the small number who were elect on this earth. The truly godly were indeed a minority in the early seventeenth century, but this does not mean that all those with religious commitment were. In the late seventeenth century, complaints from clergymen about the irreligious behaviour of their congregations have a familiar air and are no more reliable.[14]

[9] P. Burke, 'Popular culture reconsidered', *Storia della storio grafia* 17 (1990): 40–9.

[10] Exceptions include M. Ingram, 'From reformation to toleration: popular religious cultures in England, 1540–1690', in Harris, *Popular Culture*, pp. 95–123; and D. Hempton, *The Religion of the People: Methodism and Popular Religion c. 1750-1900* (London, 1996), pp. 70–1.

[11] Reay, *Popular Cultures*, p. 100. See also K. V. Thomas, *Religion and the Decline of Magic* (New York, 1971); D. Cressy, *Birth, Marriage and Death* (Oxford, 1997).

[12] C. Haigh, ed., *The English Reformation Revised* (Cambridge, 1987), esp. Introduction, ch. 1; E. Duffy, *The Stripping of the Altars* (New Haven and London, 1992). Cf. A. D. Brown, *Popular Piety in Late Medieval England: The Diocese of Salisbury 1250–1550* (Oxford, 1995), ch. 10. See also J. Obelkevich, *Religion and Rural Society: South Lindsey 1825–1875* (Oxford, 1976), pp. 271–4.

[13] Matthew 25.   [14] See chapter 8.

A second reason for questioning the dissociation of popular from official religion is that there is growing evidence of popular support for the Church of England before, during and after the Civil Wars. This evidence suggests heartfelt support for the Prayer Book and the clergy from a broad spectrum of groups in society.[15] By the early seventeenth century, many parishioners had accepted the Anglican liturgy and defined religious worship in terms of its rites and ceremonies. The strength of support for a church is often best demonstrated by its persistence during times of persecution. During the Civil Wars and Interregnum, the Prayer Book continued to be used in some parishes even though it had been proscribed by Parliament. A small proportion of parishes also continued to celebrate communions at feasts such as Easter, although this practice was discouraged.[16] The survival of these practices, although limited, compares favourably with the rapid response of parishes to the twists and turns of central ecclesiastical policy in the middle of the sixteenth century.[17] The efficiency of the enforcement of the Reformation and the Marian reaction and the chaos of the Interregnum no doubt explain some of the differences, but clear evidence of support for the Prayer Book remains, nevertheless. This support was reaffirmed by the rapid return to communion at festivals in 1659 and particularly in 1660. When ecclesiastical visitations began again in 1662, parishes moved rapidly to remedy faults left by fifteen years of enforced neglect.[18]

Recent research has employed innovative approaches to uncover further evidence for the vitality of a popular religious culture which incorporated elements of Protestant belief and practice. Tessa Watt's study of cheaply printed broadsides and chapbooks looks outside the church to the streets where ballads were sold, into houses, and even on the walls of alehouses. She finds that conservative and reformed themes were often fused in the extensive religious literature that continued to predominate in the years from 1550 to 1640.[19] Ronald Hutton's study of the ritual year returns attention to the church by focusing on its use of financial resources. His analysis of churchwardens' accounts shows how both religious and secular festive years were reformed during the sixteenth and seventeenth centuries. Although the Revolution and Interregnum had seen the temporary triumph of the long campaign of Protestant reformers against the religious and secular festive calendar, a flourishing festive culture after the Restoration

---

[15] J. Maltby, '"By this book": parishioners, the Prayer Book and the Established Church', in K. Fincham, ed., *The Early Stuart Church, 1603–1642* (London, 1993), pp. 115–37; J. Maltby, *Prayer Book and People in Elizabethan and Early Stuart England* (Cambridge, 1998).

[16] J. Morrill, 'The Church in England in the 1640s', in J. Morrill, ed., *Reactions to the English Civil War 1642–1649* (London and Basingstoke, 1982); R. Hutton, *The Rise and Fall of Merry England: The Ritual Year 1400-1700* (Oxford, 1994), p. 214.

[17] Hutton, *Rise and Fall of Merry England*, pp. 69–110; Hutton, 'The local impact of the Tudor Reformations', in C. Haigh, ed., *The English Reformation Revised* (Cambridge, 1987), pp. 114–38.   [18] See chapter 3.

[19] T. Watt, *Cheap Print and Popular Piety 1550-1640* (Cambridge, 1991), p. 126.

demonstrated the Church's 'capacity for local choice and innovation', a sign of vigour and lay support.[20] There is little evidence that the Reformation created a dissociation of popular from official religion. The religious culture of the majority of the population could not help being influenced by the Reformation as new patterns of worship emerged and became familiar. Popular religion, in other words, was not static but evolved to meet new circumstances, incorporating elements of official religion in the process, although not necessarily in a form which the Church would have recognised.

Watt finds little in pre-Civil War cheap print 'about double predestination, ecclesiastical vestments, the position of the altar, or the prerequisites for communion', although she notes that these needs may have been met elsewhere.[21] Her findings suggest that the dissociation thesis may also be criticised for placing too much weight upon the search for popular support for particular theological positions and ceremonial practices such as the sacrament of grace or doctrine of purgatory. In practice, the majority of the people had little interest in the theological debates which occupied some of the more highly educated members of the population. In this sense, at least, the dichotomy between official and popular religion is valid, but it tells us little about the religion of the people. The ambiguities within the Thirty-Nine Articles and the liturgy must, in any case, have made it difficult for many people to understand the Church's doctrinal stance. The Church's lack of doctrinal cohesion after the Restoration gave communal participation in common prayer particular importance to Anglicans.[22]

In studying the religion of the people, it is necessary to distinguish between religious belief, knowledge, experience, practice and secular impact.[23] Because these various aspects of religion are interrelated, it is natural to assume that they operate in parallel, so that one may serve as an indicator for the others. The scarcity of available evidence makes such an approach particularly attractive. Religious practice is often easier to study than belief, knowledge or experience. Yet some faiths vest greater importance in certain aspects of religion than in others. One consequence of the Reformation was to give particular emphasis to belief, through the doctrines of the priesthood of all believers and salvation by faith, and to personal piety within the family. This does not mean that this shift in emphasis was universally, or even generally, accepted. For many people, participation in church services and activities remained the single most

[20] Hutton, *Rise and Fall of Merry England, passim* (quoting p. 248).
[21] Watt, *Cheap Print*, p. 8.
[22] J. Spurr, *The Restoration Church of England, 1646–1689* (New Haven, 1991), ch. 7.
[23] R. Stark and C. Glock, *American Piety: The Study of Religious Commitment* (Berkeley, 1968), ch. 1. A similar distinction is made by C. J. Sommerville between meanings of secularisation. See 'The destruction of religious culture in pre-industrial England', *Journal of Religious History* 15 (1988): 76–93; and *The Secularization of Early Modern England* (New York and Oxford, 1992), p. 5. In portraying 'the sense of separation of almost all aspects of life and thought from religious associations or ecclesiastical direction' (ibid., p. 1), Sommerville presents an alternative formulation of an interpretation based on dissociation.

important focus for religious experience, as well as providing a forum for social relationships.

This study will investigate the social significance of religion through popular involvement in institutional religion, exploring the extent to which people were committed to the Established Church, the quality of their relations with the clergy, and the role of religion as a focus for social relationships. Historians have tended to emphasise the importance of voluntary religion from the seventeenth century onwards and the emergence of organised dissent after 1662. The confirmation of its status in 1689 may appear to confirm this interpretation.[24] Yet in sketching the evolution of the English separatist tradition, there is a danger of writing the past in terms of later developments. Dissent was created by the political and religious establishment. Relatively few people set out deliberately to separate themselves from the Church. One reason why it is so difficult to agree about the definition of 'puritans' is that they constituted a significant section of the national church, which most people found it unthinkable to leave.[25] Richard Baxter agreed that so-called 'conventicles' should be viewed 'not as a separated Church but as a part of the Church more diligent than the rest'.[26] Even after the Restoration, the great majority of parishioners wished to remain within the Church. Thus the religious census of 1676, which enumerated stubborn nonconformists, found that only a minority of the population fitted into the category. Lay officers proved reluctant to prosecute neighbours who attended conventicles or consistently stayed away from church.[27] The unpopularity of informers under the second Conventicle Act is partly explained by the fact that their net might ensnare those who attended both church and a conventicle as well as separatists. The religious societies, first formed in the 1670s, followed in the 1690s by the SPCK and later by the Methodists for many years, demonstrated the same determination to remain within the Church.[28] In short, while voluntarism was a minority instinct, the desire to remain a member of a unified church remained strong for most people, and was stronger than concern about ceremonial details or remote doctrinal debates. Indeed, this belief in the value of universal membership of one unified church was a feature of religious culture that members of all social groups shared.[29]

[24] C. Hill, *Society and Puritanism in Pre-Revolutionary England*, 2nd edn (New York, 1967), ch. 14. For an enlightening exploration of this theme, see P. Collinson, 'The English conventicle', in W. J. Sheils and D. Wood, eds., *Voluntary Religion*, Ecclesiastical History Society 23 (Oxford, 1986), pp. 223–59. See also Gilbert, *Religion and Society*, pp. 138–42; E. Troeltsch, *The Social Teaching of the Christian Churches* (London, 1931), vol. I, esp. pp. 656–71; M. Weber, 'The protestant sects and the spirit of capitalism', pp. 302–22, in H. H. Gerth and C. W. Mills, trans. and eds., *From Max Weber* (London, 1991), pp. 313–22.

[25] K. Fincham, eds., *The Early Stuart Church, 1603–1642* (London, 1993); C. Durston and J. Eales, eds., *The Culture of English Puritanism, 1560–1700* (London, 1996); J. Spurr, *English Puritanism* (Basingstoke, 1998).   [26] Collinson, 'The English conventicle', p. 223.   [27] See chapter 7.

[28] J. Walsh, 'Religious societies: Methodist and evangelical 1738-1800', pp. 279–302, in Sheils and Wood, *Voluntary Religion*.

[29] Spurr, *Restoration Church*, ch. 3; Conrad Russell, 'Arguments for religious unity in England, 1530–1650', *Journal of Ecclesiastical History* 18 (Oct. 1967): 201–26.

Parishioners expressed their commitment to membership in the Church by participating in its weekly public assemblies each Sunday and in the communal rites of baptism, marriage and burial. It may be objected that they had little choice because their observance of these offices was enforced by law and therefore was not voluntary. Until 1689 persistent absence from church could lead to prosecution and punishment by a fine. Yet it seems unlikely that for over a century the majority of the population attended church solely because they were compelled to do so. The best evidence for commitment to the services of the Church is that the laity complained when clerical neglect meant that services either were not performed or were inadequate.[30] When they were given an opportunity to contribute actively, for example by singing psalms, they did so eagerly.[31] The penal laws also present a practical difficulty, because the correctional courts which provide the best window into religious observance were heavily involved in the prosecution of nonconformists. Not everyone who appeared before the church courts or who quarrelled with their minister was a nonconformist.[32]

Worship in church had spiritual and social significance. By attending services, parishioners affirmed their membership of both the national church and the local community.[33] Interpretations which emphasise enforcement and social control understate the extent to which all members of the parish participated in institutional religion. This is not to say that the Church of England defined all popular beliefs. Popular religion constituted a blend of official and unofficial beliefs, which differed from individual to individual. A folklorised and magical world view lived alongside Anglicanism, while other ritual practices lost their religious connotations.[34] The church was a focus for social relationships. In the layout of its pews, the church replicated the hierarchical structure of society. Yet the parish church touched all sections of society. Every inhabitant, ratepayer and tithe payer had an interest in the provision of prayers and in the good government of the parish. Religion provided an important focus for negotiation between different groups in society. While it could be a force for division, it also had the potential to represent a shared culture that mediated relationships between members of different groups in society. The relationship between the parson, who was the local representative of the national church, and his congregation was particularly important.

A final reason to question the view that the sixteenth-century Reformation alienated the people from official religion is that another set of historians has identified the latter half of the eighteenth century as the crucial period when the

---

[30] Chapter 5.   [31] Chapter 10.   [32] Cf. Reay, *Popular Cultures*, p. 99, n. 107.
[33] M. Smith, *Religion in Industrial Society: Oldham and Saddleworth 1740–1865* (Oxford, 1994), p. 260.
[34] Reay, *Popular Cultures*, ch. 3; Ronald Hutton, 'The English Reformation and the evidence of folklore', *Past and Present* 148 (1995): 89–116; Obelkevich, *Religion and Rural Society*, ch. 6.

Church suffered a devastating loss of grass-roots support.[35] Alan Gilbert
describes the period from 1740 to 1800 as one of 'prolonged, rapid, and disastrous' decline for the Church of England.[36] The number of communicants in
selected Oxfordshire parishes fell by 25 per cent between 1738 and 1802. In the
north they fell by almost 18 per cent in only twenty years. By 1851, the Church
of England accounted for a minority of worshippers in most places, and even in
Anglican bastions such as the county of Wiltshire it accounted for little more
than half of those attending religious services.[37] Students of the eighteenth- and
nineteenth-century Church have long been divided between optimists and pessi-
mists.[38] The pessimistic school follows earlier reformers who viewed the eighteenth century as one of the blackest ages of church history. The Church could
not avoid the stain of 'Old Corruption', and the political alliance between the
Whig regime and the bishops made the latter appear to be little better than place-
men. At the local level, a pluralist clergy who appeared more interested in the
hunt than the pulpit must inevitably have neglected their pastoral duties. John
Wesley summed up the criticisms against the Church and its clergy, 'those
indolent, pleasure taking, money-loving, praise-loving, preferment-seeking
Clergymen' who were 'a stink in the nostrils of God'.[39] His words echoed the critique of the Whig bishop Gilbert Burnet of Salisbury half a century earlier.
Complaining that the clergy were greedy and lax and that the church courts were
corrupt, Burnet judged that the spirit of religion was 'sunk and dead'.[40] Because
the eighteenth-century Church was 'a static institution, characterised by inertia',
it proved unable to cope with the rapid demographic growth and urbanisation
that occurred later in the century, for these changes had their greatest impact in
the industrialising north where it was least able to respond.[41] The Church of
England also suffered a decline in popular support in the south, as the clergy

---

[35] Hutton observes a parallel phenomenon in studies of popular culture. *Rise and Fall of Merry England*, p. 227.   [36] Gilbert, *Religion and Society*, p. 29.

[37] R. Currie, A. Gilbert and L. Horsley, *Churches and Churchgoers: Patterns of Church Growth in the British Isles since 1700* (Oxford, 1977), pp. 22–3; Summary of Census of Religious Worship (1851), Table N; W. S. F. Pickering, 'The 1851 religious census – a useless experiment?', *British Journal of Sociology* 18 (1967): 396 (Map 1), 399 (Map 2). These figures are for the number of persons present at the most numerous service in each church or chapel. It is impossible to recover the total number of individuals who attended church on census Sunday, because of the danger of double-counting. See Smith, *Religion in Industrial Society*, pp. 250–2, and the references cited there, for a discussion of the census's limitations.

[38] The debate is summarised by K. Hylson-Smith, *The Churches in England from Elizabeth I to Elizabeth II*, vol. II: *1689–1833* (London, 1997), pp. xiii–xv; J. Walsh and S. Taylor, 'Introduction: the Church and Anglicanism in the "long" eighteenth century', in J. Walsh, C. Hayden and S. Taylor, eds., *The Church of England, c.1689–c.1833: From Toleration to Tractarianism* (Cambridge, 1993), pp. 1-64, esp. pp. 1–3; C. G. Brown, 'Did urbanization secularize Britain?', *Urban History Yearbook* (1988): 1–14, esp. 1–6.

[39] Quoted in Hempton, *The Religion of the People*, p. 83. See also Gilbert, *Religion and Society*, pp. 94–7.

[40] Burnet, *Pastoral Care*, pp. xxvi–xxvii, 117, 159; Foxcroft, pp. 329–31, quoting p. 330.

[41] Gilbert, *Religion and Society*, pp. 28, 76–81, 94–115. But cf. Brown, 'Urbanization', pp. 1–6, 11.

consolidated their alliance with landed gentry and grew more distant from their congregations. The clergy became more prosperous, self-confident and powerful, changes that were matched by the growth in pluralism and clerical magistracy.[42]

Other historians have cast the eighteenth-century Church in a more favourable light. Norman Sykes long provided the dominant account, based upon qualified optimism.[43] Sykes countered the view that the bishops were political creatures by demonstrating that they diligently performed their pastoral duties, particularly those of confirmation and the examination of candidates for the clergy. While he was not blind to the defects of the Church, he observed that many of its problems were not new. The eighteenth-century Church had many obstacles to overcome, including economic and institutional defects, many of which dated back to before the English Civil War, if not to before the Reformation.[44] More recently, historians have taken an even more optimistic stance. It has been suggested that the Church 'in the first half of the eighteenth century perhaps reached the zenith of its allegiance among the population'.[45] The use of religious patronage for political purposes appears to have been neither as pernicious nor as effective as had been thought. Historians have also found considerable potential for pastoral care and lay piety in the late eighteenth century and have stressed the vitality of local Anglicanism, even in industrialising communities such as Oldham and Saddleworth, although this depended upon local initiatives and must be set in the context of the considerable success of aggressive evangelical churches.[46]

Although recent research suggests that the Church of England coped better than had previously been thought, it nevertheless lost ground, at least relative to other churches, during the eighteenth century. Why did it suffer this erosion of support? Structural, pastoral and economic factors played a part, as did competition from the evangelical churches. Yet it will be argued in this book that the key to the decline of the Church lies in the nature of relationships between the people and the clergy. Its origins can be found in the late seventeenth and early eighteenth centuries, in the period between the Restoration and the birth of

[42] Gilbert, *Religion and Society*, pp. 80–1; P. Virgin, *The Church in an Age of Negligence: Ecclesiastical Structure and Problems of Church Reform 1700-1840* (Cambridge, 1989), *passim*; E. J. Evans, 'Some reasons for the growth of English rural anti-clericalism *c.* 1750–*c.*1830', *Past and Present* 66 (Feb. 1975): 84–109; Walsh, Haydon and Taylor, *The Church of England*, p. 28.

[43] N. Sykes, *Church and State in England in the XVIIIth Century* (Cambridge, 1934).

[44] C. Hill, *The Economic Problems of the Church* (Oxford, 1956); Brown, *Popular Piety*, pp. 70–4.

[45] W. M. Jacob, *Lay People and Religion in the Early Eighteenth Century* (Cambridge, 1996), p. 19. See also T. Isaacs, 'The Anglican hierarchy and the reformation of manners 1688–1738', *Journal of Ecclesiastical History* 33 (1982): 391–411.

[46] Smith, *Religion in Industrial Society*, *passim*, esp. ch. 2; M. Smith, 'The reception of Richard Podmore: Anglicanism in Saddleworth 1700-1830', in Walsh, Haydon and Taylor, *The Church of England*, pp. 110–23; D. R. Hirschberg, 'The government and church patronage in England, 1660–1760', *Journal of British Studies* 20 (1980): 109–39; S. Taylor, 'Church and state in England in the mid-eighteenth century: the Newcastle years 1742–1762' (unpublished Ph.D., Cambridge University, 1987). I am grateful to Dr Taylor for providing me with a copy of his thesis.

Methodism. It was in these years that the Church and its clergy revealed the rigidity of mind and the isolation from the laity that made them increasingly unable
to command popular affection. The clergy did much to overcome the pastoral
problems that confronted them. The early eighteenth century witnessed an
Anglican revival that revealed the remarkable potential of the Church to provide
the religion of the people. Yet the Church was ultimately unable to retain popular
support because it was unwilling to relinquish any control over worship to the
laity. Its problems were more psychological than structural. Indeed, its institutional defects reflected a clerical mindset that was defensive and inflexible. The
Church repeatedly showed itself unable to change to meet circumstances. The
parochial reforms of the Commonwealth were discarded. The liturgical changes
that would have allowed presbyterians to be comprehended were discarded. For
much of the period from 1660 to 1740 the Church was distracted by the threat
from dissent. The quarrel between High and Low Church that came to a head in
the reign of Queen Anne prevented the Church from confronting the real problems it faced, while making it many enemies. The SPCK, which initially sought
to involve both High and Low Churchmen, became the target of accusations of
Jacobitism. The greatest danger to the Church came not from without but from
within. The clergy turned inwards, defining themselves as a distinct profession,
determined to protect the liturgy and the monopoly over it which their unique
sacerdotal status gave them.[47] The closed mind of the Anglican clergy can be seen
in the reaction to Methodism, initially a movement within the Church. The
clergy disliked the impropriety of religious meetings held in the open, the singing
and the greater involvement of the laity.[48] Clerical inability to understand or
accept popular worship mean that clerical complaints about religious ignorance
cannot be relied upon as evidence of popular beliefs.

There are good reasons for starting this study in 1660, even though there
undoubtedly were continuities between religion and politics under the early and
later Stuarts.[49] The Restoration of the Church of England alongside the Stuart
monarchy provided it with the opportunity for a fresh start. After years of disorder, the restored Church was initially popular. Dissent created a new set of
problems, but these were more institutional than theological, and puritanism no
longer represented a serious threat within the Church. The end point in around
1740 is more controversial. The years 1688–1714 represent a continental divide
which historians are reluctant to cross.[50] It is true that 1689 marked the end of

[47] See chapter 2.   [48] Hempton, *The Religion of the People*, pp. 149–50.
[49] M. G. Finlayson, *Historians, Puritanism and the English Revolution: The Religious Factor in English Politics before and after the Interregnum* (Toronto and London, 1983); T. Harris, et al., eds., *The Politics of Religion in Restoration England* (Oxford, 1990).
[50] Many of the books cited in this chapter either stop or start in the period 1688–1714, mostly 1688, e.g. Clark; Walsh, Haydon and Taylor; Wrightson and Levine; Spurr; Hylson-Smith; Virgin; Rule. Champion, Gilbert and Smith are notable exceptions.

the Church of England's legal monopoly over religious worship. Yet the Act of Toleration did not stimulate an expansion of dissent, even though some clergymen complained that it served as a licence for non-attendance at either church or chapel. To conservative nineteenth-century commentators the psychological and ideological significance of the fracturing of the Church caused by the departure of non-jurors was enormous, and it is no coincidence that they decried the state of the Church after 1700 while praising the Restoration Church. Yet the numerical impact of the non-jurors was minuscule and had little effect upon the religious practice of the common people. The 1690s presented an important political turning point, as William III transformed England into a European power, and the tax burden grew commensurately. Yet there is now reason to doubt that the new century witnessed such significant social changes as the disappearance of the smallholder.[51] The events of the years around 1700, while significant, should not prevent one from seeing continuities between the seventeenth and eighteenth centuries.[52]

There are good socio-economic and religious reasons for stopping in the middle of the eighteenth century. Social and economic changes began to quicken at that time, as the forces of industrialisation, urbanisation and parliamentary enclosure began to change both town and countryside.[53] Norman Sykes believed that, although Addison was writing 'during the high church *régime* of Anne', he had nevertheless 'discerned the features of rural religion which persisted throughout the greater part of the century'.[54] Yet it has become clear that there was no single entity that can be called 'the eighteenth-century Church'. The Church may have reached its lowest ebb sometime around the middle of the century.[55] It was already losing contact with its popular constituency and showing signs of inflexibility. The danger signs can be found, not just in the north, but also in those southern dioceses where it was in theory relatively strong. In 1739 John Wesley and George Whitefield broke from the parochial system by preaching in the fields outside Bristol, a development which has particular symbolic significance. In July, Wesley preached for the first time in Wiltshire.[56] The birth of Methodism marked a watershed for the Anglican Church, even though the movement would formally remain within the Church for another fifty years. In the eighty years between 1660 and 1740, the Church

---

[51] J. M. Neeson, 'An eighteenth-century peasantry', pp. 24–59, in J. Rule and R. Malcolmson, eds., *Protest and Survival: Essays for E. P. Thompson* (London, 1993); D. E. Ginter, 'Measuring the decline of the small landowner', pp. 27–47, in B. A. Holderness and M. Turner, eds., *Land, Labour and Agriculture, 1700-1920* (London and Rio Grande, 1991).

[52] G. Holmes, *Augustan England: Professions, State and Society, 1680–1730* (London, 1982), p. ix.

[53] P. Hudson, *The Industrial Revolution* (London, 1992); M. Overton, *The Agricultural Revolution* (Cambridge, 1995). Gilbert provides the clearest statement of this interpretation.

[54] Sykes, *Church and State*, p. 230.

[55] Walsh, Haydon and Taylor, *The Church of England*, p. 21; cf. Jacob, *Lay People and Religion*.

[56] *The Journal of the Revd John Wesley, A.M.* (London, 1909–16), vol. II, p. 243.

and its clergy wasted the popular support that they attracted at the Restoration. They showed that they understood popular religious beliefs no better than the puritans had done, and by their intolerance of dissent and insistence upon their clerical monopoly they alienated many people. The gulf between the Church and the people grew larger in the late seventeenth and early eighteenth centuries.

This section will end, as it began, with *The Spectator*. Mr Spectator's discourse on the social aspects of worship was part of an extensive case study of life in Coverley parish. He spent a month there, rather in the manner of an ethnographer seeking to provide his own 'thick description' of an alien society and culture, and there he witnessed Sir Roger hunting and learned of his superstitious witchcraft beliefs, among many other amusing activities.[57] The author of letter no. 112, Joseph Addison, was more familiar with parish life than he may have been prepared to admit. His father, Launcelot Addison, had been rector of the Wiltshire parish of Milston in the late seventeenth century, and his grandfather also was a cleric.[58] Because *The Spectator* was political propaganda intended to ridicule the Tory gentlemen and High Church clergymen who were to be found in the country, these letters are not reliable evidence about eighteenth-century religion. Yet the methodology of the parish case study remains valid. An assessment of the social context of religion must start by looking at worship in its parishes.

It would be impossible to study all ten thousand of England's parishes, so this book will focus on the three hundred or so that lay within the county of Wiltshire in south-western England. Whether or not one regards a county as a distinct community, there is no doubt that it provides a convenient unit of analysis, since many of the records are organised on a county basis. No county can claim to be typical, of course, and recent research on the eighteenth-century Church has stressed the importance of differences between dioceses.[59] The Church was, in theory, in a particularly strong position in the diocese of Salisbury, two of whose three archdeaneries were located in Wiltshire. The parishes in the diocese were smaller and the value of its benefices were higher than those in northern dioceses. The bishopric was in the second tier of dioceses, less desirable and lucrative than Durham, London or Winchester, but preferable to Bath and Wells or Carlisle. Because the diocese was more compact than such sprawling dioceses as Lincoln and Norwich, the bishop had more opportunity to centralise power in his own hands, reducing

---

[57] *The Spectator*, nos. 115, 117. For the concept of 'thick description', see C. Geertz, *The Interpretation of Cultures* (New York, 1973).

[58] Launcelot Addison was no mere parish incumbent, however. In addition to being dean of Lichfield, he was also author of several treatises, including *Introduction to the Sacrament* (London, 1686), whose publisher claimed that many ministers had found it the fittest exposition to give to those who were poor and of mean capacity. Spurr, *Restoration Church*, p. 342.

[59] Walsh, Haydon and Taylor, *The Church of England*, pp. 12–13. Although Jacob finds no evidence of regional variations in religious practice, there were considerable differences in the effectiveness of the church courts of different dioceses. Jacob, *Lay People and Religion*, pp. 224, 135–54.

the importance of archdeacons. Salisbury was fortunate in the quality of its bishops after the Restoration. Two, Seth Ward and Gilbert Burnet, presided consecutively for no less than half a century and did so conscientiously, despite their political commitments. Until illness and a vitriolic dispute with the dean dissipated his powers in his final years, Ward, who was bishop from 1667 to 1688, brought administrative competence and concern for his clergy's cure of souls. Diocesan officials continued to use his meticulous calculations and surveys of clerical incomes throughout the eighteenth century.[60] Gilbert Burnet, who succeeded Ward as bishop from 1689 to 1715, was determined to reinvigorate the Church in his diocese. His promotion of Queen Anne's Bounty is well known, and his membership of the Society for Promoting Christian Knowledge showed his support for religious revival at a national level. In Salisbury diocese, he sought to reform the consistory court, to improve the theological training and incomes of his clergy, and to raise standards of pastoral care. Burnet personally visited many of the parishes in his diocese, where he preached and confirmed, and the significance he attributed to ordination was expressed in the care with which he examined candidates for it. Unfortunately, his reform campaign was frustrated by the refusal of the clergy to co-operate with a bishop whose Low Church politics had earned him a reputation for caring more about dissenters than the Church.[61]

If the Church depended upon the support of the landed gentry, then it was in an enviable position in Wiltshire. The county possessed a strong aristocracy and gentry, whose estates were scattered across the landscape from Longleat and Wilton in the south to Lydiard and Draycot to the north. Wiltshire, like many other shires, was divided into distinctive farming regions that were as different as chalk and cheese, a phrase that describes the contrast between the arable chalk downs to the south and the pastoral cheese country to the north.[62] This contrast had religious significance, because the northern pastoral parishes were often larger and had their population scattered between distinct hamlets, presenting the clergy with a significant pastoral challenge. It has been argued that separate family farms were more prevalent in the cheese than the chalk and that these encouraged greater independence in religion.[63] The chalk was characterised by the large estates of such magnates as the earls of Pembroke and Montgomery and the dukes of Somerset. Yet the landed gentry were a strong presence everywhere, in the chalk, the cheese and the county's many towns and boroughs.[64] The

---

[60] E. A. O. Whiteman, 'The episcopate of Dr. Seth Ward, bishop of Exeter (1662 to 1667) and Salisbury (1667–1688/9) with special reference to the ecclesiastical problems of his time' (unpublished D.Phil. thesis, Oxford University, 1951); D1/27/1/1, ff. 73–112v (Table of Benefices); D1/48/4.

[61] Foxcroft, pp. 499–503. Burnet donated £300 a year for charitable purposes which included augmenting the incomes of poorer clergymen. SPCK, AL 53.

[62] E. Kerridge, 'Agriculture c. 1500–1793', in VCH *Wilts.*, IV, pp. 43–64.

[63] J. Thirsk, 'Seventeenth-century agriculture and social change', in P. Seaver, ed., *Seventeenth-Century England* (New York, 1976), pp. 72–110; Underdown, *Revel, Riot, and Rebellion.*

[64] J. Adams, *Index Villaris* (London, 1680).

largest number of towns were in the region of clothing industry to the north-west, and these cloth towns proved to be important centres for dissent in the late seventeenth century, although the county's 4 per cent of separatists in 1676 was close to the average in the archdiocese of Canterbury.[65] Wiltshire's industry was older than most (and was now entering a period of decline), but cottage indus-try was an increasingly familiar characteristic of the English countryside.

Most of the county's gentlemen supported the Church of England, although some were Catholic and many were reluctant to proceed against nonconformity during the Restoration. A common response to James II's Three Questions was to assert the importance of defending the Church.[66] In the eighteenth century, a small number of Tory families provided the county's MPs and did so, with a few exceptions, by mutual agreement rather than by election.[67] Further research will be needed to determine whether the picture of social and religious relations pre-sented in this study was also characteristic of other English counties, although there is no reason to believe that the problems the Church faced there and the behaviour of its clerics were unique. Yet, the Church in Wiltshire was as close to a position of strength in confronting these pastoral challenges as anywhere in England, and this makes the story of the relations between the clergy and the laity there of particular interest.

THE CHURCH IN DANGER

. . . about Michaelmas last they committed a Riot in ye Church at which time two of them . . . also severall times (but especially ye Sunday before Palm Sunday) shamefully polluted with human excrements ye Church Porch to near ye quantity of a Barrowfull which they lay agt ye door & allso filled the keyhole, daub'd all ye door over with it, & thrust as much as they could into ye Church.[68]

Two weeks before Easter Day in 1676 the Revd James Garth found the porch of Hilperton church covered with human excrement. It is hard to imagine a more explicit symbolic demonstration of ill-feeling against the clergy and the Church of England of which they were the local representatives. Garth complained that his parishioners had used 'malitious invectives to blemish' him and had 'con-spired . . . To eject mee out of my Living'. The clergy felt themselves to be under attack in the late seventeenth and early eighteenth century. The cry of 'the Church in danger' was loudest in the reign of Queen Anne, but the sense of threat persisted throughout the period. The clergy's foes were legion and included nonconformity, anticlericalism and irreligion. Dissenters were the most visible threat. In the late seventeenth century their presence was a constant

[65] Whiteman, *Compton Census*, pp. 106–35.
[66] G. Duckett, ed., *Penal Laws and Test Act* (London, 1882), pp. 212–19.
[67] VCH *Wilts*, V, pp. 195–230; B. D. Henning, ed., *House of Commons 1660–1690* (London, 1983), q.v. 'Wiltshire'; *A Poll for the Wiltshire Election of 1705* (1705).   [68] D1/41/4/43.

reminder of the failure of the Restoration settlement of religion. After 1689 the issue of the treatment of dissent defined an ideological fault line between High Church Tories, who wished to restore the Church's authority and status, and Whigs, who were suspicious of its disciplinary machinery. In the 1730s Parliament debated a series of bills which appeared to constitute a concerted campaign against the Church and passed one, the Mortmain Act of 1736.[69]

The clergy and the laity alike believed that anticlericalism was widespread. At his trial in 1710 the symbol of the High Church movement Dr Henry Sacheverell grieved that 'never were the ministers of Christ so abused and vilified . . . never was infidelity and atheism itself so impudent'. The Low Church bishop Gilbert Burnet of Salisbury believed that 'None but the confederates of our enemies, and those who are deluded by them can imagine our church to be in danger'. Nonetheless, he agreed that '*priestcraft* grew to be another word in fashion, and the enemies of religion vented all their impieties under the cover of these words'.[70] Although the assault upon 'priestcraft' reached new heights in the 1690s, criticism of the clergy was already a familiar theme. In 1670 John Eachard had attacked the pretensions of the clergy in *The Grounds and Occasions of the Contempt of the Clergy*. Launcelot Addison was one of several divines who leaped to the clergy's defence, arguing that they had been held in contempt in all ages because their spiritual functions required them to express uncomfortable truths. Another contemporary agreed in 1684 that because 'Ministers tell the People of their faults . . . it is a kind of pleasing revenge to find fault with them again'. '[C]hief and leading Men in their Country', he reflected, 'seemed never more delighted, at Market or such like publick Meetings, then when they have fallen upon the Subject of reviling the Ministry.'[71] The clergy suffered as a target of Restoration wit, and in the eighteenth century they became stock figures of fun in literature and prints.[72] As a parish clerk observed, 'many people [were] glad to meet with anything ill done or ill reported of a Minister nowadayes'. The rector of Avebury, John White, agreed that 'the mobb is very apt to beleeve any reports that are raised upon ministers'.[73] The clergy and leading laymen shared the opinion that irreligion was a third enemy that was undermining the fabric of English society and could be found wherever they looked. *The Letter to a*

[69] G. V. Bennett, *The Tory Crisis in Church and State 1688–1730* (Oxford, 1975); Best, *Temporal Pillars*, pp. 103–9; S. Taylor, 'Sir Robert Walpole, the Church of England, and the Quakers Tithe Bill of 1736', *Historical Journal* 28 (1985): 51–77; N. Sykes, *Edmund Gibson* (London, 1926), pp. 149–66.

[70] Bennett, *The Tory Crisis*, pp. 19, 116; D. Slatter, ed., *Diary of Thomas Naish* (Devizes, 1965), p. 55. Many Wiltshire clergymen refused to sign an address to the queen, after the victory at Ramillies, into which Burnet tried to insert the phrase that the Church was not in danger.

[71] Launcelot Addison, *A Modest Plea for the Clergy* (London, 1677), pp. 125, 129; Anon., *The Case of Peoples Duty in Living Under a Scandalous Minister Stated and Resolved* (London, 1684), pp. 5–6.

[72] Spurr, *Restoration Church*, pp. 219, 234; Jacob, *Lay People and Religion*, pp. 44–51.

[73] D1/42/60, f. 181v; John White to Sir Richard Holford, recd 27 Jan. 1695[/6], WRO 184/1.

Convocation Man observed that 'a open looseness in men's principles and practices, and a settled contempt of religion and the priesthood have prevailed everywhere'.[74] Deism represented irreligion's intellectual guise and the impiety of the masses in city streets and country lanes its popular guise. Anxiety about irreligion and immorality manifested itself in urban areas in the 1690s in the formation of societies for the reformation of manners. The provincial clergy also bemoaned the ignorance and impiety of their congregations. One commentator claimed that concubinage was particularly rife in Wiltshire and appealed for the correction of atheism. With the support of the Society for Promoting Christian Knowledge parsons took steps to reinvigorate parish religion.[75]

   Anticlericalism must be viewed within its broader intellectual and political contexts, as exposed by the recent research of Justin Champion and Mark Goldie.[76] Freethinkers and other critics of the clergy coined the term 'priestcraft' to describe the corruption of 'true' religion by the clergy and the Established Church as an independent source of authority. The clergy were denounced for creating doctrinal obscurity and emphasising rites and ceremonies in order to ensure their interpretive and functional monopoly, for their dogmatic intolerance of heterodox beliefs, and for their use of religion for their own private aggrandisement, turning religion into a trade. Radical republicans saw clericalism as a form of tyranny which sought the spiritual enslavement of the people, while High Churchmen followed Laud and Heylyn in seeing an independent clerical estate as central to the Church's recovery of status and authority. The critique of priestcraft contributed to a debate which had both intellectual and political facets. Opposing views of the legitimacy of clerical authority differentiated Tory defenders of the Established Church from Whig defenders of liberty of conscience.

   Expressions of anticlericalism also had a social dimension. The clergy had to defend themselves from verbal and physical attack in numerous country parishes. In Damerham South two men abused and assaulted the vicar Thomas Derby in 1680. One assailant threatened the minister with his stick, although several onlookers stopped him from striking Derby. The other called Derby a 'Rogue & Rascall', threw beer in his face and struck him with his fist. He warned the vicar that he could humble him just as the parishioners of Rogborne had humbled their parson, indicating that it was not an isolated incident.[77] Thomas Twittee was

[74] Bennett, *The Tory Crisis*, p. 48; Burnet, *Pastoral Care*, p. xxii.

[75] Jacob, *Lay People and Religion*, ch. 5; W. O. B. Allen and E. McClure, *Two Hundred Years: The History of the Society for Promoting Christian Knowledge, 1698–1898* (London, 1898), p. 69. See also chapter 10 below.

[76] This paragraph draws heavily upon J. A. I. Champion, *The Pillars of Priestcraft Shaken: The Church of England and its Enemies, 1660–1730* (Cambridge, 1992), *passim*, esp. chs. 5–7; and M. Goldie, 'Priestcraft and the birth of Whiggism', in N. Phillipson and Q. Skinner, eds., *Political Discourse in Early Modern Britain* (Cambridge, 1993), pp. 209–31.

[77] A1/110, H1680/1 (Informations). The assailants were Gyles Early (or Yearly) of Damerham and Richard Early of Salisbury. Rogborne is probably Rockbourne, which lay in the parish of Martin just to the north of Damerham.

attacked at his induction into the rectory of Draycot Foliat in 1665. Inhabitants struck and knocked him over, drawing blood, and then forced him to leave the churchyard.[78] Richard Day of Dauntsey chased the rector of Brinkworth, Francis Henry Carey, into the churchyard. Day, who was on horseback, threatened Carey with his whip and called him the 'son of a whore', but two men stopped him from whipping the rector.[79] Widow Everitt verbally abused the vicar of Westport while he was performing divine service in the chapel of Charlton in 1663.[80] Mathew Clark laughed at the rector of Bremhill during divine service.[81] Attacks on individual clergymen manifested themselves in abuse and disruption of the church and its services. The inhabitants of Draycot Foliat disturbed divine service by 'making mocks & rimes at the Comon Prayer'. In Knooke parishioners threw stones at the church and boycotted communion.[82] The churchwardens and other inhabitants of Netheravon removed the cushion on which the vicar knelt at prayers and laughed at him when he complained. They also disturbed divine service on the feast day of the Holy Innocents in December 1687 'by tuning, whistleing, talking, & making terrible noises by tumbling of stones . . . about the Belfry loft'. Afterwards they left the loft and walked through the church, 'not taking the least notice of Divine Service being then in Reading, except by putting off their Hats'.[83] Thomas Chambers urinated against the pulpit of Norton Bavant church during divine service, a choice of location which was surely significant.[84]

The clergy interpreted these incidents as assaults, not just on them as individuals, but upon the entire clerical profession, a view they expressed by suing their abusers for vilification of the clergy. The Church was particularly sensitive to evidence of anticlericalism. Although it seems unlikely that the common people were aware of publications concerning priestcraft, many of the parish clergy may have been, and this can only have heightened their sensitivity to criticism.[85] The description of ministers as 'black coats' in the late seventeenth century indicates that the Restoration had not entirely extinguished views that had led the Quakers and other sects to rebel against the control of the clergy. Yet abuse of the clergy involved more than traditional popular anticlericalism, exacerbated by the turmoil of the Civil War and its aftermath, or frustrated nonconformity. The laity valued the contribution that individual clerics made to the religious and

---

[78] PRO, E 134, 23&24 Charles II, Hil 2 (testimony of Austin Hodges and George Jacques, both gentlemen from Chiseldon). Service was being read in the ruins of the church.
[79] A1/110, E1686 (Informations).   [80] D3/12, 1663.   [81] D1/54/6/3 (1674, A&P), f. 30/44.
[82] D5/28, 1665, f. 4.   [83] D5/28, 1688, f. 70.   [84] D1/54/21/4 (1708, W&W).
[85] John Lewis of Holt read widely from the writings of John Locke, as well as William Freke, *A Vindication of the Unitarians* (London, 1690). His careful selection of passages from John Walker's *An Attempt Towards Recovering an Account of the Numbers and Sufferings of the Clergy of the Church of England who were Sequester'd, Harass'd, &c. . . . in the . . . Times of the Great Rebellion* (London, 1714) may reveal his own sense of vulnerability. WRO 1981/1; Bodleian Library, MS Eng Misc f. 10, Diary 1718–60. I am grateful to Stephen Hobbs of the Wiltshire Record Office for bringing the Bodleian diary source to my attention and to Kenneth and Helen Rogers for giving me access to a copy, of which they are preparing an edition.

secular life of the community. The lack of a minister could have a devastating effect on the religious welfare of inhabitants. A particularly vivid example was Baydon, a chapelry in the parish of Ramsbury, where the curate received a stipend of only £6 a year for his maintenance. The villagers wrote a series of presentments and petitions complaining of the poor service they received as a result, 'which is notorious to the whole country'. They either had no minister at all or had a deacon who could not perform communion and who was forced 'to betake himself to the servile works of husbandry, which render the service & worship of God contemptible in the eies of the people'. Religious worship collapsed in the village as a result, 'whereby there hath ensued much error in Doctrine & profaneness in life & conversation, to the dishonour of God & the destruction of poore Souls'.[86] Similar pleas for help came from Stratton, where wardens presented that 'the church & parish for the most part is run to ruine and confusion',[87] and from Westbury where all things were 'out of joynt for want of a menester'.[88] The importance of the parson to his parishioners can be seen in the frequency of complaints about clerical pluralism and non-residence.[89]

The arrival of a minister could stimulate a dramatic revival of religious life. At Shalbourne the churchwardens reported in 1679 that 'all the parish comes to church since Mr May came, in beter order then they were formerly wont to doe'. The parish rejoiced in the replacement of the previous incumbent, who had been a common swearer, brawler and drunkard.[90] The laity wrote petitions and testimonials on behalf of ministers. The inhabitants of Swallowcliffe asked that their curate be allowed to remain with them, even though he was in trouble for performing clandestine marriages, because they had 'receaved much comfort & content by his officiating amongst us'. The dean of Salisbury answered their petition by agreeing that the curate could remain in Swallowcliffe, so long as he promised not to marry couples illegally in future.[91] The parishioners of Marlborough St Peter wrote to recommend that Farewell Perry, the curate of Mildenhall, be appointed in place of the recently deceased incumbent, and they asked that his meagre stipend be supplemented by appointment to the prebend of Winterbourne Earles, requests to which the bishop assented.[92] Churchwardens used visitation presentments, which were designed to detect moral and religious offenders, to express their satisfaction with their minister. The Downton wardens reported in 1662 that their curate preached 'to the great content of many well affected people', even though they admitted they were not

---

[86] D5/28, 1671, f. 14; 1675, f. 43; 1678, f. 34; 1692, f. 29; Tanner MS 143, f. 119; quoting D5/17/1/2.
[87] D5/28, 1674, f. 29.   [88] D25/12, May 1665.   [89] See chapter 5.
[90] D5/28, 1679, f. 55; 1678, f. 2. May was presumably a curate. A new incumbent, Daniel Stockwood, arrived in 1681.
[91] D5/28, 1668, f. 13. The curate gave a bond promising to perform no more clandestine marriages, but he soon broke his promise and tried to recover his bond.
[92] D1/14/1(d), f. 83. The bishop granted both requests and Perry's collation to Marlborough and the prebendary were recorded on 23 January 1685. D1/2/23, ff. 27v–28.

sure whether he was licensed.[93] Ministers were valued for their contributions to parish government, including the help they provided in drawing up rates, administering poor relief, and preparing presentments for ecclesiastical visitations.[94] Villagers naturally turned to the minister for help at times of crisis. Thus Roger Jarrett went to the vicar Mr Hodges for advice about what to do about his mentally unbalanced son, who kept trying to set the house on fire.[95]

Praise for individual clergymen was matched by criticism of others. Assaults against the clergy were rarely isolated incidents. They can be understood only in the context of broader disputes between the clergy and the laity. Laymen abused their minister when they were disappointed, disgusted, or angered by his behaviour. Such episodes should be seen as attacks on individuals rather than as generalised anticlericalism. The assault on Thomas Twittee as he read prayers at Draycot Foliat was the response to an extended campaign by the rector to claim tithes. By taking direct action to stop the new rector, so that he could not read the liturgy in the ruins of the abandoned church, inhabitants might be able to claim that he was not the legal incumbent because he had not fulfilled the requirements of the Act of Uniformity. Tithes were also involved at Netheravon, whose inhabitants were later to petition for a new minister because they objected to the violence and quarrelsomeness of the incumbent.[96] Matthew Whittley of Westport St Mary found himself the subject of a suit to correct his scandalous behaviour, because his drunkenness gave 'a very great offense and discouragem[en]t to the congregacon'.[97] The inhabitants of Knooke wrote to express the 'great comforte' they received from their curate, after four years of bitter conflict with his predecessor. They expressed the hope that 'he may be continued amongest us wee haveing been much profitted by him' and promised they would 'wth all cheerfullness submitt to the discipline of the Church and performe all conformity'.[98] Parishioners objected to individual clerics rather than to the clerical estate as a whole. Yet lay–clerical disputes nevertheless damaged the reputation of the Church and its clergy. They also damaged the worship of the Church, causing congregations to boycott, disrupt or ridicule church services.

A FACTIOUS, PROPHANE AND REFRACTORY PEOPLE

The parish of Hilperton in Wiltshire demonstrates the complexity of conflict between the laity and the clergy, so that issues of anticlericalism, irreligion, nonconformity, popular recreations and finance were interwoven.[99] James Garth was

---

[93] D1/54/1/4 (1662, W&W), ff. 39b, 41b.
[94] In Damerham South, for example. D1/42/59, f. 139v.
[95] The son was subsequently hauled off to prison. A1/110, T1666 (Informations). Jarrett's reference to the prison indicates that this incident occurred in Malmesbury, despite confusion over the minister's name.   [96] *WAM* 45, pp. 84–6.   [97] D1/42/62, ff. 2v–3.   [98] D5/21/1, 1671.
[99] This section is based on the following sources, unless otherwise indicated: D1/41/1/46 (12 March 1689/90); D1/41/4/43 (n.d.); D1/54/8 (18 Jan. 1675/6).

the vicar of Hilperton for thirty-nine years, from 1673 to 1702.[100] Although he was a pluralist, pastoral neglect was not a source of complaint. The vicar appointed a curate to his other parish of Keevil, and with the exception of an isolated incident when he complained that a man used opprobrious words against the clergy he encountered relatively little trouble there.[101] Garth was not so lucky in Hilperton, where he resided and officiated. He became a beleaguered and isolated figure who quarrelled with parishioners over many issues.

James Garth painted a black picture of worship in his parish, where he thought irreligion was endemic. Although there were over 200 people in his congregation who were old enough to receive communion, he observed that there were only '14 Christians amongst them (I mean Christian communicants)'.[102] Many parishioners failed to attend church regularly or to send their children to be catechised. Nonconformity was a persistent problem, for the parish was home to both Quakers and Baptists, but Garth reported in 1676 that only 35 of his 213 parishioners were nonconformists.[103] Garth's problems cannot be attributed entirely to nonconformity. Indeed, he used the courts against 'conformist' parishioners and complained when process against them ceased. The minister embarked on a solitary campaign against popular sociability and recreations. Villagers profaned the Sabbath 'by Drunkennesse, Fives-Playing, Cockfighting etc. Generally making no other use of the Lords house and day, but the one to bee the place, the other the Time of all manner of Prophanesse'. The minister presented those who sold drink without a licence and failed to keep good order 'espe[cial]ly on the L[or]ds day in times of Divine Service'.[104] He gained a Quarter Sessions order to remove a widow's cottage from parsonage land where he claimed idle persons played cards during divine service.[105]

James Garth quarrelled with members of his congregation over tithes and the use of church land. In addition to presenting them at visitations and Quarter Sessions for their neglect and misbehaviour, he was also the most litigious clergyman in Wiltshire, suing thirty-three defendants for their failure to pay their tithes.[106] Inhabitants expropriated portions of the glebe and the churchyard with the full co-operation of the churchwardens. Most of Hilperton's arable and pasture land had been enclosed by 1663[107] and Garth complained that inhabitants had 'inclos'd all the best arable Ground belonging to ye Parish, & converted it into pasture, & do still persist in inclosing more & more; & part of the best

[100] When Garth died at the age of 82 he had been ill for many years, preventing him from fulfilling his duties properly. Twelve years earlier he had complained of 'laboring under several of the infirmities of old age . . . as ye strangury, the stone, the wind, the scurvy'.
[101] D1/54/8 (16 Jan. 1675/6).   [102] By 1690 the number of communicants was down to twelve.
[103] Whiteman, *Compton Census*, p. 122.   [104] A1/110, E1680.
[105] A1/160/3, T1677; A1/160/4, T1679, E1682; A1/110, E1680.
[106] D1/39/1/59; PRO, Exchequer Bill Books, IND 1/16831, Wiltshire, case nos. 161, 162, 186, 260; IND 1/16835, Wiltshire, case nos. 14, 23, 30; WRO 1699/18, Book of Quaker Sufferings.
[107] VCH *Wilts* VII, pp. 86–7.

glebe land also purposely . . . to defraud the church of its due rights'. The church-wardens sold the church-house for use as a stable and allowed part of the church-yard to be enclosed so that the church-way was covered with dung. Individuals also allowed their sheep to feed on the parson's wheat.

The difficulty of disentangling the issues of nonconformity, irreligion, anti-clericalism and finance in Hilperton can be seen by considering Anthony Richman Sr, one of the ringleaders of those who were bitterly opposed to the minister. Garth accused Richman of 'many falce & scandalouse words against myselfe & the whole clergy', and the vicar was himself indicted for an assault on him.[108] Although Richman was persistently absent from church, an offence for which he was presented or indicted on at least four occasions between 1662 and 1684,[109] he did attend church occasionally. The magistrates sitting at Quarter Sessions were not convinced that he was nonconformist, and they freed him without trial. Richman was also involved in enclosing glebe land. His son was absent from church because he sold ale during divine service on Sundays. The bishop's consistory court excommunicated Richman, although for 'prophane-ness' rather than nonconformity, but this did not prevent him from becoming a churchwarden.

In addition to depositing excrement on the church porch, parishioners also expressed their hostility towards the vicar with verbal and physical violence. Two men struck at Garth when he told them to behave themselves in church. Two others called Garth a 'Rogue, lyer, & devill'. Parishioners tried to make the vicar's life as difficult as possible and hoped to eject him from the living. One of Garth's greatest problems was that the churchwardens sided with their neigh-bours against him, opposing the vicar on a broad range of issues. The church-wardens neglected to present nonconformists, supported popular recreations, and co-operated in the enclosure of church land. When the minister tried to stop fives-playing in the churchyard, they presented him at visitations on the grounds that he had damaged the church by removing the wire that protected its window. Garth had considerable difficulty finding support. When he appointed one of his few allies, Gifford Gerrish, as churchwarden, the other inhabitants refused to pay rates, claiming that he had been chosen against their will and was in any case too poor to hold office.[110]

The involvement of the churchwardens is one reason why so much is known about conflict in Hilperton. They presented the minister at visitations, and Garth responded with his own presentments and suits against members of his congregation, using the courts as a weapon with which to bludgeon his enemies. Hilperton thus became the site of a petty war between its minister and

---

[108] A1/110, H1682/3, indictments, f. 10. Henry Hurlbatt was also indicted for the same offence. The lack of the usual annotation suggests that the indictment did not proceed to a trial.
[109] D1/54/1/2 (1662, A&P), f. 79; D1/54/8; A1/110, T 1682, indictments, f. 11; A1/160/4, H 1682/3.
[110] D1/42/64e, ff. 1v–2.

parishioners. Garth became an isolated figure, who had antagonised his congregation and was left almost without a friend or ally. His situation was particularly bleak in the 1690s when he was ill and badly in debt. Garth suspected that the efforts to eject him were a consequence of his determination to expose religious offenders in the parish. There is no doubt about the strength of feeling against him. The vicar concluded that his parishioners were 'a People so factious, prophane, & Refractory . . . that no True Minister of the Gospell ever did or can quietly reside amongst them'.

LAY–CLERICAL CONFLICT

James Garth and his congregation suffered from a phenomenon that was far from unusual in late Stuart and Hanoverian England. Two out of three Wiltshire parishes experienced at least one dispute between the clergy and laity in the years from 1660 to 1740. In some parishes conflict was relatively short-lived, a disagreement between the minister and one or two inhabitants which was quickly resolved and almost as quickly forgotten. At the other extreme were parishes like Hilperton where an incumbent quarrelled repeatedly over many years with members of his congregation. Such disputes poisoned religious and social life within the parish and could not help but damage the authority of the Church and its clergy. Clashes of personality were often involved, yet the fact that some parishes had problems with minister after minister suggests that deeper structural and ideological problems were also involved. Those thirty or so Wiltshire parishes where lay–clerical conflict was a persistent theme of worship will be the focus of much of the remainder of this book, providing the basis for a dozen or so in-depth case studies that place us in the religious world of the parish.

Disputes between ministers and their congregations were not a new phenomenon. There is no reason to believe that lay–clerical conflict was substantially worse than it had been before the Civil Wars or would be in the early nineteenth century, when the Anglican clergy are known to have been targets for criticism. Yet, although they were common, such disputes have received relatively little attention from historians. Revisionist interpretations of such events as the English Reformation have questioned the religious significance of popular anticlericalism.[111] Among the literate, anticlericalism was an enduring theme of complaint literature from the time of Erasmus to Toland and beyond. At parish level lay–clerical disputes often appear to have been merely personal disagreements between individuals, and to have had little to do with larger religious issues. Tithes were increasingly viewed merely as property, so it is little surprise

---

[111] C. Haigh, 'Anticlericalism and the English Reformation', in Haigh, *The English Reformation Revised*, pp. 56–74; G. R. Elton, *Star Chamber Stories* (London, 1958), pp. 216–18. Cf. P. Marshall, *The Catholic Priesthood and the English Reformation* (Oxford, 1994), ch. 8.

that disputes arose over issues of payment and ownership.[112] The subjects at dispute had little to do with theological debates over such issues as the sacrament of grace, the positioning of the altar, or the wearing of a surplice. Yet they had a great deal to do with religion as it was experienced by parishioners. Conflicts might impinge directly upon church worship. The role of the minister as spiritual officiant and representative of the Church kept him constantly in the public eye.[113] A quarrel with the parson was different from any other precisely because it was with the parson, whose role as a shepherd of his flock was supposed to cause him to act as a peacemaker rather than a disputant. Disagreements inevitably influenced views of the clergy and Church, both for participants and for observers. Lay-clerical conflict is as significant to the study of parish religion as debates over doctrine, church government or ceremony. It is particularly important to an understanding of the religious and social relationship between the laity and the clergy. Lay-clerical conflict was a normal state of affairs rather than a pre-revolutionary event. The prevalence of conflict does not necessarily prove that lay–clerical relations were worsening. Yet it is possible to use particular disputes to understand the nature of these relations better.

The records left by episodes of conflict are among the few sources that document lay–clerical relations. The parish was the primary arena for conflict. Wherever parsons and parishioners met, in private homes and on public roads, in fields and alehouses, and most often in the church and churchyard, the place could be a scene for a dispute. The courts provided another arena, although their cost and inconvenience led most people to use them only as a last resort. They preferred to deal with matters within the community, if possible, rather than risk an escalation of tensions by resorting to prosecution or litigation. There were those who were quick to take offence and action, and despite the duty of charity they included clergymen among their number. Litigious ministers such as the Revd James Garth found the courts provided a weapon which came quickly to hand, but such men were the exception rather than the rule. Potential plaintiffs avoided resorting to the courts if they could and might hope that the threat of court action would be enough to cause potential defendants to settle. This was as true of the laity as the clergy. A contemporary pamphlet complained that it was 'a great failing, that all the Neighbourhood almost will agree to tell the story of such a Ministers miscarriages and sins to one another . . . but few or none have the courage or faithfulness to report it to such as may and would remedy it'.[114] The author advised nevertheless that exhortation to reform was better than court action, except in notorious cases. The decision to resort to the courts testifies to the desperation of the litigants and to the bitterness of the dispute. It is likely that many disputes left no record because they never reached the courts.

[112] P. Langford, *Public Life and the Propertied Englishman, 1689–1798* (Oxford, 1991), pp. 14–16.
[113] Burnet, *Pastoral Care*, ff. 177–8.
[114] *The Case of Peoples Duty in Living Under a Scandalous Minister Stated and Resolved*, p. 4.

Court action as often as not led to the escalation rather than the resolution of conflicts, which were then played out in suits and counter-suits, documents and court days. A churchwardens' presentment against a minister might be matched by his own counter-presentment against them. Parsons and parishioners exchanged prosecutions for pastoral neglect, non-payment of tithes and vilification of the clergy. Presentments, lists of charges, depositions, petitions and correspondence provide a detailed picture of religious and social life within the parish which is unmatched by any other source material. This rich body of sources often includes descriptions of church worship and parish life, activities about which it is otherwise notoriously difficult to find evidence. The texts of depositions and other sources include personal statements from lay people who otherwise left no record of their attitudes. These are not, of course, spontaneous expressions and cannot be taken at face value, nor are all members of village society equally likely to be represented. Visitation presentments came in response to a set of questions which was dictated by the interests of ecclesiastical authorities.[115] We are able to catch only rare glimpses of the way in which they were prepared and submitted. Depositions were also not made spontaneously but came in response to questions provided by the two parties. The testimonies of witnesses, and often presentments too, were recorded by scribes. Since in the consistory court the questions and their answers were written in Latin, language creates an additional barrier between people's voices and the documentary record. The registrar must have given the questions in English, but we cannot tell how close his translation was to the Latin original. Language was less of a problem when the answers were recorded, for the scribe's first language was English and any statement that escaped the formula was recorded in English.[116] Reading several answers to the same question rapidly makes it clear that witnesses spoke with individual voices. Petitions provide another useful source, although we do not know who took the lead or how the signatures were collected. The adversarial nature of court records introduces another interpretative problem, namely that of the bias of the sources. We cannot assume that the evidence of every witness survives or that every witness spoke the truth.

Disagreements are the business of the courts. It comes as no surprise that they provide evidence of disputes between clergy and laity, although the scale of such conflict may be surprising, particularly when it is remembered that many disputes may never have reached the courts. Court records are less effective at documenting amicable relations, which may only occasionally have been interrupted

---

[115] P. Burke, *Historical Anthropology of Italy* (Cambridge, 1987), on visitations as reflections of changing clerical concerns.

[116] In some Continental inquisition records three languages might be involved. A clerk whose first language was in one vernacular might record in Latin testimony which was given by a peasant in a wholly different dialectic. E. Le Roy Ladurie, *Montaillou* (New York, 1978); Carlo Ginzburg, *The Cheese and the Worms* (Baltimore and London, 1980).

by disagreements. There is a danger that reliance upon court records will lead us to exaggerate the significance of conflict while understating the extent of co-operation and consensus, which, as we have seen, often was present. Clerical diaries provide a complementary source that has the potential to allow experiences of conflict to be placed in due proportion with other events in a clergyman's life. Diaries have their own limitations, of course. They present a selective summary of a single person's viewpoint, which can rarely be verified from other sources. The completeness and accuracy of a diary depends upon the interests, discretion and perceptiveness of the diarist and upon whether entries were made soon after the events described or later in life. Nonetheless, clerical diaries reveal that even the most peaceable clergyman was rarely able to avoid at least a brief period of conflict during his incumbency. Indeed, these diaries have themselves been used to document the prevalence of lay–clerical conflict.[117] A dispute might occupy the thoughts and activities of a minister for several months, although only a minority of clerics and parishes were unfortunate enough to suffer disputes that pervaded their lives for a prolonged period. Those disputes that did occur underlined the fragility of the minister's position and of his relations with his congregation.

John Lewis of Great Chalfield, Holt and Atworth kept a detailed diary from 1718 to 1724.[118] Although he was a pluralist, Lewis was mostly on good terms with the inhabitants of his parishes. His diary documents his conscientious performance of his pastoral duties and his frequent visits to neighbours and to other ministers. Lewis spent most of his time in his study, reading books and preparing his weekly sermon, but he was not able to escape conflict. In 1718 he had to deal with an incident when several youths vandalised the church, requiring him to go to the next Quarter Sessions. In 1720 he brought an Exchequer bill against John Goulding for non-payment of tithes.[119] The case continued to trouble the minister for two years, and his diary shows how it distracted him from his normal regimen of reading and writing. In June and July he recorded details of the progress of his suit. He had to devote valuable time to copying documents and attending the sessions of the commission that took depositions from witnesses. In September and October his studies were disrupted completely by the business of the case, which occupied him for sixteen days. As a result, he was able to spend only five days a month reading and preparing sermons rather than the

---

[117] J. A. Phillips, 'The social calculus: deference and defiance in later Georgian England', *Albion* 21 (1989): 426–49.

[118] WRO 1981/1; Bodleian Library, MS Eng Misc f. 10, Diary 1718–60. The format and content of the diary suggest that Lewis kept it on a daily basis from 1718 to 1724, since there is an entry for each day of the month, and he recorded whether the weather was wet or dry. The first diary summarises his life until 1718. Lewis kept a less detailed and more reflective diary from 1725 to 1760.

[119] PRO, IND 1/16839, case 71, IND 1/17050, p. 364. This may have been the same Goulding who had previously disputed tithes with other ministers in Chalfield Magna and Broughton Gifford. D1/39/1/60; PRO, IND 1/16833 (case 9), 16835 (cases 41 and 42), 16837 (case 205).

fourteen days that he would normally have spent. Not until April 1722 was he able to record that he had ended his Exchequer suit.

Other clerical diaries confirm that disputes could disrupt relations between the clergy and laity, even when they were usually on good terms. The best known late eighteenth-century clerical diary is the one kept by James Woodforde, which presents a picture of leisured gentility. Yet, although Woodforde held an annual tithe dinner, even he had disputes with parishioners over tithes, and a disagreement with the choir about what they should sing caused the affronted singers to boycott prayers.[120] James Newton, the rector of Nuneham Courtenay (Oxon.), recorded in the brief entries of his diary at least nine quarrels over a span of two years. Although most concerned trivial exchanges of words with servants or villagers, Newton's efforts to remain on good terms with the local magnate Lord Harcourt were not always successful. The rector was vexed by the marked fall in church attendance that resulted from Lord Harcourt's relocation of the church and village so that he could expand his park. Their differences over tithes led the rector to seek consolation from the reflection that 'though I may have him for my Enemy, I trust I shall have God for my Friend'.[121]

Lay-clerical disputes were not everyday events, but they disturbed the lives of many clergymen at one time or another. The wise cleric took steps to avoid serious disagreement. Clerics were aware of the potential for conflict, and some sought to minimise it. James Newton resolved to 'study to do all offices of good Will toward my Neighbours, Foes as well as Friends'.[122] Wiltshire incumbents who became embroiled in disputes tried to escape their situations. William Durston tried to arrange a switch of parishes with the minister of Wilcot, explaining that 'they were such rogues at Tockenham, that he was weary of liveing amongst them'.[123] It is unlikely that he would have found the exchange, which would have cost him £70 a year, an improvement. Wilcot's minister, John Mortimer, also had difficulties with his parishioners, which led him to sue those who vilified him or failed to pay their tithes.[124] Other clergymen chose not to claim unpaid tithes in order to avoid unpleasant disagreements. The peacefulness of a parish was an attraction for clergymen considering a benefice, as can be seen from the advertisement in the *Salisbury Journal* placed by a Hampshire incumbent who wished to exchange livings. The minister sought to reassure interested

[120] James Woodforde, *The Diary of a Country Parson 1758–1802*, selected and edited by J. Beresford (Oxford, 1978), pp. 61–4 (12 Nov. to 24 Dec. 1769), 192 (3 Dec. 1782).
[121] G. Hannah, ed., *The Deserted Village: The Diary of an Oxfordshire Rector, James Newton, of Nuneham Courtnay 1736–86* (Stroud, 1992), quoting p. 110.   [122] Ibid.
[123] D1/41/4/35 (Tockenham, 1691).
[124] D1/39/1/63 (25 June 1691). Three of the five ministers who heard the testimony in this case had (or would have) personal experience of lay–clerical conflict. The litigious Thomas Twittee had already been pursuing his campaign to regain tithes for over twenty years. Farewell Perry brought his first tithe suit in 1695. Cornelius Yeate advised an Avebury landlord about how to deal with a troublesome cleric.

readers that his reasons were 'only of a private Nature, not relating to Parochial Affairs; and such as will not affect the Ease or Quiet of a successor'.[125] Yet in his haste to escape his benefice, he expressed a willingness to live in any one of four counties, suggesting that parochial affairs may indeed have been involved. Disputes with their congregations placed clergymen on the defensive and increased their sense of being members of a profession which was under attack. Members of the laity were equally troubled by disputes with their minister. As one contemporary advised, 'Sir, you will certainly find it a most uncomfortable thing to live at variance with your Pastor, a vexation like to that which the Wise Man calls a Continual Dropping.'[126] Such disputes were a constant irritation and could not help but disrupt worship. The same author warned that a quarrel with the minister would prejudice one against his doctrines and his person, and as a consequence would damage the health of one's own soul. Lay-clerical conflict revealed the depth of the gulf which lay between clergy and the laity, while contributing to the growth of the clergy's isolation from the common people and to the people's alienation from the Church. Although episodes of conflict were not everyday events, they reveal the attitudes of parsons and their parishioners which governed the behaviour of each in ordinary life. Conflicts exhibit the stresses and strains which afflicted the Church of England at their most extreme, and in particular the tension between competing visions of parish religion and of clerical authority.

Some parishes were somewhat more likely to be the site of disputes than others.[127] Because the collection of small tithes was more complicated than that of great tithes, conflicts involved vicars more often than rectors. Nonetheless, conflict was equally common on modest and wealthy benefices, although somewhat less usual on the poorest benefices where the position of the clergy was most desperate. Parishes where dissenters and their conventicles were present were also more likely to be the site of lay–clerical disputes, for two reasons. First, disputes sometimes occurred if a minister sought to prosecute nonconformists against the wishes of other inhabitants. The second, and more important, explanation is that the same conditions encouraged dissent from the Church and disputes within it. Just as scattered settlements offered dissenters a greater chance of meeting out of the sight of authorities, they also often presented an incumbent with a pastoral problem of serving two or more chapelries. Chapelries expected to be treated like parishes and frequently complained that the minister

---

[125] *Salisbury Journal*, 22 Jan. 1740.

[126] *The Case of Peoples Duty in Living Under a Scandalous Minister Stated and Resolved*, p. 17.

[127] Parishes where ministers were the subject of presentments or correctional suits, brought presentments themselves, sued for vilification of clergy, or sued five or more than five tithe defendants, and parishes with other evidence of conflict were compared with D1/27/1/1, ff. 73–99 (incomes and patronage); Browne Willis, *A Survey of the Cathedrals . . .* (London, 1742), vol. III (patronage); Whiteman, *Compton Census*, pp. 105–35; Turner, *Original Records*, pp. 106–27; CSPD 1671–2, pp. 305ff., 1672–3 (nonconformity).

was neglecting their needs. Parishes of scattered settlement often received less direct oversight from their social superiors, of which one indicator is the owner-ship of the advowson. Conflict was somewhat more likely where a relatively remote peer or the Crown was the patron of the living. It occurred less often where a local gentleman who was able to take more interest in parish affairs was patron. It should be stressed, however, that the influence of each of these under-lying factors was relatively small. In practice, lay–clerical conflict could occur virtually anywhere, and it often did. The local dynamic of social, personal and religious relations, which differed from one parish to another, was a more impor-tant determinant of disputes than any underlying factors.

It is often difficult to tell what triggered a particular episode of lay–clerical conflict, because disputes were usually well advanced by the time they reached the courts. Parsons and parishioners each complained about the other. Lay com-plaints against the clergy can be grouped into four broad categories. Most common was the charge that the incumbent or his curate had failed his cure of souls by neglecting some aspect of his pastoral role, such as reading divine service with sufficient frequency or visiting the sick. The laity also complained if some duty, such as preaching, was performed badly. Charges of pastoral neglect were often the subject of a churchwardens' presentment at the regular visitations made by the bishop and dean of Salisbury. Over eighty parishes and chapelries filed such presentments at some point between 1660 and 1740, some repeatedly; others complained that they had no minister at all. Serious cases were often heard by the consistory court, as the result of either a presentment or a complaint made directly to the ordinary such as a petition. When, as was often the case, such cases pursued the plenary instance procedures in which charges (libels), counter-charges (interrogata) and depositions were taken, they are particularly well documented. Over forty suits were brought to the consistory courts of the bishop or dean seeking the correction and reform of clergymen for pastoral neglect, scandal and solemnising clandestine marriages, among other offences. A second category of accusation was the charge that a clergyman had failed to conform to the liturgy of the Church of England. Despite official anxiety in the 1660s and 1690s, there were few accusations against nonconform-ing clergymen who sought to remain within the Church. Thirdly, clergy might be charged with scandalous behaviour, most often drunkenness or sexual inconti-nence, which rendered them unable to set a moral example to members of their congregation, and often also unfit to administer sacraments. Fourthly, parishion-ers might complain that their minister had failed to live in charity with his neigh-bours by being quarrelsome, starting fights, or even just by behaving litigiously. Such behaviour was often linked to disputes over scandalous behaviour or the payment of tithes and indicated particularly serious disputes between the clergy and the laity.

Clergymen in turn brought their own charges against lay people and in doing so they revealed not only local problems with worship but also a widely shared pessimism about standards of lay religiosity. Churchwardens were often the subject of clerical accusations that they had failed to fulfil the duties of their office, either by failing to replace church goods or to repair church fabric or by neglecting to present religious and moral offenders, including of course nonconformists. Clergymen also presented offenders themselves, including those who failed to attend church, receive communion, or adopt other rites of the Church. Such behaviour sometimes, but not invariably, indicates people who were dissenters from the Church, a nagging source of worry for the parish clergy. Serious disputes are sometimes revealed by clerical complaints against lay people who disrupted the church services. A suit for vilification of the clergy is evidence of lay abuse of an individual clergyman, and usually signals bitter conflict. The clergy brought around forty suits in the consistory courts for vilification or defamation. The clerical complaint that was the most common by far was that individuals had failed to pay the tithes and offerings they owed. Clergymen brought suits for the substraction or withholding of tithes in the consistory court or the Exchequer Court of Equity against over 850 defendants.[128] The process of dividing types of cases into distinct categories, however helpful it is for purposes of analysis, is misleading. An episode of lay–clerical conflict often involved several issues, each reinforcing the others, so that it is often impossible to determine the initial cause of disagreement. In some cases, disagreements over money or land were a constant irritant that frayed lay–clerical relations and made disagreements over other issues more likely. In others, it was the neglectful or scandalous behaviour of the minister that led laymen to withhold their tithes. The involvement of the parish minister in conflict meant that popular attitudes towards religion and the worship of the Established Church could not help but be affected.

---

[128] See chapter 6.

Clerical profiles

The eyes of contemporaries and historians alike have been caught by two clerical stereotypes, the impoverished curate and the wealthy pluralist. Eighteenth-
century prints capture these familiar figures. One cartoon portrays a greedy
pluralist who is reaching out to hold four churches at once. Another shows a fat
incumbent seated comfortably with his tithe profits in a carriage that is being
pulled by his lean curates. 'The Church was made for Me, and not I for the
Church,' the complacent parson observes.[1] One of the harshest critics of the
Church and its clergy was Gilbert Burnet, who served as bishop of Salisbury
during the crucial period from 1689 to 1715 when the political debate over religion raged most fiercely. Burnet decried the corrupting influence of 'Covetousness,
aspiring to preferments, and a restless seeking after great livings', which clergymen often sought to hold in plurality. Parsons should 'watch over and feed their
Flock, and not enjoy their Benefices only as Farms, or as Livings', a word to
which he particularly objected. Burnet nevertheless believed that the sharp contrast between wealthy beneficed clerics and starving curates did the Church no
good. The ignorance of many clergymen, which was due to the poor quality of
education they received from the universities, also contributed to contempt for
the clergy. Although Burnet disliked the clericalism of his political foes, he was
nevertheless concerned that the status of the clerical profession would be
damaged by the poor preparation of entrants, which compared unfavourably
with the intensive training required of practitioners in the remaining two great
professions, medicine and the law.[2]

Burnet was hardly an unbiased source, and his charges cannot be taken at face
value. His confrontations with High Churchmen, both within Convocation and
in his own diocese, gave him a jaundiced view of the lesser clergy. By his own
admission, he was predisposed to think badly of clergymen. He disliked what he

---

[1] J. Miller, *Religion in the Popular Prints 1600–1832* (Cambridge, 1986), plates 54 (BMC 2618) and
53 (BMC 2003). For a literary example see T. Smollet, *The Adventures of Roderick Random*
(1750), vol. I, ch. 9.
[2] Foxcroft, pp. 101, 103, 330, 500, 502, 506; Burnet, *Pastoral Care*, pp. xxvi–xxvii, 172–5, quoting
117, 159. For Burnet's implicit anticlericalism, see J. A. I. Champion, *The Pillars of Priestcraft
Shaken: The Church of England and its Enemies, 1660–1730* (Cambridge, 1992), pp. 81–2.

regarded as cruelty towards nonconformists, and the clergy in turn considered him a traitor to the Church, opposing his attempts to reform the church courts, to reduce pluralism and to provide theological training for those preparing for the priesthood.[3] Burnet's critique nevertheless introduces the main issues which must be considered in any review of the position of the clergy: their incomes, the significance of pluralism, their education and scholarship, and the extent to which the clerical profession formed a distinct and cohesive social group. The issues of the quality of pastoral care and the treatment of nonconformity, also identified by Burnet, will be considered later in this volume (see chapters 5, 7).

It is difficult to generalise about the clergy of late seventeenth- and eighteenth-century England because individual experiences differed so greatly. In a phrase that has often been quoted, Joseph Addison divided the clergy into 'Generals, Field-Officers, and Subalterns'.[4] Even within the last and largest group there was considerable variety. There was no such thing as a 'typical' clergyman. The wide range in clerical incomes made certain of that. This chapter will explore the position of the clergy with the help of three case studies, of an impoverished and unhappy vicar in the 1670s, a late seventeenth-century squarson, and a contented and well-read early eighteenth-century pluralist. As will become clear, the distinction between poor and rich, curate and pluralist, is too simple to embrace the variety of clerical experiences. The clergy's position was a function not only of their incomes but also of their birth, education, sociability and administrative role. Their social status was ambiguous. They participated in the societies of the gentry, the yeomanry and, of course, the clergy. This marginal position on the boundaries between social groups was fundamentally unstable and could generate anxiety and a sense of vulnerability. Yet many parsons found strength and comfort in their professional role in the study and pulpit and in fellowship with other clergymen.

AN ILL-LIVING MAN

Since the late seventeenth century most observers have agreed that the great majority of Addison's subalterns, the parish clergy, lived in poverty. In 1670 John Eachard argued that clerical poverty was one of the reasons why both the clergy and religion were held in contempt. He estimated that not one living in forty was worth £100. How is it possible, he asked, for a man to maintain a family on £20 to £30 a year 'without committing himself to such vileness as will, in all likelihood, render him contemptible to his people'?[5] In the nineteenth century

[3] Foxcroft, pp. 178, 317, 499–506.
[4] *The Spectator*, no. 21, 24 March 1711.
[5] *The Grounds and Occasions of the Contempt of the Clergy and Religion* (London, 1670), reprinted in *Critical Essays and Literary Fragments*, ed. J. C. Collins (New York, 1906), pp. 241–315 (passages quoted from pp. 307, 293).

Macaulay embellished Eachard's account. The clergy were a 'plebeian class', he wrote. 'Hardly one living in fifty enabled the incumbent to bring up a family comfortably. As children multiplied and grew, the household of the priest became more and more beggarly . . . His children were brought up like the children of the neighboring peasantry. His boys followed the plough; & his girls went out to service.'[6] Twentieth-century historians have often accepted these views. 'Without doubt,' Geoffrey Best argues, 'the church's main material defect in this period was the poverty that brought contempt upon so many of its clergy.' According to Eric Evans, Macaulay's 'portrait of the English clergy as labourers in the vine-yard is for the most part accurate. Few clerics in 1700 could comfortably attend to the cure of souls without working also for the provision of their daily bread'.[7]

Robert Randall was one such impoverished clergyman.[8] His example demonstrates the severe stress that poverty placed upon ministers, with unfortunate consequences for their own welfare and for the pastoral care that they were supposed to provide for their congregations. Randall might be regarded as relatively fortunate because he had succeeded in acquiring a benefice as vicar of Great Bedwyn from 1668 to 1679. Yet he was little better off than a lowly curate. In 1672 the churchwardens presented 'the smallness of our vicarage as being too small a competency to maintaine a Minister'.[9] The living was worth only £20, a sum sometimes augmented by an annual payment of £5 from the patron.[10] Great Bedwyn, which lies on the eastern edge of Wiltshire, was part of the peculiar of the Lord Warden of Savernake Forest, who was the duke of Somerset. The Seymour dukes of Somerset owned the advowson and the profits, and throughout the seventeenth century they held the land tithe-free in return for a modest annual rent.[11] The vicar was entitled to receive no tithes at all, although he sometimes managed to persuade a tenant to pay them on newer crops such as turnips and carrots. The duke generously ordered his steward to make the annual

---

[6] T. B. Macaulay, *The History of England from the Accession of James the Second* (London, 1913–15), vol. I, pp. 315, 318.

[7] G. F. A. Best, *Temporal Pillars: Queen Anne's Bounty, the Ecclesiastical Commissioners, and the Church of England* (Cambridge, 1964), p. 13; E. J. Evans, *The Contentious Tithe: The Tithe Problem and English Agriculture, 1750–1850* (London, 1976), p. 3. For an important note of dissent, see John Pruett's study, which finds that the clergy in late seventeenth-century Leicestershire were relatively prosperous. J. H. Pruett, *The Parish Clergy under the Later Stuarts: The Leicestershire Experience* (Urbana, 1978), p. 175.

[8] Unless otherwise indicated, references in this section are based on D5/22/18, ff. 17–22v, 25–8, and on another copy of the testimony in D5/22/17, ff. 12–30. For more details of Randall's extreme behaviour and of the management of the correctional suit brought against him, see pp. 97–100, 130–1, 208–9.   [9] D21/2/3, f. 80.

[10] Deponents to an Exchequer suit testified that the benefice was worth £18 or £20 a year. PRO, E134/30 Charles II East 7. By 1707, the estimated value had risen to £30. J. Ecton, *Liber valorum et decimarum* (London, 1711).

[11] The dukes of Somerset leased the tithes from the dean and chapter of Windsor in 1603 for 99 years. They paid £77 a year for tithes that parliamentary commissioners valued at £219 in 1650. 'The church survey in Wilts, 1649–50', *WAM* 41 (1920): 37–8.

payment of £5 to the vicar so long as it was recognised that this was a free gift and not a right.[12]

The impoverished vicars of Great Bedwyn were obliged to search for means of supplementing their incomes. Without tithes, the annual offerings paid by each layman loomed large. Robert Randall resorted to violence to collect overdue offerings. To the horror of a witness he threatened one defaulter, 'God damne mee if thou doth not pay mee now I will cutt off thy pricke.' He forced another, a female servant, to pay him three years' worth of offerings (rather than the single year she claimed she owed) by frightening her with threats of imprisonment. Each vicar of Great Bedwyn also sought to take advantage of the parish's status as a peculiar by performing clandestine marriages. This was a desperate step because, however popular it might be among the laity, it carried the risk of suspension for three years.[13] Randall's predecessor, Robert Billings, tried unsuccessfully to claim that he could provide marriage licences on his own authority.[14] Randall sought to evade official disapproval by using decanal or archiepiscopal licences, but he made the mistake of marrying a couple from North Tidworth, the parish served by the dean's son.[15] When these financial expedients failed, the vicars of Great Bedwyn had little choice but to try to use the courts to support claims for tithes. After nine years as vicar, Randall followed his predecessor's example by suing tenants for privy tithes. But his suit was fruitless; its only results were to incur expense and to antagonise the laity further.[16]

The pressures of poverty took their toll upon both the vicar's mental welfare and the religious welfare of the parish. Randall began the downward spiral of scandalous living and personal deterioration that would end only with his death. He turned to drink and gained a reputation for violent behaviour and language. The minister kept ill company in the inns and alehouses of the neighbourhood when, in the opinion of his congregation, his time would have been spent to better effect in his study. Randall appears to have suffered a crisis of calling, telling one person that he could preach better sermons from Aristotle than from the Bible. The intemperate minister took out his frustrations on his wife. He told his children to curse their mother, calling her a devil and a toad, and he offered to swap her for the wives of at least two other men. Randall's behaviour renders even more tragic the fact that his death in 1679 left his widow penniless, forcing her to turn first to the parish and then, when the parish refused to help, to the Quarter Sessions for relief for herself and her children.[17]

[12] PRO, E134/30 Charles II East 7; E112/535/156.
[13] See pp. 203–14 for a fuller discussion of clandestine marriage.
[14] D5/22/15, ff. 47–47v. In 1713 another vicar, William Meaden, also was presented for performing clandestine marriages. D5/28, 1713.
[15] J. W. Packer, *The Transformation of Anglicanism, 1643-1660* (Manchester, 1989), p. 54.
[16] PRO, E112/535/156; E134/30 Charles II East 7; IND 1/16829, cases 25, 55; IND 1/16831, cases 156, 282.　　[17] A1/110, M1679.

Members of Randall's congregation began to stay away from church, attending services in neighbouring parishes such as Burbage, Tidcombe and Little Bedwyn. They were particularly reluctant to receive communion from the profane vicar. When a new landlord arrived in the parish and 'enquired touching the life and conversacon' of the vicar, he was informed that the minister 'was an Ill Liveing man'. Squire Player decided to promote a correctional suit against Randall in the dean's consistory court. Robert Randall was a pitiful creature, whose experience demonstrates the damaging effects of clerical poverty. A remedy for the plight of the parish and its incumbents was slow to arrive. Although it was in order to help parishes like Great Bedwyn that Queen Anne's Bounty was established, the benefice would not receive an augmentation until 1823.[18]

THE INCOMES OF THE CLERGY

Not all clergymen were poor, although contemporaries thought that most were. The range of clerical incomes in Wiltshire was wide. It is easy to find examples of both impoverished and wealthy benefices. At one extreme, Seagry was worth only £10 and Biddestone St Peter only £13 a year. At the other, Collingbourne Ducis and Steeple Langford were each worth £300 a year.[19] How typical were these examples? The diocese of Salisbury fortunately is not short of information to answer this question. No fewer than four sets of surveys survive for the period from 1650 to 1710. The parliamentary survey of 1650 was taken to identify parishes that were candidates for merging or dividing. Because it covers only half of Wiltshire and its coverage is uneven, it cannot be trusted as a representative sample.[20] The survey most familiar to historians was taken in around 1707 in accordance with the terms of Queen Anne's Bounty and was subsequently published in a variety of versions including John Ecton's *Liber valorum et decimarum* (1711). Ecton's book is neither entirely reliable nor complete since it lists current values only for benefices worth less than £50. The Exchequer did not collect the current values of more valuable livings (except, in a separate survey, for those between £50 and £80). In a few cases these can be found in a third survey, the Notitiae Parochialis. This private survey, apparently undertaken at the instructions of Robert Harley, is unsystematic and

---

[18] C. Hodgson, *An Account of the Augmentation of Small Livings* (London, 1826), p. 415.
[19] The poverty of Seagry forced its incumbent to preach 'up and downe at other places for his livelyhood'. D1/42/61, f. 256 (1671).
[20] The survey, which covers only 136 parishes, includes at least 89 per cent of livings in Amesbury, Malmesbury and Wilton deaneries, but less than 10 per cent in Cricklade and Potterne deaneries. Benefices may have been worth less in 1650 due to disruptions caused by the Civil Wars and unwillingness to pay tithes. The manuscript copy of the parliamentary survey in Lambeth Palace is reprinted as E. J. Bodington, 'The church survey in Wilts, 1649–50,' *WAM* 40: 253–72, 297–317, 392–416; 41: 1–39, 105–28.

incomplete, making it unreliable as a source.[21] The fourth survey, kept by Bishop Seth Ward in the 1670s, is the most complete record of living values. Ward kept a table of benefices in which he recorded the value of almost every parish under his jurisdiction.[22] The source of the figures in Ward's survey is not clear, and its usefulness is reduced by the bishop's tendency to round values to the nearest £10.[23] Nonetheless, as the most comprehensive survey of benefices, both rich and poor, it provides an indispensable source of evidence on the incomes of the clergy.

The extent to which the clergy appear to have been poor naturally depends upon where one decides to draw the 'poverty line'. In September 1661 the Crown instructed bishops and deans to ensure that vicars and perpetual curates of church-owned rectories had their annual income augmented to at least £80.[24] The mandate noted in particular the many 'Rurall Prebends where the vicaridges are not sufficiently endowed', concern that the example of Great Bedwyn shows was justified. Gregory King's famous estimates of the incomes of different social groups suggest that £80 was unrealistically high. King regarded £72 as the average income of 'eminent clergymen' and thought that lesser clergymen were worth £50 a year.[25] Since £50 was also adopted as the official poverty line by Queen Anne's Bounty, it seems reasonable to accept this figure as the amount which contemporaries regarded as the bare minimum for a beneficed clergyman. Incumbents receiving less than £50 a year were discharged from the payment of first fruits and tenths and were eligible to receive an augmentation. If King's figures are to be trusted, an income of between £50 and £80 would have placed the clergy firmly within the middling sort. A cleric with £50 a year was on a par with the lesser freeholders and tradesmen. Only those who fell below this level were in danger of sharing the lowly position of labourers. A cleric worth £80 a year would have been one of the wealthiest inhabitants of the parish, with an income close to the £91 at which King rated 'freeholders of the better sort'. On the negative side of the balance, ministers had the cost of the upkeep and establishment of the parsonage, which hearth tax returns suggest was often one of the

[21] The Notitiae Parochialis includes only thirty-nine Wiltshire parishes that replied to an advertisement printed at the end of a brief distributed to parishes. Lambeth Palace Library, MSS 960–5; WRO 413/50.

[22] D1/27/1/1, ff. 73–99. The survey includes 205 parishes. Since Ward became ill in the 1680s, it most likely covers the 1670s. Most parishes include two estimates, one of which is followed by the letter 'D', suggesting an estimate made during the episcopate of either Robert Davenant (1620–40) or Brian Duppa (1641–5, d. 1660). The values are close to those found by the parliamentary survey.

[23] I have compensated for this tendency by assuming that half of the livings Ward valued at £50, £80 and £100 were worth less and that the other half were worth more.

[24] D1/27/1/4, f. 32 Some bishops responded generously to this letter, which threatened to withhold future preferment from those who disobeyed. I. M. Green, *The Restoration of the Church of England 1660–62* (Oxford, 1978), pp. 109–10.

[25] G. S. Holmes, 'Gregory King and the social structure of pre-industrial England', *Transactions of the Royal Historical Society*, 5th ser., 27 (1977): 41–68, includes a copy of King's table, which has often been reprinted. Holmes questions the reliability of King's population figures.

largest houses in the parish.[26] Most clergymen fell well below the annual income
of £280 or more that King attributed to the gentry.[27] King's figures can provide
only very rough guidelines since they make no allowance for the considerable
variations between regions. Clerical incomes in Salisbury diocese were no doubt
considerably higher than they were in northern dioceses such as Chester,[28]
although this may also have been true of lay incomes.

Ecton's *Liber valorum* is often used to document the poverty of the clergy, so it
is unfortunate that it is not entirely reliable. Comparison with the returns that
Salisbury diocese sent to Exchequer and with other sources reveal that up to ten
parishes worth more than £50 were discharged from first fruits and tenths in error.
This did not prevent three of these parishes from benefiting from the Bounty by
1740. These mistakes were the result of reading or transcription errors and lack of
familiarity with the local context. In at least one case, the Exchequer office was
fooled by a return that cleverly presented the net rather than the gross value of the
benefice, so that it appeared to fall below the £50 threshold. The return for Broad
Chalke with Bower Chalke stated that the parish was worth £83, but then sub-
tracted all charges and the cost of a curate for the chapelries to produce a 'clear
value' of £48 18s. 6d., the exact figure recorded by Ecton.[29] Since Broad Chalke was
a large parish with two chapelries, which had been split into three separate parishes
during the Commonwealth, it might be thought that it had a good case for special
treatment, yet the burdens placed upon its incumbent were far from unique.

Ecton's under-valuation of some parishes is partly compensated for by his
over-valuation of others.[30] After correction, Ecton's figures suggest that 27 per
cent of livings fell below the threshold of £50, a substantial proportion but far
less than was the case in some other parts of England.[31] Even if Ecton's figures

---

[26] The incumbents of Wylye and Wootton Bassett had eight and four hearths respectively in 1662,
placing them at or close to the top of the parish, although the latter received an exemption. PRO,
E179/259/29, ff. 97v–98; E179/259/26B, ff. 15–16. It is unsafe to use hearth tax returns to estimate
clerical incomes, because the parsonage might have been larger than the living justified. For
example, the curacy of the chapelry of Baydon was returned with two hearths in 1662, even though
it was worth only £6 a year. PRO, E179/259/29, f. 15.

[27] Cf. G. Holmes, *Augustan England: Professions, State and Society, 1680–1730* (London, 1982), p.
95.

[28] E. J. Evans, 'The Anglican clergy of northern England', in C. Jones, ed., *Britain in the First Age
of Party 1680–1750* (London and Ronceverte, 1987), pp. 225–8.

[29] D1/3/5/1. This method of calculation may have been thought to be justifiable since it was similar
to that used to calculate the 'clear value' when negotiating the fine to be paid by the leaseholder
of an ecclesiastical benefice. C. Clay, '"The greed of Whig bishops"?: church landlords and their
lessees 1660–1760', *Past and Present* 87 (May 1980): 33.

[30] Four parishes were listed among those that were not discharged of first fruits and tenths, although
other sources indicate that they were worth less than £50. Another five parishes that were probably worth less than £50 were omitted entirely from the lists, although these are balanced by the
simultaneous omission of some worth more than £50.

[31] Ecton lists 248 Wiltshire parishes, of which he says 66 were worth less than £50. According to
Evans, 51 per cent of livings in England and Wales were worth less than £50, rising to nearly 70
per cent in the dioceses of York, Chester and St David's. Evans, 'The Anglican clergy of northern
England', p. 225.

provide a reasonably accurate picture of the state of the clergy around 1700, they almost certainly exaggerate the extent of clerical poverty in the longer period from 1660 to 1740. Agricultural depression and high taxation hit the incomes of clergymen hard, particularly those with smaller benefices, in the decades immediately before and after 1700.[32] In Wiltshire the need to raise additional funds to pay the land tax prompted some desperate clergymen to perform clandestine marriages.[33] The returns to Exchequer document the difficulties in which clergymen found themselves. Many leased their glebe and tithe rights, ensuring themselves a reliable income free from the burdens of managing the land directly. Yet in the early eighteenth century they were often unable to negotiate as much rent as they would have liked. One farmer realised too late that Chicklade was worth only £40 rather than the £50 he had paid for it, but others were shrewder. Rollestone was said to be worth about £46, but it had been leased for as little as £30. Although Chitterne St Mary was valued at £35, a note reported sadly that no tenant had been prepared to offer this much.[34]

Comparison of Ecton's values with Bishop Ward's estimates of forty years earlier confirms that benefices had fallen in value. Of the 46 parishes for which figures are available for both surveys, no fewer than 25 suffered a loss in value of at least £10. For some incumbents, the decline in value was enough to push them below the £50 threshold. Ward estimated that only one in six livings was worth less than £50, whereas Ecton's lists suggest more than one in four was. Local circumstances explain the decline in value in some parishes. In Hilperton, for example, the enclosure and conversion to pasture of the best arable land left the vicar much worse off, and the resulting ill-feeling seriously disrupted religious life in the parish.[35] The incumbent James Garth fell so deeply into debt that he had to make over his benefice to a creditor. In other parishes, the bad times were themselves enough to reduce benefice values. Since the clergy depended upon the yields from their glebe and from tithes, they were affected directly by agricultural depression, and taxation of tithes was an added blow. Clerical incomes improved again in the agricultural upturn that began in 1712 and also benefited from the low level of the land tax.[36] While realising that clerical incomes were subject to change, it seems likely that for much of the period Ward's figures provided a better estimate of benefice values than Ecton's. This view receives some confirmation from the discovery that diocesan officials continued to use Ward's figures for much of the eighteenth century.[37]

Ward's survey suggests that most beneficed clergy were reasonably prosperous, while confirming the presence of inequality. The small minority (17 per cent) of livings that fell below the poverty line of £50 were balanced by a similar

---

[32] Holmes, *Augustan England*, pp. 83–4.

[33] John Hopkins of Hankerton to Francis Henry Carey, 21 Oct. 1691, PRO, C104/137.

[34] D1/3/5/1. The landed gentry also had difficulties collecting rent in these years. G. Holmes, *British Politics in the Age of Anne* (London, 1967), pp. 159–60.

[35] D1/41/4/43.   [36] Holmes, *Augustan England*, p. 89.

[37] Ward's figures are repeated in a Diocese Book begun in the 1720s and updated for the rest of the century.

Table 2.1 *Distribution of incomes of pluralists and non-pluralists c. 1683*

	Non-pluralists	Pluralists' livings	Pluralists' incomes
£1–49	31 19%	7 18%	1 5%
£50–99	45 34%	19 50%	1 5%
£100–99	54 33%	8 21%	12 63%
£200+	22 13%	4 11%	5 26%

Sources: D1/27/1/1; D1/48/2.

number (13 per cent) that were worth £200 or more, placing them on a par with the lesser gentry. Most livings fell somewhere in the middle. Around 60 per cent exceeded the threshold of £80 set by the Crown after the Restoration.[38] It must be stressed that these are figures for the values of livings and not for the incomes of individual clergymen. Furthermore, they relate only to beneficed clergymen and not to unbeneficed curates, whose situation was far less rosy. There are no surveys of curates' salaries to match those of benefices, so it is necessary to rely upon scattered references. Legislation in 1714 set the salaries of assistant curates at between £20 and £50.[39] In practice, salaries were usually between £20 and £30 a year, although there were instances of curates who received as little as £16 or even £6 a year.[40] If the forty assistant curates who were employed in 1683 are added to the thirty-five benefices worth less than £50 then as many as 30 per cent of all serving clergy in Wiltshire were in poverty.[41] Curates formed an underclass of the parish clergy who fell below the threshold set by Queen Anne's Bounty without being eligible to benefit from it.

Pluralism was not yet as serious a pastoral problem as it would later become,[42] so only a minority of the clergy had an opportunity to benefit from the increased income it could bring. Two types of pluralism, parochial and prebendal, overlapped to only a small degree.[43] At least 26 of Wiltshire's 206 incumbents held more than

[38] For comparison with other dioceses see the table in Pruett, *The Parish Clergy*, p. 105. The mean benefice in Leicestershire in 1707, for example, was worth about £86 a year. Livings in Warwickshire were worth less, about £66 a year on average. J. L. Salter, 'Warwickshire clergy, 1660–1714' (Ph.D. dissertation, Birmingham University, 1978), p. 22. (Both figures based on vicarages and rectories only.)

[39] Act for the Better Maintenance of Curates within the Church of England, 12 Anne stat. 2, c. 2.

[40] Since no survey of curates' income was taken, we must depend upon lucky survivals. The ministers of Bemerton and of Donhead St Andrew each allowed their curates £30 a year, but that of Plaitford only £16. D1/54/6 (1674); D1/54/3 (1668). In 1650 £20 was the most common stipend for a curate, as in Britford, Maddington and Oaksey ('Church survey in Wilts').

[41] The number of assistant or stipendiary curates varied from year to year. There were around fifty in 1680, excluding those in impropriate curacies. D1/48/1.

[42] P. Virgin, *The Church in an Age of Negligence: Ecclesiastical Structure and Problems of Church Reform 1700-1840* (Cambridge, 1989), ch. 8.

[43] A third type of pluralism, which occurred when an incumbent of one parish was also curate of another, is more difficult to detect.

one parochial benefice within the county, and others doubtless held benefices outside the county.[44] Twenty incumbents held cathedral stalls. Examples of stereotypical incumbents who combined two or more rich benefices were uncommon. The holders of poor and modest livings benefited more from parochial pluralism than their wealthier colleagues. Whereas one in four incumbents with a living worth less than £100 had responsibility for the cure of souls of more than one parish, only one in nine of those with livings worth more than £100 did so. Parochial pluralism had the effect of raising a number of incumbents with modest livings to reasonable prosperity. Whereas three out of four livings of pluralists were worth less than £100, their combined incomes pulled all but two of them above this level. Thirteen of fifty-one incumbents with livings at or below the £50 threshold were pulled above it by pluralism. In theory, parochial pluralists had to set against their additional income the cost of a curate. In practice, they often went without a curate, preferring to serve both benefices themselves. Curates were more often hired to help the incumbents of parishes with chapelries than pluralists.

Owners of cathedral stalls were among Addison's field officers. Prebendal pluralism was almost entirely to the advantage of wealthier clergymen. Only two of the twenty Wiltshire clergymen with a prebend in Salisbury cathedral in 1683 are known to have had a benefice worth less than £50.[45] One exception was Marlborough St Peter, worth only £28, which for a time after 1677 was commonly coupled with the prebend of Winterbourne Earles, an arrangement that was popular with the inhabitants.[46] Bishop Burnet later claimed that he was forced to abandon the unpopular plan to give prebendaries to ministers of market towns to compensate for low incomes.[47] It is difficult to be precise about incomes from prebends, which were treated as beneficial leases. The prebendary would as a matter of course have leased the associated property and would have been guaranteed a modest annual rent, which bore little relation to the true 'improved' value of the property. In addition, he could normally expect to receive every few years a fine that reflected its true 'improved' value. Such fines are rarely documented, but it is possible to estimate what they might have been so long as too much weight is not placed upon such estimates or the assumptions on which they are based. A new prebendary might find that the lease had just been extended by his predecessor and might die or exchange stalls before he had a chance to benefit. The fine itself depended upon agreement over the improved

---

[44] University alumni records suggest that as many as twenty-four Wiltshire incumbents may also have held a benefice outside the diocese, although they rarely indicate whether they held them at the same time. *Alumni Oxoniensis.*

[45] Daniel Whitby of Salisbury St Edmund (for which no value is available) may have been a third example, but since Whitby was also precentor of the cathedral he is unlikely to have been poor. Some Wiltshire clerics probably held prebends in other dioceses as well.

[46] After Sacheverell's death, the inhabitants of Marlborough St Peter asked that the rectory and prebend both be given to Farewell Perry, a request the bishop granted in January 1685. D1/14/1(d), f. 83; D1/2/23, ff. 27v–28.   [47] Foxcroft, pp. 504–5.

value, the interest rate and the term of the lease. Nonetheless, it was common for leases to be extended every seven years and for the fine to be equivalent to the 'clear value', namely the improved value minus the annual rent.[48] So, if all went well, a prebendary might receive an amount approximating the true annual value of the property every seven years or so, in addition to the annual rent. The regularity of fine income depended upon the number of leases associated with the benefice and when they were due for renewal. As prebendary of Winterbourne Earles, Joshua Sacheverell could expect to receive an annual rent of around £17 and, if he remained long enough, fines totalling around £100 over a seven-year period. His income probably averaged over £60, a modest sum but still an improvement over the £28 he received from his parish. At the other extreme was Highworth, the most valuable prebend in Wiltshire. The prebendary John Tounson, who as vicar of Bremhill also received £300 a year from his parish living, collected a yearly rent of around £60 and every seven years or so a fine of around £1,000. His income may have averaged as much as £500 a year.

Gregory King's estimates appear to be reasonably accurate, although they do underestimate clerical incomes. The average (median) income of Wiltshire clergymen in the late seventeenth century was just over £80 for those with a single living, rising to £130 for pluralists.[49] Only a minority of the clergy (many of whom were curates) fell below the poverty line of £50. Only a handful earned as little as labourers and had to labour in the fields. This is not to underestimate the position of those clergymen who were unfortunate enough to find themselves in poor and inadequate benefices, or the damaging impact of the years around 1700 on clerical incomes. Yet most clergymen were more prosperous than this. They were often among the wealthiest inhabitants of villages, with incomes second only to the gentry, able to live at or above the level of the yeoman farmers who governed the parish. Poor rates must be used with care when assessing clerical incomes, since the clergy sometimes complained that they had been over-rated,[50] yet they appear to confirm that Wiltshire clergymen might be among the wealthiest members in their parishes. In Box in 1695 only one non-gentleman paid higher poor rates than the vicar. The rate paid by the rector of Langley Burrell in 1705 was second only to that of the local squire, Samuel Ashe.[51] A small but significant number of clergymen were able to match the incomes and life styles of the gentry.

---

[48] The calculation that a fine to extend a lease for seven years was equivalent to one year's true value (less costs), based on an interest rate of just under 12 per cent, was accepted practice in the period. *Reasons for altering the method used at present in letting church and colleage leases* (London, 1739), pp. 5–19; Clay, '"The greed of Whig bishops"', pp. 128–57, esp. 132–4.

[49] These figures make allowance for the hiring of curates (at £20 each) but not for prebendal stalls (although the latter would have little effect on the median). I have used the median in preference to the mean, since it is less susceptible to distortion from a few high values. The mean living of £103 (standard deviation £71) rose to £164 for pluralists (£85). The mean value of the livings of pluralists was only £87 (£61).

[50] As in the case of Richard Bigge of Shrewton. A1/110, H1677/8, T1678, A1/160/3, H1677/8.

[51] WRO 212A/34; WRO 118/149.

A CLERICAL GENTLEMAN

Instituted to the rectory of Brinkworth in 1671, Francis Henry Carey was an early example of a squire-parson, or 'squarson'.[52] He governed the parish for forty years until his death in 1711. Carey was the son and heir of a gentleman with an estate worth £400 a year in North Leigh in Oxfordshire.[53] As befitted his gentry origins, the rector-to-be was educated at the King's School Westminster and Christ Church Oxford, matriculating in 1661 at the age of 21.[54] He received his first living (at Stow in Northamptonshire) in 1666 and added Brinkworth five years later.[55] Brinkworth was one of the plum livings of Salisbury diocese, worth £300 a year.[56] One of the largest parishes in the deanery of Malmesbury, it had the agricultural economy characteristic of the parishes in the clay vale of Wiltshire's cheese country. The parish had very little arable land but consisted primarily of enclosures of pasture ground, meadow and common of pasture and woodland. The population of 669 was divided between Brinkworth and the small hamlet of Grittenham.[57] Carey appears to have been neither a prebendary, a doctor of divinity, nor a chaplain, so Addison's classification places him among the subalterns, but his position could hardly have differed more from that of the unfortunate Robert Randall.

Carey fulfilled his pastoral duties in Brinkworth, despite his pluralism and the remoteness of his other living. To serve Stow he appointed a curate from whom he received reports. Yet family business and other business often took him away from Brinkworth. In 1677 he left the parish without cure of souls for at least six weeks, until the bishop wrote to remind him of his responsibilities. Henceforth, Carey appointed a curate even though he normally resided in Brinkworth. Carey ignored the bishop's nominee, either because he preferred to make his own choice or because he did not wish to pay the salary of £30 set by the bishop.[58] Joseph Dresser assisted as curate for at least five years, freeing

---

[52] All the information in this section is derived from PRO, C104/137/Part I unless otherwise indicated.

[53] He was not to inherit the estate until after his father's death in 1702. PRO, C104/137/Part II.

[54] Carey received his BA and MA. *Alumni Oxoniensis*, q.v. 'Francis Henry Carey'.

[55] Carey received a licence from the archbishop of Canterbury to hold both Brinkworth and Stow Nine Churches in Northamptonshire, so long as he ensured that both cures were served.

[56] D1/27/1/1.

[57] VCH *Wilts*, XIV, p. 20. Carey's papers record that the parish had 435 adults above the age of 16 (including 65 in Grittenham) and 234 under the age of 16 (including 38 in Grittenham); there were 35 dissenters. The closeness of the adult population to the figures in the Compton Census show that this paper was prepared for this purpose (while casting doubt on the reliability of the letter 'I' in Salisbury MS A as an indicator that inhabitants, and not just communicants, were counted). Whiteman, *Compton Census*, pp. 106, 128.

[58] The bishop licensed John Swaffield to serve Brinkworth without waiting for Carey's approval and, when this was not forthcoming, found him a living in Colerne. D1/22/3 (26/9/1677, 8/1/1678); D1/2/23, f. 11.

the rector to travel on business when he needed to.[59] In 1686 Carey had regret-
fully to decline the bishop's invitation to preach a visitation sermon because the
death of his mother and the frailty of his father were keeping him in
Oxfordshire. Despite his occasional absences, Carey's papers leave no doubt of
his continuing concern for the spiritual and material well-being of his parishioners and of his participation in parish administration. Alongside notes for
sermons and on the sacrament of communion,[60] they include the names of
those awaiting confirmation or in receipt of charity, marriage licences, rates
and assessments, settlement certificates, and correspondence concerning unlicensed alehouses. Carey gave annual gifts of clothing to the poor and would
leave a bequest of £50 to the poor.[61] In 1701 he joined parish officers and other
inhabitants in petitioning magistrates not to license any alehouse without a
certificate from him, due to complaints about the inconvenience caused by
excessive drinking.

Carey's lengthy incumbency was not without strife. In 1686 a horseman
chased him into his churchyard and would have struck him with a whip if two
parishioners had not interceded.[62] Tithes were an occasional irritant, and the
rector brought suits for non-payment of tithes against twelve inhabitants. Of
these it was the first suit that was the most serious because it was against Sir
George Ayliffe, the patron of the living and the lord of Grittenham manor in
Brinkworth. In the absence of the earl of Berkshire, who was lord of
Brinkworth manor, Ayliffe was the most important resident gentleman.[63] The
dispute between the two men lasted from 1677 until at least 1691 and placed
the rector in an alliance with other parishioners against the squire. Given
Carey's gentle birth, it seems likely that an element of competition for primacy
was involved. Ayliffe was in the process of taking back to himself the lands of
Grittenham manor, which had formerly been divided into small closes, so that
he could stock them with cattle, sheep and horses. The rector joined other
inhabitants in complaining against Ayliffe's depopulation of the hamlet and
refusal to pay poor rates. They complained that he had ruined almost all his
tenants and had pulled down their houses without reference to the law, forcing
them into Brinkworth. The landlord's repossession of land also led to confusion over the tithes, not least because he claimed that 400 acres of his demesne
were tithe-free. Yet Ayliffe found himself outmanoeuvred at every turn. Carey
prosecuted him for assault and battery at King's Bench and filed an Exchequer
bill against him for non-payment of tithes. Ayliffe was incensed when the
latter case went against him, and he was still complaining about the rector's
ingratitude to his patron a decade later. Carey was able to take advantage of

---

[59] D1/48/1; D1/48/2.   [60] PRO, C104/135.
[61] He also left £50 to the poor of Stow. PRO, C104/269, bundle 49.
[62] A1/110, E1686. See p. x.   [63] VCH *Wilts*, XIV, pp. 18–19.

Ayliffe's mental instability, which led to his confinement in a lunatic asylum for fifteen months.[64] This left Ayliffe vulnerable to suggestions that bad husbandry or other errors of judgement were evidence of the recurrence of his insanity. Ayliffe initially refused to obey the Exchequer decree, but he later decided it was better to pay his tithes than to offer Carey another occasion to go to law.[65]

Francis Henry Carey's horizons were not limited to his benefice. He also took an interest in county and national matters. In 1685 his friends among the gentry expected his imminent appointment to the commission of the peace. The appointment of a mere parson was very unusual in the late seventeenth century, however, and it appears that Carey ultimately did not gain appointment to the bench.[66] He was an ally of Sir James Long in 1685 and of Bishop Burnet after the Revolution, suggesting that he was a Low Churchman.[67] In 1705 an agent of Burnet solicited his willingness to stand as Proctor in Convocation. The rector wrote a poem in praise of the Whig bishop: 'Tho I can add no Glory to your Name / Yet, praising you, I may arrive at Fame . . .' Carey was proud of his social connections with the gentry and aristocracy, which he recorded in a large family tree. The tragic death of his son John in a duel in 1695 was also suitably aristocratic.[68] Carey's gentle background and education made him a natural member of the society of the county's greater gentry. With his daughter, he visited and received visits from members of the Bayntun and Long families.[69] In 1703 he sent James Long a present of venison. Although Carey was by now probably too old to hunt, this was a suitable gift of game from one landowner to another.

---

[64] An undated letter from Ayliffe to Carey documents the former's insanity, and indicates that an exaggerated fear of popery may have exacerbated his anticlericalism. Ayliffe referred to 'a booke called a paterne of popish peace . . . ending in a Bloudy massacre of many thousand protestants' and related how this massacre occurred in 1644 when Queen Elizabeth burned several Dutch Independents in Smithfield! On the fear of popery, see J. Miller, *Popery and Politics in England 1660–1688* (Cambridge, 1973); J. Scott, 'England's troubles: exhuming the Popish Plot', in T. Harris, P. Seaward and M. Goldie, eds., *The Politics of Religion in Restoration England* (Oxford, 1990).   [65] PRO, E126/13, ff. 228, 292–294d; C104/63.

[66] PRO, C104/135; Lambeth Palace Library, MS 933, f. 34, 'Reasons to induce Queen to trust some of clergy with commissions for the peace'. Carey is not in the *Liber pacis* compiled in 1685–6. PRO, C193/12/5, ff. 152–6. I am grateful to Lionel Glassey for allowing me to refer to his notes of Wiltshire commissions of the peace.

[67] Sir James Long, Bt. (1616–92) of Draycot Cerne was MP for Malmesbury in 1679 (twice), 1681 and 1690–2. B. D. Henning, *The House of Commons 1660–1690* (London, 1983), q.v. 'Sir James Long'. His answers to James II's Three Questions expressed support for toleration. G. Duckett, ed., *Penal Laws and Test Act* (London, 1882), pp. 213–14.

[68] See J. C. D. Clark, *English Society 1688–1832* (Cambridge, 1985), pp. 93–118, for his use of duelling to define the aristocratic ethos.

[69] Both were substantial landowners in north Wiltshire, the Bayntuns in Bremhill and Bromham, the Longs in Draycot Cerne and Sutton Benger.

THE STATUS OF THE CLERGY

Francis Henry Carey was unusual among the clergy in his easy acceptance by the county gentry as their social equal. He owed his social position to his birth and not to his status as a clergyman. Indeed, it was Carey's clerical status that most likely blocked his path into the commission of the peace which his friends on the bench took for granted. The social position of other clergymen was ambiguous and was far weaker in consequence. Few could match Carey's gentry birth and family estate.[70] Yet Carey's example introduces the patterns of gentry sociability in which the clergy might have hoped to participate. Members of gentry society visited one another regularly and dined together. They hunted deer and fox and met in their official capacity as members of commissions of the peace and taxation. The clergy might have an opportunity to participate in these forms of leisure and business, but their status was rarely better than marginal.

Dining and visits were important forms of gentry sociability. It might be suggested that gentlemen regarded those with whom they dined, who included clergymen, as members of the gentry. The diary of Thomas Smith, a magistrate living in Shaw in Melksham, shows that some members of the gentry socialised freely with the clergy and treated them as social equals. Smith dined regularly with other gentlemen, and a clergyman was often one of the guests. In September 1716 the vicar of Box, George Millard, joined Smith and others who dined at the house of Mr Norris in Farley. Smith also received occasional visits from local ministers. The minister of Malmesbury, Thomas Earle, visited Smith and his family in August 1717, and the Smiths returned the favour on the following day. Smith often dropped in at the vicarage for casual visits. In April 1716 he and several other parish gentlemen met at the vicarage, where they discussed private affairs, parish business and national news, including the 1715 rebellion.[71] Thomas Smith had close and fairly equal relationships with several clergymen. The cleric with whom Smith was closest was the vicar of Melksham, Bohun Fox, whose benefice of £120 per year, while lower than gentry incomes, placed him among the better-off members of the clergy. Yet Thomas Smith may have been the exception rather than the rule among gentlemen, because he and Fox had a bond with other clergymen with whom they socialised in their mutual support for the Society for Promoting Christian Knowledge.[72]

---

[70] Only 12 per cent of incumbents in 1683 are known to have been of gentle birth, although this figure rises to 19 per cent if the significant number who could not be found in alumni records are omitted from the calculation. See Table 2.2. For other examples of gentleman rectors, see Holmes, *Augustan England*, p. 98.

[71] WRO 161/70. Farley was either Farleigh Hungerford, just across the Somerset border, or Monkton Farleigh, near Bradford-on-Avon.

[72] Other corresponding members with whom Smith dined included George Millard, vicar of Box; John Rogers, minister of Bradford; and Mr Hilldrop, a Marlborough schoolmaster. WRO 161/70; SPCK, Minutes, vols. 5, 7; SPCK, Miscellaneous Abstracts, 1709–22.

Sir Richard Holford, the absentee landlord of Avebury, provides a very different model of gentry treatment of the clergy. On Holford's annual visits to his
estate, he usually dined with the vicar John White, the Reverend John Brinsden
of Winterbourne Monkton nearby, and their wives. His invitations did not indicate social equality, however. Because he visited infrequently, Holford used such
dinners to re-establish contact with his tenant and other subordinates and to
exert control over the parish. Just as on one occasion he taught the manor court
jury how to make their presentment, he used his dinners with the vicar to instruct
him in how he should serve the cure. Over dinner in 1711, he demanded that the
vicar explain 'how he prsumed to omit the Exhortacon before the Prayers' when
he read divine service.[73] Holford's attempts to regulate the behaviour of the vicar
and other clergymen extended to his personal correspondence, in which he
pressed them to charity.[74] Although Holford was later to describe White as 'a
gentleman of breeding',[75] the vicar had no doubt of his inferior social position.
He reacted angrily to Sir Richard's advice, complaining that he knew 'great men
take liberty to say anything of inferiors'.[76] James Mayo, White's successor as
vicar, was more willing to accept his inferior position. When Holford and his
wife visited Mayo, the landlord patronisingly observed the vicar's 'improvement
in his house and Garden'.[77]

Other gentlemen also instructed parish clergymen how to behave. Robert
Tyderleigh, esquire and JP, advised the vicar of Chardstock to reform before he
incurred ecclesiastical punishment.[78] Edward Keate, JP, of East Lockings warned
the rector of Chilton 'to become more friendly toward his neighbours'.[79] If
dining with the gentry conferred status, then it was a double-edged sword, for it
might apply equally to the beneficed clergy and to their unbeneficed curates. An
incident at the dinner table of the Lyneham gentleman, William Mortimer,
shows the tension created by such situations. Mortimer was familiar with several
local clergymen, and his own son was vicar of Wilcot.[80] He invited to dine both
William Durston, the rector of Tockenham Wick, and Boaz Hodges, who had
formerly been his curate. Although Durston was himself the son of a gentleman,
he found it necessary to rebuke the curate for his social presumption, and by
doing so revealed anxiety about his own social position. It appears that Hodges
had failed to follow Durston's example by eating brown bread, choosing instead
to eat the finer white bread preferred by the gentry. In the argument that ensued

---

[73] WRO 184/8.
[74] Sir Richard Holford to John White, 30 Jan. 1695[/6]; Sir Richard Holford to Mr [John] Brinsden,
21 May 1712, WRO 184/1.
[75] Sir Richard Holford to John White, 22 July 1708, WRO 184/1.
[76] John White to Sir Richard Holford, 4 April 1696, WRO 184/1. The relationship between the two
men is discussed in greater detail in chapter 6.   [77] WRO 184/4.   [78] D5/22/15, f. 2.
[79] D1/42/61, f. 142.
[80] Wilcot's value of only £30 shows that the sons of the gentry could not depend upon rapid promotion within the Church. D1/27/1/1.

Durston told Hodges that 'he was but his boy'. Sharply stung, Hodges retorted that he was not Durston's 'boy' and that he kept 'as Good gentlemen as yorself & better company'. This incident reveals the importance with which clergymen regarded their acceptance into the social circles of the gentry, however inferior their status. The rector Durston cannot have been pleased when their host interposed on the curate's behalf, calling him his friend.[81] Although the clergy wanted to be treated like gentlemen, they were all too aware of the weakness of their social position. Matthew Whittley, the vicar of Westport St Mary, revealed his own social anxieties when he was drunk, saying 'that he had as good blood in his veines as the . . . Earle of Berks', the lord of the manor. The vicar's audience expressed their own views about the relative social inferiority of the clergy by rebuking him 'for speakinge soe insolently abusively and scandalously of soe noble a person'.[82] The clergy were vulnerable to charges that they were of lowly status, particularly in the aftermath of the Civil Wars, when memories of 'mechanic preachers' were fresh. The churchwardens of Horningsham presented their curate in 1669 as scandalous and unlearned. He had never received a university degree, they believed, 'because in his junior years he exercised the trade of a Mechanicke'.[83] An enemy of Thomas Twittee, smarting from numerous suits for tithes, told the minister 'that hee was not worth ten groats before hee had their Tithes'. 'Before hee put on his Black Coate,' he said, Twittee 'went about wth a Baskett of Eggs'.[84]

The ambiguity of the clergy's social position is thrown into relief by the issue of hunting. The right to hunt was the ultimate perquisite of the gentry and one which they protected jealously. The Game Act of 1671 stipulated that the possession of freeholds worth at least £100 a year was the minimum qualification for a man to hunt legally.[85] The majority of the population were therefore excluded from the right to hunt and could be prosecuted for possessing hunting equipment such as nets, traps, guns and dogs. Poaching was endemic, however, as can be seen by the occasional flurry of prosecutions for game violations in Quarter Sessions records.[86] Since clerical benefices were freeholds, almost half of incumbents were legally entitled to hunt, yet this right did not go unchallenged.

In December 1675 clerical hunting led to an altercation in the parish of Heddington. Although the benefice was worth less than £100, its vicar Henry

---

[81] D1/41/4/35, Smith c. Durston (testimony of William Mortimer). Hodges is described as the former curate, but it is not clear whether he left the cure before or after this argument. He had become curate on 17 Sept. 1686.   [82] D1/42/62, f. 6.   [83] D5/28, 1669, f. 42.
[84] A1/110, M1668 (Informations).
[85] P. B. Munsche, 'The game laws in Wiltshire 1750–1800', in J. S. Cockburn, ed., *Crime in England 1550–1800* (Princeton, 1977), p. 211. Qualified hunters also included those with leaseholds of at least £150 a year, heirs apparent to esquires or to those of higher status, and holders of the royal franchise of a park, chase or warren.
[86] For example, see A1/110, M1676, where 22 of 36 indictments were for game offences, including 17 for keeping a greyhound, 3 for keeping a handgun, and 2 for trapping rabbits.

Rogers had recently added the living of Leigh de la Mere and therefore he was entitled to hunt.[87] No doubt to celebrate his new claim to this badge of gentle status, Rogers went coursing hare on his land, accompanied by Edward Child, an Oxford MA. When a hare they were chasing escaped to the land of a tenant of Sir Edward Bayntun, they decided to pursue it. This was a mistake, as they were shortly to discover. It was customary for gentlemen to turn a blind eye when other gentlemen hunted on their land, but Sir Edward was not likely to extend this courtesy to them.[88] A Parliamentarian during the Commonwealth, Bayntun had ambivalent views about the Anglican clergy. Although he was prepared to supplement the income of the minister of his parish of Bromham, he quarrelled with the incumbents of Bremhill over tithes and of Rodbourne Cheney over an annual stipend and repairs to the chancel. A puritan, he was appointed during the Commonwealth to the commission assessing fitness for the sacrament and was reluctant to prosecute dissenters after the Restoration.[89] As bad luck would have it, Sir Edward and two of his men rode into sight before the two clergymen could return to their own fields, having failed to find the hare. Bayntun sent his servants after the clergymen, and they rode up threateningly and demanded, 'who gave you authority to course upon my Masters ground'. When Rogers denied that he had been hunting on Bayntun's property they called him a 'lying priest'. They assaulted the minister and his dog, barely avoiding wounding the former seriously. Rogers fled to his house, chased by Bayntun and his men, who had drawn their swords and were shouting threats. They pursued the minister into his house where they abused him and his mother. After threatening to 'pinne the impudent bl[ack] coate to the wall', they finally left.[90] Bayntun's violent treatment of Rogers shows that he had very little respect for the clergy. While his puritan sympathies may have made him less tolerant than other gentry, he nevertheless expressed a common disrespect for their social position.

The ambiguity of the clergy's social position undermined their authority as parish leaders. The clergy had a natural leadership role in parish administration. They helped to draw up rates and to prepare churchwardens' presentments, and their names headed petitions and vestry resolutions. Yet any attempts to 'lord it' over their parishes outside this constrained administrative role could provoke resentment. In Wylye a dispute developed between a parishioner and the minister over agrarian matters. William Barnes alleged that the rector had removed boundary stones and that the rector's pigeons had damaged the roof of his house. He was not prepared to ignore such grievances,

[87] Heddington was worth at least £65 and Leigh de la Mere was worth £80.
[88] D. Hay, 'Poaching and the game laws on Cannock Chase', in *Albion's Fatal Tree* (New York, 1975), p. 200.
[89] PRO, IND 1/16831, n. 140 (Trinity 28 Charles II); D1/54/6/2 (1674, M&C), f. 8. See also J. Freeman, ed., *The Commonplace Book of Sir Edward Bayntun of Bromham*, Wiltshire Record Society 43 (Devizes, 1988), pp. xii, xix, 54–7.   [90] A1/110, H1676 (Informations).

Table 2.2 *Social origins at matriculation of
Wiltshire incumbents*

	1683	1730
Gentry	24 19%	28 38%
Clergy	31 25%	24 33%
Plebeian	42 34%	13 18%
Pauper puer or serviens	27 22%	8 11%
Total	124	73
Others		
Cambridge	10	8
Not recorded	16	1
Not found	57	18
Overall total	207	100*

Note
* The figures for 1730 are for a random sample of 100
incumbents.
Sources: D1/48/2; D1/48/4; *Alumni Oxoniensis*;
Alumni Cantabrigiensis. Oxford registers sometimes
failed to record father's status and Cambridge registers
almost never did so.

as he might have done had the offender been a gentleman. The authority of the clergy was not beyond challenge. As Barnes said, 'It shall not be all as the parson and clerke will have itt.'[91] The clergy sometimes found it difficult to enforce their will upon the laity, and they met with resistance and even abuse when they chastised or punished villagers or tried to collect tithes from them. Clerics might also be criticised for failing to fulfil their duty of charity, for example by withholding their poor rate. Seeing the rector of Sutton Mandeville, Augustine Hayter, on the highway, a passer-by commented, 'There goes one that will starve the Poore.'[92]

The early eighteenth century would see a moderate rise in the social status of clergymen. The clergy's improved position can be seen in university alumni registers, although this source must be used with caution. Social origins can be studied through information about the status of the father, which was often recorded when a student matriculated, particularly at Oxford, where most Wiltshire clerics were educated. Between 1683 and 1730 the proportion of incumbents of Wiltshire benefices who claimed gentry origins at least doubled, rising

[91] D1/42/60, ff. 182v, 182.
[92] D1/42/61, f. 204v. Hayter brought three separate prosecutions for vilification over a forty-year period.

to two in five in the latter year.[93] The change in clerical status was not quite as dramatic as these figures would suggest. Because the title of 'gentleman' was claimed by a wider range of people during the eighteenth century, an element of status inflation is built into matriculation records. Growing numbers of sons of urban professionals and merchants, who formerly would have been entered as plebeians, may now have claimed gentry origins.[94] To complicate matters further, a significant proportion of clerics cannot reliably be found in the registers. While some were doubtless of lower social status, others in the registers may have escaped identification because of difficulties in distinguishing between matriculants who had common names. Nonetheless, it appears that the social profile of the beneficed clergy changed markedly between the 1680s and the 1720s, particularly when it is remembered that some clerics held their benefices for forty years or longer.

The rising status of the clergy also manifested itself in their appointment to seats on commissions, including those for the land tax and of the peace. No parish clergy achieved a seat on Wiltshire's commission of the peace between 1660 and 1688, but they began to do so in the early eighteenth century. By 1728 there were five clerical magistrates and the number grew to seven a decade later and to nine in around 1760.[95] The clergy's entry on to the bench did not, however, mark unreserved acceptance into the ranks of the gentry, for reasons that were similar to those discussed with reference to university registers. It was facilitated by the declining social prestige that accompanied the office later in the century as the county gentry became less interested in taking on the duties of magistracy. Clerical entrants, while providing the commission of the peace with some of its most active members, made the gentry even less willing to participate.[96] In the long run, there would be a price to pay for the authority of magistracy, which increased the divide between the clergy and their congregations. Nineteenth-century reformers would question whether a seat on the bench was consistent with the clergy's pastoral role, at the same time as they challenged the now common stereotype of the clerical gentleman.[97] Yet these developments still lay far in the future.

---

[93] Based upon comparison of all incumbents listed in the 1683 Diocese Book (D1/48/2) and of a sample of one hundred clerics listed in an eighteenth-century Diocese Book (D1/48/4) with *Alumni Oxonienses* and *Alumni Cantabrigiensis*.

[94] P. J. Corfield, 'Class by name and number in eighteenth-century Britain', in P. J. Corfield, ed., *Language, History and Class* (Oxford, 1991), p. 107.

[95] A1/100. In 1786 there were ten clerical magistrates, including some of the most active of the justices. W. R. Ward, 'County government c.1660–1835', VCH *Wilts*, V, pp. 176–7. A similar pattern can be seen in other counties, such as Oxfordshire, where in 1775 31 per cent of 251 justices were clerics; in 1780 83 per cent of convictions recorded at Quarter Sessions bore the signature of a clerical JP. D. McClatchey, *Oxfordshire Clergy, 1777–1869* (Oxford, 1960), pp. 179, 191.

[96] P. Langford, *Public Life and the Propertied Englishman 1689–1798* (Oxford, 1991), pp. 410–36; N. Landau, *The Justices of the Peace, 1679-1760* (Berkeley, 1984), pp. 270, 318.

[97] Virgin, *The Church in an Age of Negligence*, ch. 5; E. J. Evans, 'Some reasons for the growth of English rural anti-clericism, c.1750–c.1830', *Past and Present* 66 (Feb. 1975): 101–4; B. Heeney, *A Different Kind of Gentleman* (Hamden, Conn., 1976).

While the basis of the authority of most clergymen in the late seventeenth and early eighteenth centuries was weak, they were required to live on a higher plane than others in the parish. The laity expected clergymen to live the sober life of scholars, holed away in their studies. This was one reason why they objected to scandalous behaviour by clerics. The parishioners of Chilton, one testified, 'would be well satisfyed wth the Ministry of Mr Lawrence, if grave & sober, as becomes a Clergyman'. The inhabitants of Great Bedwyn expressed similar sentiments about their vicar, whom they thought spent too much time drinking in alehouses 'when it had byn better for him to have byn in his study'. The laity accepted the unique position of the minister as a scholar. They did not expect him to do ordinary labour. Indeed, they knew that it was inappropriate for him to do so. So the inhabitants of Baydon petitioned for assistance for their curate, whose poor stipend meant that he was 'enforced to betake himself to the servile works of husbandry, which render the service & worship of God contemptible in the eies of the people'.[98] The laity accepted the intellectual divide that separated them from the parson, but his scholarship gave him only a limited authority outside the Church.

A CLERICAL SCHOLAR

The ecclesiastical authorities concurred with the laity's emphasis upon scholarship. Bishop Gilbert Burnet laid down a lengthy programme of reading, to ensure that clergymen were as well trained as members of other professions.[99] In his *Country Parson*, George Herbert recommended that a parson be well read in divinity, law and medicine.[100] John Lewis was the model of a clerical scholar. The diary that Lewis kept from 1718 to 1724 indicates that the minister spent many hours reading in his study.[101] In a single year he read from no fewer than forty books, pamphlets and sermons. His reading interests were wide. Following Herbert's advice to be a physician of the sick, Lewis took particular interest in medicine. His selections from literature ranged from Homer's *Iliad* to the *Beaux Stratagem*,[102] and included Shakespeare's *Henry VI*. As the latter suggests, he also took an interest in history, reading a *Historical Account of the Popish Plot*[103] and Burnet, and he began a programme of reading collections of county antiq-

[98] Chilton (Berks.): D1/42/61, f. 138; Great Bedwin, D5/22/18, f. 18; Baydon: D5/17/1/2.
[99] Burnet, *Pastoral Care*, pp. 162–75.
[100] George Herbert, *A Priest to the Temple; or the Country Parson*, 4th edn (London, 1701), chs. 5, 23.   [101] WRO 1981/1; Bodleian Library, MS Eng Misc f. 10.
[102] George Farquhar, *The Beaux Strategem. A Comedy* (London, 1707).
[103] This may have been Thomas Long, *A Compendious History of all the Popish and Fanatical Plots and Conspiracies against the Established Government in Church and State* (London, 1684), or Henry Care, *The History of the Damnable Popish Plot* (London, 1680).

uities with Plot on Oxfordshire.[104] Lewis read Clarendon[105] and copied extracts from Walker's *Sufferings of the Clergy*, as was consistent with his High Church opinions.[106] Acting on the principle of knowing one's enemy, he read widely from the writings of John Locke, as well as *A Vindication of the Unitarians*.[107] He also referred to guides on gardening, the law and pastoral care, including to George Herbert's *Country Parson*.[108] Not surprisingly, works of theology and published sermons provided the bulk of the rector's reading matter, ranging from Thomas à Kempis and Hooker to Stillingfleet. Although he read published sermons by Sherlock and Waterland, he nevertheless wrote his own sermons, unlike his fictional counterpart in Coverley parish. The preparation of new sermons occupied as much of his time in the study as his reading. In addition to giving weekly sermons in two of his churches, he also lectured once a month in Tetbury (Glos.). He also gave occasional funeral sermons, writing them specially for the occasion, often using a text requested by the deceased.

John Lewis embraced scholarship with great enthusiasm. He recorded with pride the bundles in which he collected his sermons and his work to prepare one or two discourses for publication. Lewis was one of several West Country clergymen who left manuscript volumes of their sermons in which can be seen how they honed the texts of sermons that they might give repeatedly in different churches.[109] Yet the clergy's scholarly role also increased the divide between themselves and the people they served. It isolated them not only physically in their studies but also culturally. The English clergy had taken great strides in their education since the Reformation, when only 10 to 20 percent of the parochial clergy outside London were university graduates. Sixteenth-century reformers had wanted to create a well-educated pastoral and preaching ministry, whose members would be able to instruct the laity and satisfy their spiritual needs. If the receipt of a university degree is used as the standard, these goals had already been fulfilled by 1640. In the Wiltshire deaneries of the diocese of Salisbury, at least 85 percent of instituted clerics had a degree, both before the Civil Wars and after the Restoration.[110] The clergy of other dioceses matched this improvement

---

[104] Robert Plot, *The Natural History of Oxfordshire*, 2nd edn (Oxford, 1705). It is not clear which work of Burnet's Lewis read.

[105] Edward Hyde, *The History of the Rebellion and Civil Wars in England* (London, 1703, and Oxford, 1704–7).

[106] John Walker, *An Attempt Towards Recovering an Account of the Numbers and Sufferings of the Clergy of the Church of England who were Sequester'd, Harass'd, &c. . . . in the . . . Times of the Great Rebellion* (London, 1714).

[107] William Freke, *A Vindication of the Unitarians* (London, 1690).   [108] Herbert, *Country Parson*.

[109] Sermon books of John Lewis, WRO 1981/2, Thomas Hochkis of Stanton Fitzwarren, WRO 1762/1, and William Skinner of Didmarton, Glos., Lambeth Palace Library, MS 1825–7.

[110] Based on the registers of the bishop of Salisbury, with corrections from Cambridge and Oxford alumni registers. In 1660–1714, only 70 percent of clerics being instituted were listed as having a degree in the Institution Books, but analysis of a small sample of them shows that at least 85 percent had a degree. The sample was of those whose surnames began with A or B. Bishop of Salisbury, Bishops' Registers, D1/2/22–5 (1660–1714); *Alumni Oxoniensis*; *Alumni Cantabrigiensis*

in the standards of the clergy.[111] The bishop of Salisbury acknowledged the improvement in the education of his clergy by distributing licences to preach to the incumbents of over 90 percent of the parishes in his diocese.[112] The Church no longer had to worry about 'dumb dogs' who fell short of the intellectual standards of the laity.

In practice, the parish clergy paradoxically were educated both too well and not well enough. Although most had received a Master of Arts, fewer than 10 per cent had an advanced degree in theology or divinity. Bishop Burnet complained that the clergy often left university knowing less than when they arrived, and he resolved to set up his own 'nursery' of students of divinity in Salisbury diocese.[113] Divinity was not part of the university curriculum, and college instruction increasingly stressed the reading of classical literature. Most undergraduates also received some theological instruction in college and would have been expected to read some divinity, particularly the Greek New Testament. The quality of theological training depended upon the tutors, some of whom took their responsibilities more seriously than others. Students would also have heard university sermons and attended chapel services.[114] The universities nevertheless produced graduates who were likely to feel more comfortable with the Greek classics than with theology. This helps to explain the frustration that lay behind the confession of Robert Randall of Great Bedwyn that 'hee could preach a better sermon out of Aristotle than out of the Bible'.[115] At the same time, the parish clergy were too well educated because they were unable to share their intellectual interests with their congregations. They were usually the only persons in the parish to have attended university, with the possible exception of a curate or a resident gentleman. Their university degree meant in theory that the parish clergy had something in common with the gentry, who accounted for half of matriculants at the end of the seventeenth century, even though many never proceeded to a degree. Unless they were themselves of gentle birth, clergymen probably had little to do with the gentry at university. Occupants of poorer livings had often been servitors or batelers and this mark of inferiority excluded

---

[111] In Worcester diocese, the percentage of clergy who were university graduates rose from 19 in 1560 and 52 in 1620 to 84 in 1640. D. M. Barratt, 'The condition of the parochial clergy from the Reformation to 1660, with special reference to the dioceses of Oxford, Worcester, and Gloucester' (D.Phil. dissertation, Oxford University, 1949), cited by C. Hill, *Economic Problems of the Church* (Oxford, 1956), p. 207. In Coventry and Lichfield, 83 per cent of newly instituted clerics had a degree in the period 1660–1714. Salter, 'Warwickshire clergy', p. 49.

[112] D1/48/1–2. In 1603, only half of the beneficed clergy in the diocese of Worcester had been trusted with a licence to preach. For the Worcester preaching licence statistics, see Hill, *Economic Problems of the Church*, p. 207.   [113] Foxcroft, pp. 500–1.

[114] L. S. Sutherland and L. G. Mitchell, eds., *The History of the University of Oxford*, vol. V: *The Eighteenth Century* (Oxford, 1986), pp. 403–11, 469–80, 502–3; R. O'Day, *Education and Society, 1500–1800: The Social Foundations of Education in Early Modern Britain* (London and New York, 1982), ch. 6.

[115] D5/22/18, f. 19 (Player c. Randall), although Randall himself appears not to have matriculated at university.

them from sociability with those of higher rank while at university.[116] The parish clergy nevertheless shared with the gentry a common intellectual grounding in the classics.

The education of the clergy set them apart from most of the laity and sometimes made them ill-suited to perform their pastoral responsibility of instruction. John Eachard probably exaggerated when he inveighed against the 'high tossing and swaggering preaching' of the clergy, which he said was intended to impress the patron rather than to instruct the poor.[117] The parish church was not the place for erudite sermons with a scattering of Greek and Latin. Bishop Burnet advised parsons that the purpose of their sermons was to edify their congregations rather than to make themselves admired as learned and well-spoken men. He advised each cleric to give shorter and simpler sermons and 'to fancy himself, as in the room of the most unlearned Man in his whole Parish'.[118] The challenge of giving sermons that a country audience could understand was too much for some ministers. One Bristol cleric memorialised the intellectual tedium of a Sunday service in a particularly bad poem about a trip to Horfield.[119] The Revd Goldney stressed Horfield's isolation, describing it as 'A place as wild, as cold, as bleak / As newfoundland or Dirby peak'. The parish clerk was barely able to sing, the congregation was small and clearly uninterested in the sermon, perhaps not surprisingly since it was 'long and dull / Adapted right to cladpates scull'. One literate youth turned to the Bible for reference, but the others either fell asleep or 'stared and listened now and then'. Both the preacher and his audience were bored by the exercise. Goldney concluded, 'Was ever Priest in such an errand sent . . . To teach sad swine in ignoramous green?' Contemporary prints present the same picture of congregations (albeit urban ones) who slept through sermons.[120] Richard Luce, the vicar of Chardstock, expressed the boredom and frustration that many parish clergy must have felt when he complained to a parishioner that if the members of his congregation 'did hear him all the daies of their lives they should not be a fart the better for his preaching'. Luce threw a Bible on the ground, 'trampled on it & then swoare severall oathes that he would burne all the bookes he had in his studdy'.[121] As Macaulay noted, 'Even a keen and strong intellect might be expected to rust in so unfavorable a situation.'[122]

John Lewis was more fortunate. He fulfilled Burnet's advice to a parson that 'His Friends and his Garden ought to be his chief Diversions, as his Study and his Parish, ought to be his chief Imployments'.[123] Although he worked in his

---

[116] *History of the University of Oxford*, vol. V, pp. 375–6.
[117] Eachard, in Collins, *Critical Essays*, p. 264.   [118] Burnet, *Pastoral Care*, p. 223.
[119] 'A Description of the reverend Mr. Goldneys journey to Horfield to preach a gift Sermon on the 23 February 1730'. WRO 1259/83. Horfield was a village just to the north of Bristol, where Goldney lived.
[120] Miller, *Religion in the Popular Prints*, plates 49 (BMC 2285) and 50 (BMC 7777).
[121] D5/22/15, f. 8v.   [122] Macaulay, *The History of England*, vol. I, p. 318.
[123] Burnet, *Pastoral Care*, p. 179.

study on most days, a fine day might draw him out to his garden. He commented in his diary when illness or visitors kept him from his study. Yet Lewis was not kept so busy in his study that he neglected his pastoral duties. He was a pluralist: in addition to holding the rectory of Great Chalfield, he also served as curate in nearby Holt and Atworth. Great Chalfield was a sinecure, with only eighteen residents in 1676. Holt and Atworth, with 540 residents between them, occupied the bulk of his time. They were two of six chapelries within the parish of Bradford-on-Avon and so were usually served by a curate. Lewis's example shows that it was perfectly possible for a pluralist to serve the cure of souls in several parishes satisfactorily, especially when they were close to one another. Although he could not afford a horse, he fulfilled his pastoral duties conscientiously, often walking from Holt (where he lived with his family) to Atworth or Great Chalfield to visit the sick, baptise an infant, or marry a couple. He had no difficulty in administering the sacrament quarterly in each of his parishes, and he used his diary to jot down plans for improving services in future. In 1722–3 he had the chancel of Great Chalfield church re-tiled and re-roofed, and he painted an altarpiece with images of Aaron, Moses and cherubim.

Despite occasional complaints when visitors kept him from his study, John Lewis was a sociable man. In a single year he engaged in over 170 social contacts, dining with, visiting and receiving visits from the gentry, tenant farmers and the clergy.[124] He dined regularly with the gentry, with whom he exchanged gifts. The gentry with whom he socialised included Thomas Smith of Shaw and Edward Lisle, Esq. At different times he sent Mr Lisle, whom he called 'my very good friend', a hamper of grapes and he laid down bottles of beer for him, and his wife received a gift of tea, cups and saucers from William Lisle. His respect for Edward Lisle can be seen in the care he took to draw out his coat of arms. Lewis emulated the life style of the gentry. Besides going shooting or coursing on occasion, he also read such books as *The Gentleman's Recreation* and *The Gentleman Instructed*.[125] The diary of John Lewis shows a man who had found his position in society and was content with it. His income cannot have been high. Great Chalfield was returned to Exchequer in 1707 as being worth only £38.[126] Bradford-on-Avon was not a rich benefice, and the incumbent is unlikely to have paid his curate more than £30. With the addition of his Tetbury lectureship, Lewis may almost have scraped the £80 which the Crown recommended as the minimum stipend for incumbents after the Restoration. Yet he appears to have found his place among the gentry, farmers and clergy in the neighbourhood.

---

[124] The number of 179 contacts was reached by counting the number of guests on each occasion and then summing them together. A dinner with five guests is counted as five contacts. Each contact with a person is counted separately. Meetings of the Clergy Club of Melksham are not included.

[125] Nicholas Cox, *The Gentleman's Recreation. In Four Parts. Viz. Hunting, Hawking, Fowling, Fishing, etc.*, 5th edn (London, 1706); William Darrell, *A Gentleman Instructed in the Conduct of a Virtuous and Happy Life* (London, 1704).

[126] This was a significant decline from Ward's estimate of £60. D1/27/1/1.

The farmers accepted his position and looked to him for help in drawing up rates. The gentry were also on good terms, and were prepared to treat him as an equal so long as he did not presume too much. He served on tax commissions and occasionally helped others to draw up rates.

Lewis felt most comfortable in the company of his colleagues among the clergy. Social exchanges with gentlemen almost always occurred in the formal context of a meal hosted by a member of the gentry.[127] Contacts with local farmers were less common and were more likely to take the form of a visit. Lewis's strongest social ties were with other clergymen. He was a member of a society of ten or so clergymen he called the Clergy Club of Melksham, most of whose members came from nearby parishes. The Clergy Club met for dinner at least once a month in the warmer months from March to October. Although no record of club discussions survives, these dinners in an inn such as The George at Melksham or at the house of a member were no doubt occasions for conviviality enlivened by political news and diocesan gossip. Club members shared High Church Tory political opinions. Their meeting on 2 May 1722, when they dined with John Ivory Talbot, MP, enabled allies of the Tory Richard Goddard to prepare for the forthcoming elections, and Lewis recorded in his diary how he canvassed support for Goddard.[128] References to news of James III suggest some Jacobite sympathies, which he may have shared with other members of the club. Several members were also members of the Society for Promoting Christian Knowledge.[129] Lewis often socialised with members of the club on other occasions, most frequently with William Hickes, incumbent of nearby Broughton Gifford. Members of the club provided each other with mutual support. Lewis sought advice from George Millard of Box on tithe matters and, at Millard's request, he drew up a rate list for another clergyman, Francis Fox, who was not a member of the club. Spiritual community and their common social and professional position, and not mere proximity, brought together the members of the Clergy Club. These patterns of sociability reveal a clergy which saw itself as a distinct social group.[130]

Some clergymen, less fortunate than John Lewis, found themselves to be relatively isolated – culturally, socially and physically. Even in the nineteenth century,

---

[127] In 1720 Lewis had around 57 social contacts with clergymen (38 of them involving dinner or breakfast), at least 21 with gentlemen (16 involving a meal) and at least 15 with farmers (5 involving dinner).

[128] *VCH Wilts.*, vol. V, p. 200; Lewis met with several freeholders on behalf of Richard Goddard and counted the number of freeholders in Holt. Bodleian Library, MS Eng Misc f. 10. Goddard was elected as a knight of the shire in a contested by-election in November 1722, after the death of Robert Hyde. R. Sedgwick, ed., *The House of Commons, 1715–1754* (London, 1970), q.v. 'Wiltshire'.   [129] See chapter 10.

[130] Rosemary O'Day argues that combination lectures, prophesyings and other meetings fulfilled a similar role before 1640, although significantly these were more vocational than social occasions. R. O'Day, *The English Clergy: The Emergence and Consolidation of a Profession, 1558–1642* (Leicester, 1979), pp. 166–9.

a bishop of Salisbury would comment on the isolation of the parish clergy.[131] It was therefore natural for them to turn to their fellow clerics, with whom they had in common their education, spiritual function and politics. Burnet advised clergymen 'to contrive ways to meet often together, to enter into a brotherly correspondence', suggesting that they hold four or five 'sober' meetings each summer. The Clergy Club of Melksham met even more often, although their dinners at an inn may not have been that sober. As a town in the relatively densely populated north-western region of Wiltshire, Melksham was particularly well placed to serve as the focus of a vibrant clerical culture. Yet there is also evidence of clerical sociability elsewhere in the diocese. John Foster, the minister of Longbridge Deverell, on the southern downs, reported in 1701 the existence of a clerical society with seven members nearby, and he said that they were 'concocting Measures to enlarge their Numbers'.[132] The SPCK, of which Foster was a member, provided a focus for clerical co-operation. The annual meetings of visitations also served to bring the clergy of an area together professionally and socially, and incidental references confirm that clerics met on less formal occasions, whether to dine or to join in signing a certificate or testimonial. As Burnet remarked, meetings of clergymen were 'a means to cement them into one body'.[133] At the same time, social trends also helped to consolidate the position of the clergy as a distinct social and professional group. Just as more gentlemen sent their sons to become clergymen, more ministers did the same thing. One in three incumbents in 1730 was the son of a minister, compared to one in four a half century earlier. In some parishes clerical dynasties were created as son followed father as incumbent.[134]

The university education of the clergy, as much as their sacerdotal status, was the basis for their authority within parishes. It defined their membership of a distinct professional group, with its own training programme, standards for entry, career structure, mechanisms for self-regulation and 'mystery'.[135] Patterns of sociability, in which the clergy were most comfortable socialising with other clerics, confirmed their separateness from the rest of society. The laity expected the clergy to spend much of their time in their studies. Yet clerical education created a cultural barrier that made it difficult for the clergy to understand lay religious beliefs. This helps to explain the contempt which the parish clergy felt for lay religiosity.

---

[131] The bishop was Edward Denison (1837–54). VCH *Wilts*, III, pp. 58–9.

[132] Longbridge Deverell, SPCK, AL 335 (12 Aug. 1701) (also excerpted in W. O. B. Allen and E. McClure, *Two Hundred Years* (London, 1898), pp. 180–1).

[133] Burnet, *Pastoral Care*, pp. 209–10.

[134] W. M. Jacob, *Lay People and Religion in the Early Eighteenth Century* (Cambridge, 1996), p. 31; Holmes, *Augustan England*, pp. 107–8. In Leicestershire the proportion of parsons who were sons of clergymen rose from 24 per cent in 1670 and 1714 to 30 per cent in 1750. Pruett, *The Parish Clergy*, p. 35. In Wiltshire, at least 15 per cent of a sample of incumbents in 1683 were sons of clerics, rising to 24 per cent in 1730. See Table 2.2.

[135] O'Day, *The English Clergy*, chs. 12, 13; O'Day, *Education*, p. 142; Holmes, *Augustan England*; P. J. Corfield, *Power and the Professions in Britain 1700-1850* (London and New York, 1995).

The common education of the clergy accentuated a process of polarisation that was already under way. The liturgy and canons provided the foundation for the 'mystery' of the clerical profession, for they defined clerical control over the rites of the Church. The Act of Uniformity provides one explanation for clerical insistence that the liturgy be followed exactly. Another is that it was in the interest of members of the profession to protect traditions of proper worship of which they alone were the true custodians and which after the Restoration came to define Anglicanism itself.[136] Any lay questioning of the liturgy represented a challenge to clerical authority. For these reasons, the divide between clergy and laity, already emerging by the middle of the seventeenth century, became wider after the Restoration. As the eighteenth century progressed, the clergy grew increasingly remote from the concerns and beliefs of ordinary villagers.

CONCLUSION

This chapter has sketched the portraits of three clergymen whose situations could hardly have been more different. Robert Randall's example shows the despair to which some clergymen were brought under the pressures of poverty, social and cultural isolation, and weak personal authority. While most soldiered on quietly, a few sought comfort from ale and alehouse company.[137] Arthur Dent observed that 'If neighbours meet now and then at the alehouse . . . I take it to be good fellowship', and Wiltshire men and women recognised that most men 'loved to take a cup now and then'.[138] Unfortunately, this relaxed view of drinking did not extend to the clergy, serving to accentuate their social isolation. As the canons made clear, the clergy were not to drink heavily or to resort to alehouses. George Herbert and Gilbert Burnet also advised parsons not to haunt alehouses.[139] Their status marginal, their incomes insufficient to support the life style of even a yeoman, let alone a gentleman, these clergymen were trapped in their parishes. The stress of their position caused some to lose their sense of calling, to turn to the bottle for solace, and in at least one case to commit suicide.[140]

[136] J. Spurr, *The Restoration Church of England, 1646-1689* (New Haven and London, 1991), ch. 7.
[137] D. J. Horton argues that 'the primary function of alcoholic beverages in all societies is the reduction of anxiety', and others have associated such anxiety with social isolation or anomie. 'The functions of alcohol in primitive societies: a cross-cultural study', *Quarterly Journal of Studies on Alcohol* 4 (1943): 223, quoted by D. B. Heath, 'Anthropological perspectives on the social biology of alcohol: an introduction to the literature', in B. Kissin and Henri Begleiter, eds., *Social Aspects of Alcoholism* (New York and London, 1976), p. 48.
[138] Arthur Dent, *The Plaine Mans Path-way to Heaven*; D1/42/61, f. 75v. See also P. Clark, *The English Alehouse* (London and New York, 1983).
[139] Herbert, *The Country Parson*, ch. 3; Burnet, *Pastoral Care*, p. 178.
[140] A contemporary note in the Institute of Historical Research's copy of the printed pollbook from the 1705 election reports that the minister of Boscombe, Robert West, had hanged himself. West served as minister from 1683 until his death in 1708. The fact that Ward valued the benefice at £100 shows that poverty was not the only source of stress, although the living may have lost some of its value. D1/27/1/1.

Such impoverished clergymen were in the minority. Although Francis Henry Carey's institution to Brinkworth came only three years after Randall's to Great Bedwyn, they lived in entirely different worlds. Their examples demonstrate how difficult it is to generalise about the position of the clergy in the late seventeenth and early eighteenth centuries. As a gentleman parson who was supremely confident of his position in society, Carey set an example that relatively few incumbents were able to match, even though the social position of the clergy was beginning to improve. John Lewis was probably far more typical of the parish clergy in this period. Despite his pluralism and his modest income, Lewis made the best of his position, enjoying socialising with a cross-section of society, especially with fellow clerics, and positively revelling in his studies. Yet, like many of his colleagues, he looked primarily to fellow clergymen for his social identity.

Although the plight of few clergymen was as desperate as that of Robert Randall, many clergymen nevertheless found themselves in a vulnerable position. Neither of the gentry nor of the people, they tried to negotiate parish life, sometimes successfully, but sometimes less so. They were not so different from their nineteenth-century successors, separated from the gentry by their inferior income, from the rural middling sort by their education, and from those below them by both.[141] In 1744, the Revd William Sterne of West Deane was to find out to his own cost how vulnerable his position was after a quarrel in church with Sir Arthur Cole about parish administration. Cole claimed that the minister had employed the poor without paying them. The implication was that Sterne had gone too far, taking on responsibilities which exceeded his status within the community.[142] 'You have no power in the parish,' Cole told the minister, '& have carried matters with a light hand.' The insulted minister Sterne sued Cole in the consistory court. Yet it was Sterne who was found guilty of brawling in church and in consequence was suspended from the ministration of his office. As this case demonstrates, the clergy could not depend upon the support of the landed gentry in their relations with their congregations. Before considering the participation of different social groups in episodes of conflict, however, it is necessary to investigate the role of the courts as forums for disputes and see how this changed over time.

---

[141] J. Obelkevich, *Religion and Rural Society: South Lindsey, 1825–1875* (Oxford, 1976), pp. 114–15.
[142] D1/41/4/3. Cole was also an Irish peer, Lord Ranelagh.

3

Arenas for conflict

Episodes of conflict between parsons and their parishioners were played out in the ecclesiastical and secular courts of the land. The church courts provided a natural source of remedy for spiritual complaints, serving both to correct offenders and as venues for interpersonal disputes. Visitations channelled offenders against the canons and statutes to the consistory court's correctional side. The court's plenary side heard complaints from plaintiffs concerning such matters as the non-payment of tithes, the neglect of the cure of souls, and vilification of the clergy. Complainants looking for a favourable hearing also had other legal venues from which to choose. The Quarter Sessions heard indictments for assault and mediated in rating disputes. Tithe disputes were brought to the Assize's *nisi prius* jurisdiction via Common Pleas, as well as to the emerging jurisdictions of the equity courts of Chancery and Exchequer. The chronology of lay–clerical conflict is closely bound up with the histories of the courts and of their competition for business. The church courts suffered a disastrous collapse in business, both correctional and plenary, and in authority in the late seventeenth century, making it difficult to assess changes in the incidence of lay–clerical conflict in the late seventeenth and early eighteenth centuries. The surviving evidence shows that disputes between clergymen and laymen continued to occur after 1700, although they were less likely than before to appear before the courts.

Any study of the decline of the church courts must be clear about which aspect of its jurisdiction is being considered.[1] The church or consistory court had two jurisdictions which were procedurally distinct.[2] As a correctional court, it prosecuted offences against canon law and, where it had jurisdiction, statute law. These offences included failure to attend church or to participate in other ceremonies, clerical neglect of the cure of souls, profanation of the church or

---

[1] For brief summaries of procedure, see C. R. Chapman, *Ecclesiastical Courts, Their Officials and Their Records* (Dursley, 1992), ch. 8; M. Ingram, *Church Courts, Sex and Marriage in England, 1570–1640* (Cambridge, 1987), pp. 48–51. For a fuller account, see Henry Consett, *The Practice of the Spiritual or Ecclesiastical Courts* (London, 1685).

[2] The administrative functions of its *negotia* side, including probate and faculties (for church modifications), represented a third category of jurisdiction.

59

sabbath, clandestine marriage, such moral offences as fornication, adultery and incest, as well as teaching in school or acting as a midwife without a licence. The correctional side of the consistory court was known as its 'office' jurisdiction, because the case was heard through the 'office of the judge' rather than being brought by another party. The procedure was summary: the judge (usually the chancellor of the diocese) examined the defendant and any witnesses orally, although of course without recourse to the *ex officio* oath. Much correctional business originated from churchwardens' presentments.

The second aspect of the consistory courts' business was their 'instance' jurisdiction, so called because causes were promoted 'at the instance' of one party against another. It was through its instance side that the court heard interpersonal disputes, similar in nature to those brought before the common law and equity courts. Issues included non-payment of tithes and other fees, defamation, vilification, pew disputes and marital disputes. The instance side of the court followed plenary procedures which were very similar to those of the courts of equity and in which full sets of charges (libels), counter-charges (interrogata) and witnesses' depositions were recorded in writing. The distinction between the consistory court's instance and office sides could be blurred, however. 'Promoted office' causes were correctional prosecutions which nevertheless took on all the characteristics of an instance cause. A complaining party rather than the judge promoted the suit, and the court followed the instance procedure. This practice, which was particularly common in cases brought to correct clergymen, recognised that, as with other instance suits, there was an injured party who was seeking a remedy from the court. The only party injured by other disciplinary matters was the Church itself. Neglectful clergymen, like defamers, disturbers of seats and withholders of tithes, injured a third party. The use of promoted office procedures provided the laity with a means of bringing a 'private prosecution' when officials might be reluctant to act. More cynically, it also gave court officials a lucrative source of income, since every document and court day increased the cost of the suit.

Historians have paid particular attention to the correctional 'office' side of the consistory court, because this dealt with puritans, nonconformists and other religious offenders. Yet the instance side has at least as much to tell about relationships between the laity and the Church, because through it lay people and parish clergy were able to use the courts for their own purposes. Complainants saw the court instrumentally and not merely as an alien imposer of discipline. It was possible for the church courts' instance side to remain vibrant and popular, even after their disciplinary function had been lost. There is no reason to assume that the office and instance functions of the court operated in parallel. Yet in practice, at least in Salisbury diocese, their decline marched in step. At the same time as churchwardens became more reluctant to present their neighbours, both lay and clerical litigants largely abandoned the church courts in favour of secular alternatives.

Although most historians agree that the church courts had suffered a significant loss in authority by the start of the eighteenth century, there is less consensus about the causes and timing of the decline.[3] One explanation attributes the decline of the courts to the Act of Toleration of 1689 and James II's Declaration of Indulgence of 1687, measures which removed their jurisdiction over the correction of dissent, which since 1662 had been one of the Church's primary concerns.[4] In practice, as we shall see, the decline of visitations was already well advanced by 1687. In any case, the Act of Toleration cannot explain the decline of the instance side, which was largely unconcerned with the prosecution of dissent. Indeed, after 1689 the instance side failed to experience an increase in activity in one of its main categories of business, suits for the non-payment of tithes, even though this offered one of the few remaining means of prosecuting dissenters, particularly Quakers. An alternative view is that courts never recovered from the loss of their powers during the Civil Wars.[5] The 'bawdy courts' had been the focus for criticism from puritans before the wars for the twin offences of providing insufficient discipline of the ungodly while persecuting the godly, at a time when their jurisdiction was also being challenged by prohibitions from the common law courts. The quickening of Anglican justice under Laud contributed to the growing unpopularity of the regime, and the church courts suffered during the 1640s in consequence.[6] In 1646 Parliament removed their jurisdiction. The Commonwealth failed to provide a general solution to the problems of discipline, however, although JPs took over some regulatory functions. When the church courts and visitations were restored in 1661, after fifteen years in abeyance, they had lost the *ex officio* oath (which had been deemed to require defendants to commit themselves to testify before they knew the charges against them) and High Commission, so that their powers to enforce conformity were reduced. Yet, although the absence of these powers may have contributed to the reduction in the authority and effectiveness of the correctional side of the courts, they should have had minimal effect on the instance business of the courts, whose collapse was if anything more dramatic. Indeed, in the enthusiasm which succeeded the Restoration, the courts initially appeared to be back to full strength, as can be seen from the buzz of activity both at visitations and in the consistory court itself. This appearance of health and vigour was to prove false, concealing a

---

[3] See W. M. Jacob, *Lay People and Religion in the Early Eighteenth Century* (Cambridge, 1996), pp. 135–54, for a more positive interpretation of the effectiveness of the church courts, which indicates the presence of significant regional variations.

[4] E. A. O. Whiteman, 'The re-establishment of the Church of England, 1660-63', *Transactions of the Royal Historical Society* 5th ser., 5 (1955): 125; G. V. Bennett, *The Tory Crisis of Church and State 1688–1730* (Oxford, 1975), p. 9.

[5] C. Hill, *Society and Puritanism in Pre-Revolutionary England* 2nd edn (New York, 1967), pp. 317–20, 331; J. Addy, *Sin and Society in the Seventeenth Century* (London and New York, 1989), pp. 201–2.

[6] D. Oldridge, *Religion and Society in Early Stuart England* (Aldershot, 1998).

fundamental malaise which was increasingly to debilitate both the correctional and the civil roles of the courts.

The courts' unpopularity has been attributed to their costliness and slowness, as well as to the increased reluctance of society to accept their role as enforcers of discipline. The general contempt for the courts is often demonstrated with evidence of the substantial proportion of people who were excommunicated for their failure to appear in court after being cited. In Wiltshire after the Restoration almost two-thirds of those who were cited failed to attend the courts.[7] By itself this is unpersuasive evidence since those prosecuting puritans had encountered much the same problem a century earlier.[8] Those facing excommunication had often already separated from a church whose authority they no longer recognised. Indeed, the Restoration is by no means the first period thought to have experienced the decline of the church courts. The church court was ineffective in London on the eve of the Reformation, when its declining popularity has been attributed to the 'secularisation' of justice.[9] According to Ralph Houlbrooke, the church courts never recovered from the blow to their authority struck by the Reformation, although the picture was not entirely negative. They showed their flexibility later in the sixteenth century by expanding their disciplinary and litigation business.[10] The eighteenth-century courts were to perform a similar trick, as recent research has established. In the diocese of Carlisle, the regulation of sexual offences increasingly dominated the business of the correctional court and kept it busy until at least 1750.[11] In the diocese of London the consistory court became a popular venue for defamation suits, which women from the middling sort brought to protect their reputations.[12] Yet these present only points of light in a generally black picture. The work of both the Carlisle and London courts narrowed considerably, as they came to specialise in issues that had once been only part of a broad range of business. Sexual regulation accounted for 99 per cent of the Carlisle correctional court's business in 1750. The experience of these dioceses only confirms the scale of the decline in authority of the church courts by the eighteenth century.

Although the Commonwealth weakened the courts, their central role in persecuting dissent caused far more serious damage. The post-Restoration period was the crucial phase in their decline of authority. The courts were too weak to

---

[7] H. Lancaster, 'Nonconformity and Anglican dissent in Restoration Wiltshire, 1660–1689' (Ph.D. thesis, Bristol University, 1995), p. 105.

[8] R. A. Marchant, *The Church under the Law* (Cambridge, 1969), pp. 205, 212.

[9] R. M. Wunderli, *London Church Courts and Society on the Eve of the Reformation* (Cambridge, Mass., 1981).

[10] R. Houlbrooke, *Church Courts and the People during the English Reformation 1520–1570* (Oxford, 1979), pp. 16, 271–2.

[11] M. Kinnear, 'The correction court of the diocese of Carlisle, 1704–1756', *Church History* 59 (1990): 191–206.

[12] T. Meldrum, 'A women's court in London: defamation at the bishop of London's consistory court, 1700–1745', *London Journal* 19 no. 1 (1994): 1–20.

survive identification with such an unpopular and divisive function.[13] After 1662 the churchwardens, upon whom the entire correctional system relied, initially responded to ecclesiastical inquiries with enthusiasm. Faced with the task of prosecuting many of their neighbours, however, their natural reluctance to present rapidly came to the fore. The decline of the courts in Salisbury was already well advanced when Gilbert Burnet became bishop in 1689. Burnet described the church courts as 'the most corrupt courts of the nation, in which they think of nothing but squeezing and oppressing people by all the dilatory and fraudulent ways that are possible . . . [and] they seem to subsist upon nothing but disorder'. He claimed that he had tried unsuccessfully to regulate the Salisbury court, reporting that he had 'found that which is crooked cannot be made straight'.[14] Although there is no doubt of the court's loss of authority during this period, Burnet's words must nevertheless be used with caution, because they remind us that the role of ecclesiastical discipline was a highly contentious political issue during his episcopate and afterwards. Despite the differences in their political outlooks, High Churchmen like Atterbury and Gibson shared the belief that the recovery by ecclesiastical courts of their disciplinary powers over the laity was important to the restoration of the status and authority of the Church.[15] Yet the church courts could not shake off their association with persecution and intolerance, and attempts at reform proved abortive. In 1733–4 they became the target of unfriendly reform bills, although these failed for lack of government support.[16] The draft legislation would have emasculated the courts both by reducing the willingness of wardens to present and by weakening excommunication.[17] Even without legislation, the authority of the Established Church was weakened further by the decision in *Middleton* v. *Crofts* (1737), in which Lord Hardwicke ruled that the laity could not be prosecuted for violating canons unless these had been confirmed by parliamentary statute.[18] This ruling confirmed a less well-known judgement made over three decades earlier. In 1703 the judges had ruled in *Matthew* v. *Burdett* that the church courts could not discipline the laity under the canons. Equally seriously, they had decided that parliamentary imposition of a temporal penalty for an offence

[13] See chapter 7 for discussion of the unpopularity of the prosecution of dissent.

[14] Foxcroft, pp. 105, 331, 503.

[15] G. V. Bennett, *The Tory Crisis of Church and State 1688–1730* (Oxford, 1975), pp. 132–3, 137, 167; G. Every, *The High Church Party 1688–1718* (London, 1956), ch. 8; T. Isaacs, 'The Anglican hierarchy and the reformation of manners 1688–1738', *Journal of Ecclesiastical History* 33 (1982): 406–7.

[16] S. Taylor, 'Sir Robert Walpole, the Church of England, and the Quakers Tithe Bill of 1736', *Historical Journal* 28 (1985): 51–77.

[17] 'A Bill for the better Regulating the Proceedings of Ecclesiastical Courts' (1734), in S. Lambert, ed., *House of Commons Sessional Papers of the Eighteenth Century* (Wilmington, Del., 1975), vol. VII, pp. 119–21. Prosecutions would have had to be made by accusation and would have required a bond to be filed.

[18] N. Sykes, *From Sheldon to Secker: Aspects of English Church History, 1660-1768* (Cambridge, 1959), p. 57.

removed ecclesiastical jurisdiction over that offence, to protect defendants against double jeopardy. This decision would have weakened ecclesiastical jurisdiction over nonconformity even without the Act of Toleration.[19] From this time onwards ecclesiastical discipline was in theory limited to the clergy, although laymen were occasionally presented for offences. In practice, the decay of ecclesiastical jurisdiction was already well advanced in Salisbury diocese by 1703.

THE DECLINE OF VISITATIONS

Visitation records are important sources of the extent and nature of lay–clerical conflict. Each parish was visited at least once a year, at which time new churchwardens took the oath of office, the incumbent exhibited his licence and, most importantly, the visitation court detected offences through the presentments of churchwardens and incumbents. The identity of the visiting jurisdiction varied from year to year. The bishop of Salisbury had the largest jurisdiction in Wiltshire, covering 245 parishes which he or his official visited every three years. Otherwise the lesser jurisdictions of the archdeacons of Wiltshire (to the north) and of Salisbury (to the south) visited these parishes at least once a year.[20] Forty-five Wiltshire parishes lay within peculiars in the largely separate jurisdiction of the dean of Salisbury, whose large domain also embraced parts of Berkshire, Dorset and Devon. The dean visited some parishes annually and others triennially; a prebendary visited in other years. The visitation records of the bishop and dean of Salisbury supply the largest and most complete sets of surviving presentments. The records of the archdeacons' visitations are sparse. Although it is unwise to read too much into their failure to survive, there is other evidence that these lesser jurisdictions were less important than their counterparts in larger dioceses such as Lincoln and York. The survival of presentments from archdeacons' visitations within episcopal court papers indicates the dominance of the bishop's consistory court.[21]

Apparitors distributed copies of the book of Articles of Inquiry to all parishes several weeks before the visitations. This provided churchwardens with a long list of questions that summarised possible offences against the canons, royal injunctions, liturgy and statutes. Churchwardens were bound by oath to present all offenders, so their presentments provide the fullest picture of religious observance and pastoral practice that is available to us.[22] The interpretation of

---

[19] F. K. Eagle and E. Younge, *A Collection of the Reports of Cases, the Statutes and Ecclesiastical Laws relating to Tithes* (London, 1826), vol. I, pp. 650–1. Ecclesiastical jurisdiction would technically have survived because of a proviso that it might remain if explicitly protected by the same legislation.

[20] Visitation courts were held in market towns and other centres within each deanery, where they were attended by officers from the surrounding parishes.   [21] D1/41/4/35.

[22] Churchwardens were also to report any recent deaths in the parish for probate purposes, and the names of schoolmasters and midwives without licences, but I have not counted these presentments.

Table 3.1 *Churchwardens' presentments, Amesbury deanery, 1662–1714*

Year	Parishes and chapels presenting	*Omnia bene*	Fabric	Absence	Number absent
1662	21	0	17	11	49
1668	20	3	10	15	74
1674	18	3	10	13	56
1683	21	7	8	10	21
1686	19	5	7	6	15
1689	17	5	7	2	9
1692	18	14	3	1	0
1698	15	12	3	1	1
1701	19	17	1		
1714	20	16	3		

Note
Omnia bene includes presentments of nothing to present, excluding the listing of deaths. Fabric includes presentments of missing books and objects, building faults in the church, churchyard, parsonage or outhouses. Absence indicates the number of presentments that mention absence from church. Number absent shows the number of named absenters (including those who also did not receive communion), recusants, sectaries and excommunicates. One parish presented dissenters in 1692 without giving names.
Source: WRO D1/54, 1662–1714, Amesbury and Chalke.

presentments is not straightforward, however. It is tempting to assume that churchwardens presented all offenders, so that the absence of any presentment indicates that all was well. Unfortunately, this assumption would be unsafe because wardens often failed to present known offences. Presentments understate the extent of religious 'crime' and tell us as much about the concerns of those chosen to represent their parish as churchwardens as they do about the state of religious practice. Yet offences usually had to occur before they could be reported. The historian must attempt to strike a balance between viewing presentments as records of religious life and as fortunate survivals.

In Salisbury diocese, as elsewhere, the first episcopal visitation after the Restoration was made in September and October 1662, under the new bishop Humphrey Henchman. The presentments from this visitation suggest little evidence of an institution in decline, while at the same time demonstrating how much reconstruction the parishes of the Church of England needed to do after fifteen years in the wilderness. Almost all parishes reported defects in church fabric or goods, including the lack of the new Prayer Book and other Anglican texts such as Jewel's *Apology* and of such ceremonial items as surplices, communion cloths and hearse cloths. Many churches and churchyards had fallen into disrepair. Churchwardens were scrupulous in their presentments. Some answered virtually every question in Henchman's unusually lengthy articles.[23]

The excellent record of 1662 was not to be repeated in subsequent years, as the example of Amesbury deanery in southern Wiltshire demonstrates (Table 3.1). In part the decline in presentments reflected the success which parishes achieved in correcting faults in the fabric of the church left by the Commonwealth. Yet it also provides a barometer of declining enthusiasm of churchwardens for the task. Defects in fabric included repairs which were required to the church, chancel or outbuildings, missing or defective books such as the Prayer Book and Bible, and missing ritual items such as communion cloths. It comes as no surprise that such presentments were at their peak in 1662, when Prayer Books and ritual items needed to be replaced and when some churches had suffered poor maintenance. Over 80 per cent of parishes presented defects in fabric in 1662, and in most cases they had many defects to report. The rapid fall in the number of parishes presenting defective fabric in 1668 suggests that much had been accomplished, although some places had more to do. Yet the decline in presentments of fabric did not stop then; it continued downwards until it reached its nadir in the 1690s. Indeed, the statistics understate the extent of the fall because they record only the incidence and not the number of faults which were reported. Whereas in 1662 most parishes presented several defects in fabric, in later years it became rare for wardens to acknowledge more than one fault and to offer more than minimal details. The presentment of Milston chapelry is typical: 'Wee have made diligent enquirey in our parish, but doe not find anything pr[e]sentable saveing that our church is out of repaire.'[24]

Presentments of dissenters followed a similar downward curve. Visitations were the main ecclesiastical route for prosecutions of dissenters who neglected to conform to the canons or to Elizabethan leigislation, particularly by prolonged absence from weekly services. Amesbury deanery was not a hotbed of dissent, but no fewer than half of its parishes were reported as housing separatists in 1676,[25] and presentments for absence ought to have remained high until the Act of Toleration of 1689. Yet churchwardens' enthusiasm for the task of presenting their neighbours was clearly waning well before then. Presentments peaked as early as 1668, the year of the first Conventicle Act, when the Cavalier Parliament's campaign against dissent was at its height. Thereafter the picture was one of steady decline in the numbers both of parishes presenting and of

[23] D1/54/1 (1662). A handful of Wiltshire presentments give the year 1661, since the presentment covered the year from Easter 1661 to Easter 1662. See also Whiteman, 'The re-establishment of the Church of England', p. 121; and I. Green, *The Re-establishment of the Church of England 1660–63* (Oxford, 1978), p. 135. Green suggests that some dioceses initially had difficulty in getting churchwardens to attend visitations (pp. 138–9).   [24] D1/54/16/4 (1698, A&C).

[25] Half of the twenty-two parishes in the deanery had dissenters in 1676, compared to a peak of 67 per cent of fifty-one parishes in Malmesbury deanery. Calculations are based upon Whiteman, *Compton Census*, pp. 104–30.

offenders presented. Even the Tory reaction of the early 1680s, when prosecution of nonconformists rose in Quarter Sessions, did little to increase presentments in Amesbury deanery.[26] Secular prosecution did not compensate for this downward trend in the presentment of dissent at visitations. Nor is there any evidence that nonconformity was declining over the same period. Across Wiltshire more parishes were the sites of dissenting places of worship after 1689 than had been known locations of conventicles in 1669–72.[27] The Act of Toleration recognised a *de facto* toleration of dissent that was already present in many parishes.

The declines in presentments of absenters and fabric were aspects of a more general reduction in the willingness of churchwardens to make any presentment at all. The Restoration period saw a rapid rise in the number of *omnia bene* presentments. No parish presented that all was well in 1662 and the number doing so remained low through the 1670s. Thereafter the number rose rapidly, accounting for 30 per cent of presentments in the 1680s. In 1701, two years before *Matthew* v. *Burdett* in theory removed ecclesiastical jurisdiction over the laity, 90 per cent of churchwardens presented that all was well. A presentment of *omnia bene* indicated either that churchwardens had no offences to report or had decided not to report any. Visitations ceased to be an effective means of detecting offenders because lay churchwardens had stopped co-operating. In the eighteenth century the failure of churchwardens to present known offenders, even though they had taken an oath to present in full, became a scandal and was deemed to discredit oaths.[28] Even when they did make a presentment, churchwardens tried to reveal as little as possible. The failure of churchwardens to present was a common complaint of clergymen. The parson's decision to present members of his congregation might exacerbate lay–clerical tensions. The churchwardens preferred to present *omnia bene* or even to make no presentment at all, perhaps because they were fearful of their neighbours. In 1673 the rector of Somerford Magna, Nathaniel Aske, submitted a presentment in the name of a churchwarden who was afraid to present his own neighbours. Aske reported that the errant warden 'knows the truth of every particular and advised with me beforhand'. He did not forget to present the warden himself for his neglect. Nathaniel Forster, rector of Allington, also stood in for his wardens in 1689, providing an unusually long presentment for that year. The names of the wardens were ultimately appended to the presentment.[29] The natural instinct of wardens was to avoid making a presentment. Ecclesiastical visitations were not the only institutions to suffer from the reluctance of parish officers to present. Secular

---

[26] Lancaster, 'Nonconformity and Anglican dissent', p. 329.
[27] Lambeth Palace Library, MS 639; CSPD, 1671–2; WRO A1/250, Dissenters' Places of Worship, 1695–1750.
[28] P. Langford, *Public Life and the Propertied Englishman 1689–1798* (Oxford, 1991), p. 111; Lambeth Palace Library, MS 1741, ff. 106–107v.
[29] D1/41/1/17 (Somerford Magna, 6 and 20 Oct. 1673); D1/54/12/3 (1689, A&C, Allington).

authorities also experienced difficulties in persuading local officials to present their neighbours, even though they asked far fewer questions of constables and juries. John Eyre reported to the bishop in 1670 that constables 'were more ready to perjure themselves than give true presentments'.[30] Complaints to magistrates acting through summary justice may have been replacing jury presentments as the primary means by which petty offences were brought to the attention of the authorities.[31]

Churchwardens' presentments were not made spontaneously. They came in response to specific questions and were subject to pressure from ecclesiastical officials. The high incidence of presentment in the 1660s was the consequence of two factors, episcopal pressure and lay support for the recent Restoration. Bishop Henchman greeted with energy the opportunity to cleanse the Augean stables left by the Commonwealth. In his extensive set of articles he asked no fewer than 180 questions divided between 81 separate articles.[32] Churchwardens took very much to heart the stern admonition that 'There must be several Presentments made to every several Article' with which he ended his articles. A generation had passed since the last episcopal visitation and, while churchwardens were uncertain how to go about the task, they were eager to please. The wardens from Amesbury parish queried whether they had the power to fine dissenters for absence from church according to Elizabethan anti-recusant legislation: 'the churchwardens humbly conceiving themselves not fully in power to levie by way of distress upon the goods of absent parishione[rs] the summe of 12 pence for every such day of their absence'. The religious chaos of the preceding fifteen years left both wardens and clerics in doubt about issues of practice and ceremony, and presented them with new problems. The wardens and rector of Allington admitted confusion about the correct positioning of the communion table: 'I cannot tell whether the table be placed as it ought, or noe. The wardens of Ludgershall asked whether their rector, Andrew Read, who had recently been restored to his benefice, should christen unbaptised older children immediately or wait until they reached the age of discretion.[33]

Unsure of their rights and powers, churchwardens took their cue from the firm guidance provided by the bishop in his articles of inquiry. Many treated the articles as a questionnaire, responding point by point to each article, even when they had nothing to report.[34] The susceptibility of wardens to episcopal influence can

[30] CSPD, 1670, p. 417. In 1675 24 of 50 hundred juries and constables had nothing to present, a non-presentment rate that exceeded that of churchwardens. The rate of presentment was much higher in 1683 during the Tory reaction, yet even then the grand jury had to summon the Melksham hundred jury for refusing to present dissenters. A1/110, 1675, 1683 T, f. 99.

[31] J. A. Sharpe, *Crime in Early Modern England, 1550–1750* (London, 1984), p. 172.

[32] *Second Report of the Commissioners . . . into the . . . Conduct of Public Worship . . .*, House of Commons Parliamentary Papers, 1867–8, vol. XXXVIII, 610–13.

[33] D1/54/1/3 (1662, A&C), f. 42 (Amesbury); f. 51 (Allington), f. 43 (Ludgershall).

[34] See, for example, D1/54/1/3 (1662, A&C), ff. 2–5 (Dinton), 22 (Chicklade), 25 (Bishop's Knoyle); D1/54/1/2 (1662, A&P), ff. 12 (Winterbourne Basset), 35 (Holt).

be seen in those presentments which even echoed the wording of articles. The presentment from Holt followed the fourth question of Article III word for word, reporting that their minister 'doth endeavour to reclaime all Popish recusants and other Sectaries to the true religion established in the Church of England'. Chicklade's version was briefer but also included the key words: the minister 'hath often indeavoured to reclaime sectaries to the true religion',[35] although the omission of any reference to recusants suggests that some thought went into the answer. If the book of articles had not survived, it could be reconstructed from such presentments. After years of uncertainty, churchwardens responded enthusiastically to the return of discipline and order under the Established Church.

The infusion of blood given by the revival of visitations after the Restoration gave the church courts a visage of rude health which they were rapidly to lose. The campaign against nonconformity was unpopular, and in the long run would prove fatal to the authority of the courts. At the 1668 visitations some wardens continued to provide detailed answers to the queries, but the number of wardens who made a presentment for every query was declining.[36] Visitation articles became briefer, with only forty to fifty articles the common number by the eighteenth century.[37] In 1674 the churchwardens of Codford St Mary were still echoing the articles, but their long presentment said that virtually everything was well.[38] Bishop Burnet was well aware of the imperfect quality of presentments when he entered the see in 1689. Before his primary visitation he wrote to his clergy to instruct them to 'take care that ye presentments may not be made wth the carelessless yt is too ordinary'. As he recognised, the failure of churchwardens to present lay at the roots of the problem, and he told his clergy to remind churchwardens of their oath to present fully.[39] As presentments became briefer and less formulaic, they were more likely to reflect lay choices than ecclesiastical pressure. Wardens' natural reluctance to present their neighbours came to the fore. Churchwardens adopted a variety of evasive tactics to pressure from visitation officials and the clergy. They might report that an offence had been committed but omit the names of offenders, perhaps requesting more time for reform or to collect details. Or they might offer an excuse for the offender. In Laverstock the wardens sought to excuse the illiteracy of their parish clerk by his poverty; in any case they claimed that he was diligent in his office.[40] In 1662 the disruption caused by the Civil War and Interregnum might itself be used to excuse any deficiencies. As the warden and rector of Allington explained, 'what soever hath been omitted through the iniquity of the late times shall hereafter bee observed'.[41] After the 1660s the reporting of an offence reflected a deliberate

---

[35] D1/54/1/3 (1662, A&C), f. 22; D1/54/1/2 (1662, A&P), f. 35.
[36] See, for example, D1/54/3/2 (1668, A&C), f. 25 (Grimstead).
[37] There were forty-three articles in Burnet's queries of 1695 and thirty-eight in 1729. D1/54/15, 1695; D1/54/31 (1729, Abingdon deanery).   [38] D1/54/6/5 (1674, W&W), f. 27.
[39] PRO, C104/63.   [40] D1/54/1/3 (1662, A&C), f. 39.   [41] D1/54/1/3 (1662, A&C), f. 51.

Table 3.2 *Presentments against clergymen to the bishop and dean of Salisbury, by decade*

Decade	Bishop	Dean
1660s*	28	7
1670s*	9	10
1680s	20	1
1690s	11	6
1700s	8	3
1710s*	2	2
1720s	4	0
1730s	6	2
1740s*	3	2

Note
*Decades marked by an asterisk had two episcopal visitations per decade, those without had three. Some of the dean's parishes were visited annually, others triennially. Presentments for failure to perform perambulation are not included.
Source: WRO, D1/54, 1662–1750; D5/28, 1662–1750.

choice made by churchwardens. Although this development makes it more diffi-cult to analyse presentments systematically, it increases their value as sources of lay belief. Moral and religious offences are particularly susceptible to 'dark figure' errors, which result from the difficulty of estimating the relationship between actual and reported crime.[42] Reform campaigns can create significant rises and falls in the reporting of offences. In the late seventeenth and eighteenth centuries churchwardens' presentments provide unreliable guides to the inci-dence and chronology of offences. They tell us as much about the presenters as the presented, if not more. Churchwardens who made presentments did so delib-erately. They had reasons for choosing to present a particular person at a partic-ular time. While some ministers complained about churchwardens who failed to present offenders, others benefited from the lay preference for keeping silent before authority.

It is in this context that the downward trend in presentments against parish clergy must be viewed. Churchwardens continued to present clergymen when they had largely stopped presenting other offences. It comes as no surprise that the largest number of presentments against clerics was made in 1662. The com-

[42] Sharpe, *Crime in Early Modern England*, pp. 47–8.

bination of instability after the Commonwealth and of the aggressiveness of episcopal inquiry made this inevitable. Thereafter, the number of clerics who were presented to the bishop or the dean remained at about the same level through the 1690s, including another brief flurry of presentments in 1689, before falling to only one or two each visitation after 1700. Given the general decline in presentment over the same period, it would be unsafe to conclude, merely on the basis of this quantitative evidence, either that the quality of pastoral care offered by the clergy had improved or that lay–clerical tensions had relaxed. It is clear that ministers were committing offences which were not being presented. Churchwardens were particularly concerned about pluralism and non-residence and about the resulting insufficiency in the provision of Sunday prayers. Yet although pluralism was a growing problem in the late seventeenth and early eighteenth centuries the number of presentments for the offence fell during the period. In 1683 29 pluralist incumbents served 56 parishes between them. By 1730 these numbers had grown to 36 clerics serving 79 parishes.[43] The incidence of pluralism had grown from one in four to one in three parishes. Pluralism was inevitably linked to non-residence, and in 1735 the archdeacons of Salisbury and Wiltshire ordered that 23 incumbents be cited for their non-residence.[44] Yet churchwardens were much less likely to present non-residence and pluralist incumbents in the 1730s than they had been half a century earlier. The bishop and dean of Salisbury received 24 presentments for these offences in 1660–99, but only nine in 1700–39. Visitations had ceased to be a reliable means of detecting even clerical offenders.[45]

Churchwardens showed discretion when deciding to present clerics, just as they did with their lay neighbours. This is most vividly demonstrated in the 1672 presentment from Colerne, when churchwardens had to be warned three times before they would present their minister, even though he was a notorious offender.[46] Such examples are by their nature rare, because ministers were themselves the commonest source of the complaints that churchwardens had failed to present. Ministers were unlikely to complain when they themselves benefited from the silence of parish officers. Yet there are several examples of churchwardens who sought to protect their minister by making excuses for him: the minister had not yet catechised because he had only recently been inducted, or he had not read common prayer because of a long illness.[47] The wardens of Winterbourne Bassett answered every question in 1662 and so perhaps felt obliged to mention that communion had not been celebrated, but they stressed that this was because the minister had been sick. In 1683 the

---

[43] D1/48/2, D1/48/4. Only those with more than one living in Salisbury diocese are counted.
[44] D1/61/1b, pp. 65–6.   [45] Cf. Bennett, *The Tory Crisis*, p. 15.   [46] D1/41/4/39.
[47] Trowbridge, D1/54/6/3 (1674, A&P), f. 13; Laverstock, D1/54/1/3 (1662, A&C), f. 39.

Table 3.3 *Summary of consistory court causes*

Offence category	1674	1716–17
Tithes	31	2
Defamation	8	22
Rates and parish payments	6	1
Fee	5	1
Testamentary/negotia	5	5
Vilification of clergy	5	
Office	2	1
Dilapidations	1	1
Not given	2	1
TOTAL	65	34

Source: WRO, D1/39/1/58–9, 69.

Stockton wardens also reported no communion because of the sickness of the minister.[48] These clearly were not examples of lay–clerical conflict, although they do indicate dissatisfaction about the level of service which the parish was receiving.

The decline in the effectiveness of visitations means that it is difficult to draw any firm conclusions about the changing incidence of lay–clerical conflict in the late seventeenth and early eighteenth centuries. Churchwardens became far less likely to present clerical offences than they had been, particularly when these were relatively trivial. Yet the continued appearance of presentments against clergymen is all the more remarkable given the decline of business. This suggests that clerical neglect remained a significant matter of concern in the 1730s, just as it had been in the 1670s. The churchwardens of a single chapelry, Bratton, presented their vicar thirteen times between 1721 and 1729 for reading prayers only once every fortnight.[49] Although eighteenth-century visitations still provided a forum for complaints against ministers, the laity sometimes preferred secular alternatives. In 1754, after a dispute over the service of Combe Bissett, the non-resident vicar Charles Barber was obliged to swear out a bond to the churchwardens that he would appoint a curate or serve the cure himself.[50]

THE FLIGHT FROM THE CONSISTORY COURT

At the same time as ecclesiastical visitations found it increasingly difficult to secure the cooperation of lay churchwardens, the instance side of the consistory

[48] Winterbourne Bassett, D1/54/1/2 (1662, A&P), f. 12; Stockton, D1/54/10/3 (1683, A&P).
[49] D25/12. These presentments were made at the precentor's visitations (held twice a year) and are not included in the figures for the dean and bishop.   [50] WRO 539/11.

Table 3.4 *Tithe suits in the consistory court of the bishop of Salisbury,*
1663–1720

Decade	Tithe acts (defendants)	Tithe citations	Total
1660s		138	138
1670s	108	18	126
1680s	43		43
1690s	29		29
1700s	21		21
1710s	12		12

Note
Each cause is counted only once, even if multiple citations survive.
Source: WRO, D1/39/1/55–72 and D1/39/3/1–5 (act books), D1/41/1/6–13 (citations).

court was suffering a corresponding decline in business. Clerical and lay litigants made heavy use of the court's services in the decades which followed the Restoration, particularly for such issues as non-payment of tithes. Yet the late seventeenth and early eighteenth centuries were to see a dramatic fall in the case-load of the bishop of Salisbury's court, as it lost business to competitors. In the first instance, most litigants took their business to the competing jurisdiction of the Exchequer Court of Equity, with the clergy leading the way. When in 1696 two acts gave justices of the peace summary jurisdiction over tithes, the flight from the church courts was already well advanced.[51] Some clergymen turned to summary jurisdiction, although the shortage of surviving records makes it difficult to document this transition. The increasing tendency of the clergy to lease their tithes and the use of summary justice meant that tithes became somewhat less likely to generate lay–clerical conflict.

The decline in tithe business was part of a larger fall in consistory court business. Relatively few cases proceeded far enough for sentence to be decreed, so court activity is best studied through the act books, which provide the official record of the progress of each cause. The court's activity can be studied by counting the initial entries of causes, when the citation against the defendant was issued. Citations were filed if they were returned by the apparitor, and these files provide an alternative guide to activity which can be used when act books are missing or incomplete.[52]

[51] 7&8 William III, c. 6, c. 34.
[52] Citations can be used to plug the gap from 1661 to 1671 when the Salisbury act books unfortunately omit details of the issue at dispute. Citations and act books may not be directly comparable. It is theoretically possible that citations were issued and returned for some cases which were never recorded in an act book, e.g. if the case was dropped quickly. On the other hand, some citations were never returned to the court, as can be seen in the occasional survival of a citation *viis et modis* when the initial citation is missing.

Comparison of the caseload for the bishop of Salisbury's consistory court for two years from the late seventeenth and early eighteenth centuries documents the dramatic fall in both the scale and range of business handled by the court. In 1674 tithes accounted for roughly half the court activity on the instance side and was one of six issues at dispute in five or more suits. Forty years later, in 1716–17, only three issues were raised more than once and the most common, defamation, accounted for over two-thirds of the business. Tithes, by far the most important issue in the 1670s, had virtually disappeared from the caseload by the 1710s. The consistory court continued to serve a function, but its authority and activity had narrowed significantly.

Figures for individual years can be unreliable because of the possibility of annual variations. Yet the reduction of activity in the consistory court can be tracked decade by decade by studying the numbers of defendants in suits for non-payment of tithes.[53] Litigants greeted the return of the spiritual court's jurisdiction with enthusiasm, delighted to see the restoration of the natural forum in which to defend their rights and incomes, and the court remained busy throughout the 1660s and 1670s. This high level was in part a legacy of the Commonwealth. The sequestration of ministers during the Civil Wars and Interregnum created doubts over the ownership of tithes, particularly where excluded ministers were still alive to return to their benefices in 1660. Ministers like Walter Bushnell of Box sought to recover the income they had lost on the grounds that they had been legally instituted and so were entitled to it.[54] After 1680 the court's tithe caseload fell sharply, long before the early eighteenth century when the combined effects of Toleration, the 1696 tithe acts and *Matthew* v. *Burdett* signalled the reduced authority of the courts. Whereas in the 1670s on average 12.6 people per year were forced to defend actions for tithes, in the following decade the number fell to only a third of that number, and the decline continued into the eighteenth century. By 1696, when summary jurisdiction began, there were only three cases a year. The clergy, who, as holders of petty tithes, had the most to gain from the act, had already led the flight from the consistory court.[55] Litigants abandoned the consistory courts for other jurisdictions because they found them to be more effective. Before the Wars the ecclesiastical courts had faced competition from advocates in the common law courts who used prohibitions to poach cases.[56] After the Restoration, the ecclesiastical courts faced more serious competition from the equity courts, and particularly from the Exchequer Court of Equity.

[53] For sources, see Table 3.4.   [54] PRO, E112/533, case 28.

[55] Cf. Staffordshire where clerics favoured the ecclesiastical court and laymen the Exchequer. E. J. Evans, 'A history of the tithe system in England, 1690–1850, with special reference to Staffordshire' (Ph.D. thesis, Warwick University, 1970), pp. 109–10.

[56] Hill, *Society and Puritanism*, p. 331. Levack argues, however, that competition between common and civil lawyers has been overstated. B. P. Levack, *The Civil Lawyers in England, 1603–1641* (Oxford, 1973).

Tithes were a relatively new jurisdiction for the Exchequer. The jurisdiction had its origins in the court's right to hear complaints from debtors to the Crown, who included clerics who paid first fruits and tenths on the grounds that their ability to pay the Crown might be impaired by the withholding of tithes. The abolition of church courts in 1646 created an opportunity which the equity court grasped with both hands by developing the legal fiction of debtorship to the Crown to expand its jurisdiction to all tithe-owners, both clerical and lay.[57] In the 1650s alone the Exchequer Court of Equity received bills against over two hundred Wiltshire defendants. In the absence of the church courts, some plaintiffs also pursued tithes as unpaid debts through the county or hundred courts, which had jurisdiction over debts, although not specifically over tithes.[58] In the late seventeenth and early eighteenth centuries, it was the ecclesiastical and Exchequer courts that were used most frequently against tithe defaulters and were most feared by them. Although Chancery had its own equity jurisdiction, this received relatively few bills for tithes.[59] A case begun in Chancery might still be moved across to Exchequer even if the process was well advanced.[60] When the Quakers lobbied for the 1736 Quaker Tithe Bill they named the Exchequer and church courts as the main threats to Friends, and the bishops strenuously resisted this assault on their jurisdiction.[61] In Salisbury, at least, the tithe jurisdiction of the church courts was already defunct. The Court of Exchequer was far more important as a threat to Quakers than the church courts were.

[57] R. M. Ball, 'Tobias Eden, change and conflict in the Exchequer office, 1672–1698', *Journal of Legal History* 11 (1990): 70–89; D. B. Fowler, *The Practice of the Court of Exchequer upon Proceedings in Equity* (London, 1795), vol. I, pp. 1–6.

[58] N. Morgan, *Lancashire Quakers and the Establishment 1660–1730* (Halifax, 1993), p. 202. A sheriff's county court is described by S. A. Peyton, ed., *Minutes of Proceedings in Quarter Sessions . . . 1674–1695*, Lincolnshire Record Society 25 (Lincoln, 1931), p. xvii. During the Interregnum tithe-owners used the jurisdiction of the county court to sue for distraint of amounts under 40s. Quaker sufferings record prosecutions in the county court, hundred court, Common Pleas, Exchequer and the bishop's court. Some sufferers had their goods confiscated without being taken to court. WRO 1699/18; Friends' House Library, Great Books of Sufferings, vol. II, Wilts., pp. 1, 8, 11, vol. IV, part 22, pp. 448, 453–4, 455, 464–5.

[59] Tithes accounted for fewer than 1 per cent of Chancery decrees in 1785, although it is true that Chancery had much more business than Exchequer. H. Horwitz and P. Polden, 'Continuity or change in the Court of Chancery in the seventeenth and eighteenth centuries?', *Journal of British Studies* 35 (1996): 24–57. The indexing of Chancery records makes it impossible to create a comprehensive time-series for a county. Most of the indexes of the Six Clerks cover the whole of England, provide no topographical information and record only the surnames of the parties, so that discovering that there was a suit is a matter of luck, and there is little chance of finding cross-suits, such as Ewen c. Twittee, allegedly brought to Chancery in 1671. 'The Society's MSS – Chiseldon and Draycot', *WAM* 30 (1898): 51–4. The samples for 1685 and 1735 in H. Horwitz and C. Moreton, *Samples of Chancery Pleadings and Suits*, List and Index Society vol. 257 (Richmond, 1995), include no Wiltshire tithe cases.

[60] *Townson v. Hungerford*, Eagle and Younge, *A Collection of the Reports*, vol. I, p. 551. The similarities in procedure between the two courts meant that Chancery depositions could be used in the Exchequer proceedings.

[61] Friends' House Library, Minutes of Yearly Meetings, vol. II, 1733, p. 386, quoted by N. C. Hunt, *Two Early Political Associations* (Oxford, 1961), p. 71.

Table 3.5 *Exchequer bills (defendants)*
for tithes prosecuted by clergy and laity,
1650–1730

Decade	Clergy	Laity	Total
1650s	115	101	216
1660s	158	26	184
1670s	86	59	145
1680s	96	86	184
1690s*	101	35	136
1700s*	10	4	14
1710s*	37	22	59
1720s*	36	48	84

Note
*The issue was incompletely recorded from
the 1690s onwards. The bill books for the
1730s–50s record only twelve cases for tithes,
but are almost certainly not complete.
Source: PRO, IND/1 16827, 16829, 16831,
16833, 16835, 16837, 16839, 16841.

Because the equity courts' procedures were similar to those of consistory courts they were familiar to litigants.[62] A case began when the complainant exhibited an English bill of complaint. The defendant was summoned by subpoena to submit his personal answer and the receipt of a satisfactory answer marked the end of the pleadings stage. The depositions of witnesses were taken in writing, usually by a commission sent into the county. A decree by the barons of Exchequer ended the case, but very few cases reached this advanced stage.[63] The court's activity can be studied by counting entries in its bill books, which listed each bill of complaint according to the county of the complainant and so provide an index to pleadings.[64] Each bill is listed once with details of the year

---

[62] For Equity proceedings, see D. B. Fowler, *The Practice of the Court of Exchequer upon Proceedings in Equity* (London, 1795). Henry Horwitz, *Chancery Equity Records and Proceedings 1600–1800* (London, 1995), ch. 1, provides a convenient summary of the analogous procedure in Chancery.

[63] There were decrees or dismissals for only around one in six of the 283 bills listed in the reign of Charles II. PRO, IND 1/17050, pp. 361–2; IND 1/16829, 16831. The discussion above simplifies the procedure considerably. Subpoenas might be issued before the bill was filed. The defendant might employ various pleas, and the pleading stage might involve further stages of rejoinders. Cases might need to be revived if a party died.

[64] For sources, see Table 3.5. To assist comparison with the consistory court, defendants rather than bills will be counted. Whereas the act books treat each defendant as a separate cause, the practice of the Exchequer was to consolidate cases into a single bill, as for example in cases 158, 180 and 182 in PRO, IND 1/16839. Fowler, *Practice*, vol. I, p. 244; vol. II, p. 46. For the application of a similar technique to the other central courts, see C. W. Brooks, *Pettyfoggers and Vipers of the Commonwealth* (Cambridge, 1986), ch. 4.

and the names of the parties and usually also the issue, parish and parties' ranks. Unfortunately, the quality of the listings slips from the 1690s onwards when Exchequer clerks became more careless about recording complete details in the bill books, most likely because they found this information was not necessary for their work.[65] These omissions severely restrict the usefulness of the bill books, so that a comparable count can be produced only by referring to the original bills, a much slower process.[66]

Tithe suits were central to the expansion of the Exchequer court, accounting for 60 per cent of its business during the reign of Charles II.[67] The restoration of ecclesiastical jurisdiction in 1661 did not dent the court's activity. Indeed, the equity court shared the rise in business after 1660, when it heard more business than the consistory court.[68] Unlike the consistory court, the Exchequer remained a popular venue for tithes at least into the next century.[69] Although the bill books appear to show a sharp fall in business, reference to the original bills establishes that this is entirely an artefact of the source, because clerks often omitted the rank of the complainant and the issue at dispute. One might have expected the Exchequer Court of Equity to lose some of its business after 1696, when Parliament passed acts which enabled tithe-owners to use summary justice in order to reclaim their tithes. Yet in the 1690s and 1700s the court continued to be just as busy as it had been previously. Indeed, the Exchequer managed to delay a general loss of business which affected other Westminster courts, including King's Bench, Common Pleas and Chancery, from the 1680s onwards, which may have indicated a decline in litigiousness.[70] The complete failure of the consistory court to participate in this activity confirms its infirmity.

The new acts were not entirely without effect, as we shall see. At the same time, economic and fiscal developments were increasing the pressure on tithe-owners and payers. The last decade of the seventeenth century saw the conjuncture of a significant increase in the burden of taxation to pay for the new monarchs' continental wars and of a succession of bad harvests from 1693 to

---

[65] The omission of such information in most of the contemporary indexes kept by the Chancery Six Clerks is one of the main reasons why the records of that court are much less accessible.

[66] Bills are also organised by monarch and county. Because depositions and decrees were taken for relatively few cases, listings of them provide an unacceptably incomplete picture of court action over tithes.

[67] Based on the number of tithe bills recorded for Wiltshire. However, tithes accounted for only 38 per cent of decrees in 1685. Horwitz and Polden, 'Continuity or change'.

[68] I have ignored the distorting effect of a single 1656 case with sixty-nine defendants. This complex case was brought by the Trustees for the Maintenance of Ministers and concerned the attempt of an impropriator of a neighbouring parish to claim tithes for a portion of Savernake Forest formerly payable to the Dean and Chapter. E112/343, case 78.

[69] Cf. Staffordshire, where the ratio of ecclesiastical to Exchequer suits was 4:1. Evans, 'A history of the tithe system', pp. 94–5.

[70] C. W. Brooks, 'Interpersonal conflict and social tension: civil litigation in England, 1640–1830', in A. L. Beier, David Cannadine and James M. Rosenheim, eds., *The First Modern Society*, (Cambridge, 1989), pp. 357–99; Horwitz and Polden, 'Continuity or change', pp. 24–57.

Table 3.6 *Exchequer bills (originals) for
tithes, 1690–1709*

Decade	Clergy	Laity	Total
1690s	131	41	172
1700s	53	122	175

Note
These figures are derived by combining the
information from the bill books and the
original bills.
Source: PRO, IND 1/16835, 16837; E112/759,
907–12.

1700.[71] Rents fell and some landlords were obliged to allow tenants to accumulate arrears. Tithes become more difficult to collect than ever, while tithe-owners
themselves faced an increased tax burden. In Avebury the farmer William Skeate
pleaded to be allowed a reduction in rent of £100 'in consideration of the bad
times & my losses'. Skeate also embroiled himself in a dispute over tithes with
the vicar.[72] Clerical tithe-owners in Wiltshire must have experienced the same difficulties as their Norfolk colleagues, who found to their despair that, despite
their poverty, they were being taxed on the same basis as the gentry; some had
books distrained to pay tax arrears, and others experienced the rough side of
Exchequer.[73] As a result, some clerics resorted to the courts even to recover very
small sums.

Two tithe acts passed by Parliament in 1696 provided a new venue for tithe-
owners. One act allowed all tithe-owners to recover up to £10 in tithes from
Quakers by recourse to two justices of the peace. If the Quaker remained recalcitrant, magistrates could issue a warrant authorising the distraint and sale of
goods in order to recoup the lost tithes. The second act provided similar procedures for claiming unpaid tithes from all categories of tithe-payer, although it
was limited to owners of petty tithes who wished to collect unpaid tithes up to
only £2 in value.[74] The latter act was always likely to have the greatest impact
upon clerics, who usually owned petty tithes. The advantages of summary justice
were clear, given the potentially high costs of a suit, and research on other counties has shown that these new summary powers were used to good effect against

[71] J. Brewer, *The Sinews of Power* (Cambridge, Mass., 1990); J. Thirsk, ed., *Agrarian History of
England and Wales* (Cambridge, 1985), vol. V.2, p. 57.
[72] WRO 184/1, Letter from William Skeate, 17 May 1695. Skeate estimated that he had lost £300.
[73] 'The case of the poor country clergie with respect to the execution of the late poll-acts and land-
taxes represented and humbly submitted to the judgment of wise and good men', Tanner MS 80,
ff. 121–121v.
[74] 6&7 William III c. 6, c. 34; Evans, in *Agrarian History of England and Wales* V.2, p. 403.

Quakers.[75] Relatively little direct evidence of the use of summary justice for tithes survives for Wiltshire, but entries in the notebook of JP William Hunt indicate that the procedures were used more extensively in the mid-eighteenth century than can be shown from official records.[76] One cleric who tried the new summary procedures was William Bath of Purton, who in around 1699 summoned four tithe defaulters to appear before justices. Bath had taken ten defendants to Exchequer or the consistory court between 1669 and 1697, but he did not use these courts again.[77] Another examination of Tables 3.5 and 3.6 reveals that he was not alone, for clerical use of the Exchequer court dropped rapidly in the first decade of the eighteenth century. In each decade from 1650 to 1700 clergymen always brought more suits for non-payment of tithes than laymen did. In the 1690s the clergy brought bills against three times as many defendants as the laity did. Yet in the following decade the proportions were completely reversed. More cases were now brought by laymen than clerics. One reason for this complete change was that clerical tithe-owners increasingly chose to farm their tithes out to laymen, thus easing themselves of the irritation of collection. Clerical debts, often exacerbated by the land tax, may have left them with little choice.[78] This trend is, however, insufficient on its own to explain the dramatic decline in clerical tithe cases. It was the 1696 act which relieved clerical owners of petty tithes of the necessity of resorting to the courts in order to reclaim their tithes.

It did not take long for Wiltshire ecclesiastics and tithe-payers to become aware of the act. In February 1698 the archdeacon of Wiltshire, Cornelius Yeate, explained in a letter to Sir Richard Holford of Avebury that the new act provided an easier means of recovering tithes than the Exchequer.[79] The archdeacon must also have informed others of the new procedure. In Holford's case the information was almost certainly unnecessary. As a Master of Chancery and frequent litigant, it seems likely that Holford already knew the terms of the legislation. Indeed reference to the Act in 1698 by a defendant of an Exchequer tithe suit suggests that it had already become general knowledge. Joseph Hayward was aggrieved that the vicar of Avebury had gone to Exchequer for such a small amount when he had 'a much easier Remedy by virtue of an Act of this present Parliament'. He claimed that the vicar had not pursued the easier and cheaper route of summary jurisdiction because he had 'a design to oppress and undoe'

---

[75] Morgan, *Lancashire Quakers*, ch. 6. In Staffordshire, there was a sharp decline in the number of Quakers being imprisoned for tithe sufferings in 1697. Evans, 'Our faithful testimony', p. 144.

[76] E. Crittall, ed., *The Justicing Notebook of William Hunt 1744–49*, Wiltshire Record Society 37 (Devizes, 1982), entry 111. Hunt noted that the two men did not appear as summoned. The failure of the complainant to pursue them indicates that the summons was all that was required to produce payment.

[77] A1/260 (dated from adjacent certificates). The only other summary conviction for tithes to survive resulted from the complaint of the rector of Wilton on 19 Sept. 1747.

[78] The litigious James Garth of Hilperton was apparently forced to sign over his glebe without rent in order to repay debts. D1/3/5/1.

[79] WRO 184/1, Dr Cornelius Yeate to Richard Holford, 28 Feb. 1697[/8].

him.[80] By 1703 clerical litigants had discovered the advantages of the Act, and henceforth the number of lay complainants always exceeded that of clerics. The 1696 act did not, however, provide a complete solution since it excluded the more lucrative great tithes which were usually owned by clerical and lay rectors. The owners and farmers of rectorial tithes continued to provide Exchequer with a considerable amount of business.

The consistory court of the bishop of Salisbury failed to recover after 1700, but instead saw its own tithe caseload continue to fall to one or two cases a year.[81] The explanation for the relative popularity of Exchequer lies partly in the procedural advantages of equity over the common law and church courts. Unlike the consistory courts, the equity courts were not subject to common law prohibitions. The case could be referred to the common law courts for a trial at law if an issue of property right arose, and the verdict would then be returned to the equity court for judgement.[82] The equity jurisdiction was initially intended for plaintiffs unable to gain remedy at the common law. Whereas common law litigants had to purchase the correct writ, those filing an equity bill could adjust it later as circumstances dictated.[83] Equity litigants found the plea of discovery particularly valuable, since this enabled them to create an official record from personal answers, depositions and other documents. Many suits were brought for the purposes of discovery rather than to win a decree, in order to obtain evidence which might be useful in subsequent legal proceedings.

A more important reason for the unpopularity of the consistory courts lay in the widespread perception that they were ineffective. Litigants take their business to courts in order to achieve their objectives, which may include a favourable judgement, the discovery of evidence, or the overpowering or financial ruin of defendants. When one court is perceived as ineffective, then litigants take their business elsewhere. Tobias Eden, Deputy King's Remembrancer for much of the late seventeenth century, seems to have sought to attract business to the court by making it more useful to litigants, enhancing the powers and income of his own office at the same time.[84] One commentator advised clergymen not to sue for tithes in the church courts because they would 'find the methods there used to be sufficiently tedious and troublesome, deletary and chargeable'.[85] The abandonment of the consistory court for Exchequer can be seen in the behaviour of individual Wiltshire tithe-owners who resorted to the courts repeatedly through the years. Many launched suits in the consistory courts early in their careers, but over

[80] PRO, E112/758/176. The personal answer was sworn on 2 Feb. 1697[/8].
[81] Cf. Norwich consistory court, which saw an increase in tithe cases in the 1720s. Jacob, *Lay People and Religion*, p. 38.
[82] For an example, see Eagle and Younge, *A Collection of the Reports*, vol. I, p. 763.
[83] H. Horwitz, *Chancery Equity Records and Proceedings 1600–1800* (London, 1995), pp. 2–4.
[84] Ball, 'Tobias Eden', pp. 70–89.
[85] 'The great grievance of the Clergy stated', Tanner MS 80, ff. 122–123v. Prohibitions were an additional inconvenience.

time switched their business to the Exchequer. Thomas Twittee of Draycot Foliat and Chiseldon was one of the most experienced clerical litigants in Wiltshire.[86] Since his tithe campaign required him to establish title, he started in the common-law courts. Title secured, he tried the consistory court but he found it unsatisfactory for reasons that become clear in the documentation for a 1673–4 case in which he sought the dismissal of his parish clerk. To Twittee's disgust the cause was dismissed for lack of evidence even though it had been initiated on the instructions of the bishop. Apparently, poor weather had prevented Twittee from getting his witnesses to Salisbury, a process that was much simpler in an Exchequer suit because a commission took evidence in a local inn. He wrote to the Chancellor to complain: 'I should have taken it as kindly, if he calld mee foole.' Twittee feared that if others he prosecuted got off equally lightly, then 'farewell authority of your court, & indeede ye Church'. He was not prepared to take this risk, and thereafter he avoided the consistory court, using Exchequer instead.[87] Sir George Hungerford was also disappointed by his experiences of the consistory court. In 1673 he succeeded in obtaining a favourable sentence in a correction suit against the rector of Bremhill, only to have the matter delayed for a decade by an appeal to the Court of Arches. This may explain why he finally turned to Exchequer for help in forcing the minister to provide a curate, casting the issue as one of failure to pay a debt.[88]

The decline in presentments and tithe business by the ecclesiastical courts was reflected in other issues as well. The number of suits clerics brought against laymen for vilifying or slandering them fell sharply, from a total of twenty-nine between 1660 and 1700 to only nine between 1700 and 1730. This demonstrates the increasing incapacity of the ecclesiastical courts to handle business, particularly when laymen were the defendants, and says little about tensions between the clergy and laity. Visitations suffered a similar loss of credibility. The problem was less that discipline was unfashionable than about whether it was suitable for ecclesiastical authorities to exercise it. JPs and (outside Wiltshire) societies for the reformation of manners took on the role themselves.[89] Analysis of churchwardens' presentments and tithe prosecutions has confirmed the pessimistic interpretation of ecclesiastical courts after the Restoration. The decline of the church courts stemmed in part from their association with the unpopular campaign against dissent and in part from their inefficiency. The courts were briefly able to re-establish their claims to their disciplinary and judicial functions in the

---

[86] Twittee's campaign, which lasted from 1665 to 1702, is described by J. H. Stevenson 'Will a man rob God?', *WAM* 72/3 (1980): 151–3. Twittee brought suits in the consistory court, at common law and Exchequer, and had to defend a Chancery bill.
[87] Twittee claimed that the parish clerk had assisted in the funeral of an excommunicate. D1/41/1/17.
[88] PRO, E112/609/48.
[89] Sharpe, *Crime in Early Modern England*, pp. 154–6; R. B. Shoemaker, *Prosecution and Punishment: Petty Crime and the Law in London and Rural Middlesex* (Cambridge, 1991), ch. 9.

1660s after the Interregnum. Thereafter they began to suffer the flight of litigants. The bishop's consistory court lost its tithe business to equity because it was perceived as being ineffective by potential litigants. No longer overawed by the authority of visitations and reluctant to present their neighbours, churchwardens came to perceive presentment as a matter of choice rather than obligation. The church courts' decline was well advanced by 1700, and the Church's loss of this aspect of its authority could not help but weaken the position of the parish clergy. Nonetheless, the courts were not entirely moribund, for they still provided services which complainants found useful well into the eighteenth century. Visitations continued to receive a trickle of reports of fabric in need of repair, as well as presentments against ministers. Correctional suits against clergymen provide a means of studying the extent to which the gentry and the common people participated and co-operated in religious action.

4

The management of disputes

Religion is one sphere of activity often thought to be inevitably under the control of the squire. The country gentry had an interest in defending the Established Church, just as the Church supported the social and political hierarchy, a marriage of church and state that J. C. D. Clark has termed the 'confessional state'.[1] Sir Roger de Coverley provides the archetypal example of the relationship between the gentry, the clergy and the people. The church that Sir Roger ornamented provided an arena for the confirmation of his authority. At the end of services, the congregation showed their respect for the squire by forming a double row through which he processed and bowing to him as he passed. The squire and parson co-operated in governing the parish. The latter mediated local disputes on behalf of Sir Roger and sought favours for members of the congregation. Yet, as Addison observed, the social relations in many parishes were not as amicable as they were in Coverley.

Disputes between the clergy and the laity had serious implications for eighteenth-century society. Their occurrence may appear to cast into doubt the robustness of the 'confessional state'. John Phillips has argued that the clergy were faced with an individualistic population who required very careful handling and whose deference was illusory.[2] We should not assume that a rigid alliance between the gentry and the clergy prevailed. As befitted their position of social leadership, the gentry often took the lead in disputes with the clergy. Particularly in the years following the Restoration, some were reluctant supporters of the religious establishment. Nor should we assume that the people merely deferred to the squire's wishes, worshipping as he did because it was in their interest to do so. It is in the nature of the sources that they provide much fuller evidence about the views of the gentry who governed the county and of the substantial farmers who governed the parish than they do about those of the common

---

[1] J. C. D. Clark, *English Society 1688-1832: Ideology, Social Structure and Political Practice during the Ancient Regime* (Cambridge, 1985).

[2] J. A. Phillips, 'The social calculus: deference and defiance in later Georgian England', *Albion* 21 (Fall 1989): 426–49. Cf. J. C. D. Clark, 'England's ancien regime as a confessional state', *Albion* 21 (Fall 1989): 450–74, who observes that hegemony does not require absolute control.

people. Yet episodes of lay–clerical conflict reveal the extent of co-operation between different groups of society. Religion was a sphere of activity in which every person had an interest.

DEFERENCE

Most historians would agree that relations between the gentry and the people in eighteenth-century England were marked by deference, a word used here in preference to analogous terms such as 'paternalism' and 'patriarchalism'. Paternalism considers social relationships from the standpoint of the governing classes only, and carries connotations of nineteenth-century attempts to improve the poor for their own good.[3] Patriarchalism, the word which Clark prefers, describes the ideology which legitimised the superiority of the gentry, while failing to explore the social relationships through which this superiority manifested itself.[4] The characteristics of deference and how it operated in practice have received surprisingly little study. A familiar image shows the squire in his country estate, presiding over the surrounding countryside through a set of mutually reinforcing relationships in which he is always the superior: as father, master, landlord, magistrate and clerical patron.[5] E. P. Thompson criticised this image. He argued that gestures of deference often concealed secret resentments that might be expressed through such acts of rebelliousness as hedge-breaking, poaching and anonymous letter-writing, what Keith Snell writing more recently has called 'deferential bitterness'. 'Deference', Snell says, 'often covered a deep-rooted sense of grievance, of social bitterness, which had to be censored because of the very precarious circumstances of livelihood.' What was so exciting about Thompson's critique was that it restored to the common people their own voice. Yet it still assumed (indeed it emphasised) the one-sided nature of social relations, which were marked by naked power and sullen retaliation, not by negotiation. Thompson and Snell are describing, not deference, but subservience. The social divide was too wide for deference to be appropriate for the relations they describe. Theirs is as much a top-down picture as that of the 'confessional state' in which the Established Church supported the gentry's claims to superiority.[6]

The concept of 'deference' describes a two-way relationship based upon reciprocity. In the classical theory of deference which J. G. A. Pocock derives from

---

[3] See, for example, D. Roberts, *Paternalism in Early Victorian England* (London, 1979), which discusses attitudes towards the poor but not those of the poor.

[4] Clark, *English Society*, pp. 64–93; G. J. Schochet, *Patriarchalism in Political Thought* (Oxford, 1975).   [5] H. Perkin, *The Origins of Modern English Society 1780–1880* (London, 1969).

[6] E. P. Thompson, 'Patrician society, plebeian culture', *Journal of Social History* 7 (1974): 382–405, reprinted in an extended form in his *Customs in Common* (London, 1991), ch. 2; K. D. M. Snell, 'Deferential bitterness: the social outlook of the rural proletariat in eighteenth- and nineteenth-century England and Wales', in M. L. Bush, ed., *Social Orders and Social Classes in Europe since 1500* (London, 1992), pp. 158–84.

Harrington, deference is a relationship between independent actors involving the voluntary acceptance by some individuals of the natural leadership of others.[7] Those who do not belong to the elite are nevertheless 'sufficiently free as political actors to render deference not only a voluntary but also a political act'. Although they do not have the capacity for leadership, they have an 'intelligently critical attitude' towards their leaders. In early modern England the natural leaders were the aristocracy and the gentry, and Pocock describes the yeomanry as the non-elite. The ownership of property was the basis of a partnership in which each group respected the contribution of the other. Deference was a reciprocal relationship; it was not the same as unquestioning and servile obedience. It involved a delicate balance of the interests and wishes of the governors and the governed. Howard Newby has described this balance as the 'deferential dialectic'. The deferential dialectic involves tension between two competing pressures, which Newby calls 'differentiation' and 'identification'.[8] The identification of interests is necessary to maintain deference as a relationship based on partnership. Too much identification, however, can weaken the hierarchical social differentiation upon which deference relies. Newby stresses that deference ideally should be studied through interactions rather than behaviour. He defines deference as 'a form of social interaction which occurs in situations involving the exercise of traditional authority'.[9]

Deference has been studied in a number of social contexts. Thompson and his followers propose the criminal law as the stage for the theatre and counter-theatre of social conflict.[10] It is here that the naked power of the governing classes is most cruelly exposed. In the 'dependency' model, the 'social control of the ordinary squire manifested . . . itself in the inevitability with which [tenants and villagers] followed his religion and politics'.[11] Electoral politics provide a familiar context for such students of electoral deference as D. C. Moore and Lewis Namier.[12] According to this interpretation, deference is viewed as one aspect of the web of interest and patronage which ensured that a landlord could deliver the votes of his tenants at the polls. The debate between Namierites and their

---

[7] J. G. A. Pocock, 'The classical theory of deference', *American Historical Review* 81 (1976): 516–23, esp. 522–3. Cf. D. Spring, 'Walter Bagehot and deference', *American Historical Review* 81 (1976): 524–31.

[8] H. Newby, 'The deferential dialectic', *Comparative Studies in Society and History* 17 (1975): 149–51.   [9] Ibid., p. 146.

[10] Thompson, *Customs in Common*, ch. 2. Although Thompson paints a bleak picture of deference, he also stresses its reciprocity. See also P. Griffiths, A. Fox and S. Hindle, eds., *The Experience of Authority in Early Modern England* (Houndmills, Hampshire, 1996).

[11] Perkin, *The Origins of Modern English Society*, p. 42.

[12] D. C. Moore, *The Politics of Deference* (Hassocks, Sussex, 1976). Students of twentieth-century politics also use the concept of deference to explain why electors voted against what might be perceived as their class interest. B. Jessop, *Traditionalism, Conservatism and British Political Culture* (London, 1974). L. Namier, *The Structure of Politics at the Accession of George III* (London, 1957).

critics is similar to the question we have posed about religion. Did electors have a free choice about whom they voted for or did they vote according to the preferences of their social superiors? Recent research has suggested that this question has been posed too simply.[13] Electors exercised a degree of choice, even when they opted to vote in accordance with the preferences of their landlord. Frank O'Gorman has proposed a mutual theory of deference. Although his new model, like Namier's, is based on electoral interest, it does place more emphasis upon reciprocity than recent Namierite interpretations do. O'Gorman sees reciprocity in the squire's exploitation of patronage in exchange for electoral support from his tenants.

Although religion is also thought to have been under the control of the squire, religious deference has received far less attention from historians. J. C. D. Clark presents the strongest case for the social and intellectual alliance between church and state in eighteenth-century England. He describes England as a 'confessional state' in which the Established Church supplied the ideological underpinnings for the political establishment. He makes no attempt to explore the alliance between the gentry and the clergy which his interpretation suggests must have been present, a significant omission. Religion provides a good context in which to explore deference for other reasons, also. The parish church touched all sections of society, not only through attendance at services but also through the administration of local government. The gentry, the clergy and the parish elite all had a claim to involvement in the administration of the parish and its church. Religion therefore provided an important focus for negotiation between different groups in society. It also provided a forum for conflict.

FOXHAM

Foxham, a hamlet in Bremhill parish, was the scene of a religious dispute fought out between the vicar, the landlord and other inhabitants for almost thirty years after the Restoration.[14] The litigation which was the visible manifestation of the dispute provides insights into the management of such cases and the nature of co-operation between gentleman governors and those they governed. The social interactions of deference were played out in the management of the suit and are

---

[13] S. W. Baskerville, P. Adman and K. Beedham, 'The dynamics of landlord influence in English county elections, 1701-1734: the evidence from Cheshire', *Parliamentary History* 12 (1993): 126–42; F. O'Gorman, 'Electoral deference in "unreformed" England: 1760-1832', *Journal of Modern History* 56 (Sept. 1984): 391-429; N. Landau, 'Independence, deference, and voter participation: the behaviour of the electorate in early-eighteenth-century Kent', *Historical Journal* 22 (1979): 561–83; Landau, *The Justices of the Peace, 1679–1760* (Berkeley, 1984).

[14] The material in this section is based on the following sources, unless otherwise indicated. D1/42/61, ff. 228v–222v; D1/39/4/38; D1/39/1/58, ff. 179v, 224v, 239; D1/39/1/61, f. 61; Lambeth Palace Library, Court of Arches, Personal Answers, Section Ee, ff. 537–8; PRO, C5/167/113; E112/609/48; E112/536/246.

documented in bills and depositions. Sir George Hungerford, an MP and member of one of Wiltshire's leading families, owned land scattered across the northern half of the county. His seat was at Cadenham House in Foxham, a chapelry of Bremhill. Sir George's pre-eminence was recognised during the reign of William III by his election as one of Wiltshire's knights of the shire.[15] The vicar of the parish was the Revd John Tounson, DD. The son of a bishop and the holder of a prebendal stall, Tounson was a self-confident member of the clerical elite. He had first been instituted to Bremhill in 1639 but the benefice was sequestered during the Civil Wars.[16] No doubt this experience made him more determined than ever to assert his rights and to protect his income and that of his successors, for he was one of the most litigious ministers in post-Restoration Wiltshire. Tounson brought numerous prosecutions for non-payment of tithes in the ecclesiastical court and at Exchequer, including a suit against Sir George Hungerford himself.

At issue was the pastoral care of the hamlet and the cure of the souls of its inhabitants. Foxham was one of two chapelries within the parish of Bremhill, and every Sunday these three churches presented its incumbent with a practical problem. Clearly he could not officiate in all three at the same time. The inhabitants of Foxham had a simple solution: the vicar should appoint them a curate. After all, Bremhill's other chapelry had one of its own, even though it had fewer inhabitants. Furthermore, previous vicars had given them their own minister. An elderly inhabitant was able to name no fewer than eleven curates who had served the chapelry since before the Civil Wars. This solution did not appeal to the vicar. Although he combined one of Wiltshire's richest benefices with a valuable prebend, the vicar saw no reason to pay out the £20 a year it would have cost him to appoint a curate. He claimed that the inhabitants of Foxham were responsible for hiring a minister themselves. The income from a bequest of land and other moneys were already available to meet the cost.

The dispute began in 1666 when Sir George and several inhabitants asked Tounson to supply a curate. The vicar refused, and he challenged his opponents to prove that he was responsible for doing so. In the unlikely event that he was proved wrong, however, he agreed to pay any sums incurred to hire a minister (or at least so Hungerford later alleged). In 1672 Hungerford was one of four men who jointly promoted a suit for correction of manners against Tounson in the bishop's consistory court. In the following year the court passed sentence against the vicar, who was ordered to supply a curate and to pay costs. Unfortunately, this did not end the matter. Tounson appealed to the Court of Arches where the suit was still languishing a decade later when Hungerford revived it with another consistory court suit. In 1687 he tried another tack, by filing an Exchequer bill

[15] B. D. Henning, ed., *House of Commons 1660–1690* (London, 1983) 'Sir George Hungerford', q.v.
[16] D1/2/21, f. 47; Matthews, *Walker Revised*, p. 381; *DNB*, q.v. 'Robert Townson'.

against the vicar. The Exchequer Court of Equity was in the process of stealing a large proportion of the consistory courts' tithe business. Hungerford imaginatively sued Tounson for debt, because he had failed to repay the moneys expended to hire curates. In doing so he revealed that he had himself been hiring ministers for Foxham church for many years and perhaps since the 1660s. Unfortunately, Tounson died before the matter could be resolved.

CONFLICT

John Tounson was one of over forty Wiltshire ministers who were the subject of consistory court suits intended to reform their behaviour during the late seventeenth and early eighteenth centuries. Suits against the clergy might be promoted in one of two ways. Roughly one in four followed the church courts' office jurisdiction. These cases, which usually concerned specific canonical offences such as non-residence and solemnising clandestine marriages, were heard by the judge using summary procedures and have left little in the way of documentary evidence. Most suits against the clergy were heard through the courts' promoted office jurisdiction. Because such cases followed the plenary instance procedure, they have often left extensive written evidence in the form of libels, answers and depositions. The role of promoter was a natural extension of the office of churchwarden, particularly when a presentment at visitations brought the offending minister to the attention of ecclesiastical authorities. Although churchwardens could draw upon parish funds to bear the often considerable costs of court action, a suit could easily outlast their one-year term of office.

The gentry, and particularly the greater gentry, were natural promoters of court action against the clergy. Gentlemen were plaintiffs in almost half of the promoted office suits brought to correct clergymen, and they were involved in other suits as well. The relative deepness of their purses, their familiarity with the law and law courts, and the extra-local contacts which enabled them to serve as brokers with the larger world all pointed to gentry promotion. Recent research has somewhat dented the image of gentry predominance in the courts and has established that their contribution to litigation was probably declining during our period.[17] Nonetheless, the gentry were by far the largest distinct social group of litigants in the great courts of Westminster, making regular use of the courts to defend and assert claims to property. Their significance as complainants far exceeded their actual numbers in the population.[18] Sir Richard Holford of

---

[17] C. W. Brooks, *Pettyfoggers and Vipers of the Commonwealth: The 'Lower Branch' of the Legal Profession in Early Modern England* (Cambridge, 1986); Brooks, 'Interpersonal conflict and social tension: civil litigation in England, 1640–1830', in A. L. Beier, D. Cannadine and J. M. Rosenheim, eds., *The First Modern Society* (Cambridge, 1989), pp. 384–7.

[18] Gentlemen and above may have accounted for between 25 and 11 per cent of complainants at Common Pleas, considerably more than their representation in the population. Brooks, 'Interpersonal conflict', p. 384, Table 10.5.

Avebury and Middlesex expressed a common, if overly optimistic, faith in the law when he wrote, 'the Law is an Englishman's birth right, & must putt an end to all controversies'.[19] A Master of Chancery, he found his own court to be a weapon which fitted very comfortably into his hand. Holford was a legal bully who used his court to harass those who crossed him. Between 1689 and 1713 he exhibited at least fifteen bills of complaint in Chancery. Holford was probably atypical, but other gentlemen also made frequent use of the courts, even if they were not always able to match his success. In addition to his consistory court and Exchequer suits, Sir George Hungerford of Foxham exhibited at least seven Chancery bills. Sadly, he became the victim of a bitter dispute over an inheritance which cost him an estimated £2,700, an extreme example of court expenses.[20]

Gentlemen also had the advantage of their education. A period at the Inns of Court, either after or in place of university, remained part of the training of a typical gentleman during the Restoration, although it was to become less so in the eighteenth century. Despite a small decline in their representation in the second half of the seventeenth century, from 1700 to 1709 gentlemen, esquires and peers still accounted for 77 per cent of entrants to the Inns of Court.[21] Both Hungerford and Holford were members of Lincoln's Inn. Indeed, Holford was a bencher and member-officer.[22] A sixteenth-century author advised that gentlemen ought to have some knowledge of the law 'for the better furtherance of their neighbours just causes, to give unto them good counsel freely, to make an end of debates and stryfes'.[23] The historian of the Inns of Court has questioned how much practical legal knowledge amateur students acquired in view of the complexity of the common law and the lack of any tutorial system to guide students.[24] The gentleman student was even less likely to have learned about the canon or civil law used in ecclesiastical courts unless he studied civil law at university. Yet we should recognise the advantages, not least in self-confidence, bestowed by contact with legal circles, however brief. Just as important as any book-learning were the social contacts a gentlemen established at university or the Inns from whom he might later be able to seek advice.[25]

The Inns of Court also provided professional training for sons of the gentry, who were thereby placed in a position to assist relations, friends and neighbours,

[19] WRO 184/1, Richard Holford to James White, 10 Nov. 1708. See chapter 6.
[20] *Index of Chancery Proceedings, Bridges' Division, 1613–1714* (Lists and Indexes, vol. 39, etc.); *House of Commons 1660–1690*, q.v. 'Sir George Hungerford'. PRO, C5/355/32 provides an example of Holford's harassment. See also chapter 6 for his relations with the clergy.
[21] W. R. Prest, *The Inns of Court under Elizabeth I and the Early Stuarts 1590–1640* (Harlow, 1972), pp. 44–5.
[22] *The Records of the Honourable Society of Lincoln's Inn: The Black Books*, vol. III, *From AD 1660 to AD 1775* (Lincoln's Inn, 1899, reprinted 1991), pp. 168, 187, 192, 200.
[23] Prest, *The Inns of Court*, p. 23, quoting B. L., The Institution of a Gentleman (1555), sig. Diii^{vv}.
[24] Ibid., p. 151.
[25] Clerics also might seek legal help. Nathanial Aske considered writing to Doctors' Commons for advice. D1/41/1/17.

including those from lower social backgrounds, with lawsuits and to offer the
benefits of their contacts in London society. Richard Knapp Jr, a gentleman,
played a crucial role in the preparation and presentation of the correction suit
against Thomas Lawrence, the rector of Chilton (Berks.).[26] The nephew of one
of the suit's yeoman promoters,[27] the 24-year-old Knapp was at Oxford for two
years and had already spent six years as a student at the Inner Temple at the time
of the suit. He resided at the Inner Temple during terms but spent vacations at
home living in the house of his father. Knapp's studies bore fruit, for two years
later he was called to the bar.[28] The young Knapp was therefore the obvious
person for the parish to turn to for help in bringing a suit against their minister.
The inhabitants had been unhappy about their minister for a while and his misbehaviour had become a talking-point in the parish. Now a 'great part of the
parishioners' asked Knapp to present their grievances to the bishop of Salisbury,
Seth Ward, and to request his help in obtaining a curate. Knapp's familiarity with
the law proved invaluable, and so did his regular visits to London, near Ward's
residence in Knightsbridge. His training was in the common law, and he confessed that he knew little about the very different procedures of the civil law used
in the ecclesiastical courts (although he could not resist criticising the Latin used
in the minister's *interrogata*). Fortunately, the bishop was able to advise. Ward
instructed the young gentleman to have parishioners bring him articles against
the minister, saying that he would then arrange for formal proceedings against
the minister in his court. Accompanied by his cousin, Knapp travelled to Oxford
to retain a proctor to draw up the articles. He then returned to Knightsbridge
with two parishioners, who presented the articles to the bishop. Ward had the
articles sent to the Registrar, Sir Edward Lowe, and Knapp travelled to Reading
in order to pay for the process against the minister to be issued. He and his cousin
also met two proctors of the court in Abingdon to make arrangements for
himself and the other witnesses to give their testimony.

 This narrative underlines the obstacles that lay in the way of the promotion of
a suit against the minister. The preparation of the articles, issuing of process,
payment of fees, employment of proctors and planning of witnesses all involved
considerable advance preparation, expense and travelling. Richard Knapp was
neither promoter nor did he pay travel or other costs in the case; these were borne
by the parish. Yet his education, expertise and contacts proved invaluable in the
effective preparation of the suit. Income, familiarity with the courts and with the
law, and their network of contacts meant that the gentry were natural promoters

---

[26] D1/42/61, ff. 148–137v.
[27] The absence of any rank for the promoters suggests that they were not gentlemen. At least one
   promoter was most likely a yeoman, because this was the status ascribed to his son, a witness, who
   managed his estate.
[28] Knapp appears to have pursued a legal career and achieved bencher status in 1708, despite some
   confusion concerning the name of his father, which is variously recorded as 'Richard' (at matriculation) and 'George' (at acquisition of bencher status). *Alumni Oxonienses*, q.v. 'Richard Knapp'.

of court suits against offending ministers, as well as being obvious sources of advice and assistance. Perhaps the most important reason for their primacy, however, was their position of leadership within both parish and county. Leadership involved the fulfilment of duty to the community as well as the exercise of power. In their various patriarchal roles as father, master, landlord, justice of the peace, and on occasion member of Parliament, the gentry had a responsibility to protect those over whom they exercised authority. These responsibilities extended to care for religious worship. It is customary to deprecate the motives behind such care in terms of self-interest, particularly in accounts of eighteenth-century religion. By lowering rents, providing charity, and treating, the gentleman gained electoral interest, or so the standard account goes. We hear of gentlemen whose method of supporting the Church was to chastise or remove tenants who were absent from services. A strong Church was a bulwark against social and political collapse. Sir Henry Herbert was not alone in thinking that 'the best foundation of the state is Religion . . . it makes men more peaceable and better subjects'.[29]

Yet there is a more positive side to this picture. The gentry were responsible for the men and women under their authority. They had their own idea of how the locality should be governed and they expected others to follow their lead. Thus Sir Richard Holford instructed the jury of his manorial court how to make their presentments and expressed disappointment when they failed to live up to his expectations.[30] In addition to the general social responsibilities of the gentry, particular roles might enhance their sense of duty: as lords of the manor, of course, and so responsible for their tenants, servants and labourers; sometimes as impropriators of the great tithes and so perhaps responsible for part of the minister's income; certainly as tithe-payers themselves. The landlord might also own the advowson and so be patron of the living, although this last aspect should not be overstated. Patronage is often viewed largely in political terms. The pastoral role of patronage has less often been considered, except to assume that the local landlord would own the advowson and would make sure he placed the living in hands he trusted. This is what Sir Roger de Coverley and Lady Catherine de Burgh do, but they are of course merely fictional characters. In Salisbury diocese private gentlemen owned fewer than half of the advowsons. The balance was in the hands of the Church, the peerage, the Crown, and educational institutions. The earl of Pembroke and Montgomery, with his fourteen Wiltshire livings, had extensive patronage, but he is too powerful and remote a figure to fit the image of a local governor, the parish his small kingdom. Advowsons were property, and property was not necessarily packed into tidy bundles in which the manor, major landholdings and advowson were all owned by the same person.

---

[29] Quoted in F. Heal and C. Holmes, *The Gentry in England and Wales, 1500-1700* (Houndmills, Hants., 1994), p 232.   [30] WRO 184/8.

The Hungerford family owned several advowsons, but they were not patrons of Bremhill; the bishop of Salisbury was.[31]

The gentry took responsibility for the worship of their social inferiors. In Avebury Sir Richard Holford instructed the minister to pay children who learned their catechism. Elsewhere the gentry contributed to charity schools, as in Box where Lady Rachel Speke left a bequest of £100 for use in teaching poor children to read and instructing them in the knowledge of Christian religion.[32] Thomas Gore of Alderton fought to protect the parish's separate status, entitled to its own minister, against attempts to merge it with Sherston Magna.[33] It is in this context that Sir George Hungerford's involvement in obtaining a curate for Foxham should be seen. In addition to launching several suits against the minister, Sir George also made regular payments to curates over a number of years. For at least fifteen years he appointed ministers himself and paid them 10s. a week for officiating.[34] In theory, these payments were made on behalf of the vicar, and this was the rationale for Hungerford's 1687 Exchequer bill. Yet the court evidence suggests that Hungerford hired ministers before his first suit and that this was part of family tradition that went back to the Civil Wars, if not earlier. Witnesses admitted in 1672 that Sir George and Lady Hungerford had 'intreated such ministers as have of late come accidentally to their house to give the Inhabitants a sermon'.[35] The minister claimed that the family had traditionally paid gratuities to curates to preach there. The wording appears significant. The Hungerfords paid ministers to preach a sermon. It is possible that witnesses sought merely to protect their squire from prosecution for violating the Act of Uniformity. Yet there may also have been a puritan connection. Sir George was too young to have been politically active during the Commonwealth, but his family was involved on the Parliamentary side. A strong anti-Catholic, he favoured exclusion in 1679–81 and was one of those whom Shaftesbury described as 'twice worthy'.[36] Hungerford's support for preaching may signal his own religious views. In the past, his family had paid ministers for their preaching. The Bayntun family had even left a bequest and other property to support a minister. Sir Edward Bayntun had served as a Parliamentary committee-man during the Interregnum, and his attitude to the Anglican Church and its clergy was ambivalent at best.[37] The emphasis upon preaching suggests that these gifts

[31] D1/27/1/1; Browne Willis, A Survey of the Cathedrals . . ., vol. III (London, 1742). See also P. Langford, Public Life and the Propertied Englishman, 1689–1798 (Oxford, 1991), p. 18.
[32] WRO 184/1; John Mayo to RH, 16 June 1715; 'Four Letters written by the Rev. George Millard, A.D. 1712–18', WAM 31 (June 1900): 34, 35, 41. Other gentry patrons of religious education included John Kyrle Ernle and Lady Bruce. W. O. B. Allen and E. McClure, Two Hundred Years: The History of the Society for Promoting Christian Knowledge, 1698–1898 (London, 1898), p. 4; SPCK, AL 14, 9599.   [33] WRO 84/43, 84/44.
[34] Other records confirm that Foxham had curates in at least the years 1679–80, but they do not say whether they were appointed by Hungerford or Tounson. D1/48/1; D1/22/3.
[35] D1/42/61, f. 224v.   [36] House of Commons 1660–1690, q.v. 'Sir George Hungerford'.
[37] Ibid.; J. Freeman, ed., The Commonplace Book of Sir Edward Bayntun of Bromham, Wiltshire Record Society 43 (Devizes, 1988), pp. xii, xix, 54–7.

by two leading gentry families should be seen in the context of the puritan programme to finance preaching. The Hungerford family received regular visits from ministers. Their puritanism gave an added edge to their religious leadership within the hamlet, although there was no question of leaving the Church. There is an irony in the Anglican minister's determination that puritan funds should be used to free him from his pastoral responsibilities.

I have been arguing for the genuine commitment of the gentry to serve as leaders, both socially and religiously, in the late seventeenth century. There is, nevertheless, a paradox in this argument, for the same gentry who were prepared to commit money to support worship and who made gifts to the clergy also fiercely defended tithe suits. Yet there is no necessary contradiction between these forms of behaviour. The explanation for this apparent paradox lies in the difference between investment and expenditure. The gentry were prepared to donate moneys as long as such payments did not jeopardise the future income or capital value of their lands. Sir George paid a curate, but he was careful to deny that he was obliged to do so. The payments were made on behalf of the vicar, who was expected to refund them. Hungerford subsidised the court case against the minister, in the knowledge that if he were victorious he could expect his reasonable costs. Indeed, the judge taxed Tounson for his costs, although Hungerford probably found it no easier to collect this money than the other sums he was owed. A landlord might be prepared to make an occasional gift of money to an impoverished minister, as the duke of Somerset did in Great Bedwyn, but he was careful to make this an *ex gratia* payment which did not represent a concession that he owed the vicar any tithes for his land.[38] There was no contradiction between the gentry's willingness to fund improvements in worship and their determination not to pay any more tithes than they rightly owed.

THE MANAGEMENT OF COURT ACTIONS

The main objective of a clerical defendant who was faced with a reformation suit was to attempt to discredit the case against him. He might simply deny that he owed any service at all, as John Tounson tried unsuccessfully to do. Or he might allege that the suit was malicious. One common defence was to allege that the complainants were part of a confederacy or conspiracy against clergymen. A 'confederacy' is a value-loaded description for an alliance of parishioners united by their resistance to an offending minister. As the defendant of one tithe suit observed, a confederacy was a sound tactic.[39] How did the gentry and other promoters put cases together? Let us return to Foxham to find out.

The recruitment of witnesses was itself an important part of the tactics of a suit. Sir George Hungerford promoted the suit against John Tounson jointly with three other inhabitants. He took the lead personally, as was to be expected

---

[38] PRO, E134/30 Charles II East 7.   [39] PRO, E112/758/176.

given his exalted social status. Hungerford also asked the three witnesses to testify. It was generally recognised that he was prosecuting the case and would bear the costs himself. He had the full support of the promoters and of 'all ye conformable part of the Inhabitants' on whose behalf he was prosecuting the suit. The vicar John Tounson had difficulty in finding any allies in the parish. In 1685 he was forced to choose as churchwarden a man who was unacceptable to the rest of the parish because, they alleged, he was only a poor day-labourer and therefore not fit to collect rates and handle parish accounts.[40] Nonetheless, Hungerford's leadership role did not go entirely unchallenged. This can be seen in testimony on two issues raised by Tounson's set of *interrogata*, i.e. the questions which the vicar stipulated should be asked of all witnesses as part of his attempt to discredit the case against him.[41] Who, Tounson asked, was paying the costs of the suit? This was a standard method of discrediting witnesses. If they were poor and dependent and could be proved to have been rewarded, then obviously their testimony had been bought and was worthless. Two of the witnesses were in no doubt about their answer to this question. As one bluntly said, they 'came to testifie at the request of Sir George Hungerford & at his charge'. The third witness, William Rylye, told a somewhat different story, revealing that the 'parties promovent & all the . . . Inhabitants . . . would be willing to beare their share in the Expenses of this suit'. Rylye's testimony must be treated with care, since it came in response to questions whose main purpose was to suggest that the promoters were bribing the witnesses. Yet it shows that the inhabitants were more than passive participants in a case launched by their landlord. William Rylye had personal reasons for asserting the contribution of his fellow inhabitants since his father was one of the promoters. Although none of the witnesses appears to have been a gentleman,[42] the elder Rylye had his own estate and was on good terms with Cadenham House. William Rylye recognised the delicacy of the matter, for he declared that 'he should willingly beare his own charges *if Sir George will permitt it*'. Ultimately, he accepted that Sir George 'for the good of the said Inhabitants wilbe at the sole charge himself'.

Tounson's second tactic was to argue that Foxham had traditionally paid its own curate. So he asked witnesses to say who had made payments in the past. The witnesses not only revealed the details of the Hungerford family's payments but they also asserted their own role. William Rylye wisely denied that the inhabitants of Foxham had ever levied a rate or collected contributions to maintain a minister. But the other two witnesses revealed past occasions when payments had been made. Thomas Harris testified that Cadenham House had given a gratuity to the curate of Foxham before Tounson came to Bremhill. At around the same time, Henry Scott remembered, his father had sent a chine of bacon to the curate.

---

[40] D3/12, 1686.   [41] D1/42/61, ff. 225–222v.

[42] In the depositions, one witness is identified as a maltster and, unusually, the ranks of the others are not recorded. The three were defendants in an Exchequer suit in 1674, when none was identified as a gentleman, as would have been usual if they could claim this status.

More recently, during the Commonwealth before the new incumbent 'would be brought to provide a curate', Thomas Harris's father and some neighbours had 'of their own love & voluntary charitie give[n] something' to a minister who preached among them. Given that the purpose of the question was to discredit them, the witnesses appear to have been surprisingly frank, although they were careful not to confess to any payments during Tounson's incumbency. All three witnesses asserted the active participation of non-gentle inhabitants in action against the minister and more generally in the support of religious worship in the chapelry. Their views can be seen as part of a process of negotiation.

Hungerford's care for worship in Foxham was an expression of the patronage that was a crucial part of the reciprocal relations of deference that he had with inhabitants. His negotiations with the minister over the provision of a curate and his own appointment and payment of curates were performed for the good of the community and confirmed the legitimacy of his authority. Hungerford was reasserting a traditional claim to authority, for his ancestors had also made gifts to previous clerics. His family's puritan background gave additional religious purpose to their social responsibility for the worship of their fellow inhabitants of the hamlet. It might be suggested that he was acting out of self-interest rather than in the interest of his subordinates, ensuring that he and his family could attend services in Foxham. Self-interest and patronage are not, of course, mutually exclusive. But it seems unlikely that Hungerford was simply trying to ease his Sundays. Although we do not know where he worshipped, the family vault was in Bremhill church, demonstrating his family's long-standing commitment to the parish church. Hungerford's promotion of suits against the minister was itself a form of patronage. His assertion of authority did not go entirely unchallenged, revealing the delicate balance of a deferential system.

It is significant that Sir George Hungerford was not the only promoter of the suit. He was joined by three other men from Foxham. It is not clear how the other promoters were chosen, but they were most likely members of the parish elite.[43] They had their own estates although they were not described as gentlemen. Hungerford could have proceeded on his own. The addition of the other promoters may even have damaged the case against the minister since it prevented them from acting as witnesses. Yet their inclusion expressed social relations as a partnership between men who, although not social equals, shared the same cultural interests and had an equal part to play. Their involvement helped Hungerford to secure the support of his social subordinates, a key aspect of a system of deference.[44] The selection of witnesses, apparently also from the chief inhabitants, was part of the same process of partnership.

---

[43] The 1662 hearth tax returns include a Robert Hawkins with three hearths and a Robert Ryley with one, with no mention of the fourth promoter, John Jenkins, although twelve years was plenty of time for property to change hands. PRO, E179/259/29, f. 48.

[44] Newby, 'The deferential dialectic', p. 149; K. Wrightson, 'The politics of the parish in early modern England', in Griffiths, Fox and Hindle, *The Experience of Authority*, p. 32.

There was no doubt in any of the witnesses' minds that Sir George Hungerford was promoting the case and that he would expect to bear its costs. Yet, as we have seen, there is evidence that others would have preferred to share the costs. The witnesses understood very well the delicacy of the matter. Hungerford was willing to share involvement in the suit, but it was important for his overall leadership to be unambiguous. This could be done by taking sole responsibility for the costs of the suit. To have done anything else would have been to risk weakening the legitimacy of his authority. This dilemma arose from tensions which can be understood in the terms of Newby's 'deferential dialectic'.[45] Hungerford promoted the *identification* of interests between himself and other inhabitants by joining with three others in promoting the suit, but the witnesses understood that he would wish to maintain *differentiation* by paying the costs. He needed an opportunity to express patronage in order to preserve the reciprocal nature of deference. His witnesses were therefore quite right to defer to his wish to bear the costs. This element of tension does not disprove the fact that this was a deferential relationship. The tension was resolved by one witness's acceptance that, despite his own wishes, he would defer to the knight's wish to pay the costs. This demonstrates the flexibility within deferential relationships and the degree of negotiation which took place within them.

There was also tension over another issue, namely the provision of support for curates. As we have seen, by providing for a curate, albeit on an *ex gratia* basis, Hungerford was following a family tradition of benevolent concern for the religious worship of Foxham. The exchange of gifts is an important aspect of gentry society,[46] reinforcing the community of the gentry and hierarchy at the same time. Members of the gentry exchanged gifts with one another, although the character of the gifts might itself express finer distinctions of rank within the elite class. The gentry also gave gifts to those not in the elite, but this was an expression of condescension and strengthened differentiation. To receive gifts without giving them was to reveal one's subordinate position. This was most obviously true of charity to the poor, but might also apply in other contexts, such as gifts to the clergy.

One witness asserted a family tradition of supporting curates, recalling, as we have seen, how his father had given bacon to a curate. The focus of his story is somewhat blurred. It appears that the curate was also the witness's schoolmaster, and it is possible that the 'gift' was payment for his teaching. Nonetheless, it is significant that the witness chose to mention this incident in the context of past payments to ministers, including those by the Hungerford family. Indeed, he also remembered that the inhabitants of Foxham together, and not just the Hungerford family, had contributed to the support of the curate, doing so out of

[45] Newby, 'The deferential dialectic', pp. 149–51.
[46] For example, see A. Fletcher, *A County Community in Peace and War: Sussex 1600–60* (London and New York, 1975), pp. 52–3. See also Newby, 'The deferential dialectic', pp. 161–3.

'love and charitie'. The witness was asserting his family's own participation in an elite which supported the clergy by giving them gifts. This was not intended as an explicit challenge to Hungerford's authority, although it did represent a claim to participate in acts of patronage.

Why was negotiation necessary? The answer lies in the context of the episode, namely the regulation of parish religion. Religion was a boundary area, in which two distinct social groups had competing claims to govern. The claims of the county elite, the gentry, as we have seen, derived from their ideological status as natural governors and indeed from being governors in fact – as MPs, justices of the peace, impropriators and patrons of advowsons. A visit to any parish church provides ample evidence of the gentry's sense of ownership over the physical space in which they worshipped, in the form of funereal monuments. If the numerous pews and galleries which they built were still standing, this point would be even clearer.[47] These monuments underlined the close connections between a gentry family and the local community, connections which were central to the family's position of religious leadership. The consistory court recognised this when, in 1719, it dismissed a case brought against the rector, John Shuttleworth of Fifield, on the grounds that the promoter, George Penruddock, Esq., was not resident in the parish and had no interest there.[48]

A second elite also had a claim to regulate local religion. This was the parish elite, which contemporaries described as the substantial inhabitants, the wealthier individuals who held parish office. This was not necessarily a tightly knit group, since individuals tended not to hold office for more than two or three years. As churchwardens, they were responsible for making presentments at visitations, for keeping the church in good repair, and for managing parish funds. Court cases were promoted by churchwardens as well as by gentlemen. In short, deference did not apply equally to all spheres of activity. The parish elite could reasonably expected to govern their parishes with minimal interference. This is not to say that they questioned the ultimate authority of the squire. They accepted his authority, while asserting their own.

GREAT BEDWYN

The example of the parish of Great Bedwyn casts that of Bremhill into relief. Great Bedwyn was part of the large holdings of the duke of Somerset, who also owned the advowson of the parish. In 1677 Mr Parker bought one of his farms. We know little about the new landlord except that he was entitled to place 'esquire' after his name. Not long after his arrival, Parker asked the sitting tenant, Edward Hall, about the minister's fitness. Hall had good reason to be unhappy

---

[47] As in St Mary's church in Lydiard Tregoze, where the St John family pew dominates the others. For the erection of pews, see the bishop's register of faculties, D1/61/1a–1c.

[48] D1/39/1/69, 23 June, 22 Sept. 1719.

about the vicar, Robert Randall. Randall's scandalous life style and drunkenness were a matter of general concern within the parish.[49] Edward Hall had personal experience of the vicar's misbehaviour. On one occasion when the vicar was in his cups he made sexual overtures to Hall's wife. Hall and his sub-tenants were also in dispute with Randall over tithes.[50] Upon learning of the vicar's 'ill liveing', Parker resolved to make a complaint against him. Although he would promote the suit, he asked his tenant to handle the entire business, arranging for witnesses to testify and paying any necessary expenses on his behalf.

The list of witnesses included an unusually large number who were of lower status; the biographies for the twelve witnesses record no fewer than six husbandmen, a blacksmith, a maidservant, a spinster, a widow, plus a yeoman (Hall) and his wife. Hall did not have complete control over the selection of witnesses. One of the dean's officials had asked four witnesses, including three of the husbandmen, to testify to an additional charge of clandestine marriage.[51] Dean Pierce had personal reasons for supporting the case since the couples who married illegally came from North Tidworth where his son was rector.[52] Another witness had until recently been Hall's servant, and he, the maidservant, Hall's wife and Hall himself were the only witnesses to a drunken exhibition by the vicar which occurred in Hall's own house. The other two 'husbandmen' (*agricolae*), both from Wilton, might be better described as labourers. One said of himself that he was 'a poore labouring man and getteth his liveing by his labour, and is worth little or nothing', and the other also testified that he was worth little but his daily labour. John Leadall, who had until recently been Hall's servant, testified with some pride to the four shillings he had paid in poll tax earlier in the year, evidence that he had earned £3 in wages;[53] although still a labourer, he estimated that he was worth £10. Hall personally asked most of the witnesses to testify, and he offered to pay their necessary expenses, as he had been instructed to do by the promoter. The witnesses did not attempt to hide either the fact that Hall had asked them to testify or that he had agreed to pay their expenses, and they even affirmed their hope that Squire Parker would win the case. However, they denied that their testimony was being purchased by payment of a reward. Nevertheless, Hall was not above threatening the stick as well as offering the carrot. In addition to promising to refund the charges of Edward Laurence, one of the labourers, he also 'told him that if hee would not come by faire means hee could compell him to come'. He also threatened to have the other labourer, Francis Street, cited if he did not go to testify voluntarily.

[49] Unless otherwise indicated, this section is based on D5/22/18, ff. 17–22v, 25–8; and D5/22/17, ff. 12–30. See also chs. 2, 5, 9.
[50] PRO, E112/535/156; E134/30 Charles II East 7.
[51] See chapter 9 for a discussion of clandestine marriage.
[52] J. W. Packer, *The Transformation of Anglicanism, 1643-1660* (Manchester, 1989), p. 54.
[53] 29&30 Charles II c. 1. In addition to the standard rate of 1*s*. a servant was to pay 12*d*. for every 20*s*. per year payable in wages.

The witnesses in Great Bedwyn appear to have been subjected to more pressure than most, and their evidence was not given entirely voluntarily. Yet Hall's threats should not be given too much weight. The citation of witnesses to appear in court was not uncommon, just as in the criminal courts complainants and witnesses might be bound by recognisance to appear at the next Sessions. Witnesses may have been reluctant to testify, in part because they were daunted by the prospect of repeating their testimony in the presence of ecclesiastical officials and other clerics. A trip to Marlborough would also cost them at least a day's wages. Hall had to agree to pay the wages of his former servant and to hire a substitute in his place. It is striking how the landlord put together his suit in a highly traditional fashion, through a chain of authority which reached down through his tenant farmer to the lowliest members of society. The case against Robert Randall included representation from four distinct layers of village society. At the top was the promoter himself, Squire Parker, and below him was his yeoman tenant farmer, Edward Hall. Twelve of Hall's sub-tenants did not testify in this suit but were also involved in disputes with the minister; they were prosecuted for substraction of tithes in 1677. At the very bottom were the labourers, apparently landless and dependent.

The recruitment of witnesses in Great Bedwyn differed from that in Foxham in three ways. First, although the case was promoted by the squire, it was managed by his tenant farmer. This represented another partnership between a gentleman and yeoman, but the similarities with Foxham were only superficial. Edward Hall acted as the agent of his landlord, and he was in a subordinate position. His involvement introduced an intermediate layer between the promoter and witnesses. A second difference was that the witnesses were largely drawn from the lower ranks of village society. Although described as husbandmen, they were in fact wage labourers, and several were dependants of Hall. There was no doubt that they expected their costs to be paid. Thirdly, in Great Bedwyn some witnesses were pressured, whereas in the Foxham case they appear to have been eager participants. The combination of these three features of the management of the suit against Robert Randall was not coincidental.

As a tenant farmer Hall was unable to call upon the legitimacy of the authority of a gentleman, even though he had been a tenant for ten years. Although there is no evidence that any of the witnesses questioned his authority, he may not have felt entirely confident about his position. Squire Parker's own status as a new landlord may also have meant that he could command less authority than either Sir George Hungerford, whose family's seat had been in Foxham for generations, or the previous owners of the Great Bedwyn estate, the dukes of Somerset. At the same time, the menial social standing of several of the witnesses also meant that the balance of deferential relationships was different, so that greater emphasis was placed upon authority and less upon partnership. It was

essential for the tenant farmer to maintain his authority. In threatening some witnesses, Edward Hall made a mistake that one of his social superiors would not
have made.

When action was required against the parson, the natural governors of the community took the lead. The squire was often at the head but he acted in partnership with the yeoman farmers who formed the parish elite. It is more difficult to
detect the involvement of the lower orders of society in such action, as it is with
their involvement in the religious life of the Established Church more generally.
Yet there is evidence that the common people, by which is meant those below the
parish elite, also participated in communal action against negligent and troublesome clergymen.

The parish elite, defined as those who held parish office, was itself a relatively
large group. Pewsey is an example of an open-field parish characteristic of those
found in the nucleated parishes of the Wiltshire chalk country. In the thirty years
from 1690 to 1720, no fewer than twenty-nine Pewsey men held the office of
churchwarden, with most serving for only one or two years. Half of those who
paid rates in 1705 served as either churchwarden or overseer during this period.
The number of those participating in the parish vestry was also high: forty-six
different lay signatures subscribed to vestry resolutions. A similar picture prevailed in Clyffe Pypard, a parish in the pastoral cheese country, characterised by
less centralised patterns of settlement. In Clyffe Pypard twenty-eight people
served as churchwarden between 1692 and 1714, almost exactly the same number
as in Pewsey; most served for only one or two years.[54] Landholders shared the
office of churchwarden between them, with each farm taking its turn, a procedure that ensured that the richest farmers did not monopolise parish office. The
churchwardens who, in the first instance, bore responsibility for presenting negligent clergymen might be drawn from the smaller landholders.[55]

Parish officers were, however, drawn only from those with enough land to pay
rates. Practical considerations reinforced social objections to the exercise of office
by those who did not have a propertied stake in the community. The office was a
position of authority and responsibility, and it required someone who was literate and who could be trusted to account for considerable sums of money. Parish
office involved the assessment and collection of rates, the disbursement of parish
funds, and the keeping of funds. As we have seen, the inhabitants of Foxham
objected to the selection as churchwarden of someone they characterised as 'a
poor day labourer haveing noe house nor tenement or any visible estate in the

[54] WRO 493/49; 895/30.
[55] The sparseness of social evidence unfortunately makes it very difficult to assess systematically
whether poorer wardens were less likely to present than their wealthier neighbours.

parish'.[56] Whether or not their charges were accurate, they provide a fair description of the accepted requirements for parish officers. These social considerations tended to keep parish office in the hands of more substantial inhabitants. In Pewsey at least half the churchwardens were drawn from the wealthiest quartile of ratepayers who farmed half the land in the parish. The officeholder elite, although not tightly defined, was largely drawn from the substantial inhabitants.

The poorer inhabitants had other opportunities to participate in community action against the clergy, either as witnesses in court or as supporters of petitions that appealed for help from the bishop or dean. Reliance on either source is hazardous. As we have seen, the means by which deponents were brought to give testimony was subject to challenge on the grounds that they had been suborned. Since it was not in the interest of witnesses to confess to pressure, even the hint of coercion in Great Bedwyn casts doubt on whether testimony expressed willing participation in a suit. Even less is known about the process by which support was gained for petitions. Nonetheless, the evidence from depositions and petitions does suggest popular participation in court action. Gentry promotion of a suit was not in itself enough to guarantee success. Support was also needed from other inhabitants because success in court depended upon their testimony.

Each deposition was headed by a brief biography of the witness, taken primarily to document how long he or she had known the parties to the dispute. This biography usually recorded the rank or occupation of the witness. Occupational descriptions of this sort are not entirely reliable, since a particular rank might be used to describe men of very different status and wealth and was subject to the natural tendency to inflate one's social standing. Gentleman, yeoman and husbandman were the most commonly used ranks, but the variety of ranks that are employed suggest that they may be more reliable descriptions than the small number used in criminal records.[57] It is also sometimes possible to supplement the rank with socio-economic information that witnesses provided to counter attempts to impugn their reputations.

Those of higher status were better represented among witnesses than those of lesser status. While there were some husbandmen, labourers and servants, witnesses were more often drawn from the gentry and the middling sort of yeomen, tradesmen and craftsmen. In Tockenham Wick, for example, no fewer than fourteen witnesses testified against the minister, including a weaver, his wife, and one or two husbandman. Most were substantial members of the community, including at least three yeomen, a gentleman, a curate and his wife, an innkeeper and a blacksmith.[58] Six of eleven witnesses in Chardstock (Dorset) were drawn from

---

[56] D3/12, 1686.

[57] J. S. Cockburn, 'Early modern assize records as historical evidence', *Journal of the Society of Archivists* 5 (1975): 215–31.

[58] D1/41/4/35 (1691). One witness was described variously as a yeoman and a husbandman, showing the vagueness of these social descriptions.

the gentry and middling sort. The witnesses against Thomas Lawrence of Chilton (Berks.) included a gentleman, a yeoman, a maltster and a shepherd-husbandman.[59] The relatively high representation of the gentry and more substantial parishioners does not, however, mean that they were the only ones who were concerned about clerical neglect. There was a bias in favour of the testimony of those of higher status, whose independence was more difficult for defendants to challenge. Depositions often referred to the views of the 'cheifest' or 'more substantiall' inhabitants of the parish. Promoters and their agents took considerable care in selecting their witnesses. It was in their interests to call witnesses of higher status, since their evidence was likely to carry more weight. Members of the lower ranks were sometimes called upon to testify because they were the only witnesses to particular offences. Depositions do, nevertheless, document popular concern about clerical misbehaviour, not least in testimony itself. The disgusted inhabitants of Chardstock who refused to receive communion from their drunken minister also included a husbandman, a labourer and an illiterate clothworker.[60] A widow who testified against Robert Randall of Great Bedwyn reported that she had heard complaints about the vicar not only by 'some of the most substantiall parishioners' but also 'by most of the vulgar sort'.[61] Petitions against the clergy provide further evidence of popular participation.

We the inhabitants of the parish of Colerne within your Lordship's Diocese, whose names are underwritten, do beseech your good honour that whereas Mr Thomas Latimer our Vicar hath by his notorious vicious life & conversation; which we know can & do hope will be made appear to your Lordship) rendered himselfe so obnoxious, that it is impossible for hym to benefitt us any longer as minister of our said parish; That it would please your honor so effectually to provide for your humble petitioners, by removeall of this obnoxious person, that we may be once more putt into a capacity of serving God within this Church, of which we are yett members; & which we are unwilling to desert without a just cause.[62]

In around 1671 28 inhabitants of Colerne submitted a petition to the bishop of Salisbury in which they requested the removal of their vicar Thomas Latimer because of his scandalous misbehaviour. This is one of several petitions that can be used to assess the extent of popular support for action against the clergy. Unfortunately, there is little evidence about how people were recruited to join these petitions and how voluntarily their signatures were given. The gentry are known to have participated in only two petitions, from Colerne and Alderton. The Colerne petition was part of a larger dispute between the vicar and Thomas Harris, Esq., who was to promote the correctional suit which resulted

---

[59] Chardstock: D5/22/15, ff. 1–18v (1667); Chilton: D1/42/61, ff. 148–137v (1680).
[60] D5/22/15, ff. 5, 6, 15.   [61] D5/22/18, f. 19v.
[62] This section is based on material in D1/41/4/39. A modern dating of 1671 appears in pencil on the petition, but the date of Latimer's court appearance on 16 July 1672 suggests 1672 is more likely. The bundle also includes a churchwardens' presentment (to the archdeacon of Wiltshire), the initial charges, depositions and the agreement.

Table 4.1 *Support for Wiltshire petitions*

	N names (males / females)	N adults, 1676	% males supporting (est.)	N marks (males/ females)	% marks (by males)
Hurst, 1731	54/0	—	—	7/0	13
Baydon, n.d.	42/0	—	—	0/0	0
Netheravon, 1681	34/1	—	—	—	—
Somerford Keynes, 1735	34/5	128	45	10/1	31
Sherston Magna, 1730	33/0	300	22	4/0	12
Colerne, 1671	27/0	300	18	11/0	41
Highworth, c.1679	25/0	—	—	0/0	0
Alderton, 1676	16/0	137	23	2/0	12
Somerford Magna, 1673	13/1	60	40	0/0	0
Winterbourne Stoke, c.1678	10/1	101	18	3/0	33

Note
The ratio of men to women is assumed to be 1:1.
Sources, as listed: D5/28, 1731; D5/17/1/2; *WAM* 45 (1930): 84–6; D1/41/4/36;
D1/61/1/42; D1/41/4/39; D5/17/1/1; WRO 84/44; D1/41/4/39; D1/41/1/21. Population
figures from Whiteman, *Compton Census*, pp. 106–35.

from the petition. Harris was a member of the greater gentry, serving as a land tax commissioner and probably as a magistrate.[63] Harris also discouraged inhabitants from paying their tithes. Although he took a leading role in the suit, there is no evidence to suggest that popular support for the petition was not voluntary.

The analysis that follows will consider ten petitions, of which nine complained about the misbehaviour of an individual clergyman and one appealed for a curate. Unlike depositions, petitions provide little information about the status of those whose names appear at the bottom, and it is rarely possible to link these names to other social data.[64] Yet two crude indexes of popular involvement can be used. The number of names at the bottom of petitions allows the scale of support to be assessed, demonstrating that petitions often received support from a substantial proportion of inhabitants. Since supporters might either sign or mark their name, their illiteracy provides a second index of involvement. Both the scale and illiteracy of petitions suggest that support for action against the clergy often reached below the parish elite.

---

[63] Harris was a land tax commissioner in 1677. 29 Charles II, c. 1. He may also have been made JP in 1671. The presence of two Thomas Harrises (one explicitly of Colerne) in the list of land tax commissioners leave the identity of the JP ambiguous.

[64] This is a particular problem for Wiltshire, because of the limited survival of hearth tax returns, so that reliance must be placed on the lucky survival of a timely rate list or similar source. However, survival of a hearth tax list from the right time might also prove difficult in counties with better records.

Table 4.2: *Illiteracy rates by social status in the*
dioceses of Exeter, Norwich and Salisbury
(Wiltshire only) in the 1670s

	Wilts.		Exeter		Norwich	
Gentlemen	0%	(24)	—		—	
Yeomen	7%	(15)	27%	(130)	17%	(24)
Crafts/Trades	39%	(39)*	48%	(314)	35%	(149)
Husbandmen	56%	(54)	73%	(203)	82%	(56)

Notes
Rate is percentage of number in sample (in brackets) who
were unable to sign.
*Wiltshire figures include craftsmen only.
Sources: D1/42/ 61, 1671–8; David Cressy, *Literacy and the*
Social Order (Cambridge, 1980), pp. 146, 150, 152.

The names of churchwardens and overseers were usually prominent among those listed with petitions against ministers, as is to be expected. The signatories to the Colerne petition included a churchwarden and an overseer. Yet the large number of names on some petitions indicates that a considerable proportion of the population participated in action against offending clerics. There were fifty-four names on the Hurst petition requesting better service in 1731 and forty-two names on a late seventeenth-century petition from Baydon asking that the dean of Salisbury augment the stipend of the curate so that the village could attract a better minister.[65] This exceeded the number who would have participated in parish office or in the parish vestry.[66] In parishes for which information about population size is available, every petition had the support of at least one in five male adults.[67] Two were supported by over 40 percent of males. Support for these petitions came from individuals who otherwise had no involvement in parish government and were not members of the parish elite, an interpretation that is confirmed by relatively low rates of literacy among petitioners.

[65] Unfortunately, there are no reliable population figures for Baydon or Hurst in 1676 (since both were chapelries). We do know, however, that Baydon had 31 hearth-tax-paying households in 1662. If we assume that there were about 5.5 adults for every household, as there were in Pewsey in 1662 (71 households listed in hearth tax return and 389 adults), Baydon had about 170 adults in 1676, so that about one-half of adult males signed the petition. D5/17/1/2; PRO, E179/259/29, ff. 15, 20–20v. According to the Hurst petition, the parish had a population of 4,000 souls, although this seems high. D5/28, 1731.

[66] In Pewsey, for example, individual vestry resolutions were likely to be signed by ten or fifteen people at most. Three vestry resolutions in 1699 (2) and 1710 were signed by 15, 19 and 12 people. The middle figure was probably higher than usual because it concerned the type of rate the parish should use in future. WRO 493/49.

[67] The Compton Census usually enumerated those able to take communion, i.e. aged about 16 or older, but sometimes enumerated all inhabitants. Since young communicants are unlikely to have signed a petition, the figures in Table 4.1 most likely understate the scale of participation in the petitions.

The ability to sign one's name is only a rough indicator of literacy, which depends for its accuracy upon whether children were taught first to write or to read. Evidence from autobiographies suggests that children usually learned to read before they learned to write, at around the age of 6, suggesting that someone who could write could also read.[68] Even so, the ability to sign is not irrefutable proof of functional literacy. The same person might sign some documents and mark others. What are we to make, for example, of the 62-year-old witness who testified to attending school in his childhood but who used a mark rather than signing his name at the bottom of his deposition? Although illness might provide the explanation, the quality of Henry Scott's 'T', written clearly and with a flourish, suggests that he deliberately chose to mark rather than sign and probably could write and read.[69] Despite these caveats, the use of marks provides one of the few scraps of information we have about these petitioners and should not be disregarded lightly.

Illiteracy statistics from the dioceses of Norwich, Exeter and Salisbury in the 1670s demonstrate a correlation between the ability to sign one's own name and rank in society. While gentlemen and clergy were 100 per cent literate, over half of husbandmen were unable to sign their own names. Making the transition from these aggregate figures to the evidence from individual parishes is fraught with dangers. Each parish must be considered as a distinct sample. If these were random samples, substantial variation in the percentages able to sign their name would be expected, particularly since each sample is relatively small. The diocesan samples show such variation, with the proportion of husbandmen using a mark ranging from 56 per cent in Salisbury to 82 per cent in Norwich. In practice, the samples are not random and may show even more variation from the effects of such factors as the distribution of schools. Although the results can only be indicative, they do suggest that participation in action against the clergy penetrated below the elite.

Support of petitions was not limited to those able to sign their name and in some cases included a substantial percentage who only used a mark. Petitioners therefore included some people who were not able to read the Bible, catechisms or other published guides such as *The Whole Duty of Man* to support worship by their families in their homes. Attendance at Sunday services must have constituted these people's main form of worship, and this reliance upon church services helps to explain their dissatisfaction with the minister. Participation also often extended below the yeomanry into the husbandmen and labourers who represented the lower strata of village society. This was most apparent in Colerne, where two in five supporters used a mark, well above even the most pessimistic estimates of yeoman illiteracy from the Exeter diocese. The Salisbury signature data suggest that the meaner sort of people were also involved in such parishes as Somerford Keynes and Winterbourne Stoke.

---

[68] M. Spufford, 'First steps in literacy: the reading and writing experiences of the humblest seventeenth-century autobiographers', *Social History* 4 (Oct. 1979): 407–35. See also Spufford, *Contrasting Communities*, pp. 181–3.   [69] D1/42/61, f. 223v.

CONCLUSIONS

It could be argued that the case studies explored in this chapter document the dependency system in action. In Bremhill and Great Bedwyn, it may seem, the squire marshalled his villagers in a manner reminiscent of a medieval tenant-in-chief summoning his men-at-arms. Clergymen who refused to accept their subordinate position were brought before the courts. Yet this interpretation does not do justice to the social co-operation which characterised relationships between the gentry and the people in these parishes. The example of Sir Roger de Coverley proves to be unsatisfactory, because it portrays the relationship between the gentry and the common people only from the top down. Gentry leadership in promoting court action to correct clergymen should not obscure the participation of those below them. Court action expressed the shared concern of the whole village for the quality of religious worship. As is often the case, the views of the lower ranks of village society are hardest to detect, but there is enough evidence to suggest that there was popular participation below the level of the parish elite. Complaints against the clergy represented cultural co-operation between rich and poor in village society. However distinct popular and elite cultures may have been, they shared an interest in protecting worship in the parish church.

There was a sense in which the squire and the parish elite were partners. The management of court actions reveals a process of negotiation that is unimaginable in Coverley parish. Religion was not merely another strand of the web of social control. The people participated willingly in the official religion of the Church of England; it was not imposed upon them. They did not face a stark choice between conformity and dissent; they had much more room for manoeuvre. We should not, however, construct too sentimental and monolithic a model of eighteenth-century English society. Social cohesiveness should not be exaggerated. Villagers and the squire co-operated in order to deal with particular crises, but this did not preclude conflict on other occasions and over other issues. The gentleman who sought to reform the minister might also assert his own interests over tithes or hunting rights. A parish that united in support of a petition against a negligent minister might at another time divide (and even present competing petitions) over the wisdom of licensing an alehouse.[70] Religion was one of several social contexts, alongside others such as crime, electoral politics and the administration of the poor law. Co-operation in action against a minister did not guarantee agreement over every aspect of worship or parish life.

Whether or not one accepts the concept of the 'confessional state', it is clear that religion should take centre stage in discussions of deference. Just as religion helped to define eighteenth-century political ideologies, it also contributed to

---

[70] As occurred in Rowde, A1/110, E1682, T1682.

social interactions at parish level. Villagers asserted their rights to participate in the government and exercise of religion, while respecting the natural position of leadership of the gentry. The gentry, in turn, took care to involve the people and to fulfil the responsibilities of leadership. The process was one of negotiation rather than exchange or coercion. Deference was not the same as dependence.

5

Pastoral care

Contemporaries and modern commentators alike have had few good words to say about the quality of pastoral care provided by the clergy in the eighteenth century. Clergymen were at best thought to be more devoted to hunting than to their spiritual duties, and at worst were regarded as covetous and lazy. Bishop Gilbert Burnet made himself few friends within the Church by publishing his view that the general neglect of pastoral care was one reason for the contempt in which the clergy were held.[1] 'It is not easy to bring the clergy to desire to take pains among their people,' he complained; 'they seem to have no great sense of devotion, and none at all of the pastoral care.'[2] The importance which Burnet placed upon pastoral care can be seen in his statement that his *Discourse of the Pastoral Care*, published in 1692, was the book he had written that pleased him the most.[3] When the new bishop arrived in his Salisbury diocese he sought to put his principles into practice. Before his primary visitation he wrote to his clergy with instructions about their duties in their parishes and at visitations, which he followed up at subsequent visitations.[4] In addition to discouraging pluralism, he encouraged clergymen to make frequent visits to houses in their parish and placed particular emphasis upon careful catechism, supported by instructional discourses.[5] Burnet also took steps to stimulate the spirit of religion directly by embarking on an ambitious programme of visits to parishes in the diocese at which he preached, catechised and performed confirmations.[6] Despite the resistance of some clergymen, Burnet's reforms assisted the reinvigoration of Anglican worship which, with the bishop's support, the Society for Promoting Christian Knowledge also encouraged in the early eighteenth century.[7]

Burnet's *Discourse of the Pastoral Care* was criticised for exposing the defects of the Church to the nation, so clergymen may have been reluctant to turn to it

---

[1] Gilbert Burnet, *A Discourse of the Pastoral Care* (London, 1692), pp. xvi–xxx; Foxcroft, p. 506.
[2] Foxcroft, p. 330.   [3] Ibid., p. 506.
[4] PRO, C104/63; *A Letter from the Bishop of Salisbury to the Clergy of his Diocese. To be read at the Triennial Visitation in May, 1711* ([London, 1711]).
[5] Foxcroft, p. 501; Burnet, *Pastoral Care*, pp. 186–8, 205–8.
[6] Foxcroft, pp. 329–30, 498–500. Burnet reported that he had visited 275 parishes in the diocese.
[7] See chapter 10.

for advice.[8] Some ministers looked instead to George Herbert's *A Priest to the Temple* for guidance.[9] The country parson had three types of pastoral duty to perform. His sacerdotal function, which set him apart from the laity, required him to officiate at church services, to administer the sacraments of communion and baptism, and to use his sermons and catechism to educate the congregation. He also performed burials, churchings and marriages. His responsibility for the souls of his congregation took him into private homes, for example when he visited the sick and dying. Finally, he was to set a good example through his pious and moral life. The parson was expected to spend much of his time in his study, writing sermons, reading and praying. The detection of parish clergy who were negligent or scandalous or who failed to conform to the Church was one function of ecclesiastical visitations. Despite their decline in the late seventeenth century, churchwardens' presentments provide rare windows into standards of pastoral care within and outside parish churches. Although the reluctance of churchwardens to present means that their presentments cannot provide a comprehensive picture of the quality of the clergy, it also increases the value of these sources as evidence of lay expectations and concerns, revealing which aspects of pastoral care the laity valued most. The most shocking cases involved clergymen whose scandalous behaviour disturbed worship. These damaged the reputations of the clergy concerned, while undermining the authority of the Church. Although the possibility that accusations of scandal were malicious cannot be ruled out, examination of individual cases suggests that they were usually genuine. Complaints about scandalous behaviour were infrequent, however. Far more common were presentments of pastoral neglect, although these should not necessarily be taken as evidence that clerical laxity was widespread. Many country parsons fulfilled their pastoral duties conscientiously, and poor service often resulted as much from the structural defects of the parochial system as from the negligence of individual clergymen. Such presentments nevertheless expressed lay demand for pastoral care and support for worship within the Established Church. They acquired additional religious significance because presentments and court actions had the potential to cause local disputes to escalate, leading to serious disruption of parish worship.

KNOOKE

When the curate Gervase Bland arrived to officiate at Knooke church on Palm Sunday in 1669 he found that its doors had been locked against him.[10] Bland was

[8] Foxcroft, p. 506.
[9] George Herbert, *A Priest to the Temple, or, The Country Parson his Character* (1632; 4th edn, London, 1701). The Revd John Lewis of Holt noted in his diary on 5 June 1721 that he was reading Herbert. Bodleian Library, MS Eng Misc. f. 10.
[10] The details in the following paragraphs are based on D5/28, 1666, ff. 3–4, 1668, f. 11, 1669, ff. 39–41, 1675, f. 33; D5/19/43, f. 10v; D5/21/1, 1671.

barred from the church again a week later on Easter Sunday. On this most important festival of the Christian calendar when every adult in the village should have received communion, the minister was prevented from celebrating the sacrament. The lockout disrupted worship, and it also hit Bland's pocket by preventing him from collecting his Easter offerings. These events were the culmination of an increasingly bitter dispute between the minister and villagers which lasted for at least three years and ultimately led to the curate's dismissal. It is unlikely that many adults would have participated in communion that Easter even if Bland had been able to gain entry to the church. The previous year the churchwardens had reported that because of the quarrel with the minister few were willing to accept the sacrament from him. Only four adults had received on Christmas Day. Villagers had taken active steps to disrupt prayers, throwing stones at the church, ringing the bells, and banging the church door during services. Bland complained that they had prevented the parish clerk from assisting him during prayers so that he had to officiate without help. Locking the curate out of the church was the final and most effective barrier placed in his way.

The village of Knooke suffered a virtually complete breakdown of worship. The villagers' main complaint was that Bland was a pluralist. In addition to being curate of Knooke, he also served as vicar of the parish of Chitterne All Saints, where he had been instituted in 1661. Bland's pluralism meant that he was able to read divine service only once each Sunday and that he was absent during the week. The wardens alleged that the curate had refused to co-operate at a funeral. Knooke's single service had as much to do with the structural inadequacies of the Church of England as with the neglect of one man. Despite the churchwardens' denials, Knooke was a chapel of ease within the parish of Heytesbury and was therefore unlikely to gain the services of a full-time minister. Gervase Bland retaliated against his congregation by using visitations to file his own charges. In addition to reporting lay failure to receive communion and disruption of services, he also complained that the churchwardens had failed to provide him with a satisfactory Bible or to make full presentments of offenders against the canons. He claimed that the Bible was so badly torn that sometimes he was unable to read the day's lesson and had to read a different lesson in its place. He was also concerned about his failure to receive Easter offerings for several years, since these were a valuable supplement to his small stipend.

Knooke appears to have owned a copy of the new Prayer Book and other ceremonial items such as a surplice and communion cloth. There is no reason to believe that the villagers had any principled objections to the restored liturgy. Yet the Commonwealth had left its mark on the person of the minister himself. Gervase Bland had been the incumbent of Laverstock before the Civil War until he was ejected by the Wiltshire committee in 1646 on political and religious grounds.[11] Bland had remained to preach against the rebellious Parliamentarians, even after his removal from the benefice, unlike some colleagues who fled their parishes for Oxford or another royalist garrison. He had stubbornly insisted upon using the Prayer Book, although this had been banned in 1645, and as a result had attracted many people from nearby Salisbury who wished 'to receave the Sacrament after the old manner (wth out any Examination at all)'. The exclusion of the unfit from communion was a central objective for Presbyterians, so that Bland's promiscuous administration of the sacrament was as shocking to puritans as his use of the liturgy.[12] His determined use of the pulpit and liturgy demonstrates a personality which cannot have been soothed by fifteen years in the wilderness. Bland's temper must have exacerbated tensions in Knooke and ultimately led to his dismissal from the curacy in 1669. He reacted to the questioning of ecclesiastical authorities in much the same manner as he had done to that of the county committee twenty years earlier. Bland angrily denied the authority of the dean, insisting that 'I will serve the cure of Knooke in despite of you doe what you cann', and he tried to officiate even after he had been dismissed from the curacy in May. His stubborn support for the Anglican liturgy in 1646 suggests that the explanations for his behaviour lay in his personality and experience rather than in any opposition to episcopacy. By this time in his seventies, Bland once again found himself opposed by the authorities and his congregation, and he reacted angrily to their betrayal.[13] By 1671 the chapelry had a new curate, and the inhabitants wrote to thank the dean. They reported that they had 'been much profitted by' the new minister and promised to conform to the Church 'with all cheerfullness'. Unfortunately, the structural origins of the dispute remained, and in 1675 the wardens reported again that prayers were being read only once each Sunday.

The popular perception that the minister was neglecting his duty of pastoral care could damage lay–clerical relations. The quality of the clergy was an important issue for ecclesiastical officials and local parishioners alike. The former wished to ensure that ministers conformed to the Act of Uniformity and to ritual requirements laid down in the canons, particularly in the years immediately following the Restoration. The laity were more concerned that their minister fulfilled his cure of souls and set a good example by living an unimpeachable life. The presence of a neglectful or scandalous minister could have serious consequences for worship. The visitation court and and its procedures became involved in the conflict between the inhabitants of Knooke and their minister. In 1666 the churchwardens and curate submitted counter-presentments. Bland

[11] BL, Add. MS 22,084, f. 10; Matthews, *Walker Revised*, q.v. 'Gervase Bland'.
[12] W. A. Shaw, *A History of the English Church during the Civil Wars and under the Commonwealth 1640–1660* (London, 1900), vol. I, pp. 260–79.
[13] Gervase Bland received his BA from Cambridge in 1617. *Alumni Cantabrigiensis*, q.v. 'Gervase Bland'.

managed to get his hands on the wardens' presentment, and he angrily scored through the complaint against him before signing his name. There were competing presentments again in 1669 when the wardens simply denied that they had a minister.

VISITATIONS AND THE REGULATION OF THE CLERGY

Visitations provided congregations who were having difficulties with their minister with an opportunity to seek a remedy by bringing the problem to the attention of the authorities. Roughly one in five active churchwardens' presentments expressed dissatisfaction with the clergy.[14] That churchwardens were more likely to present absence from church or problems with fabric is to be expected in a period in which dissent was a widespread problem and ceremonial items needed to be restored after years of neglect during the Commonwealth. Yet presentments against the clergy were far more common than those against moral offenders. Because churchwardens exercised a degree of choice about whether or not they presented, a systematic analysis of presentments can provide clues about which aspects of clerical misbehaviour were of greatest concern to the laity. The quantification of churchwardens' presentments is not without difficulties. The queries distributed in advance of visitations were long and, as we have seen, churchwardens soon stopped trying to answer every question. As a result, presentments varied greatly in length, some saying little more than that their minister was non-resident, while others detailed every omission. Churchwardens' selection of which questions to answer and use of their own language to describe offences increase the value of presentments as sources of lay opinion, but they make them less regular and therefore less amenable to systematic analysis. The figures that follow must therefore be regarded as indicative rather than definitive.[15] Parishes submitted 127 presentments against ministers at visitations of the bishop and dean of Salisbury.[16] Unless a presentment was made maliciously, it resulted from the combination of two circumstances: clerical neglect or misbehaviour, and the decision of the lay officers to reveal this offence to the authorities.

Visitations helped ecclesiastical authorities to keep a watchful eye on the clergy. In the years following the Restoration, they were particularly concerned to exclude from the Church any clergy who hoped to be able to avoid conforming

[14] This statement is based upon an analysis of presentments in the deanery of Amesbury in 1662–1714. See Table 5.1. Active presentments are those in which wardens presented at least one offence and did not state simply that all was well (*omnia bene*).

[15] The figures in Tables 5.1 and 5.2 were calculated by listing and grouping the issues mentioned in each presentment. Each issue is counted only once per parochial presentment, even if it is mentioned more than once.

[16] This figure omits another twenty-six presentments to peculiars or an archdeacon. Table 5.2 is limited to the visitations of the bishop and dean since these are the only ones to provide consistent long-term series.

Table 5.1 *Issues presented by churchwardens from
Amesbury deanery, 1662–1714 (by parish)*

	Frequency
Clerical neglect	20
Lay offences	
Defects in church fabric or furniture	72
Lay absence from church	62
Failure to baptise or to observe ceremonies	34
Money	11
Sexual and moral offences	4
Other	12
Number of active presentments	111
Number of parishes presenting *omnia bene*	84

Notes
'Failure to observe ceremonies' includes failure to baptise
children, to come to be churched, or to take communion
although present at church. 'Money' includes non-payment
of tithes, offerings and wages. 'Sexual and moral offences'
include incontinency, drinking or serving drink during
service and swearing.
Source: D1/54, Amesbury and Chalke, 1662–1714.

to every detail of the Prayer Book, even though they were prepared to compromise their principles by assenting to the Act of Uniformity. The act accomplished the departure by St Bartholomew's Day 1662 of over 900 incumbents around England, including 29 in Wiltshire, but there remained some who had been instituted during the Interregnum and might prove unreliable.[17] The familiar example of Ralph Josselin of Earls Colne demonstrates that a puritan clergyman might with luck survive for many years. In Wiltshire relatively few incumbents at the end of the Commonwealth retained their livings for long. Of those who survived, 27 had been instituted before 1645, so there is no reason to believe that they were puritans. In only 16 per cent of parishes did a Civil War incumbent remain after 1665.

Bishop Humphrey Henchman's set of visitation articles for 1662 devoted almost one-third of its questions to the clergy, more than to any other single topic.[18] 'Doth your Minister distinctly and reverently say Divine Service upon Sundaies . . . And doth your Minister duely observe the Orders, Rites and

[17] Another 824 ministers, including 31 in Wiltshire, were ejected in 1660–2. Matthews, *Calamy Revised*, pp. xii–xiii.
[18] *Second Report of the Commissioners . . . into the . . . Conduct of Public Worship . . .*, House of Commons Parliamentary Papers, 1867–8, vol. XXXVIII, pp. 610–13.

Table 5.2 *Churchwardens' presentments against parish clergy, 1662–1750*
(by parish)

	Frequency	Scandalous behaviour	Frequency
Neglect or poor performance		*Ill life*	
Non-residence	58	Dilapidations, money	10
Divine service	44	Troublesome	7
Catechism	23	Clandestine marriage	6
Communion	11	Scandalous behaviour	5
Preaching	10		
Baptism, burial, visiting sick	8	*Conformity*	
General neglect	6	Failure to conform	23
Other issues	14		
Parishes presenting clerics	127		

Notes
Some presentments mentioned more than one issue so the sum of issues shown is greater than the number of parishes that presented clerics. 'Non-residence' includes complaints that there was no curate. 'Communion' includes complaints that congregations were not warned in advance of its performance. Presentments of ministers who failed to perform perambulation have been omitted from the table.
Source: D1/54 and D5/28, 1662–1750.

Ceremonies prescribed by the said Book of Common-Praier. . . ?' his questions began, and they continued for another 21 articles. Many of the articles reveal the Church's concern to identify reluctant conformists. Does the incumbent wear a surplice? use a ring at marriages? instruct youths in their catechism? Henchman was concerned that the clerical lecture meetings known as prophesyings might be continuing, and he paid particular attention to preaching: was the incumbent licensed and did he preach strange doctrines or admit strange ministers to preach? Concern about clerical conformity receded in time, although it was to be an issue again for a short time after 1689. Yet bishops continued to take particular care for the quality of the clergy, particularly under Burnet. Thirty-two of the ninety-eight questions in his articles for 1695 concerned the clergy.[19]

Although churchwardens were urged to present those who failed to conform, visitations detected few non-conforming clerics. Clerical behaviour which might indicate lack of conformity to the Church included failure to declare assent to the Act of Uniformity, refusal to use the liturgy or omission of parts of it, failure to have a licence, and after 1689 the failure to pray for the new monarchs or to read acts or proclamations. Nine parishes complained about such offences in the 1660s, but thereafter complaints were rare and were most often associated with

---

[19] D1/54/15 (1695).

curates who had failed to get a licence rather than with a principled refusal to conform. Indeed, the success of the St Bartholomew's Day ejection can be seen in the shortage of ministers revealed by the visitations of 1662. No fewer than twenty-three parishes presented that they had no minister, while another twenty filed a complaint against their minister. The numbers fell sharply thereafter as order returned to the Church.

The first episcopal visitation, in September and October 1662, was well timed to pursue those puritan ministers who remained, and very few survived afterwards. The minister of Easton Gray was presented at the episcopal visitation in 1662 for his failure to assent to the Act of Uniformity, and he was duly replaced in the following year. Three other ministers indicted at Quarter Sessions early in 1662 also did not survive St Bartholomew's Day. One survivor of 1662 was Paul Latham of Warminster, who was presented to the Quarter Sessions in January 1661, before the Act of Uniformity, for his failure to use the old Prayer Book. Latham conformed thereafter and in 1672 became a cathedral prebendary.[20] Two other ministers who were suspected of being puritan survivors were in fact guilty of negligence or scandal. The churchwardens of West Harnham presented their minister John Chappell in 1668 for omitting sections from divine service, behaviour which might suggest reluctant conformity. Yet their complaints about his laughably bad sermons indicate that incompetence rather than puritanism lay behind his omissions. The accusations against Thomas Latimer of Colerne were more serious. The lord of the manor prosecuted Latimer in 1671 for his failure to assent to the Act of Uniformity, and two years later the bishop ordered the minister's arrest for preaching in Trowbridge church without a licence.[21] Although Latimer subsequently lost the benefice, his alleged nonconformity was the least of his offences. Failure to observe the liturgy was tacked onto a lengthy list of grievances, including scandalous behaviour and litigiousness. Latimer lost his benefice as much for his misbehaviour as for his non-uniformity. Clerical conformity was also not a serious problem after the accession of William and Mary. Wiltshire had only four non-juring incumbents and only a couple of others who were presented for their attempts to avoid praying for the new monarchs.[22]

Lay congregations were much more concerned about pastoral neglect than they were about clerical conformity. Churchwardens were aggrieved by the behaviour of ministers whom they perceived to be neglecting their pastoral duties. Non-residence and pluralism were the most common causes of complaint, accounting for almost half of the presentments filed against the clergy. Unless the

---

[20] B. H. Cunnington, ed., *Records of the County of Wilts.* (Devizes, 1932), p. 234.

[21] D1/41/4/39. Latimer was still the incumbent of Colerne in 1673 when his arrest was ordered, but he was replaced in 1674. D1/2/22, 5th foliation, f. 16v.

[22] The non-jurors were William Beach of Orcheston St George (replaced 1695), Francis Giffard of Rushall (replaced 1703), Nathaniel Spinckes of Salisbury St Martins, and Thomas Stampe of Langley Burrell (replaced 1702). J. H. Overton, *The Nonjurors* (London, 1902), pp. 471–96.

incumbent took measures to supply a curate in his place, pluralism made it virtually impossible for him to read divine service twice on Sundays and to fulfil pastoral duties during the week. A curate might himself be a pluralist, as in the case of Gervase Bland of Knooke and Chitterne All Saints. The provision of regular Sunday prayers was the issue of greatest concern to churchwardens, followed by the performance of other priestly duties such as catechism, preaching and the administration of communion. Despite the infrequency of communion – only three times a year – the requirement to administer communion on specific feast days caused difficulties for non-residents. Other pastoral duties such as visiting the sick also suffered from non-residence, but these were less likely to be mentioned. Parishes that were served by pluralists or non-resident clergy were not always troubled by the fact. Clergymen such as John Lewis of Great Chalfield, Holt and Atworth and George Millard of Box, Hazelbury and Calstone Wellington served their livings to the satisfaction of their congregations, aided by the proximity of their churches and by the small size of some of the congregations. These two clerical friends demonstrate that pluralism was not inconsistent with pastoral devotion. Yet two presentments from Froxfield, separated by only three years, show that lay patience wore thin on occasion. In 1671 churchwardens reported that although the vicar was not resident he lived 'distant two little miles', suggesting that they perceived this to be only a minor problem. Three years later their successors complained that the vicar's non-residence was 'very inconvenient to the Parishion[e]rs', because they had no service or sermon on Sunday mornings 'and sometimes none till five of the clock in the afternoone'.[23] It was the lack of divine service which was of greatest concern to the laity, even though half of those complaining heard prayers on average once a week. The laity insisted upon their right to two services each Sunday, enabling them to choose which service they would attend. The unpredictability of times of service led to complaints about prayers at unseasonable times. Yet even in a southern diocese like Salisbury, the fault for such poor service lay as much with the structural deficiencies of the Church as with negligent clergy.[24] Most complaints about single service came from chapelries, whose congregations might only be able to get two services each Sunday if they went to the mother church. The incumbent of a parish with chapelries was not technically a pluralist and was not obliged to provide a curate. Yet he was held responsible for the failure of chapelries to receive the same number of services as parishes, as chapelwardens made clear in their presentments at visitations. Comparisons might be made with predecessors who were remembered to have read prayers regularly or to have supplied a curate. Curates were more likely to be appointed to serve chapelries than the second livings of pluralists. The parish of Bradford-on-Avon, which had

[23] D1/54/4/1 (1671, C&M); D1/54/6/2 (1674, C&M), f. 30.
[24] For inadequacies of the parochial structure before the Restoration, see A. D. Brown, *Popular Piety in Late Medieval England: The Diocese of Salisbury 1250–1550* (Oxford, 1995), pp. 70–4.

six chapelries, more than any other Wiltshire parish, always had at least two curates. Chapelries were a source of considerable ill-feeling between laity and clergy, as Gervase Bland found to his cost.

Although the main task of preparing presentments fell on the shoulders of the churchwardens, according to the canons they shared this responsibility with the parish clergy. Canon 113 gave the incumbent a formal duty to present offences when the wardens neglected to do so themselves. It was common for ministers and churchwardens to co-operate in preparing the presentment. The articles included one section about the churchwardens themselves, and churchwardens sometimes left these questions to be answered by the minister.[25] The fullest example of co-operation is provided by the 1662 presentment from Tockenham Wick, demonstrating how ministers and churchwardens, perhaps building upon experience gained during the Interregnum, might use visitations as part of an effective system of discipline. The churchwardens organised a meeting in the church to prepare their presentment at which they asked the minister 'to read unto them those articles that concerned them'. The minister took this opportunity to admonish his congregation to be careful to keep the canons and he singled out those who had been negligent.[26] Churchwardens sought the advice of the minister in other parishes also. The rector of Ludgershall was one of several who certified 'that the said churchwardens have taken a sufficient time to draw up these their presentments And therin consulted with me'; he also added his own signature to the presentment.[27] A clerical signature at the bottom of a present-ment is fairly common evidence of co-operation. The churchwardens sometimes used visitations as an opportunity to praise the minister. The detailed answers provided by the chapelry of Milston and Bromston included the assurance that 'Our minister is a man of unblameable life & conversation'.[28] Ministers and wardens occasionally even co-operated in filing a presentment which mentioned some aspect of clerical neglect. More often, however, the fact that wardens were prepared to file a complaint about their minister implied at least a minor dis-agreement. Seven parishes testified to open conflict by presenting their minister for being troublesome.

Canon 113 carried within it the seeds of direct confrontation if the minister did not agree with the presentment, often because he felt that the wardens had failed to report serious offences, an increasingly common problem as wardens become more reluctant to present. The minister might submit his own present-ment or amend the one submitted by the churchwardens. Clashes were particu-larly likely if the minister was presented himself or if he identified the wardens as the main offenders in his parishes, as occurred in Knooke. Clashing

[25] As happened in Codford St Mary. D1/54/6/5 (1674, W&W), f. 27.

[26] D1/54/1/2 (1662, A&P), f. 17.

[27] D1/54/3/2 (1668, A&C), ff. 12 (Ludgershall), 11 (North Tidworth), 25 (West Grimstead).

[28] D1/54/1/3 (1662, A&C), ff. 46–7.

presentments might reflect a disagreement between the churchwardens and minister over who was responsible for remedying problems with church fabric, particularly immediately following the Restoration. In 1662 the bishop's visitations received conflicting presentments from both Overton and its chapelry, Fifield. The vicar Anthony Popejay and the churchwardens presented one another for failing to provide a surplice, a communion table cloth and other ornaments. Overton continued to expect its minister to provide these items at subsequent visitations.[29] If the churchwardens failed to present other offenders, particularly those who had absented themselves from church, the minister might present both them and the wardens. A clergyman's decision to present members of his congregation might rapidly result in direct conflict with the churchwardens and in disapproval when he returned to his parish. Edward Northey of Berwick Bassett felt that his conscience required him to write to complain about the church abuses, including a torn Bible and a nasty church full of rubbish, but he received only abuse for doing so from his parishioners.[30] Even if the minister and wardens agreed about what to present, other issues might cause conflict. For example, in 1668 the new wardens of West Grimstead refused to pay the costs of the rector's visitation dinner.[31]

The relationship between the minister and the churchwardens was central to the religious and administrative life of the parish. It is not surprising, then, that the annual appointment of new wardens sometimes also led to conflict. In many parishes it was customary for the minister and the congregation each to choose one warden.[32] Sometimes one party was unwilling to allow the other to choose or was unsatisfied with the choice they made. When William Meaden, the vicar of Great Bedwyn, a parish with a long tradition of lay–clerical conflict, was excluded from the election in 1714 he wrote to the dean with his nomination. The previous year the wardens had presented Meaden for performing clandestine marriages. The inhabitants of Somerford Magna complained in 1673, in the midst of a heated dispute that found its way into several courts, that the rector had chosen the churchwarden to side against the parish even though, they alleged, he was not a resident. Since the rector had taken at least half of the male adults of the village to court, he may have been unable to find any resident who would serve for him. In 1700 the people's warden from Clyffe Pypard accused the cleric's warden of desecrating graves.[33]

The dispute between the minister and churchwarden of Sutton Mandeville in 1668 demonstrates how visitations could provide the focus for conflict.[34] The first

---

[29] D1/54/1/2 (1662, A&P), ff. 14–16; D1/54/6/3 (1674, A&P), f. 41; D1/41/1/22 (WCP); D3/12, 1695.
[30] D5/31/1 (2 Aug. 1699).   [31] D1/54/3/2 (1668, A&C), f. 25.
[32] The description of the Revd. John Tounson of Bremhill from 1674 provides one example of a more widespread custom. In this case the archdeacon nullified the private election because a woman was selected. D1/54/6/3 (1674, A&P), f. 30.
[33] D21/2/5 (Great Bedwyn); D1/41/4/39 (Somerford Magna); D1/41/1/28 (Clyffe Pypard).
[34] See also p. 166.

few lines of the churchwarden's presentment were unexceptionable. Apparently written by a visitation clerk, they included references to seven recusants, six other absenters and a missing hearse cloth, while other aspects of the fabric and goods of the church were reported to be in good order. The final presentment, against the rector Augustine Hayter for his 'ill language to his Neighbours', has been scrawled through, apparently by the rector himself, for his signature appears immediately below. Hayter submitted his own presentment, devoted entirely to allegations against the wardens and one of the sidesmen. He charged one of the wardens, Salathiel Deane, with being a nonconformist and with seeking to turn the parish against the rector and to deprive him of his living. Although animosity between the minister and nonconformists heightened tensions within the village, other issues were also involved. Hayter complained that the churchyard was deliberately left unfenced so that Deane and others could keep pigs there. Testimony from a vilification suit he brought in 1674 reveals that he was thought to to be 'one that will starve the poor' because he refused to pay his poor rates. When Hayter promoted several tithe suits, his unpopularity increased, because he was perceived to be grasping and litigious.[35]

Visitations also provided a forum for conflict in the parish of Tockenham Wick in the 1680s. Relations had deteriorated considerably since an earlier minister and wardens had co-operated to prepare their presentment in 1662. The churchwardens presented that all was well in 1683, the year in which William Durston was instituted as rector.[36] Unfortunately, this happy position did not last for long. Durston was a pluralist who had another living in Worcestershire, where he had been born of a gentry family. He travelled back and forth from Worcestershire, spending only one day a week in Tockenham. By the next episcopal visitation three years later the parish had lost patience with their absent minister, and the churchwardens presented him to the bishop for his failure either to reside or to provide a curate. Durston retaliated by presenting the wardens for their own neglect of the church and churchyard bounds, claiming that the church tower was in danger of falling down. The exchange had the positive effect of forcing Durston to provide a curate, but he virtually abandoned his Wiltshire living. The warden Robert Smith complained in 1689 that Durston had not appeared within the parish for three years, since the previous visitation. Unfortunately, the curate left in 1690, when the rector was presented again, this time to the archdeacon of Wiltshire. In 1692 Smith reported that Durston had almost wholly deserted the cure and had visited only once in the preceding six months. By this time, however,

[35] D1/54/3/2 (1668, A&C), ff. 27, 28; D1/42/61, f. 204v.

[36] The material in the following paragraphs is based on these sources, unless otherwise indicated. D1/2/23, f. 24; D1/54/10/3 (1683, A&P); D1/54/11/3 (1686, A&P), ff. 21–2; D1/54/13/3 (1692, A&P); D1/41/4/35; D1/39/1/63. The presentments for 1689 and 1690 were both bundled with the court papers and depositions, suggesting that they led to the lawsuit. The use of the bishop's court rather than the archdeacon's suggests the weakness of the latter.

the churchwarden had taken a more serious step. In February 1691 he had pro-moted a consistory court suit for the correction of the absent minister.

The repeated presentments demonstrate how concerned parishioners were about the rector's neglect of his cure of souls and about the impact that this was having on the religious life of the parish. The remoteness of Durston's other living meant that he had only had time to officiate once on Sunday morning, and members of the congregation complained that he sometimes rushed through the service. If a christening or burial was needed urgently during the week, then friends and neighbours might have to turn elsewhere for help, and there was no minister to visit the sick. One inhabitant related how a mother had gone crying to the churchwarden asking him to find someone to bury her dead child. Although he was in the middle of harvesting, the warden had to fetch a minister from a neighbouring parish. The willingness of other clergymen to come in such emergencies presents a positive picture of pastoral care which helps to counter the rector's own neglect (although they may also have wished to earn a fee). The incumbents of Wootton Bassett and Clyffe Pypard each performed burials in Tockenham. The rector of Seagry was sometimes able to officiate on Sunday, although he was not licensed to do so and his parish was six miles away. Clearly assistance from neighbouring ministers could not provide a satisfactory long-term solution.

The inhabitants of Tockenham Wick also complained that their rector was quarrelsome. Indeed, he had disagreements with numerous individuals, often over money. He failed to pay the parish clerk his wages and the curate his salary. Although Durston leased his tithes, this did not prevent disputes. These financial disagreements damaged the quality of worship further. On one occasion the rector evaded the collector of the land tax by ordering the church bells to be rung for service, while he hid in an alehouse. Durston used his pulpit to abuse his enemies in the congregation, 'reflecting on, and distinguishing his parishion[e]rs by pointings from his pulpitt'. He removed the communion plate from the parish so that the sacrament could not be administered without him. The wife of a former curate concluded that 'Mr Durston hath many angry neighbours'. Unidentified parishioners threw stones through the chancel windows, which it was of course the rector's responsibility to repair (although they claimed that wind had done the damage). The parishioners asked only that the rector 'would behave himself quieter with his parish and settle a good curate there, w[hi]ch might please and constantly attend'. Durston would have preferred to abandon the cure entirely, and he sought to exchange livings with the incumbent of Wilcot.[37]

Given the failure of visitation officials to bring the rector to heel, the dispute was bound to wind up in the bishop's consistory court. Churchwardens

---

[37] D1/39/1/63.

presented Durston to the bishop and archdeacon no fewer than four times in seven years. Durston was one of over forty Wiltshire ministers who were prosecuted in the consistory court for the correction and reformation of their behaviour during the late seventeenth and early eighteenth centuries. The instance procedure created and preserved numerous documents describing clerical behaviour which went far beyond the relatively brief details found in presentments. Where depositions and other court papers survive, they often provide extensive documentation of the allegations brought against clergymen. Neglect of the cure of souls was the most common complaint, followed by scandalous behaviour and clandestine marriage. Disputes that reached the consistory court may appear more serious simply because we know more about them. The infrequency of episcopal visitations, occurring only every three years, sometimes made it easier to resort directly to the consistory court.[38] This can be demonstrated by comparing the experience of two parishes within the jurisdiction of the dean of Salisbury: Knooke, which lay within the dean's primary jurisdiction and was visited annually, and Great Bedwyn, which the dean visited only every three years because it lay in a prebendal peculiar. Whereas the dispute between the inhabitants of Knooke was fought out at visitations, the complaint against the vicar of Great Bedwyn was taken directly to the dean's consistory court.[39]

It is nevertheless likely that the consistory courts heard the worst cases. The infrequency of visitations was only a problem when a complaint was serious. Churchwardens were even more reluctant to resort to the consistory court than they were to present offenders at visitations. Court action caused personal inconvenience because it required travel to Salisbury rather than to a neighbouring parish and was likely to be costly. Although churchwardens sometimes did promote suits (presumably with the financial backing of the parish), this was more often done by local gentlemen, itself a sign of the seriousness of the matter. Court action might also be divisive, and could cause a dispute to escalate. Indeed, this is what happened in Tockenham Wick. William Durston quickly retaliated against his accusers. Two weeks after Robert Smith launched proceedings against him, the rector launched a counter-suit against Smith. Later in 1691, he also sued one of the witnesses against him, the parish clerk Edward Heath, for vilification of clergy. The charges related to an exchange of words between the two men which occurred in the chancel one Sunday at the end of morning service. Durston objected to a psalm which had been sung and laid hands on the parish clerk. Heath was aggrieved because the rector had failed to pay him his wages. He also criticised his behaviour, saying 'Goe to Marlburg, and be drunk again; and lett the Country

[38] Archdeacons and prebendaries visited at least once a year, but their jurisdictions were weak and laymen appear to have preferred to refer matters to the bishop or dean. Even cases presented to an archdeacon might subsequently be heard in the bishop's court.
[39] See pp. 97, 111 for further details. The Knooke case ultimately reached the consistory court because the curate made the mistake of questioning the dean's authority to discipline him.

people sett you up againe on your horse. You a parson: You a Parson for the Whore of Babylon; I'le doe your businesse for you.' Heath observed that he would still be parish clerk when Durston was no longer the parson, a prophecy that was to be fulfilled. Bishop Burnet took a personal interest in this example of clerical pluralism and scandal, and the consistory court cases ended with judgement going against Durston, who was suspended from the living in 1692.[40] A new rector was instituted to Tockenham Wick in 1693 after ten years of bitter strife.

SCANDAL

Accusations of scandal provide potentially the most serious indictment of the quality of the clergy. Scandalous behaviour could affect the quality of worship, while causing great damage to a minister's reputation. Lay reactions to such behaviour therefore offer valuable insights into the beliefs of the people and to their attitudes towards the clergy. Descriptions of clerical behaviour may also reveal information about the morale of the clergy. Yet such evidence must be analysed with caution. William Durston was one of several ministers who claimed that the charges against him had been brought maliciously. Rather than describing clerical misbehaviour, accusations of scandal may have been the result of antipathy to a particular minister or to general anticlericalism. The drunken and fornicating priest has been a stock image of critiques of the clergy from the time of Erasmus to the modern day. A closer examination is required in order to assess the reliability both of charges of scandal and of complaints against the clergy more generally. Fortunately, cases involving scandal are often well documented because their seriousness led them to be brought before the consistory court. Charges of such scandalous offences as sexual incontinence and drunkenness occurred infrequently in visitation records. Two of the five presentments filed in the visitation records of the bishop and dean of Salisbury were brought against William Durston. Durston was first presented as scandalous and disorderly in 1686, and a presentment to the archdeacon of Wiltshire four years later revealed that his offence was drunkenness.

The definition of scandal encompassed any aspect of clerical behaviour which was unbefitting the clerical estate, dignity and liturgical status. The 75th Canon condemned alehouse-haunting, servile labour, the playing of unlawful games, drinking, riot and idleness. Such behaviour prevented ministers from setting the laity a good example and undermined both their own authority and that of the Church. George Herbert reminded the country parson that he was Christ's deputy and should 'be exceeding exact in his life'. He was to be 'very circumspect in all companyes . . . knowing himself to be both suspected, and envyed'.[41] Burnet

---

[40] D1/39/1/63–4, 10 Feb. 1690/1 – 24 Jan. 1692/3.
[41] Herbert, *Country Parson*. The quotations are from his *Works*, ed. F. E. Hutchinson (Oxford, 1941), pp. 225, 227, 237.

agreed, observing that people paid more attention to how a minister lived than to what he said. Because a cleric was 'more watched over and observed than all others . . . He must not only not be drunk, but he must not go to Taverns or Alehouses, except some urgent occasion requires it'. In short, clergymen should 'shine as lights in the world'.[42] Whether or not accusations of scandal were accurate, the damage to a cleric's reputation was a matter of concern to his congregation. Thus the Tockenham wardens complained in 1689 that William Durston was 'a defamed person'. Scandalous behaviour was often accompanied by pastoral neglect, and drunken performances of spiritual duties shocked a number of congregations.

Accusations of scandalous behaviour tended to follow a common pattern. They were often part of a cluster of charges against a minister. As Herbert recognised, drinking was the most popular vice to which the clergy were prone. Scandalous clerics were most often charged with drunkenness and haunting alehouses. Presence in an inn or alehouse constituted inappropriate behaviour in itself and was easier to prove than drunkenness. This placed clergymen in a difficult position since inns were increasingly being used by the gentry both for sociability and for official duties such as petty sessions and tax commissioners' meetings, to which the clergy might contribute. The inn might be the only public space available for such meetings. The clergymen around Melksham often held their monthly dinners at a local inn.[43] Pluralist clergymen might need to lodge in inns, particularly if the parsonage in one parish had been destroyed or leased. William Durston had little choice but to lodge in an inn when he visited Tockenham, since he resided at his other living in Worcestershire. Durston travelled to Wiltshire on Saturday, spent the night in an inn, where he ate his meals, and officiated in Tockenham church on Sunday morning before departing again. He stayed variously at the Royal Oak in Wootton Bassett, Gillard's Inn in Tockenham, and another alehouse between the two parishes. Other ministers were private drinkers. It was alleged that the minister of Netheravon reserved some of the communion wine for his own drinking so that often he consecrated too little for the administration of communion itself. Another minister insisted on buying port for use in communion so that he could drink it himself. A third was said to have gone from house to house asking for a drink. The vicar of Great Bedwyn offered to accept mead in lieu of the offerings due to him from one parishioner. His debtor firmly told him that the money he received later would be better for him than any mead that was paid now.[44] It was rare for clergymen to be seen drinking, so witnesses were more likely to testify to the consequences

---

[42] Burnet, *Pastoral Care*, pp. 177–8; 'Injunctions to the Arch-Deacons of the Diocess of Sarum to be delivered by them to the Clergy in their Easter Visitations, 1690 . . .', p. 5, Wiltshire Archaeological and Natural History Service, Devizes, WT 52.
[43] WRO 1981/1; Bodleian Library, MS Eng Misc. f. 10.
[44] *WAM* 45 (June 1930): 84–6 (Netheravon); D5/28, 1731 (Hurst); D1/42/61, ff. 148–137v (Chilton, Berks.); D5/22/18, f. 20 (Great Bedwyn).

of drunkenness. Falling off a horse, falling over while walking, and dirtying clothes might be interpreted as evidence that the minister was drunk. Durston was one of several clergymen who was accused of falling off his horse because he was drunk. An inhabitant of Tockenham related how he had met some people riding from Marlborough market who were laughing and whooping because, they said, Durston had fallen off his horse and broken his neck. Although the rector appears not to have been injured physically, his reputation was seriously damaged by the incident. Ministers often denied that they had been inebriated and sought to provide other explanations for such accidents. Durston claimed that a broken saddle girth had caused him to fall from his horse.

Drunkenness was viewed as an evil in its own right, for such behaviour was considered to be inappropriate to the clergy's spiritual position. As the example of William Durston shows, drunkenness caused serious damage not only to the reputation and authority of the individual but also to that of the clerical profession. Although lay people took a relaxed view of the good fellowship which led most men to 'take a cup now & then', they did not extend the same tolerant attitude to the clergy.[45] Ministers should be moral examples and not keep bad company in alehouses. Drinking was also decried for its consequences, particularly if drunkenness interfered with the performance of the cure of souls. Several ministers, it was alleged, fell asleep in the middle of reading divine service, lost their place in the service book, or repeated or omitted portions of the liturgy. William Willis had to seek help from the parish clerk when performing a funeral. Matthew Whittley belched while administering communion, to the disgust of his congregation. John Butler fell asleep during service and when he woke asked what trumps were, indicating that his drinking had accompanied a sociable evening over cards. Another minister asked to be excused from visiting a dying woman because he was too drunk.[46] On such occasions a village might have to ask the minister from a neighbouring parish to officiate. Abusive language and violent behaviour were other unfortunate consequences of drunkenness. Most charges of scandal included allegations of blaspheming by swearing profane oaths, of abusiveness and viciousness, of being quarrelsome and litigious, and even of physical assault. William Durston was said to be 'a frequenter of alehouses, a prophaner of the Lords day, a Quarrellsome person'. He suffered the indignity of being expelled from an alehouse after calling its keeper's wife a whore. The vicar of Netheravon, when in 'his carowseinge cups', abused his parishioners, calling them cheating rogues. He threatened a parishioner with a knife when tithing, and he entered a nearby house and assaulted the householder's son.[47] In extreme cases, parishioners chose to stay away from church services, particularly if communion was to be administered, and to worship in

---

[45] D1/42/61, ff. 75v, 78v.
[46] D1/42/69 (Anderston, Dorset); D1/42/62 (Westport), ff. 2v–3; D1/41/1/6 (Lydiard Tregoze); D1/41/1/21 (Winterbourne Stoke).   [47] *WAM* 45 (June 1930): 84–6 (Netheravon)

another parish. The Church advised against this practice, fearing that it might sanction nonconformity or celebration of the Sabbath in an alehouse, and argued that the efficacy of the sacraments did not depend upon the moral character of the officiant.[48]

Ministers charged with scandal were often also embroiled in dispute with parishioners over money or other matters. Disagreements over the payment of tithes, mortuaries and other offerings were frequently mentioned in connection with scandal. Charges might also accompany conflict over such issues as the performance of communion or the exploitation of the churchyard. Since drunkenness had a detrimental effect on a minister's ability to perform his sacerdotal and pastoral duties, he was likely to be presented for neglecting the cure of souls. In some cases, ill living was the final straw from a minister who was already nonresident. Others were presented for performing clandestine marriages, itself a canonical offence. At the very least, testimony that the parson was violent, quarrelsome, or litigious suggests that there may have been deeper causes of disagreement. There is evidence of conflict over another issue in every case of scandal, a conjuncture, it may be thought, unlikely to be a coincidence. This raises doubts about the reliability of accusations of scandalous behaviour. Is it possible that parishioners simply added drunkenness to the list of charges against a minister they already disliked in the belief that these charges would be the crucial factor in procuring his ejection?

In the years immediately following the Restoration one alleged case of malicious prosecution for scandalous behaviour resounded across the county, although it concerned events that had occurred during the Interregnum. Walter Bushnell became vicar of Box in February 1645, one of the last ministers to have his institution recorded in Bishop Duppa's register before the abolition of episcopacy.[49] Despite his support for the liturgy, Bushnell managed to survive as incumbent for ten years, with the protection of friends among the county gentry with whom he socialised. He made no secret of his illegal use of set prayers. Indeed, he defended their advantages. Bushnell's run of good luck finally ended in 1655 when he was summoned to appear before the newly formed county commission for scandalous and ignorant ministers.[50] Bushnell was charged with political, religious and scandalous offences. He was ejected in the following year, and a new incumbent was appointed in his place.[51] Yet Bushnell did not give up the fight lightly, and he claimed the fifth that would normally have been paid to his wife had he been married.[52] Bushnell was still alive in 1660 when he was restored to his

---

[48] *The Case of Peoples Duty in Living Under a Scandalous Minister Stated and Resolved* (London, 1684), pp. 12–38.   [49] D1/2/22, 1st foliation, f. 3v.
[50] A Wiltshire committee was given powers to summon, examine and remove scandalous, ignorant and insufficient ministers by an ordinance on 28 August 1654. C. H. Firth and R. S. Rait, *Acts and Ordinances of the Interregnum, 1642–1660* (London, 1911), vol. II, 968–90.
[51] The new incumbent, John Sterne, sued Bushnell for dilapidations. PRO, IND 1/16827.
[52] This was made possible by an ordinance of 26 June 1657. *Acts and Ordinances*, vol. II, 1266–7.

living. The recovery of his benefice did not silence the vicar, who immediately took steps to recover both the income he had lost and his good name. That summer he filed an Exchequer bill claiming lost tithes.[53] In July Bushnell published a lengthy account of his ejection in which he alleged that much of the testimony against him was false. He had been ejected, he claimed, in order to make a profit for corrupt members of the committee. Our knowledge of the incident comes largely from Bushnell's book. This is admittedly a biased source, for it appeared at a time when those who had been sequestered needed to defend themselves against puritan claims that only those who were scandalous had been ejected.[54] Yet the weakness of the reply by Humphrey Chambers, a clergyman assisting the committee, adds to the plausibility of Bushnell's account. Chambers, who as a survivor of the Restoration needed to defend his own position as incumbent, could do little more than point to minor inaccuracies in the book.[55]

The charges of political disaffection brought against Bushnell were weak and were based purely on association. There seems little doubt that he was guilty of the religious charges of using set prayers and baptising with the sign of the cross, offences which in themselves were sufficient to lead to his ejection. Yet the vicar was most aggrieved by the charges of scandalous behaviour, which he claimed were entirely false and malicious. Witnesses testified that he was guilty of haunting alehouses, drunkenness, attempted fornication, and playing cards and dice. It was said that, besides frequenting alehouses, on one occasion Bushnell had been unable to read the service plainly and distinctly, and that on another he was too drunk to preach. He had also been seen to sway while riding a horse, a charge which would be familiar to consistory courts after the Restoration. Bushnell vigorously denied the charges against him, pointing out that there could be other explanations for the behaviour with which he was charged. Printing errors in the book, poor lighting or a dark afternoon might all have caused him to read indistinctly, although he denied that he had done so. The vicar also challenged the accuracy of testimony that he had been too drunk to preach one afternoon, claiming that he had preached a funeral sermon on the same afternoon. The alleged witness had been absent from church then because he was attending a revel in another parish. Bushnell admitted that he had gone to inns and alehouses, but said that this had been to conduct parish business (the parish clerk kept an alehouse) and to mediate in a dispute, ironically on behalf of one of the witnesses against him. He wryly pointed out that his most recent visits to inns had been to appear before the commission, which always met in an inn.

[53] PRO, IND 1/16829; E112/533 (case 28).
[54] I. Green, *The Re-establishment of the Church of England 1660–1663* (Oxford, 1978), p. 37.
[55] The details in this and subsequent paragraphs are derived from the following sources unless otherwise indicated. W. Bushnell, *A Narrative of the Proceedings of the Commissioners . . . for Ejecting Scandalous and Malignant Ministers* (London, 1660); H. Chambers, *An Answer of Humphrey Chambers . . . to the Charges of Walter Bushnel* (London, 1660). Chambers was ejected from Pewsey in 1662. Walker, *Calamy Revised*, p. 107.

Bushnell's most serious claim was that the charges against him were malicious and were brought deliberately in order to make a vacancy for another minister. He questioned the motives of promoters, witnesses and members of the commission. This was a risky business, since one of the Wiltshire MPs to whom he dedicated the book, Sir Anthony Ashley Cooper, had been a member.[56] One witness had a personal grudge against the minister. Others had received instructions about how to testify after being either bribed or threatened. Bushnell alleged that commission members and the clergy who advised them were part of conspiracy which had 'made ejecting of Ministers a kind of a trade'. Apparently, the clerk of the committee demanded a fee from the candidate for the living. Bushnell claimed that unbeneficed ministers loitered like vultures near commission meetings in the hope that a vacant living would come their way. Charges of conspiracy are difficult to prove and Bushnell's account did not go unchallenged, as we have seen. Yet the evidence against him appears to have been largely circumstantial. Although several witnesses claimed that he had behaved in a manner which might be explained by drunkenness, not a single eyewitness testified that he had seen him drinking.

The Bushnell case shows how vulnerable the clergy were to charges of scandalous behaviour. It was easy enough to discredit a minister with charges of inappropriate behaviour and, it appears, to support these charges with the help of false testimony. Yet incumbents after the Restoration were not nearly as vulnerable as the vicar of Box had been. Bushnell's account documents the confused state of religion during the Interregnum. In 1645–6 the Wiltshire county committee had already ejected thirty-seven incumbents for disaffection to Parliament, religious innovation and scandalous living.[57] The charges of corruption remain uncorroborated, but it is still true to say that no incumbent was safe. Bushnell was particularly vulnerable because of his support for the Anglican liturgy, and it seems likely that it was this charge, rather than drunkenness, which led to his ejection. Parliamentary ordinances provided a means to eject unpopular ministers and an army of unbeneficed ministers created pressure for vacancies. The situation was very different after the Restoration. A minister's benefice was regarded as freehold property, and deprivation and suspension were rare. Indeed, scandal was not itself grounds for dismissal. There was little advantage in falsifying such allegations, except to humiliate the minister. Ecclesiastical authorities were more likely to take seriously charges of nonconformity, neglect of the cure of souls, or solemnising clandestine marriages.

---

[56] The book was also dedicated to John Ernle MP.

[57] The Wiltshire county committee was given power to examine and remove ministers by the association ordinance passed on 19 August 1644. *Ordinances and Acts*, vol. I, p. 495. Royalism and, to a lesser extent Arminianism, were the most common charges, although scandalous living was alleged in one-third of cases. BL, Add MS 22,084.

Malicious prosecution for scandal was nevertheless sometimes still alleged after the Restoration, and such charges must be considered on a case-by-case basis. An allegation of malice was often based on the perception that those making the complaint were sectaries. In 1688 petitioners from Netheravon who complained about the drunken and violent behaviour of their vicar made the mistake of threatening to worship privately if nothing was done about him. This was all the dean needed to prove that the complainants themselves deserved corrective justice. In a similar case from the 1660s, parishioners spread malicious gossip about a minister whom they wished to get rid of. In 1664 two men alleged that Richard Randall, the curate of Holt and minister of Trowbridge, was guilty of fornication. Witnesses testified, however, that they had admitted that they wished to disgrace the minister in the hope that he would be replaced by a puritan. The case occurred only two years after Black Bartholomew's Day had swept hundreds of clerics from their livings. A curate was particularly vulnerable to accusations of scandal, since he had no freehold in his position. Most of the details of this dispute emerge, not from the complaint which was brought against the cleric, but from the prosecution he brought for vilification of clergy, which he ultimately won with support from local gentlemen and ministers.[58]

The Holt case also has another significant difference from most other charges against allegedly scandalous clergymen – it concerned fornication rather than drunkenness. Indeed, another of the rare charges of fornication also appears to have been malicious. In 1683 the churchwardens of Chiseldon presented the Revd Thomas Twittee for fornication and fathering a bastard. Twittee, who combined livings as vicar of Chiseldon and rector of Draycot Foliat for half a century, was one of the most litigious clerics in Restoration Wiltshire. The occupiers in his parishes had good reason to dislike the minister, who was engaged in an extended legal campaign, involving numerous suits, to overturn a 1563 tithe agreement. His parishioners resisted vigorously by bringing counter-suits and by taking direct action, including assault and verbal abuse. The charge of fornication was most probably launched in the attempt to discredit the minister, particularly since the presentment did not lead to a correctional suit in the bishop's consistory court.[59]

William Durston of Tockenham Wick also claimed that the charges against him were malicious, and Elizabeth Shropshire, the wife of his former curate, agreed that the minister was, 'no doubt, abused in many cases, as particularly in the story of falling off his horse'. She thought that many of the ill reports against him arose from prejudice. Durston's allegations were not well founded and can be viewed rather as a standard ploy of a defendant to discredit the suit against

[58] *WAM* 45 (June 1930): 84–4; D1/42/58, ff. 62–3; 59, 26v–28; D1/41/4/47. This episode is described in more detail in chapter 7.
[59] D1/54/10/2 (1683, C&M), f. 45; PRO, E134, 23/24 Charles II, Hil 2; J. H. Stevenson, 'Will a man rob God?', *WAM* 72/3 (1980).

him. He was right that the promoters would have dropped the prosecution against him if he had supplied a curate, for they said the same themselves. Despite her words of support, Elizabeth Shropshire believed that the rector deserved many of the ill reports against him. It would be rash to discount all prosecutions which sought to correct the behaviour of scandalous clerics. The sheer bulk of the testimony against some ministers suggests the need for a closer look. Several cases are supported not only by lists of charges but also in the lengthy depositions taken from eyewitnesses, providing detailed descriptions of events that occurred on named days. There were often several witnesses to the same event. Witnesses may have colluded against the cleric, agreeing a fabricated story in advance, or might have been bribed to testify in a particular manner. If this were the case, we might expect testimony to be very similar in detail. In fact, the detailed testimony from the cases that survive has an air of verisimilitude. The depositions differ in the manner one would expect when individuals each give their own account of what they witnessed rather than agreeing in advance what to say. Despite small differences in their testimony, the witnesses told much the same story.

Thomas Latimer became vicar of the parish of Colerne in June 1671.[60] It did not take long for him to fall out with his parish, for in 1672 the churchwardens presented him for excessive drinking and assault, although they did so reluctantly. Initially, the wardens tried to present that all was well in the parish, and they presented the vicar only after receiving three warnings from the archdeacon that they must name any offenders. In the opinion of a court officer, they had presented the minister 'by way of revenge and in malice'. However, other documents suggest that Latimer was guilty of scandalous behaviour and of other offences as well. A petition submitted the previous year had already accused Latimer of being 'a Drunkard, a notorious lyar & comon swearer, a Quarreller & Striker, & Railer & defamer of his neighbours'. The villagers said that the vicar was so obnoxious that it was impossible for them to benefit from him, and they threatened that they would desert the church if the bishop did not replace him. Latimer was charged with neglecting his pastoral duties, performing clandestine marriages and, as we saw earlier in this chapter, failing to conform to the liturgy. Tithes were also at issue, and depositions reveal that a local gentleman, Thomas Harris, had organised a tithe strike against the minister, encouraging parishioners not to pay the tithes due to him. The vicar claimed that Harris made trouble for all clerics in his parish: 'he had served him no worse than he used all other ministers which had gone before him, & that he never suffered any to live quietly'. This charge is not confirmed by other sources. No other Colerne vicar encountered difficulties with Harris. In the end, Latimer signed an agreement in which he confessed his guilt and promised to behave himself in a manner

[60] The details in this and the following paragraphs are based on D1/41/4/39.

befitting a minister of the Gospel. He was canonically admonished and warned that the prosecution against him would be revived if he offended again. In return, Harris and other parishioners agreed to drop their charges and pay their tithes. There is little doubt that Thomas Latimer was guilty of scandalous behaviour as charged. It did not take long for him to get into trouble again, and in 1674 Colerne gained a new vicar after Latimer was prosecuted for preaching in another parish without a licence. The congregation and the bishop were both no doubt pleased to see the back of this troublesome minister.

The charges against Robert Randall, the vicar of Great Bedwyn, fitted the common pattern, and involved drunkenness, swearing, threatened assault, clandestine marriage and disagreements over both tithes and offerings.[61] Although promoted by the local squire, the case against the vicar was managed by one of his tenants, Edward Hall of Sudden Park. Both Hall and others had reasons to dislike the vicar. Randall brought a futile and unjustified suit for tithes against twelve of Hall's sub-tenants in 1677. Two witnesses testified that the vicar had threatened them if they did not pay offerings owing to him.[62] Several witnesses were members of Hall's family (including two servants). He promised to pay the expenses of the servants and labourers, and pressured the latter to testify. Witnesses also testified that the vicar had made sexual overtures to Hall's wife, and this incident at the promoter's house was the subject of the most detailed testimony against the vicar. The only witnesses appear to have been Hall's wife, two servants and Hall himself, although he arrived late. According to their depositions, the vicar Randall came to the house at about nine in the evening in a drunken state, making so much noise that he frightened the women and children, who were alone in the house with the servants. John Leadall, a servant who was returning to the house, found the minister outside lying in the dirt. Leadall helped him into the house, where a drink of warm milk was given to the minister and a bed was made up for him. When Randall was asked where he had been, he could not remember, but later he said that he been drinking brandy with a friend in Burbage. Both servants went out at different times to look for the minister's horse and hat, but it later emerged that he had left the horse in Burbage and had walked to Sudden Park. When Mistress Hall suggested that the vicar go to bed, he said he would go only if she accompanied him. At this point, her husband returned home and was told what the vicar had proposed. Hall had more success in getting Randall to go to bed.

Comparison of the depositions of the four witnesses suggests that this incident happened as described. The fact that the statements are not identical itself indicates that the story was not made up. The differences between the witnesses are slight and suggest genuine differences in memory rather than a carefully constructed and rehearsed false case. The witnesses were not all present at the same

[61] D5/22/18, ff, 17-22v, 25-8.   [62] See chapters 2 and 4.

time. Initially, the women were alone with the children. Not surprisingly, they were frightened by the arrival of a strange man who was shouting. Each witness remembered different details. Mistress Hall told how she was afraid that someone was trying to steal a horse, since another horse had been stolen in the village that week. Initially she put out the candle, but later she questioned the man at the window. The maidservant remembered locking the door against the intruder. Mistress Hall and the servants all remembered Randall's sexual proposition, which was his most offensive action that night, although there are again slight differences between their accounts. Leadall recalled that Mistress Hall told the vicar that she could not sleep with him because her husband would be angry; the vicar replied that Hall could lie with his own wife. Mistress Hall testified she had told the vicar that, even if she had wanted to go to bed with him, he was not in a fit state. Edward Hall did not himself report the vicar's pass at his wife, although other testimony suggests that he had been told about it. Instead, he reported that on their way upstairs the vicar had asked to lie with the maid. Randall may have been looking for another partner, or perhaps Hall transposed events to protect his wife's good name. These minor disagreements indicate that Randall really did descend upon Sudden Park in a drunken state one evening and proposition the lady of the house. If the story had been fabricated, one would have expected to find more agreement in the testimony of different witnesses. Their evidence is confirmed by the testimony from someone else of a separate occasion when Randall had offered to change wives with another man. Margery Pyke, another witness with no known relationship to Edward Hall, testified that she had heard Randall say that he could preach better sermons out of Aristotle than the Bible, a detail which seems unlikely to have been fabricated. It is impossible for us to know for certain how reliable the evidence against Randall was; the task would have been difficult even for a contemporary judge. On balance, however, it appears likely that he was guilty of drunkenness and scandalous behaviour.

Although it is true that the Halls and the other witnesses had reason to dislike the vicar, this was because of the offences they described in their testimony. Details of lost hats, mead and Aristotle seem unlikely to have been invented. Cases of scandal often involved testimony of similar complexity, including details of eccentric clerical behaviour, which seem unlikely to have been fabricated. William Durston, as we saw earlier, had the church bell rung for prayers and then hid in an alehouse in order to avoid a tax collector. Another minister threatened to burn all the books in his study. A third told fortunes and compared himself to the earl of Berkshire.[63] Such testimony suggests that unsatisfactory, unhappy and even disturbed clergymen served some parishes. Charges of

---

[63] D1/41/4/35; D5/22/15, f. 8v (Richard Luce of Chardstock); D1/42/62, f. 6 (Matthew Whittley of Westport St Mary).

scandal often did follow a common pattern. The conjuncture of charges of scandal, pastoral neglect and quarrelsome behaviour, rather than being suspicious, points to the damage which scandalous behaviour could cause to the quality of religious life in a parish. This does not mean that every charge made against a clergyman was true or that there were no malicious prosecutions. Allegations of scandalous behaviour must be judged individually, by relating as much information from different sources as can be found. Yet ill-living clerics were relatively rare. However damaging scandal might be, perceptions of pastoral neglect, the payment of tithes, and the prosecution of nonconformity were far more likely to be the cause of damaging disagreements between parsons and their parishioners.

6

Tithes and religious conflict

The payment of tithes was the issue over which parsons and parishioners quarrelled most often in the century after the Restoration.[1] Tithes were not a new source of disagreement. Disputes over tithes had revealed lay–clerical tensions on the eve of the Reformation.[2] An increase in the number of tithe suits, it has been argued, was one consequence of the clergy's loss of prestige after the Reformation.[3] The two thousand clerical tithe cases recorded in Lichfield diocese in the first half of the seventeenth century increased the laity's identification of the parish clergy with the unpopular consistory courts.[4] Christopher Hill argues that difficulties in collecting tithes contributed to the economic problems of the Church on the eve of the Civil Wars.[5] The Restoration did not resolve these economic problems, and tithes remained a major grievance in the late eighteenth and early nineteenth centuries, when they are credited with contributing to anticlericalism, declining Church influence, and the weakening of the alliance between church and state.[6] Although relatively few people refused to pay tithes for reasons of religious principle, disputes over payment nevertheless had considerable significance for lay–clerical relations and for religion more generally. Their collection had the potential to poison

---

[1] There is an extensive literature on tithes. See C. Hill, *Economic Problems of the Church from Archbishop Whitgift to the Long Parliament* (Oxford, 1956), chs. 5, 6; E. J. Evans, *The Contentious Tithe: The Tithe Problem in English Agriculture, 1750–1850* (London, 1976); E. J. Evans, 'Tithing customs and disputes: the evidence of glebe terriers, 1698–1850', *Agricultural History Review* 18 (1970): 17–35; E. J. Evans, 'Tithes', in *Agrarian History of England and Wales*, vol. V.2 (Cambridge, 1985), pp. 389–405; E. J. Evans, 'A history of the tithe system in England, 1690–1850, with special reference to Staffordshire' (Ph.D. thesis, Warwick University, 1970).

[2] R. M. Wunderli, *London Church Courts and Society on the Eve of the Reformation* (Cambridge, Mass., 1981). Cf. G. R. Elton, *Star Chamber Stories* (London, 1958), pp. 174–220, esp. 216–18. Tithe disputes were rare in Salisbury diocese in the Middle Ages. A. D. Brown, *Popular Piety in Late Medieval England: The Diocese of Salisbury 1250–1550* (Oxford, 1995), p. 81.

[3] R. Houlbrooke, *Church Courts and the People during the English Reformation 1520–1570* (Oxford, 1979).

[4] R. O'Day, *The English Clergy: The Emergence and Consolidation of a Profession 1558–1642* (Leicester, 1979), pp. 191, 198, 205.

[5] Hill, *Economic Problems of the Church*, pp. 79–99, 157–9.

[6] Evans, *Contentious Tithe*; E. J. Evans, 'Some reasons for the growth of English rural anti-clericalism c. 1750–c.1830', *Past and Present* 66 (Feb. 1975): 84–109. See also J. C. D. Clark, *English Society 1688–1832* (Cambridge, 1985), *passim*, esp. pp. 372–9.

relations between the clergy and the laity. Clerical dependence upon tithes for much of their income made it difficult for them to heed Bishop Burnet's advice that they keep their responsibility for the souls of their parishioners more in mind 'than so many scores of pounds, as the living amounts to'.[7] Impoverished clergymen had little choice but to seize any opportunity to maximise their incomes, even if this was at the expense of their congregations. Their more prosperous colleagues in other parishes confidently used the courts to defend their rights and those of their successors. The result was to do considerable harm to lay–clerical relations, making the clergy appear more like wolves than shepherds of their flocks.

AVEBURY

The parish of Avebury is best known for the standing stones, rediscovered by John Aubrey, which dominate the centre of the village. For almost twenty years around 1700 this quiet village just inside the Marlborough downs was the scene of an extended and bitter conflict over tithes, complicated by nonconformity and allegations of clerical neglect. The central figures in the dispute were the vicar and a leading landlord. John White had been vicar of Avebury since 1671. Although he was a pluralist, non-residence was not a cause of complaint. White resided in Avebury and provided a curate for his other benefice of Manningford Bruce. He brought several suits to reclaim tithes during the first twenty-five years of his incumbency, but these do not appear to have led to serious conflict.[8] All this changed in 1695 when Sir Richard Holford purchased Avebury manor.[9] A Master of Chancery, Holford resided in London and leased out his new estate. The survival of his voluminous correspondence, supplemented by the records of consistory, Exchequer and Chancery courts, means that that the resulting dispute is unusually well documented.

Holford sought advice from the vicar White on his first visit to the village, and he departed satisfied that they had established a firm friendship.[10] It did not take him long to discover his error. On his next visit in the summer of 1695, Holford was disturbed to find that differences over tithes had created a bitter atmosphere in the village. He was particularly concerned to see that the dispute had damaged worship in the parish, observing 'which is worst of all a seperacon in the publick worship of God & participation of the holy & blessed Comunion of our Lords Supper'.[11] Holford sought to resolve the dispute. He urged the vicar to practise Christian charity and to set a good example. By doing so he was sure that White

---

[7] Burnet, *Pastoral Care*, p. 159.

[8] D1/2/22, f. 9 (5th foliation); D1/27/1/1; D1/39/1/59, f. 118; D1/39/1/61, ff. 30, 67v, 77.

[9] [Richard Holford] (hereafter RH) to John Adams, 28 May 1695, writing to complain of delay in responding to his offer of £7,500. WRO 184/1. The correspondence in this chapter is from WRO 184/1, unless otherwise indicated. Holford was a Master of Chancery from 1693 to 1702. E. Foss, *The Judges of England* (London, 1864), vol. VII, p. 295.

[10] PRO, C5/294/6.   [11] RH to Mr [John] White (hereafter JW), 11 Jan. 1695[/6].

would 'perswade them to pay to you the respect due to your quallity & ffunc-
tion', so that they would pay 'their dues with cherefullness'. Instead the conflict
deepened. 'I saw the heats increased & blowne into a flame & a mutuall inclin-
acon to unneighborly squabbles,' the landlord later wrote. Despite his attempts
to serve as peacemaker, Holford soon became a combatant himself. His quarrel
with the vicar ended only with the latter's death in 1712.

Two disagreements over tithes lay behind the Avebury dispute. The first was
between the vicar and the tenant of Avebury Farm, William Skeate.[12] For several
years the farmer had paid £4 in composition for the tithes of the land Holford
was now purchasing. In 1695 Skeate rented another estate, but it appears that he
tried to avoid paying the additional 10s. in tithes for this land. Instead he accused
the vicar of increasing his demands, reporting that he had refused to accept less
than the full amount in payment. These were hard times for Skeate and other
farmers, and he may have hoped to make a small gain from the confusion. He
had already been obliged to beg for a reduction in his rent from the previous
owners of Avebury Farm, because of the bad harvests that plagued England in
the 1690s. Unfortunately, arbitration by a local gentleman only added to confusion over the dispute.[13] Holford became directly involved because he feared that
he was being charged for tithes that were due from another man's estate. Since it
was Skeate, not Holford, who owed the tithes, White could not understand the
latter's involvement in the dispute.[14]

Holford's involvement led to the escalation of conflict. The vicar now declared
his intention of collecting tithes in kind in future. The legalistic landlord wanted
to know what documentary evidence the vicar had to support his tithe claims
and his rights to collect in kind. How much was the vicar entitled to collect in
kind? Over the next sixteen years he pursued a campaign through the courts in
order to try to obtain the documentary evidence that would answer these questions. Collection in kind suited the vicar because it gave him greater control over
what and when to harvest. In addition to small tithes, White claimed that 'I may
choose two ell ridges of wheat when it is ripe containinge by estimation one acre
& cut & carry them away'.[15] Holford insisted upon independent evidence of the
size of an ell ridge. The harvesting of these ell ridges would cause repeated problems. In 1699 White sued the new tenant John Rose because he had failed to
inform the vicar that the tithe wheat was ready to collect, so that it sat in the
fields until finally some of the village poor took it for their own use.[16] White sent
his own reapers into the fields in the following year, and when Rose tried to
obstruct them he found himself charged with riot at Quarter Sessions.[17]

---

[12] Skeate's surname is spelled variously as Skeat, Skeats, Skeates and Skeate.
[13] Richard Smith of Kennet, the vicar's father-in-law, set the debt at £4 but left unclear whether this
was for the farm alone or for both estates. [14] PRO, C5/294/6.
[15] JW to RH, 29 Jan. 1696[/7]. [16] WS to RH, 29 Jan. 1699[/1700].
[17] William Smith of Calston (WSC) to RH, 6 July 1700.

A second dispute over tithes broke out in the summer of 1697, leading the vicar, John White, to file an Exchequer bill against nine Beckhampton men for withholding their tithes.[18] Holford took an interest in this dispute also, although it did not concern him directly. The vicar claimed that the defendants had withheld their privy tithes and offerings from him for four years. If the solitary defendant's answer is to be believed, White was at fault this time for attempting to increase the amount he received in composition for garden tithes. Joseph Hayward probably did not deserve the description of yeoman given after his name in the bill of complaint, but there is no doubt of his industriousness. He described himself as 'a poore man' who 'lived by his Industry and Labour'. Hayward rented a cottage and a small garden with a few apple trees in 1694. By 1697 he had added a messuage and meadow and also kept 'a little shop of small wares [such] as Tobacco, Candles and Tape Thread'. The amounts at dispute were trivial. In 1694 Hayward paid 2*d.* in offerings, plus tithe apples and a 'customary charge' of 1*d.* for tithes of garden stuff. The vicar sought to benefit from Hayward's growing prosperity. He kept a close eye on the apple trees, checking them every time he passed the cottage. Then in 1696 he demanded that he be paid 12*d.* for garden tithes, a twelve-fold increase, although he moderated his demands to only 6*d.* in the following year. White took Hayward and his neighbours to the court of Exchequer for this small amount. Hayward complained that the case was vexatious. He alleged that the vicar had often declared his intention of resorting to the courts to put them to excessive charges and expenses, and had used Exchequer rather than the new summary procedures offered by the 1696 act in order to ruin the defendants. Reflecting on the case a decade later, Sir Richard Holford still found it difficult to forgive the vicar for the common law and Exchequer suits which had impoverished Hayward and his family.[19]

The vicar of Avebury defended his right 'without breach of charity' to make 'use of what means the Law directs for the recovery of my just dues'.[20] With benefices worth around £150 a year (of which £20 to £30 would have paid a curate), White had an interest in maximising his tithe income.[21] Yet he paid a high price for his determination to collect the tithes due to him, because he gained a reputation for being litigious. William Skeate had few kind words to say about the vicar, who 'will be trobelsome to all his neighbours'.[22] Joseph Hayward insisted that he had always been careful to pay White his full dues to avoid trouble, 'knowing the complainant to bee of a very passionate temper'.[23] Sir Richard Holford chastised White for his 'boysterous haughty & uncharitable words & accons', which he said exposed him to the malice of ignorant men and were unworthy of his status. His language 'would better become a man of a lower & meaner educacon & of any other profession'. Holford referred the minister to

[18] PRO, IND 1/16835, case 176; E112/758/176.   [19] RH to JW, 22 July 1708.
[20] JW to RH, 27 Jan. 1695[/6], 4 April 1696.   [21] D1/27/1/1.   [22] RH to JW, 11 Jan. 1695[/6].
[23] PRO, E112/758/176.

three passages in the Bible in the hope that these would 'put you in a better temper'. These expressed his view that it was best for members of the clergy to suffer in silence, rather than to worry too much about the collection of tithes. The first passage was a familiar exhortation to charity from St Paul's first letter to the Corinthians: 'Charity suffereth long, and is kind . . . Doth not behave itself unseemly . . . is not easily provoked, thinketh no evil.'[24] The consequences of conflict could be dangerous for the parish community and the minister alike, as the next text warned: 'Abstain from strife, and and thou shalt diminish thy sins: for a furious man will kindle strife. A sinful man disquieteth friends, and maketh debate among them that be at peace.'[25] The final passage warned White not to be so involved in the daily grind of agriculture, including the collection of tithes, but to turn his thoughts to higher matters: 'The wisdom of a learned man cometh by opportunity of leisure . . . How can he get wisdom that holdeth the plow . . . and whose talk is of bullocks?'[26]

Holford's admonitions to the vicar were disingenuous, for he was quick to use the courts to defend his own interests.[27] If the Master of Chancery believed that 'the Law . . . must putt an end to all controversies', it was perhaps because he knew how to use it to his own advantage.[28] He brought at least ten Chancery bills in Middlesex, and in Westonbirt (Glos.), where he also had a manor, he and the minister were allies in a dispute with much of the rest of the parish.[29] Holford pursued his campaign against White with almost obsessive determination. The *casus belli* were the vicar's attempt to collect the full tithes from William Skeate and his decision to receive them in kind in future. Holford was displeased that the vicar appeared to be breaking his word and was determined to establish the correct amount that his farm owed in tithes. He feared that uncertainty would reduce the value of his investment, making it more difficult to attract a tenant in future. He was keen to get value for money or, as he expressed it, to get 'a pennyworth for a penny'.[30] Holford's standard tactic was to demand a written set of particulars from his opponent and to keep on badgering until he got what he wanted.[31] In September 1696 he requested a full account of what was due to the minister but failed to receive a satisfactory answer.[32] 'Why won't hee then gratifie me in my request,' he enquired in the margins of a letter from White. Next he turned to Chancery, filing a bill in order to force discovery of the vicar's dues. If this was successful, the documentation exposed by the suit might be invaluable in rebutting any subsequent excessive demands from the incumbent.

[24] 1 Corinthians 13, quoting verses 4–5. The quotations in this and the following notes are from the Authorised Version.   [25] Ecclesiasticus 28: 8–10.   [26] Ecclesiasticus 38: 24–5.
[27] *Index of Chancery Proceedings, Bridges' Division, 1613–1714*, Lists and Indexes, vol. 39, etc.
[28] RH to JW, 10 Nov. 1708.
[29] D. Rollison, 'Property, ideology and popular culture in a Gloucestershire village 1660–1740', *Past and Present* 93 (Nov. 1981): 70–97.   [30] RH to JW, 22 July 1708.
[31] He used the same tactic in an attempt to gain details of another property he purchased in Avebury. PRO, C5/355/32.   [32] RH to JW, 30 Sept. 1696.

White greeted the news of the Chancery suit with alarm: 'I have children enough to bestow what I have upon without feeding Lawyers.'[33] To Holford's frustration, it proved no easier to get a satisfactory answer to his bill than it had been to his letters. He wrote more letters demanding an answer and used Chancery procedures to harass the vicar.[34] He could not pass up an opportunity to pursue the suit even in a letter sent to express his regrets for the tragic death of White's son: 'God who governs the world knows best what is fit for us, & we must submit to his will, & let me take this opportunity to ask why you are pleased to delay your answer to the Bill.'[35] Chancery rejected White's first personal answer because it omitted letters from Holford which the bill had requested. His second answer enclosed the letters but was likewise rejected because White had failed to have them engrossed on parchment. The engrossment of the letters increased their value in future court proceedings, but it also increased the vicar's costs. Before witnesses were examined, White promised to pay costs and be a good neighbour if the action was dropped, and Holford consented.

Yet the landlord continued to pursue his campaign to be certain of the dues owed to the minister, threatening him with another Chancery suit in 1711, even though White was now too ill to preach.[36] To his astonishment he learned that the vicar had exhibited a terrier, precisely the type of documentary evidence he had been seeking for fifteen years, and he demanded to see a copy. John Brinsden, who was substituting for White in Avebury church,[37] was horrified to learn of the threatened suit. He reported that neighbouring gentry and clergy thought it incomprehensible that Holford 'should raise such batteries agt . . . such a poore feeble viccaridge as Avebury & then to sue in Chancery to have it more infeebled'.[38] It was Holford's turn to be advised to follow a course of peace and charity and to show his desire for good neighbourhood by stopping his 'thunderings & thretnings of lawsuits'. White was dangerously ill in May 1712 and he died in October.[39] Holford had hoped that Brinsden would become the next incumbent, but he had already obtained another benefice. Although Holford was to live another decade, he had no problems with the new vicar, John Mayo, who was instituted into the benefice in November 1712.[40]

[33] JW to RH, 29 Jan. 1696[/7]; RW to JW, 4 Feb. 1696[/7].
[34] Holford made White file additional answers. PRO, C33/289.   [35] RH to JW, 29 April 1697.
[36] Holford wrote that he had shown White the subpoena but initially had agreed not to serve it. This bill is not listed in the index for Bridges' Division, Holford's favourite, so perhaps it was never exhibited. *Index of Chancery Proceedings, Bridges' Division, 1613–1714*, Lists and Indexes, vol. 39, etc.
[37] RH to JW, 4 Oct. 1711 (from Avebury); JR to RH, 23 Feb. 1711[/12].
[38] John Brinsden (JB) to RH, 1 Nov., 13 Nov. 1711, 1 Jan. 1711[/12]; RH to JB, 22 Nov. 1711.
[39] RH to JB, 21 May 1712; WRO 1176/1.
[40] RH to JB, 21 May 1712. See WRO 184/8, 12 Aug. 1711, for praise of a Brinsden sermon. Brinsden was instituted to Tockenham Wick in September 1712. D1/2/25, ff. 1, 2. The Crown was patron of Avebury, Winterborne Monkton and Tockenham Wick. D1/27/1/1.

The personalities of the participants were partly responsible for inflaming tithe disputes in Avebury. Sir Richard Holford's pursuit of the vicar through the courts almost to the day he died was obsessive. Holford was an arrogant and pedantic man who was determined to control the actions of others. Nor did he limit his interference to religious affairs. Rather than leaving manorial affairs to his steward, he visited his manors annually, enabling him to attend their courts. In October 1700 he provided a dinner for the Avebury jurors and attempted to instruct them about how to make their presentments. To his disappointment, the jury's presentments were still very imperfect.[41] The patronising tone of his letters was guaranteed to offend their recipients. A letter to John Brinsden advised him to read 1 Corinthians 13, the same verses on charity towards which he had pointed John White, and was filled with advice about clerical duties, which must have been unnecessary for the son of a parish clergyman.[42] Holford's pedantic thoroughness was doubtless enhanced by his legal training. A bencher and member-officer of Lincoln's Inn, in 1700 the Society's Council asked him to procure a certificate of their coat of arms from the Herald's Office. Holford learned that the arms the Society was using were actually those of the earls of Lincoln, and he succeeded in obtaining a certificate of the authentic arms to hang in the Council Chamber.[43] Holford kept not only the letters he received but also a copy of every letter he sent, and he referred back to this correspondence regularly. He attached several of White's letters to his Chancery bill and asked that White's answer also be supported by letters.[44] Holford's punctiliousness left him constantly dissatisfied with those he perceived to be his inferiors: 'I cannot say that Avebury is peopled with many . . . whose conversasion is very desirable,' he wrote in 1701.[45] His attempts at control did not end with his death, for his will sought to stipulate to whom his heirs should bequeath his estates.[46]

John White, the vicar of Avebury, was not blameless. He showed himself to be unable to take criticism of any sort. His letters are filled with vitriolic and insulting language, leading Holford to comment early in the dispute, 'Good God! how unwilling should wee bee to bee snatched out of the world with such thoughts in our hearts or such words in our mouths.'[47] Holford sought help from the bishop, and he reported to the vicar Burnet's disapproval of 'your haughty & passionate behavior' and 'your bad example directly opposite to the doctrine & example of our blessed Savior'. Bishop Burnet was 'trouble[d] that his visitacon [in 1695] & pastoral care & advice had no better effects'.[48] It did not take White long to take offence at Holford's admonitions, although the landlord initially made every effort to soften his words. He could not meet Holford without falling into a

[41] WRO 184/8, Wednesday, [3] Oct. 1700.   [42] RH to JB, 21 May 1712.
[43] *The Records of the Honourable Society of Lincoln's Inn: The Black Books*, vol. III: *From AD 1660 to AD 1775* (Lincoln's Inn, 1899; repr. 1991), pp. 207–8.
[44] PRO, C5/294/6.   [45] RH to WS, 22 Feb. 1700[/1]; PRO, C5/355/32.
[46] PRO, PROB 11/564, sig. 119.   [47] RH to JW, 20 Jan. 1695[/6].
[48] RH to JW, 11 Jan. 1695[/6].

passion and complained about him when he was absent. In 1699 Holford was advised 'to bring a good soarde with you for the parson is in a greate rage against you'.[49] White's reviling language and arrogant behaviour made him few friends. William Skeate worried in 1700 that if White won his latest tithe suit he would 'almost think himselfe the next man unto a king'.[50] Holford held his poor example responsible for much that was wrong with worship in Avebury.[51] White was determined to protect his rights and income, and was quick to go to law. Like Holford, he used the courts as a weapon against his enemies. He deliberately set out to ruin John Rose and succeeded in impoverishing Joseph Hayward. Holford reflected in 1701 that he had always pitied the vicar's wife and children.[52]

White's economic and social position placed him under considerable stress, and this may account for some of his angry behaviour.[53] The low values of his livings obliged him to be a pluralist, and this made him responsible for the service of two different parishes. Curates were not a complete solution, since if they were deacons they could not preach or administer communion. They often remained in posts only briefly, so there must have been gaps when White had to serve both cures on his own as well as find a new curate to assist him. The low value of his living was also responsible for his determination to protect his income and his rights by collecting the full tithes owed to him. White also invested in land and lent out money,[54] and he took every opportunity to claim moneys owing to him by suing not only for tithes but for bonds and other debts. He was determined not to be cheated. Insecurity about his social position con-tributed to White's over-sensitivity to criticism. He felt that he was Holford's social inferior and resented his patronising manner, even though Holford took care to praise the vicar's status and education. Conversely, Skeate's own confi-dence and increasing wealth caused chagrin to the vicar, who thought the farmer needed reminding of his modest social origins.[55]

The last seventeen years of the incumbency of John White as vicar of Avebury show how both villagers and ministers used the courts. In addition to Exchequer and the consistory courts, John White also used the common law and criminal prosecutions to pursue debts and protect his rights. Sir Richard Holford's use of the courts comes as no surprise. As a bencher of Lincoln's Inn and Master of

---

[49] WS to RH, 12 May 1699.   [50] WS to RH, 19 Feb. 1699[/1700].
[51] RH to WS, 22 Feb. 1700[/1].   [52] RH to WS, 22 Feb. 1700[/1].
[53] See chapter 2.
[54] At White's death his moveable estate was valued at £531, of which £450 was in debts. Will and inventory of John White of Avebury, archdeaconry of Wiltshire probate records. Compare Ralph Josselin of Earls Colne, who also had success in using his benefice as the basis for the accumula-tion of land. A. Macfarlane, *The Family Life of Ralph Josselin* (Cambridge, 1970).
[55] RH to JW, 30 Jan. 1695[/6]; RH to JW, 22 July 1708. White's degree is not recorded in the bishop's register, but he was probably the John White who took a Cambridge BA in 1668–9 and an MA in 1673. Although Venn suggests that this graduate was vicar of Shepreth, Cambridgeshire, his Dorset origins make it more likely that was he was vicar of Avebury. D1/2/22, 5th foliation, f. 9; *Alumni Cambrigiensis*, q.v. 'John White'.

Chancery, he knew how to use this court to force discovery of information. He was also able to use his contacts both formally and informally with the ecclesiastics and civilians in the ecclesiastical courts. Even his farmer, William Skeate, learned the advantages of a subpoena against an enemy. A simple dispute over tithes could have serious consequences for the religious life of the parish, undermining the efforts of the minister to be a pastor and damaging his relations with his parishioners.

THE SIGNIFICANCE OF TITHES

The events at Avebury were far from unique. Wiltshire clergymen brought suits for the substraction or withholding of tithes against over 850 defendants in the two most popular venues available to them, the bishop's consistory court and the Exchequer Court of Equity. Over half of Wiltshire's parishes experienced at least one clerically promoted tithe suit in the period. This was only the tip of the iceberg. Some disagreements were resolved before they came to court. The courts were regarded as a last resort by plaintiffs and were feared by defendants.[56] Even the threat of court action might be enough to induce payment. Other legal venues were also available to plaintiffs, including the common law courts and, after 1696, justices of the peace.[57] The superior courts had the advantage of paying double or treble damages to a successful plaintiff (although plaintiffs sometimes waived these rights), but the costs of bringing a suit were also higher.[58]

Tithes were an inescapable fact of life for rural people, and their annual payment was a regular part of the agrarian calendar. To villagers they were another drain on their incomes, and may have appeared little different from taxes and rent. Under William and Mary England became one of the most heavily taxed nations in Europe, having previously been taxed relatively lightly. Confronted with a growing variety and burden of new taxes, people naturally tried to avoid payment, just as smugglers evaded customs duties.[59] The familiarity of tithes did not make them any less resented. Before the Civil Wars, Martin Ingram observes,

[56] Criminal prosecutions also were often brought only as a last resort. J. A. Sharpe, 'Enforcing the law in the seventeenth-century English village', in V. A. C. Gatrell, B. Lenman and G. Parker, eds., *Crime and the Law* (London, 1980), p. 107.
[57] Legal title could be established only through the common law courts, where the issue could be tried by jury. D. B. Fowler, *The Practice of the Court of Exchequer upon Proceedings in Equity* (London, 1795), vol. I, p. 311. The nature of the records makes it very difficult to locate common law suits from a particular county, but incidental references among Quaker Sufferings and other sources indicate that Common Pleas and county and hundred courts were occasionally used to recover tithes and that goods were sometimes confiscated without reference to the courts. Wiltshire Sufferings, WRO 1699/18; Friends' House Library, Great Books of Sufferings, vol. II, Wilts, pp. 1, 8, 11, vol. IV, part 22, pp. 448, 453–4, 455, 464–5.   [58] 2&3 Edward VI c. 13.
[59] D. Hay et al., *Albion's Fatal Tree: Crime and Society in Eighteenth Century England* (London, 1975).

actions were mostly either debt suits or related to specific disputes over tithing customs, and rarely 'reflect[ed] principled objections to, or anticlerical resentment of, the payment of tithes as such'.[60] Tithes became a politically significant 'issue of blood' during the Commonwealth, and in June 1659 inhabitants of Wiltshire joined those of other south-western counties in presenting a petition against tithes to Parliament.[61] Yet radical hopes for the abolition of tithes, and for their replacement by voluntary gifts from congregations, were disappointed. After the Restoration, once again, few objected on principled grounds to the payment of tithes, with the notable exception of the Quakers. Tithes may therefore appear to have little religious significance but be primarily an issue of property. The distinction between property and religion should not be drawn too sharply, however. It is a foolish defendant who criticises the legal system, while the wiser one builds his case on those facts and points of law which are to his advantage. The significance of tithe disputes lay not in criticism of the system but in the friction which they created, friction which frayed lay–clerical relations and ultimately made it impossible for some clerics to fulfil their pastoral role.

Lay ownership of tithes blurred their identity as an important element in the income of the parish clergy, turning them into just another form of rent, with the added drawback for the payer of being based on gross yields.[62] The widespread ownership of impropriate rectories which monasteries had owned before the Reformation meant that in many parishes laymen collected the great tithes (usually those for corn and hay), leaving the clerical vicar with only the privy tithes on other crops, livestock, wool and smaller items. Privy tithes were more likely to cause disagreement because they could be difficult to collect; the division between great and privy tithes could itself be a matter for dispute. Contemporaries estimated that 3,845 of England's 9,284 parishes had a lay impropriator.[63] Clerical tithes might themselves be collected by a layman if the incumbent decided to relieve himself of the headache of collection by farming the tithes out to someone else, as the vicar of Broughton Gifford did.[64] Yet the significance of lay ownership of tithes can be overstated. In Wiltshire 57 per cent of great tithes were in the hands of clerical rectors, a figure which was close to the national average.[65] It is sometimes suggested that rapacious lay

---

[60] M. Ingram, *Church Courts, Sex and Marriage in England, 1570–1640* (Cambridge, 1987), p. 109. Cf. Hill, *Economic Problems of the Church*, pp. 124, 163.

[61] M. James, 'The political importance of the tithes controversy in the English Revolution, 1640–60', *History* 26 (June 1941): 1–18; Hill, *Economic Problems of the Church*, pp. 164–6.

[62] James, 'The political importance of the tithes controversy', pp. 6, 9; P. Langford, *Public Life and the Propertied Englishman, 1689–1798* (Oxford, 1991), pp. 14–16.

[63] Hill, *Economic Problems of the Church*, p. 144.

[64] F. K. Eagle and E. Younge, *A Collection of the Reports of Cases, the Statutes and Ecclesiastical Laws relating to tithes* (London, 1826), vol. I, p. 618; PRO, IND 1/16835, case 42. The unfortunate farmer encountered problems in obtaining tithes from the same man, John Golding, whom the vicar had been obliged to take to court three years earlier for substraction of tithes.

[65] D1/48/2. This 1683 Diocese Book covers 240 of Wiltshire's 280 parishes.

impropriators and tithe farmers were more likely than clergymen to turn to the courts to maximise their yield from tithes.[66] Yet clerics more than held their own in the courts, bringing three-fifths of Exchequer bills and two-thirds of consistory court acts for tithes.[67] The figure was even higher in the decade after the Restoration, when the clergy accounted for three-quarters of the citations for substraction of tithes. It was the clergy rather than the laity who were most determined to protect their rights and had the greatest need to do so, and for this reason it was the clergy who were most likely to be identified with problems over payment.

Clerics faced greater resistance to tithes despite their religious claims. Not only did they bring more cases, but each individual case tended to involve more defendants, providing a rough index of the seriousness of disputes. The average clerical bill at Exchequer named 2.5 defendants; lay bills named on average only 1.8 defendants. A case brought against a single defendant was most likely to be an isolated disagreement, although the case may have provided an example to others. Sixty per cent of lay cases were brought against only one defendant, compared to less than half (49 per cent) of clerical cases. Bills naming several defendants indicate more serious disputes and perhaps even collective resistance to tithes. The largest clerical bill named fourteen defendants, and this was not that unusual; seven bills named ten or more defendants. That nine of the eleven most litigious tithe-owners (listed in Table 6.1) were clergymen shows that there were good reasons for the popular image of clerics as quarrelsome and litigious.

The Quakers were the people most strongly identified with the principled refusal to pay tithes.[68] Their testimony against tithes, like their refusal to swear oaths, became both a leading cause of persecution and a central testimony of faith. The Quakers had no difficulty in recognising the religious aspects of tithes, despite connotations of lay property. Their beliefs did not allow them to make payments intended for the support of an established ministry which intervened between worshippers and God. Many Wiltshire Quakers suffered for their failure to pay tithes both during the Interregnum and thereafter. Records of sufferings include 171 for non-payment of tithes between 1656 and 1700.[69] Yet in those

---

[66] Evans, 'Some reasons', p. 86; and F. Heal, 'Economic problems of the clergy', in F. Heal and R. O'Day, eds., *Church and Society in England: Henry VIII to James I* (London and Basingstoke, 1977), p. 110.

[67] D1/39/1 (1670–89); PRO, IND 1/16829, 16831, 16833.

[68] Recent contributions to the extensive literature on the Quaker testimony against tithes include N. Morgan, *Lancashire Quakers and the Establishment 1660–1730* (Halifax, 1993); and C. Horle, *The Quakers and the English Legal System 1660–1688* (Philadelphia, 1988). See also N. C. Hunt, *Two Early Political Associations* (Oxford, 1961); E. J. Evans, '"Our faithful testimony": the Society of Friends and tithe payments, 1690–1730', *Journal of the Friends' Historical Society* 52 (1969): 106–21.

[69] WRO 1699/18, Wiltshire Sufferings; Friends' House Library, Great Books of Sufferings, vol. II, Wilts. Research on other counties has found that sufferings remained important until at least the 1730s. Morgan, *Lancashire Quakers*, ch. 6. Cf. Hunt, *Two Early Political Associations*, p. 67, n. 15.

Table 6.1 Litigious tithe-owners in Wiltshire, 1660–1740

Plaintiff's forename	Plaintiff's surname	Parishes	Clerical or lay	No. of defendants	First year	Last year	Duration
Thomas	Twittee	Draycot Foliat and Chiseldon	clerical	33	1669	1706	38
James	Garth	Hilperton and Keevil	clerical	33	1676	1690	15
Richard	Watson	Pewsey	clerical	26	1668	1676	13
John	Tounson	Bremhill	clerical	19	1664	1683	20
John	White	Avebury	clerical	18	1675	1710	36
Henry	Dudley	Broad Hinton	clerical	17	1670	1687	18
John	Bennett	Heywood	lay	16	1675	1683	13
John	Fishlake	Fisherton Anger	clerical	16	1695	1718	24
Walter	Bushnell	Box	clerical	16	1660	1670	11
Elizabeth	Garrard	Broad Town	lay	15	1680	1680	1
Edward	Cuthbert	Cricklade St Sampson	clerical	15	1717	1723	7

Sources: WRO 1/39/1, 1/41/1; PRO, IND/1 16831–41, E112.

parishes where clergymen had the greatest difficulty in collecting tithes, it appears that Quakers were not responsible. It is true that in Bremhill the Revd John Tounson, one of the most litigious clerics in Wiltshire, brought several suits against Quakers. Yet Bremhill was the only parish listed in Table 6.1 that housed a Quaker meeting.[70] Even in Bremhill, Quakers represented a small proportion of defendants. According to the records of sufferings, Tounson focused his attention on Joane Hale, the leader of the Quaker meeting, as his Interregnum predecessor, James Crump, had done before him.[71] Similarly, in Hilperton the litigious vicar James Garth prosecuted the Quaker William Stovy on several occasions, but none of the other defendants is mentioned in the sufferings.[72] Although the Quakers were not necessarily diligent in recording their sufferings for tithes,[73] comparison of court records with the names of those known to be Quakers confirms that Friends accounted for only a small proportion of defendants in tithe suits. A list of Quaker families and parishes can be compiled from registrations of births, marriages and deaths, as well as from records of sufferings. Comparison with details about defendants reveals that at most 8 per cent of them may have been Quakers.[74] Even if other dissenters also sometimes withheld tithes, it seems likely that most of those who were prosecuted for non-payment remained within the Church of England.

If it was natural for people to try to avoid paying tithes, it was equally natural for clergymen to wish to protect their incomes. They faced a difficult choice between defending their standard of living and the peace of the parish. In 1747 John Butler, the rector of Lydiard Millicent, chose to overlook the withholding of tithes, perhaps wisely since the defaulter was the lord of the manor and the patron of the living. When the rector finally raised the matter, he was presented at visitations for poor performance of divine service. He suspected that the presentation had been made because the patron 'has just reason to conclude (as he knows I am able) that I shall prosecute him for it [non-payment of tithes]'.[75] Court costs were another disincentive to going to law for all but the most quarrelsome cleric. The expense of a risky suit might be more than the sum that

[70] Turner, *Original Records*, pp. 106–27, esp. 109.
[71] WRO 1699/18; Friends' House Library, Great Books of Sufferings, vol. II, Wilts., p. 11.
[72] WRO 1699/18; A1/110, E1680; D1/39/1/59, f. 140v.
[73] The Wiltshire Quarterly Meeting recorded difficulties in obtaining a full account of sufferings, for example on 2 July 1705. Friends' House Library, 'The Minute Book of Wiltshire Quarterly Meeting 1678–1708', transcr. N. Saxon, p. 246.
[74] Families, rather than individuals, were linked to maximise the number of matches. Even if a Quaker landholder neither married, had children, nor died during the period, it is likely that a family member did so. A list of known Quaker families was compiled using standardised forms of surnames and parishes of residence. These records were then linked with standardised surnames and parishes from consistory court and Exchequer records. Only 9 per cent of Quaker families suffered from prosecution in these courts. Quaker registrations are reprinted in N. Penny, ed., 'Quakerism in Wiltshire', *Wiltshire Notes and Queries*, vols. 2–7 (starting 1899–1901).
[75] D1/61/1/46 (c. 1747). The patron was one Mr Askew.

was owed. The 'remedy is worse than the disease', one commentator observed. If he encountered a defendant with 'a purse equal to his obstinacy', then the poor clergyman should 'expect to come off with great loss both of time and money, and the scandal of a litigious man into the bargain'. The unidentified author cited a case in which the tithe-owner spent £60 to recover tithes worth only £8. If the clergyman won, then he might find he had to sue for tithes every year.[76] The wise cleric looked for cheaper and quicker remedies. He might try threatening court action in the hope that this would bring defaulters either to pay or to accept arbitration, although we often learn about such tactics only because they failed.[77] The minister could use his pulpit to challenge and threaten his opponents over tithes or other issues. The minister of St Breward (Cornwall), who used the courts to claim tithes from labourers for their wages, abused his congregation in sermons, complaining that 'I poor man am sent to an impudent, stiffenecked people'.[78] Often the initial citation or subpoena had the desired effect, as indicated by a note in the act book that the parties had come to an agreement.[79] The publication of a citation in church appeared to demonstrate ecclesiastical support for the minister's claims. Abel Sheppard had only to initiate action in the church court in 1663 to bring three defaulters to pay their tithes.[80] When presentments of the impropriator and others failed to force them to pay the full stipend and other moneys owing to the vicar of Charminster in Dorset, as a last resort he named 'some of the most obstinate offenders' to Exchequer. This had the desired effect, for one offender immediately paid money in composition, while another agreed to allow the matter to be resolved by arbitration.[81] Statements from witnesses that they had been prepared to pay more than they owed to avoid a suit demonstrate how much they feared court action, although a professed willingness to pay was also a sensible defence.[82] The tithe-owner may also have felt that such people were paying, not too much, but what they owed. Another possible line of attack was to take the tithes without permission, by force if necessary, although this may have been more likely where Quakers were involved.[83] Some desperate ministers, like Robert Randall of Great Bedwyn, even threatened

---

[76] 'The Great Grievance of the Clergy stated, with some Remedies propounded . . .', Tanner MS 80, ff. 122–122v.

[77] PRO, E134, 26 Charles II Easter 11. See Barnes c. Carter, 1670, D1/42/61, ff. 60–3, for the unsuccessful attempt of a lay tithe-farmer to gain arbitration of a tithe dispute.

[78] Devon Record Office, CC178, Box 197. The ministers of Somerford Magna and Tockenham Wick also criticised opponents in sermons, although tithes were not necessarily involved. D1/41/4/39; D1/41/4/35.   [79] Several act book cases contain notes of 'pax' or 'concordantur'.

[80] D5/28, 1662, f. 26. The absence from church of one defaulter suggests that he was a nonconformist.   [81] D5/28, 1674, f. 66; D5/28, 1678, f. 11.

[82] Barnes c. Carter, D1/42/61, f. 60 (1670).

[83] Force was used against Quakers in Lancashire and Staffordshire, where Evans estimates that tithes were taken without official legal proceedings in 93 per cent of Quaker sufferings. Evans, 'Our faithful testimony', pp. 110–11; Morgan, *Lancashire Quakers*.

defaulters with personal violence.[84] The threat of court action or violence undoubtedly meant that some disputes were resolved before they reached the courts, but they nevertheless must have left a legacy of ill-feeling.

A minister sometimes embarked on action in the courts in the hope that taking a firm line and making an example of a defaulter would lead others to conform and so 'would make Peace and good Neighbourhood for the Term of my Life', as a minister from Stebbing wrote.[85] The large number of 'one-off' prosecutions suggests that this strategy often worked. Others were not so fortunate and found that resorting to the courts carried many risks. At best, the minister might lose popularity and gain a reputation for being litigious, placing a barrier between himself and the congregation for whose souls he was responsible. At worst, court action might cause the dispute to escalate. Eric Evans summarises the position well: 'The dilemma for conscientious clergymen was acute. Either they tried to realise their full tithe income (and many calculated that they collected little more than half their dues) and risked fracturing pastoral relationships, or they effectively connived at lowering the value of an estate in which they were only life tenants by forgoing legitimate claims.'[86]

The nature of tithe collection made conflict likely. The assessment of tithes generated numerous occasions for disagreement; these complexities are exposed by the range of issues brought before the courts. It was common for defendants to claim that their estates had formerly been monastery demesne land and were therefore tithe-free.[87] Compositions for tithes created many disputes. If the minister wished to change the rate or collect tithes in kind, defendants might counter by claiming a sixteenth-century modus, which had the force of custom and could not be changed. Rights and customs of collection might differ between different holdings in the parish. The borderline between great and small tithes was also not clear-cut. Some vicars received tithes for wheat from at least some land. Sheep and other stock might be pastured in more than one parish, leading to questions about the ownership of wool and lambs.[88] Tithe assessment was dictated by local custom, as recorded in the terrier. The intricacies of custom and differing memories created countless opportunities for petty disagreement. Few parishes were able to avoid dispute over tithes once in a while, for they had as much to do with the agrarian economy of the parish as with its religious life.

Where tithes in kind were received, the process of setting out was particularly prone to disagreement. The tithe-owner had a right to view the tithe alongside the rest of the yield, and disagreements about the quality of the tithe might result. The cleric might have his servants collect the tithes, although this itself could lead

[84] D5/22/17, ff. 12–30. See p. 33.
[85] *A Defence of the Examination of a Book etc.* (London, 1737), pp. 6–7, quoted by Hunt, *Two Early Political Associations*, p. 69. [86] Evans, 'Tithes', p. 399. [87] 31 Henry VIII c. 13.
[88] These examples are drawn from individual Wiltshire disputes in PRO, E134.

to dispute over payment of the servants' wages.[89] We have seen how the attempt to collect tithes in kind in Avebury led to a fight between the tenant, his men and the vicar's servants. Some ministers became directly involved in collection. A disagreement over the amount set out might lead to an undignified squabble and even violence, generating an atmosphere of ill-feeling which might be slow to dissipate. An incident in Netheravon in 1688 illustrates this point and provides deeper insight into the motivations of clerics. The source of the details is a petition from parishioners who asked for a new minister. The petitioners reported that their vicar Richard Lewis had drawn 'a dangerous weapon' at lamb tithing and threatened to stab a parishioner with it. Determined to protect his rights, he checked every sheaf at wheat tithing and, it was claimed, took the largest in each shock. Lewis insisted on taking only weaned pigs, fearful that a younger pig might die; he was prepared to go into a farm and carry away a pig to settle tithes. The parishioners claimed that the incident over lambs arose when Lewis collected 'more than his due'. Lewis saw things rather differently and called his congregation 'cheateing baggerly rogues'. The minister had to be careful to ensure that he was not cheated, that he received the correct tithes and was not fobbed off with the runt of the litter or with small or rotten wheat sheaves. To his congregation, however, such behaviour made him appear grasping. The Netheravon dispute resulted from a simple disagreement about the amount of tithes to be collected; there is no suggestion that petitioners questioned the principle of paying tithes. Yet it shows the extent to which tithe disputes could poison parish life. A dispute of this sort might have larger consequences both for religious life and for attitudes to the clergy. In Netheravon it resulted in a lay petition against the minister in which villagers threatened to hold private religious meetings if they were not sent a suitable minister. If the petitioners were 'Clergy-Haters', as they were described by the dean of Salisbury, it was the tithing system which had made them so.[90]

Composition eliminated squabbling at the setting-out stage and must have seemed a sensible way to reduce complexity and controversy. Although there was the danger that a composition might later come to be regarded as a modus, it was much safer in the era of stable prices which followed 1660 than it had been in the inflationary sixteenth century.[91] Sadly, many compositions also wound up in the courts. In these circumstances the minister might find the farming out of tithes an attractive alternative because it reduced opportunities for conflict. James Garth, who as vicar of Hilperton was one of the most litigious clerical incumbents, finally decided to lease his tithes. The unfortunate farmer was still chasing unpaid tithes after the vicar's death.[92] If the complexities of collecting

[89] As occurred in Pewsey (see below).
[90] 'Netheravon petition against the vicar, 1681', transcr. C. R. Everitt, *WAM* 45 (June 1930): 84–6. R. A. M. Green, *A Bibliography of Printed Works Relating to Wiltshire 1920–1960* (Trowbridge, 1975), dates the petition in 1688.   [91] Hill, *Economic Problems of the Church*, pp. 93–5.
[92] PRO, E112/907/4.

tithes disrupted the parish once, then they were likely do so again. In Avebury, conflict between the vicar and landlord over tithes erupted again in 1756, after a hiatus of over forty years. James Mayo (the son of the man who succeeded John White) had recently succeeded to the vicarage and was determined to increase the composition for the tithes on Avebury Farm, which remained £4 a year. When Staynor Holford, Sir Richard's grandson, objected, the vicar threatened to collect the two ell ridges of wheat tithes in kind. Holford and Mayo both lived in Avebury, but they corresponded nevertheless. On one memorable day, they sent one another no fewer than three letters, in which the vicar threatened to take his tithes by force and the landlord warned him to stay off his land. Staynor Holford also turned to the extensive documentary evidence and files of correspondence left by his grandfather, only to find that history was repeating itself. The dispute did the reputation of the Church and its clergy no good. Holford complained that he found 'the temper and disposition of the parson to be so intollerably troublesome'.[93]

The minister had to combine two incompatible social roles, those of pastor and tax man. Comparisons between tithes and taxes turned the parson into a tax collector, a familiar target of hatred in early modern Europe, thus tainting both himself and the Established Church.[94] It was precisely the similarity between tithes and taxes which damaged the clergy. Tithe disputes contributed to an atmosphere of tension within the parish. Their influence surpassed the penny-pinching nature of individual disputes. Tithes contributed to the image of parish clergy who held themselves separate from local society and used their position and the courts to persecute the laity in their own interests. As a contemporary author explained, one factor in the readiness of people to think badly of the clergy was their 'taking Tyth, which you know in this sacrilegious Age is a most unpardonable crime'.[95] The failure to pay tithes may not indicate anticlerical resistance to the principle of tithes, but tithe disputes helped to create anticleri-cal villagers, leading them to dislike their minister, the clerical estate of which he was a member, and the Church which he represented.

Disputes over tithes were often linked to other issues. Tithes became far more than a petty irritant eroding lay–clerical relations, for they could have serious implications for the quality of local religious life. By seeking to enforce their rights and incomes and those of their successors, clerics risked acquiring a rep-utation for being litigious, as John White learned to his cost. Some clergymen richly deserved this reputation. Thomas Twittee of Draycot Foliat and Chiseldon

---

[93] WRO 184/2/1; WRO 184/1, Peter Holford to Staynor Holford, 11 Dec. 1756. Peter advised Staynor to consult someone with great experience in the Exchequer (although it was noted that Chancery was hearing more cases then).

[94] Y.-M. Bercé, *The History of Popular Revolts* (Ithaca, N.Y., 1990) P. Burke, *Popular Culture in Early Modern Europe* (New York, 1978).

[95] *The Case of Peoples Duty in Living Under a Scandalous Minister Stated and Resolved* (London, 1684), p. 6.

fought a long and concerted campaign through the courts, lasting over forty years, to recreate tithe rights for himself; he brought over thirty defendants before various courts. He paid a heavy price for his victories, suffering physical assault, verbal abuse and, as we have seen, charges of immorality.[96] Richard Watson, rector of Pewsey, repeatedly sued members of his congregation for their failure to pay tithes and even quarrelled with his servants over the wages they should receive for collecting them.[97] The determination shared by these two clerics is understandable. Tithes were an important part of their income. They were protecting their rights and life style, as well as those of their successors. Whereas a gentleman tithe-owner would usually have other sources of income, the clergy did not. Although for some parish clergy the glebe provided a steady source of income, they were nevertheless substantially dependent upon their parishioners for their livelihood, for tithes and other offerings. Lay contributions were not voluntary; the clergy had recourse to law but could only use it at the cost of lay resentment. Their experience suggests that reformers may have been too optimistic in their belief that congregations would support the ministry voluntarily.

The ten most litigious clerics accounted for one-third of the tithe actions in the bishop's court and the Exchequer Court of Equity. Eric Evans is right to warn us against the impression that tithe-owners were involved in incessant battles.[98] Nonetheless, some clearly were, not only about tithes but also about other issues. Significantly, all but one of the ten most litigious clerics were involved in dispute over another issue as well. Richard Watson, for example, did not limit his forays into the courts to suing for tithes. He quarrelled with parishioners over Sunday work and had difficulty attracting them to either divine service or communion, and he presented these offences at an episcopal visitation. There was considerable personal animosity between the rector and a gentleman farmer, Ralph Smith, and the two men locked horns on several occasions.[99] James Garth of Hilperton filed several lengthy sets of charges against his parish, and was himself the subject of a number of visitation presentments.[100] One in four clerics who brought a suit for substraction of tithes also had a dispute with parishioners over at least one other issue.

John White of Avebury was no exception. His lengthy and bitter disputes with Sir Richard Holford and his tenants over tithes also had religious implications, affecting worship from the start, as we have seen. In 1711 John Ponting and

---

[96] Twittee succeeded in overturning the sixteenth-century merger of the two parishes. J. H. Stevenson 'Will a man rob God?', *WAM* 72/3 (1980): 149–53; 'The Society's MSS. Chiseldon and Draycot', *WAM* 30 (1898): 53; PRO, E134/23&24 Charles II Hil 2; WRO A1/110, M1668; D1/54/10/2 (1683, C&M), f. 45.

[97] A1/110, H1665, f. 149, M1665, f. 180, M1668; A1/160/2, H1664/5; A1/160/3, M1669.

[98] Evans, 'Tithes', p. 398.

[99] D1/54/3/1 (1668, C&M), ff. 4a–5d; D1/39/1/56, f. 132; D1/39/1/57, ff. 76v, 253v.

[100] See chapter 1.

Richard Carswell, whom White had recently sued for withholding tithes, brought the vicar before the bishop's consistory court to answer charges of neglecting his cure of souls. White was charged with neglecting catechism, omitting prayers, refusing to bury Presbyterians and others whom he did not think were worthy, including a 'lewd woman', and refusing to christen others.[101] Presbyterianism contributed to White's dispute with Holford's tenant William Skeate, whom he claimed had set up a conventicle. He accused the farmer of trying to take away his good name as part of a more general attack on the clergy. Skeate was 'such a crosse fellow & hath so great an antipathy against that Clergy', he wrote, that he doubted that he would pay his tithes unless forced.[102] Holford was not, of course, a nonconformist himself. When he found a new tenant, he bent over backwards to accommodate the vicar's dislike of dissenters by refusing a Quaker, even though he thought he would have made a good tenant. With some reservations Holford chose William Rose instead, although his illiteracy was a considerable disadvantage for a landlord who conducted so much business through correspondence.[103] Holford took a personal interest in Anglican worship within the parish. He was displeased that the vicar failed to preach in church when he and his wife made a brief visit in 1696.[104] During his long dispute with the vicar, Holford sought advice from two ecclesiastics, Bishop Burnet and the archdeacon of Wiltshire Cornelius Yeate.[105] There is reason to believe that he encouraged the 1711 correctional suit, for it was most likely his influence that led the Chancellor, Registrar and Proctor to travel to Avebury in August, during one of Holford's annual visits, to take testimony from witnesses and to hear the parties, not the usual practice for such important and busy men. The Chancellor awarded costs to the plaintiffs and warned the minister that if he received further complaints he would compel him to do his duty. Holford's attempts to persuade White that he had been treated fairly and should improve his prayers met with a predictably angry reply from the vicar.[106] With the arrival of a more cooperative incumbent, Holford took steps to promote church worship. He instructed the new vicar James Mayo to attract children to catechism by paying them to attend and promised to refund the minister's expenditure.[107]

It was perhaps inevitable that tithe disputes would find their way into the church and would affect religious life. Some clerics brought them into the church by using their sermons to threaten members of their congregations with court action. Parishioners might make the link themselves, refusing to receive communion from a minister with whom they were out of charity or even to attend

---

[101] D1/39/1/67; D1/42/68. See chapter 9.   [102] JW to RH, 27 Jan. 1695[/6].
[103] RH to Richard Chandler, 2 June, 15 June 1709; RH to WS, 23 Feb. 1709[/10], RH to John Rose (JR), 7 June 1710.   [104] JW to RH, received 12 Oct. 1696.
[105] WRO 184/1, RH to JW, 11 Jan. 1695[/6], Cornelius Yeate to RH, 28 Feb. 1697[/8].
[106] WRO 184/8. Holford refused White's request to mediate in the dispute.
[107] John Mayo to RH, 16 June 1715. Mayo reported that he doled out 8s. 5d.

church when he was officiating.[108] At Edburton (Sussex) a dispute over tithes led parishioners to stay away from church. They told the minister that they would not take the sacrament unless he accepted the amount of tithes they were prepared to pay. The minister, George Keith, related their obstinacy directly to anti-clericalism: 'they so little value the Gospel and the ministry of it that they think what they pay, or are comanded to pay of Tithe, is meer Oppression, and a sort of Robbery'. Keith remained obdurate; the tithes they had offered were 'farr Inferiour to the true value and had I consented to them would have been a great injury and ['wrong' crossed out] loss to my sucesse[r]s as well as to me'.[109] Conversely, the proper payment of tithes or of other moneys owing to the minister might facilitate the restoration of clerical services in a parish, particularly when non-payment had made it impossible to maintain a minister. In Charminster clerical poverty, exacerbated by the failure of inhabitants to pay what they owed, had damaging results upon religious worship, so that communion was administered only once in twenty years. The arrival of a more persistent minister led to the return of regular services, and the minister William Willis and the churchwardens reported that proper observance of the sacrament had already attracted fifty-five communicants. Thereafter, as we have seen, Willis had some success in pursuing his rightful income.[110]

Parishioners might also refuse to pay tithes to a minister whom they regarded as unworthy to receive them on account of his pastoral negligence or scandalous behaviour. This was not a new idea. In 1604 the House of Commons had passed a bill which would have allowed congregations to withhold tithes from any minister who was unable to provide a testimonial to his moral conduct and ability to preach.[111] Although this bill was rejected by the Lords, it expressed the principle that clergymen received tithes and offerings in return for the pastoral and sacerdotal services that they provided. In the words of a maxim cited by Gilbert Burnet, 'the Benefice is given for the Office'. So, the bishop reasoned, 'men will not have great Scruples in denying the Benefice, where the Office is neglected, or ill performed'.[112] The clergy themselves made the link between offerings and offices when they insisted upon payments for burials, marriages and baptisms. Parishioners resented such fees and occasionally presented a minister for refusing to perform these services until they had been paid. The coincidence of Easter offerings and communion might also lead the two to be linked. Incumbents were entitled to tithes because these were among the property rights of the benefice in which they had a life interest, but the distinction between the benefice and its pastoral duties was easily blurred. The canons already specified clerical offences

[108] See chapter 8.
[109] Bodleian Library, MS Rawl C743, f. 19, 11 Oct. 1712. Keith is better known for controversy with the Society of Friends, of which he had formerly been a member.
[110] D5/28, 1674, f. 66; D5/28, 1678, f. 11. The documents leave unclear whether this case concerned tithes or other payments.   [111] Hill, *Economic Problems of the Church*, p. 160.
[112] Burnet, *Pastoral Care*, p. xxvii.

which could lead to sequestration from the benefice. During the Civil Wars and Commonwealth, the sequestration of 'scandalous' and 'malignant' clerics seeemed to confirm the view that parsons who misbehaved did not need to be paid, even though their replacements, lay tithe-owners and the Trustees for the Maintenance of Ministers continued to collect tithes.[113] Some people drew the conclusion that those thought to be guilty of political, religious or moral offences were not entitled to receive their tithes, even if they had not been ejected. Thus John Brownjohn of Stowford in Wingfield refused to pay his tithes because he alleged that the cleric Edward Cornelius was a royalist. Brownjohn read articles against the minister in church, and he went from house to house forbidding other residents to pay their tithes and threatening those who did so with gaol.[114] Parishioners might also refuse tithes to a minister who excluded them from communion.[115] The principle that tithes were paid for clerical services survived the Restoration. The inhabitants of Foxham chapelry were reluctant to pay their tithes to their vicar because he would not provide them with their own curate.[116] It was no coincidence that the obstruction of communion by the residents of Knooke left their pluralist and non-resident curate without his Easter offerings.[117] In Colerne the squire organised a tithe strike against the drunken, abusive and violent incumbent, which he ended only when the minister confessed his faults, was canonically admonished, and promised to reform.[118] Tithes and offerings were so closely bound up with religious issues in such cases that it is difficult to separate them.

Although the security of the clergy in their benefices was restored after 1660, the Act of Uniformity nevertheless added new requirements to those that a minister had to fulfil in order to be eligible to hold a benefice and receive its tithes. In 1697 in the Wiltshire case of *Harris v. Adye*, the Exchequer confirmed the principle that tithes were a fee for services. Joseph Adye claimed that the rector had no right to his tithes because he had not read the Thirty-Nine Articles at his induction as required by the Act of Uniformity. Although there was evidence that the Revd John Harris had indeed not read the articles, the barons found for the rector on the grounds that 'having done the work he ought to have the wages'. Adye's argument had been turned on its head; the fact that his neighbours had paid their own tithes was seen as evidence enough that Harris was the rightful rector. The link between the clerical cure of souls and the receipt of tithes could

---

[113] James, 'The political importance of the tithes controversy', pp. 8, 10. See A1/160, vol. I, M1649, for a complaint that many were behind in paying tithes.

[114] E134, 13 Charles II, Mich 4, Edward Cornelius c. John Brownejohn. Brownejohn told others that if they paid Cornelius, they would have to pay him as well. Cornelius had been instituted by Duppa in November 1645. D1/2/22, f. 1v.

[115] As occurred in St Bartholomew, Exchange, in London, where a minister withheld the sacraments from parishioners who refused to worship with the Independent 'intruders' accompanying him, and they retaliated by withholding their tithes. W. A. Shaw, *A History of the English Church during the Civil Wars and under the Commonwealth 1640–1660* (London, 1900), vol. II, pp. 132–3. [116] See pp. 86–7. [117] See pp. 109–12. [118] D1/41/4/39.

not have been made more clearly.[119] In 1722 it was claimed that payment was not required when the minister was non-resident.[120]

The unpopularity of tithes could not help but affect the position of the parson in his parish, while confirming the prejudice that members of the clergy were more interested in personal profit than in the souls of those under their care.[121] There was potential for conflict in every parish where tithes were collected, and in some places disputes occurred repeatedly. In practice, tithes did not cause trouble in every parish, but references to disputes in the diaries of such eighteenth-century clerics as John Lewis, James Woodforde and James Newton suggest that conflict of some sort was a common experience.[122] The minister had to choose between his income and a quiet life. Pursuance of tithes through the courts could give him a reputation for being litigious and might have ill effects for worship, and the laity might retaliate with their own court actions and presentments. The reliance of ministers, both rich and poor, upon tithes for their income was a structural weakness in the Church. Concentration upon the minutiae of tithe collection distracted the parson from his pastoral duties and could poison social relations and worship, enhancing the unpopularity of the clergy and the Church. Although this was not a new problem after the Restoration, such disputes contributed to a climate in which people were prepared to think badly of the clergy, confirming their reputation of being quick to resort to the courts, whether concerning tithes or nonconformity.

[119] Eagle and Younge, *A Collection of the Reports of Cases*, vol. I, p. 624; PRO, IND 1/16835 (case 183). The defendant's name is variously spelled Adge, Ady and Aey. Harris appears to have been presented to Easton Grey twice, in 1683 and 1697, and the failure to be inducted properly the second time was used as the pretext for non-payment.

[120] The defence cited 13 Elizabeth c. 20. Eagle and Younge, *A Collection of the Reports of Cases*, vol. I, p. 816.

[121] Compare J. A. I. Champion, *The Pillars of Priestcraft Shaken: The Church of England and its Enemies, 1660–1730* (Cambridge, 1992), p. 195.

[122] WRO 1981/1; J. Woodforde, *The Diary of a Country Parson 1758–1802*, ed. J. Beresford (Oxford, 1978); G. Hannah, ed., *The Deserted Village: The Diary of an Oxfordshire Rector, James Newton, of Nunton Courtenay 1736–86* (Stroud, 1992), pp. 37, 171.

7

The nonconformist threat

Throughout the century after the Restoration nonconformity appeared to many clergymen to represent the greatest threat to the Church of England. Separatists were a constant reminder of the failure of the Restoration settlement of religion.[1] After 1689, the issue of the treatment of dissent remained important as an ideological fault line dividing the political elite between High Church Tories who wished to restore the monopoly of the Church establishment and anticlerical Whigs who decried the intolerance of churchmen. Nonconformity was defined by the refusal to accept the patterns of worship laid down by the liturgy of the Church of England. The 1662 Prayer Book confirmed such contentious elements of worship as saying set prayers, wearing priestly vestments, making the ritual sign of the cross at baptism, and showing reverence at the name of Jesus, to which the puritans had objected before the Civil Wars. The Act of Uniformity made the Prayer Book central to the definition of Anglicanism, and the Church sought to stamp out separatism by detecting and disciplining anyone who failed to attend church or to observe church ceremonies.[2] The Test and Corporation Acts in turn elevated the importance of communion, particularly after the passage of the Act of Toleration. Yet this insistence upon uniformity had negative effects, for it contributed to the unpopularity of the Church, both locally and nationally. In country parishes, the clergy were determined to stamp out sectarianism and they embarked on a campaign to return separatists to the Church, if necessary by force. They were disappointed to find, however, that they were able to attract relatively little support for the persecution of dissenters from the laity. This not only undermined the clerical campaign, but it also isolated the clergy from the parish community and increased their own vulnerability.

[1] T. Harris, P. Seaward and M. Goldie, eds., *The Politics of Religion in Restoration England* (Oxford, 1990).
[2] J. Spurr, *The Restoration Church of England, 1646-1689* (New Haven and London, 1991).

RAMSBURY

The parish of Ramsbury, in eastern Wiltshire, was a focus for nonconformity.[3] In 1669 Ramsbury housed a Presbyterian conventicle with which no fewer than seven different teachers were associated.[4] The conventicle grew from between 50 and 60 hearers in 1669 to 160 in 1715, when it included a number of leading parishioners.[5] The leadership of Henry Dent from the Restoration until Toleration gave the meeting much of its stability. Dent had been incumbent of Hannington during the Commonwealth. After his deprivation in 1660, he went to Ramsbury, where the incumbent John Wild gave him a warm welcome. Wild allowed Dent to assist him and to teach children in the church, but Dent 'was excus'd from reading the Prayers, which Mr. Wild took wholly upon himself'.[6] John Wilson, who succeeded as rector in 1664, was far less sympathetic to the Presbyterians, and he sought to suppress the conventicle that Dent kept 'publiquely & openly upon Sundayes at times of [divine] service'.[7] Yet Wilson was unable to secure the cooperation of the churchwardens and constables. He complained that 'none of the officers will do anything to sup[press] except a poore tythingman, and what can he doe a[lone]'.[8] Although officers presented a few Quakers,[9] they were reluctant to prosecute Henry Dent and his Presbyterian meeting. The wardens refused to present Dent in 1670, and in 1682 the Quarter Sessions Grand Jury presented a constable for failing to present the conventicle and for attending it himself.[10] Wilson found that he had to take action himself in order to get the Presbyterians prosecuted. On one occasion, he called upon the constable and churchwardens to break up the conventicle and refused to begin divine service until they had done so.[11] In 1669, on the instructions of the dean of Salisbury, Wilson presented Dent and five others for holding private meetings in their homes,[12] and he instigated further presentments in 1674, 1677 and 1680.[13] Yet prosecution failed to stop the meetings. Dent was excommunicated three times, but each time he was able to buy absolution.

---

[3] Turner, *Original Records*, p. 126; CSPD, 1671–2, 1672–3; Evans List, 1715–29, Dr Williams's Library, MS 38.4, f. 124.

[4] Turner, *Original Records*, p. 126. Since it lay in the jurisdiction of the dean, Ramsbury was not included in the Salisbury diocese returns for the Compton Census of 1676, so figures for the number of conformists and nonconformists are not available.

[5] Turner, *Original Records*, p. 126; Dr Williams's Library, MS 38.4, f. 124. Supporters in 1715 included three gentlemen, three yeomen, nine farmers and twenty-one traders.

[6] Matthews, *Calamy Revised*, pp. 162–3.

[7] Dent also preached regularly in the neighbouring county of Berkshire and, on occasion, in fields and woods. D5/28, 1675, f. 3; Matthews, *Calamy Revised*, pp. 162–3.   [8] D5/28, 1675, f. 3.

[9] E.g. in 1662, 1662, 1668, 1669, 1670 and 1673. D5/28.   [10] A1/110, M1682.

[11] Matthews, *Calamy Revised*, pp. 162–3.

[12] Thomas Freemen and three others were tried in the dean's court for holding conventicles in 1669, apparently as a result of the presentment. D5/22/15, ff. 92v–98.

[13] The churchwardens appear, however, to have presented Presbyterians on their own initiative in 1675 and 1676. D5/28.

The vicar came to regret his presentment in 1669 of those who held conventi-cles, for he found himself presiding over a hostile parish. In the following year he turned to the dean for assistance, writing: 'It also behoveth me to looke to my owne safety, there are some in my parish, who . . . will be ready enough to take advantage if they see me act contrary to law, because at yo[u]r Wor[shi]ps comand I set my hand to a presentm[en]t exhibited against them for holding con-venticles.'[14] John Wilson had to ask the dean for help again six years later after his surplice was stolen. Since the wardens 'delay to provide another' he was obliged to officiate without a surplice in violation of the canons. Wilson was anxious that his failure to wear a surplice would provide his parishioners with a pretext to discredit him. 'If I continue to officiate without one,' he wrote, 'I feare some will endeavour to doe me a prejudice: I live in a parish much divided, and though many will not obey the Law yet I feare they will make use of i[t to] doe me hurt.'[15]

THE CLERGY AND NONCONFORMITY

The Compton Census, conventicle returns and licences in 1669–72, licences for dissenters' places of worship after Toleration, and court prosecutions all point to the presence of a substantial core of nonconformity in Wiltshire.[16] Dissent was a widespread problem for the Church, affecting both urban and rural par-ishes. Seventy percent of parishes listed in the Compton Census identified at least one person who failed to conform. Sixty-nine parishes had at least one conventicle in 1669–72. In the twenty years after the Act of Toleration seventy-one parishes requested a licence for a meeting place. Dissent was not evenly distributed, of course. It was strongest in towns, in larger pastoral parishes where control from above was weak, and in clothing parishes, although it was not limited to such places.[17] These factors coincided in north-western Wiltshire, an area of heavy clay soils suitable for pastoral farming, where the putting-out system employed workers in rural parishes and encouraged com-munications between a cluster of towns such as Trowbridge, Bradford-on-Avon, Melksham and Chippenham. This was the 'cheese country', where the

[14] D5/31/1 (22 Sept. 1670).   [15] D5/28, 1675, ff. 2–3.
[16] Whiteman, *Compton Census*; Turner, *Original Records*; CSPD 1671–2, pp. 305ff., 1672–3; A1/250, printed in *Wiltshire Dissenters' Meeting House Certificates and Registrations, 1689–1852*, ed. J. Chandler, Wiltshire Record Series 40 (Devizes, 1985); Evans List, 1715–29, Dr Williams's Library, MS 38.4, f. 124. Nonconformity in Wiltshire is the topic of a valuable recent thesis. H. Lancaster, 'Nonconformity and Anglican dissent in Restoration Wiltshire, 1660–1689' (unpub-lished Ph.D. thesis, Bristol University, 1995). I am grateful to Martin Ingram for drawing this work to my attention.
[17] D. A. Spaeth, 'Parsons and parishioners: lay-clerical conflict and popular piety in Wiltshire vil-lages, 1660–1740' (unpublished Ph.D. thesis, Brown University, 1985), ch. 7; G. C. Smith, '"The knowing multitude": popular culture and the evangelical revival in Wiltshire, 1739-1850' (unpub-lished Ph.D. thesis, University of Toronto, 1992).

land was 'low and flat, being a rich, enclosed country, full of rivers and towns, and infinitely populous'.[18] The antiquarian John Aubrey thought that its inhabitants fed 'chiefly on milke meats, which cooles their braines too much, and heats their inventions. These circumstances make them melancholy, contemplative and malicious', encouraging religious zeal and litigiousness.[19] Historians have agreed that the cheese country was a region of economic and cultural independence.[20] The Presbyterians and Quakers were particularly strong in Wiltshire. The county was one of the few in England to establish a system of classes during the Commonwealth, and 60 per cent of licences went to Presbyterians after the Declaration of Indulgence.[21] The Quakers naturally requested no licences in 1672, but the census of conventicles in 1669 and their own records indicate that they had as many as thirty meetings in Wiltshire.[22] Baptists were also present in force, although there were fewer Independent meetings. Conventicles such as the one in Warminster where Presbyterians, Independents and Anabaptists were said to meet promiscuously suggest that in 1669 the differences between sects might be slight.[23] Wiltshire was also home to 250 or so Catholics, who were largely concentrated in a few parishes in the south-western corner of the county where they had support from recusant gentry families.[24]

Despite the concern of ecclesiastical authorities, few reluctantly conformist clergy who might have been sympathetic to separatists remained in benefices after 1662.[25] Examples of amicable co-existence between Anglican incumbents and ejected nonconformists, such as existed for a short time in Ramsbury, were rare.[26] The parish clergy took vigorous action against separatism, seeking to prosecute those who stayed away from church or attended conventicles. There were several reasons for their strong action against dissent. They were shocked by the transgression of the laws of church and state, which violated the principle of uniformity of worship. Thus Abel Sheppard of Burbage asked that one antagonist be prosecuted 'in the court that he may know there is a law for such contemners of gods service'.[27] They were also concerned that dissent would lead to the growth of faction in their parishes, a worry that was understandable in the

[18] Daniel Defoe, *A Tour through the Whole Island of Great Britain* (Harmondsworth, 1978), p. 260.
[19] John Aubrey, *Natural History of Wiltshire* (New York, 1969), p. 11.
[20] J. Thirsk, 'Seventeenth-century agriculture and social change', in *Seventeenth Century England: Society in an Age of Revolution*, pp. 72-109, ed. P. S. Seaver (New York, 1976); D. E. Underdown, *Revel, Riot, and Rebellion: Popular Politics and Culture in England, 1603–1660* (Oxford, 1985).
[21] Lancaster, 'Nonconformity and Anglican dissent', p. 1; CSPD 1671–2.
[22] From references to meetings in WRO 1699/18; Quaker registrations reprinted in N. Penny, ed., 'Quakerism in Wiltshire', *Wiltshire Notes and Queries*, vols. 2–7; and the catalogue of Monthly Meeting records in Friends' House Library.
[23] Turner, *Original Records*, p. 121.
[24] J. A. Williams, *Catholic Recusancy in Wiltshire 1660–1791* (London, 1968), pp. 253–60.
[25] See pp. 114–15.   [26] Cf. Lancaster, 'Nonconformity and Anglican dissent', p. 84.
[27] D5/28, 1662, f. 26.

immediate aftermath of the Interregnum.[28] Nonconformity threatened the spiritual unity of the parish according to which all parishioners were members of the same church and worshipped together, a situation which allegedly had existed before the Civil Wars. It seems likely that some incumbents wished for revenge, particularly if they had suffered during the Commonwealth. More importantly, prosecution was part of a strategy intended to stamp out separatism and to bring dissenters back into the Church, where in time they might become faithful participants. After all, nonconformity of the scale being experienced at that time was unprecedented. Many clergy must have believed that it was only a matter of time before these prodigal sons and daughters found their way back to their mother church. The basis of the clerical strategy was the belief expressed by the Revd Nathaniel Aske that 'constant hearers doe many tymes become conscientious hearers'. This position was consistent with the Protestant view that divine service and sermon were not just intended to worship and praise God, but were a means of edification and conversion as well. Thus proper religious observance and correct religious beliefs were closely related. As Aske wrote, 'being in Gods walk it is usuall for God to meet them'.[29]

Clerics tried to reclaim sectaries through informal persuasion, as they were encouraged to do by the episcopal visitation queries of 1662.[30] Committed dissenters treated these overtures with scorn and abuse, as Sheppard found when he chided Peirson for his absence from church.[31] Thomas Lambert exhorted Mary Caraway of Boyton 'to return to the unity of the Church, & to state those scruples (that had caused her dissent) to her own Parish Minister, who was able to give her satisfacon in her doubtings'. Caraway spoke for many in her reply: 'If the blind lead the blind both will fall in the Ditch.'[32] When informal methods failed, parish clergy were obliged to resort to harsher tactics. Their experience is summed up well in the example of Nathaniel Aske, who was rector of Somerford Magna. Aske believed that nonconformity was a serious problem in his parish, and he prosecuted seventeen inhabitants in 1672–3. Although there is reason to doubt that he was correct in thinking that all of those whom he presented were nonconformists, the letters he wrote to episcopal officers nevertheless provide insight into his motivations and those of the clergy more generally.[33] In October 1673 he wrote to explain why he had brought the prosecutions. Aske reported that he had long delayed presenting his parishioners, hoping 'to overcome them by love', but had had little success. 'If that would availe,' he wrote, 'they had all

---

[28] See, for example, A1/110, M1681 (Barford St Martin) and D1/54/11/4 (1686, Subdean, Salisbury St Martins).   [29] D1/41/1/17 (6 Oct. 1673).

[30] 'Second Report of the Commissioners appointed to inquire into the rubrics, orders and directions for regulating the course and conduct of public worship . . .', *Parliamentary Papers, House of Commons*, 1867–8, vol. XXXVIII, pp. 610–13, esp. title 3, query 4; D1/54/1/3 (1662, A&C), f. 22.

[31] D5/28, 1662, f. 26.   [32] D1/54/1/4 (1662, W&W), f. 32b. See also D5/28, 1662, f. 26.

[33] D1/41/1/17. Aske's poor relations with his congregation, who claimed that they were loyal to the Church, are discussed in chapter 8.

been my staunch freinds ere this day.' Instead, his forbearance had had the opposite effect, and 'taught them so to contemn mee'. Others had the same experience. Henry Johnson of Devizes observed that those who stayed away from
church deserved 'litl favour for they be groud the more obstinate by indulgence'.[34] Aske drew the conclusion that 'I dare not handle these Nettles gently
lest they sting mee', and it was for this reason that he turned for help to the 'court
of reformacon'. Since dissenters would not come to church on their own, ministers used prosecution and the ultimate punishment of excommunication to force
them to come.

Yet this did not necessarily mean that they tried to punish every dissenter. The
threat of punishment and the possibility of its relaxation were carefully used as
stick and carrot. Clergymen feared that if they presented every dissenter, then
they might all obstinately stand together against the Church. Thus Aske decided
that he 'would not present too many att a time lest it should encourage them all
to be contumacious'.[35] Some offenders were prosecuted as examples to the rest,
in the hope that the threat of prosecution would return them to the Church.
James Garth of Hilperton presented a few 'Phanaticks' and entreated the bishop
'that they may be prceded against wthall speed that they may be exemplary to
others'.[36] Edward Wells of Corsham adopted different tactics. He named eighty-
seven offenders and asked for them all to be excommunicated, so that he could
then announce the excommunication of individuals selectively. Wells agreed that
dissenting leaders made the best examples.[37] Nathaniel Aske directed special
attention to the matriarch Rebecca Mayo: 'She is the main fomenter of
Phanatacisme in the parish,' he reported, 'and if reclaimed would have many followers.'[38] Prosecution was a delicate tool that could be used to sway doubtful
parishioners. Bartholomew Shorthose of Bishops Lavington was convinced that
presentment had been crucial in helping persuade Francis Norris to bring his
7-year-old child to be baptised, making it possible for him to conform without
shaming himself in the eyes of other dissenters. 'Sir,' he wrote, 'I verily beleeve
that hee was partly glad thereof, as supposing that his presumed feare of the
vi[si]tation should take away or at least diminish the shame of his yeelding now
unto the church in that wch had bin soe long forborne.'[39] If prosecution set an
example, so also did mercy to those who reformed. Despite his belief in the need
for firm action, Henry Johnson of Devizes asked that an offender who had conformed be discharged so that his example 'may be an incouragement to some
others to reforme'.[40]

The clergy's hopes were ultimately to be disappointed, for prosecution failed
to bring dissenters back into the Church of England. The Act of Toleration

[34] D1/41/1/41 (8 Jan. 1664/5).   [35] D1/41/1/17 (18 July 1673).   [36] D1/54/8 (18 Jan. 1675/6).
[37] D1/54/6/1 (1674, M), f. 76 (Corsham); D5/31/1 (Horningsham). Wells noted that there were many
    other offenders. The churchwardens presented none of the absenters, naming only two bastards.
[38] D1/41/1/17 (29 Nov. 1673).   [39] D1/41/1/41 (10 Oct. 1664).   [40] D1/41/1/41 (8 Jan. 1664/5).

confirmed their separation from the Church. The number of parishes that licensed a place of worship in the years following Toleration was virtually unchanged from the number with a conventicle in 1669–72. There were several explanations for the failure of prosecution. Excommunication, the Church's only weapon against nonconformity, was largely ineffective against those who had already chosen not to attend church and might force partial conformists into full nonconformity. For this reason, the Calne wardens declared their intention of suing for a writ *de excommunicato capiendo*, 'for otherwise a bare Excommunication would be but a Cloake for their not coming to church'.[41] Excommunication was weakened further by its widespread use against both dissenters and those who were merely rendered contumacious by their failure to respond to court citations. Those who wished to escape the civil penalties of excommunication could purchase absolution with an ease which alarmed prosecutors and amused dissenters. In Devizes the congregation was astonished that 'such noatorious offenders should have such favor from my Lords court whoe maketh it their buesnes both since & before to disgrace it'. After their absolution was read in church the dissenters 'bouldly went to their meeting laffing & skofing at those of the Church of England'. The warden Ewan Walker wrote to express his anxiety about the ill consequences of the failure to execute the laws made against such 'phannatiks'.[42]

The ineffectiveness of excommunication was an old problem; the Elizabethan Church had experienced the same difficulties.[43] Yet it cannot provide a complete explanation for the failure of prosecution after the Restoration because the secular courts, which had harsher punishments at their disposal, were even more ineffective. The inconsistency of ecclesiastical and secular superiors was a more serious problem.[44] The clergy were confused by the ecclesiastical courts' tendency to blow hot and cold, which was matched by similar inconsistency from Whitehall. Although the clergy were encouraged to prosecute offenders, court officials sometimes stopped the processes they had begun. Clerics expressed their frustration in letters to court officials, advising that leniency would not bring dissenters back to the Church. Nathaniel Aske wrote to complain about the bishop's 'unparelled patience, and meekness which he exercised towards my neighbors'. 'Alass, I fear that is not the way to deal with such rough dispositeons as theirs are.'[45] Clerics could not understand the failure of the courts to deal firmly with dissent, particularly when they had presented in response to ecclesiastical instructions. William Meaden wrote to the dean, 'I beseech you, consider the many journeyes, & the great expence, & charge I have been at, & the

---

[41] D5/28, 1683, f. 1. The writ ordered the sheriff to arrest and imprison the offenders.
[42] D1/41/1/22 (1671).
[43] R. A. Marchant, *The Church under the Law* (Cambridge, 1969), pp. 226–7.
[44] JPs and even Assize judges were unenthusiastic about prosecuting dissent. Lancaster, 'Nonconformity and Anglican dissent', pp. 109, 114–15, 120, 342.
[45] D1/41/1/17 (6 Oct. 1673).

occasion of all is, for obeying yo[u]r comands, in prsenting the conventicles, &
other disorders.'[46] To add insult to injury, ministers sometimes found themselves
blamed for the presence of dissenters in their parish. Edward Wells of Corsham
tried to persuade the bishop and his officials to excommunicate the long list of
dissenters he presented, for in his opinion the bishop's 'sparing them in this much
has done great harme'. Wells was confused about the lack of support he was
getting, and he asked to be informed 'if I have urged anything inconvenient'. If
the court failed to act, then 'pray say noe more 'tis my fault I have irregulars in
my parish: as you intimated to me when last at Salisbury'.[47]

The years 1670–2 exemplified the inconsistency of prosecution. The Second
Conventicle Act of 1670 initiated a brief period of severe prosecution in the
secular courts in which conviction based on the reports of informers played an
essential part.[48] Yet Charles II's Declaration of Indulgence led to the licensing of
numerous conventicles and, in the opinion of some, emptied the churches. Two
months after its publication, the vicar and wardens of Westbury noted 'the great
defect of receiving the Sacrament of the Lords Supper since the Kings
Proclamation of Indulgence'.[49] Nathaniel Aske complained that 'This late declaration of indulgence hath made the church empty'.[50] Although this was not the
full story, the Declaration confirmed clerical doubts about the political will of
their superiors to prosecute nonconformity.

Even more serious was the failure of parish clergymen to secure support for
their campaign against dissenters from the laity, and particularly from churchwardens and other local officers. Churchwardens were in theory the clergy's
natural allies in the parish, and the courts relied upon their co-operation. Yet
complaints about the neglect of churchwardens were common. Wardens were
often reluctant to present their neighbours, particularly when nonconformity
was concerned. Indeed, repugnance against the persecution of their neighbours
contributed to the decline in effectiveness of visitations. The failure of churchwardens to co-operate should not be overstated. Some wardens did present
parishioners who were absent from church or failed to receive communion.
Evidence of the negligence of wardens was sometimes provided by fellow
wardens or sidesmen. The negligent warden of Devizes St John was compared
unfavourably with a warden of the neighbouring parish of Devizes St Mary who
was 'an honest man . . . & one that made a conscien[ce] of his oath'.[51] Ewen
Walker, who was a warden for Devizes St John in 1678, acknowledged that there
was a long-standing problem of non-presentment and offered his assistance in
'the reforming of many of them whoe have slept secuerly under the neglect of
endeferent churchwardens preseeding'.[52] A Westbury warden presented that his
'partner churchwarden Stephen Blatch is falce forsworen he haveing not

[46] D5/31/1.   [47] D1/54/6/1 (1674, M), f. 76.   [48] 22 Charles II c.1.
[49] D25/12 (30 May 1672).   [50] D1/41/1/17 (18 July 1673).
[51] D1/41/1/41 (7 Oct. 1664, 24 Oct. 1664).   [52] D1/41/1/20 (c. 1678).

prsented' offenders.[53] The Calne wardens urged the court to take action quickly while they were still in office, presumably because they feared that their successors would be less co-operative.[54] These examples in themselves demonstrate how little reliance the parish clergy could place upon the churchwardens to present religious offenders. The vicar of Latton thought that the wardens took 'no care at all to see who of the parishioners are absent from divine service and sermon for they thems[elves] are peccant herein' and reported that 'they have not as yet presented any that come late to Church'.[55] Henry Johnson complained that the wardens of Devizes St John pretended there were 'none that Refuse to baptize their children, very few of those that absent themselves from church, noe Annoyances about the church'.[56]

The secular courts experienced similar problems in persuading constables and juries to make presentments. JPs attempted to use petty sessions to stimulate greater diligence in local officers, with disappointing results. In 1670 John Eyre reported the failure of a petty sessions he had held with Sir Edward Hungerford to detect those who absented themselves from church. He wrote, 'We found, as we have often before, that the officers were more ready to perjure themselves than give true presentments, by which your lordship may judge that the tumultuous meetings will hardly be suppressed by neighbouring officers.'[57] A decade later Sir James Long was to try petty sessions again.[58] The Second Conventicle Act exposed the failure of constables by allowing convictions on the basis of reports from informers. In 1671 informers brought 281 prosecutions before Wiltshire magistrates for attendance at conventicles. Edward Hungerford, JP, certified the convictions of ten officers for failing to disperse conventicles in Chippenham and North Bradley on the testimony of two informers, and another constable was indicted for neglecting to suppress conventicles in Bromham. The clergy were not slow to see the potential of the new legislation to authorise them to take direct action. The rector of Luckington, William Hieron, summoned the tithingmen to break up a conventicle in the parish. Edward Cornelius, the incumbent of Wingfield, was one of three men whose information led to the conviction of a conventicle in nearby North Bradley.[59] Yet the unpopularity of informers meant that they could not be an effective long-term solution. Nine of the ten parish officers appealed against their convictions and were cleared at the next Sessions.[60] Local support for prosecution continued to be absent even at the height of the Tory backlash which followed the Exclusion Crisis. In 1683 the jurymen of Alderbury hundred were presented for refusal to present a Quaker meeting. Aware of the limitations of their own officers, the Quarter Sessions Grand Jury appealed to the bishop and dean to instruct

[53] D25/12 (July 1682). [54] D5/28, 1683, f. 1. [55] D1/54/3/1 (1668, C&M), f. 16.
[56] D1/41/1/41 (24 Oct. 1664). [57] CSPD, 1670, p. 417. [58] A1/110, T1680.
[59] A1/110, T1676, T1671.
[60] A1/110, H and M1671 (convictions of conventicles certified by JPs, and appeals); A1/110, H1671 (indictments).

their ecclesiastical courts to excommunicate all dissenters within the diocese, 'that they may have noe share in the government of this kingdome unlesse they will conforme to the lawes in Church and State'.[61]

A look at the quantitative evidence confirms that the ecclesiastical courts were far more effective than their secular counterparts except when the latter were supported by the Conventicle Act. In 1674 churchwardens presented 745 people for absence from church at the bishop's triennial visitations.[62] At the Quarter Sessions for the same year the hundred constables and juries presented only 65 people for absence from church.[63] This was a particularly bad year for the secular courts, and they did better a decade later in 1683 when hundred constables and juries presented 271 people for absence from church, attending conventicles, or popish recusancy. In the same year, churchwardens presented 583 absenters.[64] Even in 1683, when the political significance of religion was at the forefront of many minds, the church courts proved more effective than the secular courts in detecting dissenters.[65] These figures explain why the Grand Jury felt it necessary to appeal for action by the ecclesiastical courts.

Yet the visitations still succeeded in detecting only a minority of offenders. Churchwardens presented only around one in five dissenters, and they often presented fewer.[66] Because Quarter Sessions presentments often repeated the same individuals, they added little to this total.[67] It might be suggested that this is exactly the result one would expect from a prosecution strategy that was based upon presenting a few individuals as examples to the others. Yet many churchwardens avoided presenting anyone at all, even though dissenters were present. The bishop's visitation in 1674 elicited presentments against nonconformists from 86 parishes, including those where the minister joined the churchwardens in making the presentment. Two years later the Compton Census revealed nonconformists in 156 parishes. Almost half of parishes where dissenters were present had failed to present them in 1674. Visitations were almost as ineffective in 1683, when only 91 parishes presented any dissenters. Parishes where nonconformity was strongest were less likely to present nonconformists than those where it was weak.[68]

---

[61] A1/110, Hil 1683.   [62] These figures comprise 644 dissenters and 101 popish recusants.
[63] Individuals who were presented by both constables and hundred juries are counted only once.
[64] These figures comprise 516 presented for absence or non-receipt of communion, 21 popish recusants, and 46 negligent churchmen.
[65] For a more detailed chronology of prosecution see Lancaster, 'Nonconformity and Anglican dissent', chs. 5, 12.
[66] This calculation is based on the total of around 3,000 dissenters recorded in the Compton Census's totals for Wiltshire. Since some incumbents counted the entire population while others included only those who had reached the age of communion, the totals provided in the census are not entirely satisfactory. Whiteman, *Compton Census*, pp. 106–11, 118–19.
[67] In 1674, 48 of the 65 absenters named at Quarter Sessions were also presented to the bishop.
[68] In parishes where nonconformists were present but comprised less than 5 per cent of the population, over half (53 per cent) of the presentments mentioned dissenters. In those where nonconformists comprised more than 10 per cent of the population only one-third (32 per cent) of presentments mentioned dissenters. Calculations are based on Whiteman, *Compton Census*, and

In some cases the failure of churchwardens to present can be explained by their fear of their neighbours, for they knew that presentment would not be popular. In the years following the Restoration they faced violence or prosecution for doing their duty. Samuel Cusse, a Berwick St John warden, was assaulted and had his clothes torn from his back when he tried to expel a deprived minister in 1662, and a Wokingham warden was prosecuted for forcibly removing a dissenter's hat in church. Nathaniel Aske wrote that his churchwarden would not present absenters: 'through the fear of o[u]r neighbours he refuses although hee knows the truth of every perticuler and advised with mee beforhand'.[69] A Devizes churchwarden who failed to present offenders in 1664 also 'aspersed Mr Strong [another warden] . . . for making his presentmt as being too forward', that is, for presenting dissenters.[70] As a result, some people refused to execute the office of churchwarden, particularly if they received pressure from their neighbours. Two Collingbourne Kingston dissenters disturbed the visitation of the dean of Salisbury in 1674 'by counselling one Nicholas Butler one of the churchwardens elected to this present yeare . . . not to take his oath for the due execucon of his said office'.[71]

Others who sympathised with dissenters or attended conventicles themselves found that the power of local office could be used to protect their neighbours and even to sabotage Anglican worship. One tactic was to present *omnia bene*, although this carried with it the danger of subsequent prosecution for being forsworn. As the century progressed, churchwardens became increasingly reluctant to present anything but *omnia bene* at visitations.[72] Another tactic was to admit that there was a problem but to plead ignorance about the details and request more time to determine the names of offenders and attempt their reformation. Other wardens made excuses for parishioners who failed to attend church. Thus in 1674 the wardens of North Bradley and Trowbridge, cloth towns with strong dissenting meetings, presented that they had a few who were absent from church because their parishes were so 'wide', but they failed to name them.[73] Evidence survives of at least fourteen parishes which had wardens who dissented, failed to attend church, or in other ways obstructed church services. This evidence might be provided by the minister himself or by other wardens and sidesmen. The vicar of Rodbourne Cheney complained in 1683 that one of the old churchwardens had attended a Baptist meeting and was seldom present at church. Thomas Pearce told witnesses 'why he would goe to a meeting rather than come to church' and disturbed church services several times. He and his partner had failed to present or fine those absent from divine service and communion and had

D1/54/6, 1674. The percentages are of those who made any presentment and does not include the fourteen parishes that did not return a presentment in 1674.
[69] D1/54/1/3 (1662, A&C), f. 27 (Berwick St John); D5/28, 1664, ff. 1, 3 (Wokingham); D1/41/1/17 (Somerford Magna, 6 Oct. 1673).   [70] D1/41/1/41 (24 Oct. 1664).   [71] D5/28, 1674, f. 3.
[72] See chapter 3.   [73] D1/54/6/3 (1674, A&P), ff. 27, 40

done nothing to repair the decaying church besides repainting it against the wishes of the vicar.[74] The sidesmen of Sherston Magna presented one warden 'for frequenting conventicles' and the other 'for giveing in his presentment contrary to our minds and consent'. The latter presentment has not survived but presumably did not name any dissenters.[75] A churchwarden might use force to try to prevent a zealous minister from presenting dissenters himself. In 1668 Richard Scory of Aldbourne sought to stop presentment by 'Tareing [the vicar's] prsentment in peaces when [he] would have prsented such offenders' at the archdeacon of Wiltshire's visitation. At the following year's episcopal visitation, Scory refused even to accept the book of visitation articles. When the vicar gave it to the other warden, Scory cried out, 'burne it, burne it'. Scory and his fellow warden ultimately chose to present *omnia bene*.[76]

Ministers responded to the negligence of their churchwardens by joining in the presentment themselves or by submitting their own presentment. By applying pressure they succeeded in improving the rate of presentment, particularly where dissent was strong.[77] They paid a heavy price for their determination. As the minister of Aldbourne learned, clerical presentments of offenders which were made against the wishes of the churchwarden could lead to direct conflict. The avenging parson might be seen as dividing the community. At the very least, his efforts might meet with passive resistance and refusal to present. At worst, he succeeded in poisoning the atmosphere of parish life and might even lead villagers to try to obtain his expulsion from his living. Augustine Hayter of Sutton Mandeville was one of several ministers whose efforts to suppress nonconformity resulted in attacks upon his position. The previous incumbent as rector had been the Presbyterian Thomas Rosewall, who was deprived in 1662 for his refusal to conform to the Act of Uniformity. Rosewall moved to Donhead St Andrew, where he preached at a conventicle that attracted people from his old parish.[78] Hayter complained in 1668 that the churchwarden Salathiel Deane had not only entirely neglected to perform his duties but had promoted conventicles, seeking 'to dissuade others from hearing of it [divine service] read unto them'. Deane had also tried 'to raise comotions & jarres & combinations against the minister . . . saying that if possible hee with the rest or some of his parishioners would find a way & meanes utterly to bereave him of his spiritual promotions & livelyhood in the church'. Deane's receipt of a licence for a meeting house after the Declaration of

[74] D1/54/10/2 (1683, C&M), f. 33.
[75] D1/54/6/1 (1674, M), f. 77. Sherston Magna was reported as having only four nonconformists in 1676, who the 1669 conventicle returns indicate met in each other's houses. A Presbyterian meeting was licensed in 1672. Whiteman, *Compton Census*, p. 129; Turner, *Original Records*, p. 108; CSPD 1671–2.   [76] D1/54/3/1 (1668, C&M), f. 32.
[77] In parishes where over 5 per cent of the population dissented, five of six joint presentments mentioned dissent compared to only 40 per cent (twenty of forty-nine) of presentments by wardens alone.
[78] Matthews, *Calamy Revised*, p. 418; Turner, *Original Records*, p. 119. He also preached at Tisbury.

Indulgence confirms his nonconformist sympathies.[79] In 1668, joined by his fellow warden, he sought to use the bishop's visitation to undermine the rector's position, presenting 'Augustine Hayter Rector of our parish to be a person of a scandalous behaviour vizt for ill language to his Neighbours', a charge which the rector angrily scored through.[80] The rector showed that he was well able to defend himself. He was to remain incumbent for another forty years, during which time he brought no fewer than four prosecutions for vilification of clergy or defamation and initiated several court actions for non-payment of tithes.[81]

Other ministers also suffered attempts by nonconformists and their sympathisers to deprive them of their livings in the years following the Restoration. In 1664 William Harding and William Moone of Holt spread a rumour that the curate Richard Randall had committed adultery, although they admitted that their real motive was to have the cleric expelled from the cure so that he could be replaced by someone else.[82] As one witness testified, he hoped that 'this would be a meanes that the sayd Randoll should leave the sayd cure & that . . . Barcrofte (a factious person) might be brought in to serve that cure in his roome'. Whereas Randall was 'a royall & conformeable minister', the witness continued, 'the said Barcraft is a schismaticall person, & not any way conformeable to the church & church-gover[n]m[en]t'.[83] John Barcroft had been rector of nearby Broughton Gifford until 1660 and was now living in Melksham. He was described as 'A warm Independent who was not for Baptizing any children but such whose Parents . . . were communicants with him at the Lord's Table'.[84] Harding was determined to get rid of the minister, but he did not help his case by abusing him verbally. He went to Holt church and sat through prayers making nods and 'sneeringe and scornfull smiles' at him. As Randall left the church, Harding called out 'come out thou Rogue, thou Preist, thou black Coate Ile rout thee if it cost me five hundred Pound'.[85] The campaign was revived in 1666 when two other dissenters conspired to bring a correctional suit against the curate.[86] Randall was fortunate in having the support of the Earles, a prominent local family, who testified on his behalf, and of a number of county gentlemen and clergy who provided him with a testimonial, and this enabled him to discredit his opponents.

The curate William Meaden of Horningsham also found that his efforts to suppress nonconformity resulted in isolation and threats of ejection. Horningsham had a long tradition of separatism that could be traced back to the sixteenth century, and it was a hotbed of dissent after the Restoration. A Presbyterian conventicle meeting in Alexander Cray's barn was reported as having as many as 700 hearers in 1669, more than any other conventicle in

[79] CSPD 1671–2, p. 578.   [80] D1/54/3/2 (1668, C&A), ff. 27, 28.
[81] D1/31/1/59 (1674), 62 (1687), 66 (1707).   [82] See p. 128.
[83] D1/42/58, ff. 62–3 (Randoll c. Harding).   [84] Matthews, *Calamy Revised*, pp. 27–8.
[85] A1/110, T1664, f. 158.
[86] D1/42/59, ff. 26v–28v (Smyth c. Randoll); D1/41/4/47. Matthew Smyth apparently conspired with John Brownejohn to bring the suit.

Wiltshire.[87] Meaden received little support from the churchwardens in his
attempts to suppress nonconformity. In 1669 he charged that the wardens
Richard Caraway and George Guyer were themselves inclined towards dissent
and that Caraway regularly attended the conventicle himself.[88] The wardens did
their best to protect the Presbyterian meeting. On 19 June 1670 they 'went from
home on purpose' because the conventicle was meeting in the barn, even
though this meant missing divine service. Yet only three days before they had
joined the curate in presenting that the conventicle no longer met and that no
one refused to attend divine service. It appears that they left the parish in order
to avoid being witnesses to an illegal conventicle.[89] Later in the month the two
wardens went to the conventicle and told Cray that the only warrant they
needed to be there was the Conventicle Act. Their presence appears to have
been meant as a warning rather than as a genuine attempt to prosecute dissent.
Cray promised to disband the meeting and the wardens left without arresting
anyone, at which point the meeting simply moved to the next parish. Guyer and
Caraway later refused to fine those present on the grounds that they had met
outside the parish.[90] The wardens retaliated against Meaden for his charges by
seeking to have him ejected him from his curacy. In 1669 they presented that the
curate was only a 'Mechanick' preacher whose 'deeds speake him peccant in
several particulars wch have blasted his reputation by his scandalous conversacon, & alienated the affections of (almost all) the parishioners'. Besides accus-
ing him of being non-resident and of badly neglecting his clerical
responsibilities, they tried to fix responsibility on him for the theft of the
Common Prayer Book.[91]

In parishes such as Horningsham and Ramsbury, clerics lived in fear of their
parishioners. They were isolated and had to accept help from wherever they
could find it. William Baily sent his report of a recent Horningsham conventicle
with the only man he could trust: 'I cannot think of one more in this our deceit-
full and treacherous parish in whome I may confide except this fellow.' Yet the
bearer only co-operated because Baily had threatened that he would be prosecuted if he did not.[92] Edward Wells of Corsham asked that the churchwarden
who bore his presentment of dissenters not be informed of its contents, because
''tis not convenient'. Wells must have spoken for many clerics when he wrote,
'You may imagine what encouragement a minister is like to find, who lives amidst
such a nest of wasps.'[93]

[87] Horningsham was returned twice in 1669, as within the dean's peculiar and (in error) Wylye
deanery. The estimates of the numbers attending varied between 400–500 and 600–700. It seems
unlikely that such a large number of hearers could have fitted into a barn at one time. Turner,
Original Records, pp. 121, 126.   [88] D5/28, 1669, f. 27.   [89] D5/28, 1670, ff. 12, 14.
[90] D5/31/1 (7 July 1670). These events were witnessed by a boy from the retinue of Sir James Thynne
who was sent in disguise to spy on the conventicle but whose evidence was later considered insufficient to convict Cray.   [91] D5/28, 1669, f. 42.   [92] D5/31/1 (7 July 1670).
[93] D1/54/6/1 (1674, M), f. 76.

In Horningsham, the minister even found it difficult to retain control over the church. In 1665 dissenters occupied the churchyard for the burial of a fellow religionist from North Bradley, preparing the grave and apparently performing the ceremony themselves.[94] Two years later a nonconformist minister performed the marriage of Alexander Cray's daughter, once again in the parish church. Although nonconformists were required to marry and bury in the parish church, the ceremony was supposed to be performed by the Anglican minister using the service laid down in the Prayer Book. On at least one Sunday in 1667 the Horningsham Presbyterians held their own meeting in the parish church. The curate William Meaden was obliged to officiate in both Horningsham and Rodden chapel, reading morning service in one and afternoon service in the other. The nonconformists took advantage of his absence to occupy the parish church for their own service. When Meaden returned to Horningsham, he 'found his church filled up wth people hearing of an inconformist minister . . . preaching'. He later reported that 'the company was soe numerous' that he 'could not gett to his place of reading prayers nor preaching'. Unable to take control of the service, he left the church, accompanied by 'severall others of his parishioners who would not stay at such meetings'. Most of those who were present remained in church. The fact that some of those who normally attended divine service on Sunday saw nothing wrong, at least until the curate arrived, in hearing a Presbyterian minister demonstrates how difficult it could be for contemporaries to draw a firm distinction between conformity and nonconformity.[95]

DEFINING NONCONFORMITY

The binary opposition of the language used to describe religious allegiance makes the distinction between nonconformists and conformists appear starker than it actually was.[96] Although the clergy and some separatists accepted this black and white picture, most parishioners saw shades of grey instead. Some of those who went to dissenting meetings also attended church on occasion. Others remained entirely loyal to the Church, but earned the suspicion of the clergy for failing to conform in one way or another. According to the Compton Census around 4 per cent of the population in Wiltshire failed to conform to the Church in 1676, a figure that was close to the average for the province. The smallness of this figure is not surprising. Those who had continued to worship in the parish church during the Commonwealth had grown used to changes in the liturgy and in the personnel within the pulpit. Indeed, the replacement of one minister by another was a normal (if infrequent) occurrence in parish life, albeit one which usually happened only after an incumbent's death. So it was natural for most lay

[94] D1/41/1/41. [95] D5/22/15, ff. 90–90v (Frome c. Cray).
[96] Whiteman, *Compton Census*, pp. xxvii, xxvix; Lancaster, 'Nonconformity and Anglican dissent', p. 23.

people to continue to attend services in the parish church after 1662, even if their minister had been ejected. Only a minority who felt particularly strongly about the liturgy and church government or who were particularly loyal to a deprived minister were likely to remove themselves from the state church. It is tempting to denigrate those who remained in the Church for their weakness, but we should not let value judgements interfere with our understanding of their position. Some may have welcomed the Restoration as an opportunity to reassert their support for the Prayer Book and the Anglican Church. Others simply wished to worship with their neighbours in the parish church. The same instincts led them to feel sympathy for neighbours who attended conventicles and even to attend such meetings themselves on occasion.[97]

The Compton Census asked ministers to identify those who 'obstinately refuse' to conform and so probably omitted those partial conformists who on occasion attended both the parish church and a conventicle.[98] It can be difficult to distinguish between dissent and slack religious observance, between nonconformity and conformity. James Garth of Hilperton attributed many of his difficulties to nonconformity, and he complained about the injuries his parishioners had caused 'since the late & unhappy Rebellion'. The parish was home to the meetings of Anabaptists and Quakers; the latter may have drawn as many as a hundred people in 1680. Yet in 1676 he returned only 35 nonconformists, although he claimed that 200 adults did not receive communion.[99] The phrase 'partial conformists' describes those who attended conventicles regularly but who also attended their parish church on occasion.[100] After St Bartholomew's Day those who worshipped under a Presbyterian during the Commonwealth faced a choice between loyalty to their parish church and to a minister whose conscience had prevented him from conforming. Ministers took the lead, as Edmund Calamy later reported to Burnet: 'We told his lordship, that the communicating with the Church of England was no new practice among Dissenters, nor of a late date, but had been used by some of the most eminent of our ministers ever since 1662, with a design to show their charity towards that Church, notwithstanding they apprehended themselves bound in conscience ordinarily to separate from it.'[101] In Ramsbury Henry Dent preached at his Presbyterian meeting in the morning and attended church in the afternoon, although he would

[97] Cf. Lancaster, 'Nonconformity and Anglican dissent', pp. 25, 30, 318, who argues that adherents of a Low-Church tradition held their own small meetings.
[98] Whiteman, *Compton Census*, p. xxvii.
[99] D1/41/4/43; A1/110, E1680; D1/54/10/3 (1683, A&P), f. 61; Whiteman, *Compton Census*, p. 22. See also chapter 1.
[100] J. D. Ramsbottom, 'Presbyterians and "partial conformity" in the Restoration Church of England', *Journal of Ecclesiastical History* 43 (1992): 249-70; Lancaster, 'Nonconformity and Anglican dissent', pp. 160, 193–4. In Nottingham archdeaconry it was reported that half of the conventiclers continued to attend their parish church.
[101] Quoted by N. Sykes, *From Sheldon to Secker: Aspects of English Church History, 1660-1768* (Cambridge, 1959), p. 96.

not receive communion.[102] By the standards set by the Elizabethan penal laws (intended originally to detect recusants, of course), nonconformity was defined by prolonged absence from the parish church. Yet court records provide indirect evidence that dissenters may sometimes have attended church prayers, because they document other offences they committed while there, such as refusing to remove their hat or leaving before communion. Quakers were known for their principled objection to doing 'hat honour', but they were not the only people to commit this offence. Mark Stoneham of Aldbourne, who probably went to the Presbyterian meeting of Christopher Fowler, attended church twice a year, but he would not remove his hat during divine service or receive communion.[103] Similarly, four Calne men not known to be Quakers were presented for wearing their hats during divine service.[104]

The language we use to describe the religious beliefs of Restoration men and women is primarily that of the Established Church and state. When discussing 'conformists' and 'nonconformists', it is difficult to avoid the divide which they dictate. The term 'partial conformity' is itself not entirely satisfactory because it implies a tactical decision of nonconformists to make some gesture towards conforming. Many lay people may not have been aware of choosing between conformity to the Church and separatism from it. They saw relations between those who were members of the community in much more fluid terms. Yet the clergy imposed a binary definition of parish worship by prosecuting dissent. In doing so they alienated many supporters of the Established Church.

CONCLUSION

Nonconformity was a divisive force in many parishes, widening the gap between clergy and laity. As far as many parishioners were concerned, the nonconformity of their neighbours to the Church of England did not sever their connection with the village community, particularly given the indistinct definition of nonconformity. Clerics found that popular sympathy with dissenters meant that their attempts to prosecute dissent alienated them from the rest of the parish. If this was so before 1689, it was even more so afterwards. The Act of Toleration removed the powers of the Church to prosecute nonconformists. It was not

---

[102] Matthews, *Calamy Revised*, pp. 162–3. Dent was presented in 1680 for failing to receive communion for sixteen years and again for non-receipt in 1684. D5/28, 1680, f. 25, 1684, f. 10.

[103] D1/54/3/1 (1668, C&M), f. 32. Stoneham was excommunicated in 1671 and remained so in 1674. D1/54/6/2 (1674, C&M).

[104] The four are not named as Quakers and do not appear in Quaker records (D5/28, 1683, f. 1). The Presbyterian John Burden of Donhead St Mary often went to Berwick St John church, where he insisted on keeping on his hat. Since Berwick church had been the scene of the violent expulsion of the puritan incumbent in 1662, Burden's irreverence was probably deliberate. D1/54/1/3 (1662, A&C), f. 27. Two Sutton Benger Quakers attended church in 1683, one of whom kept his hat on. D1/54/10/1 (1683, M), f. 3.

intended to license irreligion, however, and there remained a slow trickle of presentments against those who went neither to church nor to any other religious meeting.[105] Although most clergymen accepted the new order, a few did not. In Avebury, for example, the vicar John White objected to the 'hellish, factious, scandalous & schismatical conventicle' that he believed had been set up 'in opposition' to himself, and in 1698 he presented its minister to the bishop. There had been a Presbyterian meeting in the parish since at least 1669, and the meeting was licensed after Toleration. When his antipathy to dissenters led White to refuse to bury Presbyterians, the churchwardens brought a correctional suit against him that resulted in his admonishment.[106] The vicar's objections to the Presbyterians had done little but increase his unpopularity among his congregation.

Churchmen found it difficult to distinguish their friends from their enemies. Bishop Burnet believed that the clergy of Salisbury diocese had opposed his measures of pastoral reform because they thought that he was guilty of betraying the Church to the dissenters.[107] In country parishes the clergy tended to interpret any omission in religious observance as separatism and any challenge to their authority as an assault upon the Church and the clerical estate. The increased defensiveness of the clergy reinforced the inflexibility of the Church of England, which was determined to protect the Anglican liturgy and the clerical estate, and which resisted any significant contribution to worship from the laity. This intolerance and insistence upon the Church's monopoly over religion hurt the Church because it impaired its understanding of popular religion.

[105] See, for example, presentments from Stert and Berwick St James (1703), D1/54/18; Chicklade, D1/54/25 (1716, A&C); and Seend, D1/54/30/5 (1726, W&W); among others.
[106] WRO 184/1, John White to Richard Holford, received 27 Jan. 1695; D1/54/14; Turner, *Original Records*, p. 109; A1/250 (1707 and 1710); D1/42/68; WRO 184/8. See chapter 5.
[107] Foxcroft, pp. 499, 502.

8

Popular observance

On 1 October 1673 fourteen people from Somerford Magna appeared before the bishop's court charged with failing to receive communion. The previous year, during the period of the Declaration of Indulgence, the rector Nathaniel Aske had tried to present many of the same villagers for absenting themselves from services or coming late. Yet, despite this evidence of nonconformity, the villagers professed their conformability to the church government and their willingness to participate in church services. They explained that they had been reluctant to receive communion from their minister because he had behaved in an unsuitable manner. In response to the rector's presentment, the villagers submitted their own lengthy list of charges against him and petitioned the bishop to replace him with some other honest minister.[1] This episode demonstrates the difficulties of studying popular religious observance within the Church of England after the Restoration. Clergymen were unable to understand non-observance as anything but dissent or irreligion, which they regarded as two sides of the same coin. It is hard for historians to avoid sharing their assumptions. The same court processes that detected nonconformists, whose principles would not permit them to accept the patterns of worship laid down in the Prayer Book, also detected others who offended but remained loyal to the Church. It is, nevertheless, just possible to detect the outlines of popular observance of the liturgy beneath the outward appearance of nonconformity. Lay observance of every detail of the liturgy was far from complete. In part, this reflected the impact of the Civil Wars and Interregnum, which had disrupted Anglican practice and which could not help but influence popular definitions of accepted practice. Popular Anglicanism blended Interregnum practices with the restored liturgy of the Church of England.

The legislation which has come to be known as the Clarendon Code, including the Conventicle Acts, demonstrated the determination of the Cavalier Parliament to suppress religious dissent. However, nonconformists were more often prosecuted under the laws that had been put in place during the sixteenth

---

[1] D1/41/1/17; D1/41/4/39.

century to catch recusants, and they were brought to the attention of authorities, alongside petty offenders, by the presentments of local officers at visitations and Quarter Sessions. The study of observance is complicated further by the fact that the records of these courts are fullest for the years from 1662 to 1689, before the Act of Toleration placed the seal on the decline of the discipline of the church courts. As clergymen observed, the new act provided a screen behind which all varieties of neglect could hide.[2] Yet not all those presented for absence from church services and communion or for other lapses were dissenters. Hidden within their midst were conformists who stayed away from church out of negligence or choice. A presentment described as 'Churchmen, but negligent' forty-six Fugglestone inhabitants who had failed to receive communion in the preceding year.[3] A communion certificate for Ambrose Powell advised the Quarter Sessions to be gentle with him 'for in truth he was never a Reall fanatick, but did it out of neglect & sloth'.[4] Absence from church sometimes also resulted from the deliberate choice of those who were in dispute with the minister.

SOMERFORD MAGNA

Somerford Magna is a small parish lying in the 'cheese country' of north-west Wiltshire. The petitioners represented a substantial part of the community, including roughly half of the adult male population. Twelve were householders, among the chief inhabitants of the parish. At least one had formerly been a churchwarden. The emptiness of the church after the Declaration of Indulgence seemed to confirm that dissent was a significant problem. Aske complained, 'I warn comunions & none appears, & often tymes read prayers to the walls.'[5] The Compton Census of 1676 provides independent confirmation that there were nonconformists living in the parish, but suggests that they were not involved in the petition. They accounted for only eight adults, and no conventicle met in the parish.[6] In fact, the nonconformists enumerated in 1676 were almost certainly the Quakers who were presented at Quarter Sessions four years later, none of whom signed the petition against the rector.[7] Even the rector had to admit that his parishioners' love of good fellowship was not consistent with nonconformity: 'A Paradoxe to speake it a Drunken Swearing Puritan'. Furthermore, six minis-

---

[2] See, for example, Chicklade, D1/54/25 (1716, A&C).   [3] D1/54/10/5 (1683, W&W).
[4] A1/110, E1683.
[5] The details in this and subsequent paragraphs are, unless otherwise indicated, derived from D1/41/1/17; D1/41/4/39.
[6] Based on examination of conventicle returns (1669), licences for meeting houses and preachers (1672), and certificates of dissenters' places of worship after Toleration. Turner, *Original Records*, pp. 106–27; CSPD, 1671–2, 1672; and Quarter Sessions, Certificates of Dissenters' Places of Worship, 1695–1745, A1/250; Whiteman, *Compton Census*, p. 129.
[7] Nine Quakers were presented in 1680. A1/110, T1680.

ters from nearby parishes signed a declaration in support of the petitioners. The church court judge discharged the fourteen defendants forthwith, while warning them to receive communion when it was next administered at Christmas. Most petitioners obeyed this admonition. By the end of December the rector had certified the submission of two of his opponents. But he refused to acknowledge the obedience of the rest, leaving them with little alternative but to write to the registrar themselves, certifying that they had received the sacrament at Christmas.

In their petition the parishioners charged the minister with numerous offences, including neglecting the pastoral duties of baptism and burial, refusing to allow corpses to be brought into the church without payment for a sermon, and using the churchyard as a pasture for cattle and pigs. They also questioned his own conformity to the Church.[8] Aske's worst offence was that he 'hath demeaned himself very troublesome & vexatious', and it was for this reason that many parishioners had stayed away from church and felt that they could not 'with a good conscience receave the Sacrament from his hands', although they said they longed to receive it. The rector had used the courts to harass members of his congregation 'by severall suits comenced against them . . . and by indeavouring to procure & abets one Neighbour . . . to sue an other'. It was Aske who brought the dispute into the church, using his privileged position in the pulpit to threaten his congregation with further persecution: 'vizt that he had made a beginning with us, And those that were left out should drinke of the same cupp for hee was resolved to fill the courts with presentments against us'. This desecration of the church was the last straw, and the villagers drew up their petition on the next day.

Nathaniel Aske asserted the hope that in his 'presentments there shall not be one drop of revenge, No such vinegar or gall in our ink'. Yet other evidence confirms the villagers' belief that their minister was a troublemaker who was only too happy to use the courts to get his way and to harass his enemies. Shortly after his induction, he sued his predecessor's widow and daughter for dilapidations. When an inhabitant of the neighbouring parish of Dauntsey, angered by the suit, charged the minister with simony, adultery and drunkenness, Aske responded with a suit for vilification of clergy. He turned to the courts again four years later, first bringing an Assize charge for vexatious suits against John Atkins, and, when Atkins complained, suing him for vilification.[9] The minister was outraged by the church court's dismissal of the charges against his congregation, and five days later he renewed his prosecution.[10] The atmosphere within the parish grew worse. An 80-year-old widow whom Aske regarded as a leader

[8] Although parishioners claimed that both he and the members of his family had themselves not received communion for two years, the sermon preached at Aske's funeral leaves little doubt of his conformity. John Clark, *A Sermon Preached at the Funerall of Mr. Nathaniel Aske, Late Rector of Somerford-Magna in North-Wilts.* (London, 1676).
[9] D1/39/58, ff. 7, 23v, 62; D1/39/59, f. 37v; D1/42/61, ff. 260v–255v, 84v–87, 88–9.
[10] Aske's prosecution tactics are discussed more fully in chapter 7.

of those who were arrayed against him continued to refuse to take communion from the minister and rarely went to church except to attend christenings and funerals. Another petitioner laughed and whispered to his neighbours in church, while a third refused to pay his church rates. The rector prosecuted two others for failing to pay their tithes.[11] In short, a significant number of people withdrew their support from the Church. Memories of conflict were still strong when the minister of nearby Malmesbury, John Clark, preached Aske's funeral sermon in 1676 to an audience that included both the laity and the clergy. Clark blamed the parish for the recent troubles, commenting 'That had he met with a more obliging people, he might have proved a more usefull Pastor'. But he was well aware of the rector's faults, for he expressed the hope that his friend's behaviour 'may well allow of a better construction then [sic] altogether contentious'.[12]

THE IMPORTANCE OF COMMUNION

Behind Nathaniel Aske's presentments of apparent nonconformists there lay a bitter and prolonged struggle over religious worship in Somerford Magna. Most parishioners had no wish to leave the Church. They were reluctant to receive communion from their rector because they thought his litigious behaviour made him unfit to administer the sacrament. Although they would have preferred a new minister, they told the clergy of neighbouring parishes that they were willing to receive communion from Aske 'if he shall lay by his Contention and inconvenient Disputes of Secular Affaires'.[13] This attitude was consistent with the doctrine of the Church as expressed in the liturgy, although the Church frowned upon their withdrawal from participation in services. The rubric to the communion service instructed the minister not to allow 'those betwixt whom he perceiveth malice and hatred to reign' to partake of the sacrament 'until he know them to be reconciled'. The laity were warned that it could be dangerous to their souls to receive without first reconciling themselves with their neighbours.[14] Parishioners and clerics alike took this admonition seriously. The vicar of Compton Chamberlayne forbade two of his parishioners to receive communion because they were embroiled in a lawsuit, and he threatened them with suspension from the Church if they tried to receive. When one of them expressed a desire for reconciliation, the vicar promised to readmit him to communion. Some people disbarred themselves from communion voluntarily, making a clerical prohibition of this sort unnecessary. After Robert Mortimer of Calne was involved in a fight which led to a suit at law he 'could not with a safe & quiet conscience come to the Holy Communion'. Only when the suit had been ended

[11] D1/39/1, f. 37v; D1/54/6/1 (1674, M).
[12] Clark, *A Sermon Preached at the Funerall of Mr. Nathaniel Aske*, pp. 23–6.   [13] D1/41/4/39.
[14] Book of Common Prayer (1662).

did Mortimer feel that he could safely receive the sacrament again.[15] Richard Strong of Downton also testified that he had not received communion for three years because he had 'bin often perplext with law suites'.[16] To have allowed quarrelling parishioners to receive communion would have violated the spiritual function of the rite, for both communal and individual reasons. In addition to assisting the 'continual remembrance of the sacrifice of the death of Christ', the sacrament of communion symbolised membership in the Church and fellowship with all other members, and disagreements among communicants disturbed this amity. Anyone who was quarrelling with his neighbours was not behaving with sufficient charity, despite warnings in the liturgy and in scripture.

If lawsuits with other laymen prohibited people from taking communion, how much more a legal dispute with the minister who was administering the sacrament must have done. How was it possible to receive the body and blood of Christ from a man who had taken one to court? And if being out of charity with one's neighbours prevented one from receiving communion, how much more, it must have seemed, that it should prevent anyone from administering the sacrament. In addition to their concern about the safety of receiving communion from a man with whom they were in dispute there must have been some concern about the efficacy of receiving from an unworthy minister, despite the assurances contained in the 26th Article of Religion that the benefits of the sacrament were not diminished if it was administered by 'evil men'. By using his sermons to make threats, Aske had fatally compromised the role of divine service in affirming community and peace. We can see the choleric rector shouting threats at his congregation: 'If the first court will not doe it, I will have you in the second: and if the second will not due it the third shall.'[17] It was natural for the congregation to react emotionally against such an abuse, which would have made it unpleasant to receive the holy sacrament from the rector. In the same manner, inhabitants of other parishes refused to receive communion from ministers whose behaviour seemed to desecrate the sacrament. In Charlton people were scandalised by the behaviour of their vicar, who was a drunkard and sometimes fell 'acrying and belching as though he would vomits and the like at the Administracon of the Sacrament therby making himself rediculous'. These antics gave 'a very greate offence and discouragement to the congregation in soe much that . . . divers . . . cannot frequent the said church in time of divine service and participate of the sacraments with any comfort'.[18] Reluctance to receive communion from the minister was often a feature of episodes of lay–clerical conflict. The villagers of Knook prevented the administration of the sacrament

---

[15] D1/54/6/4 (1674, A&C, Compton Chamberlayne); D5/31/1 (Calne, 3 Oct. 1669). For evidence of a similar connection between the resolution of legal disputes and the ability to take communion, see D. W. Sabean, *Power in the Blood: Popular Culture and Village Discourse in Early Modern Germany* (Cambridge, 1984), pp. 37–60, esp. 47–51.   [16] D1/42/61, f. 211.   [17] D1/41/4/39.
[18] D1/42/62, ff. 2v–3.

by locking the minister out of church.[19] In Somerford Magna the parishioners also found an imaginative way to avoid having to receive from the hands of their objectionable rector. On Whitsunday 1674 the churchwarden John Mayo failed to provide enough wine for communion to take place properly.[20] Such behaviour provides insight into the respect with which people regarded communion and into their fear of receiving it in an unworthy fashion.

The Church recognised that it was natural for individuals to wish to stay away from services officiated over by a minister whose behaviour rendered him scandalous,[21] but it could not sanction absence from one's parish church under any circumstances, even to attend the church of another parish. To do so would be to accept the dangerous principle that people were at liberty to attend any form of worship they wished, leading inexorably through Presbyterianism, Independency, Anabaptism and Quakerism to atheism. As a 1684 treatise observed, 'the first step to Apostasy is the forsaking of Publick Assemblies'. The Civil Wars provided a recent example, still fresh in the memory, of the consequences of the principle that one should leave a wicked pastor, 'which ended in the Ruin of King and Laws, Religion and Church, for a time'. In any case, such behaviour might have more immediate practical consequences. A minister could make life very uncomfortable for those who stayed away from church, because the laws were on his side.[22] This was a truth to which the inhabitants of Somerford Magna could testify from personal experience.

The clergy saw little difference between nonconformity and irreligion, for the one led to the other, and they regarded both as features of a concerted attack upon the authority of the Established Church. Complaints about non-observance therefore became part of a long tradition of clerical complaints about the ignorance, irreligiosity and immorality of the people.[23] Before the Restoration, such views had often been expressed by puritans. In 1655 the Presbyterian cleric Peter Ince had complained, 'The greatr part of my poore people that will have their Children Baptized hate instruction, & are as ignorant of C[hris]tianity, I meane of the plainest principles . . . as if they had never heard of them.'[24] After the Restoration, the Anglican clergy expressed similar opinions.

---

[19] D5/28, 1668, f. 11; 1669, f. 41.   [20] D1/54/6/1 (1674, M).
[21] Bishop Henchman asked in 1662 whether any refused to receive communion from the minister, 'taking exception against him'. 'Articles to be Enquired of in the Diocese of Salisbury . . . 1662', House of Commons, *Parliamentary Papers*, 1867–8, vol. XXXVIII, pp. 610–13, title 6, query 5.
[22] *The Case of Peoples Duty in Living Under a Scandalous Minister Stated and Resolved* (London, 1684), pp. 7–19, quoting pp. 12, 14.
[23] C. J. Sommerville, *The Secularization of Early Modern England* (New York and Oxford, 1992), p. 185; and C. G. Brown, 'Did urbanization secularize Britain?', *Urban History Yearbook* (1988): 1–14. Brown's observation that 'churchmen have been voicing this concern almost continuously from the 1780s down to the present day' (p. 1) might easily be shifted back to the seventeenth century, if not earlier.
[24] Letter to Richard Baxter, 1 March 1655, Dr Williams's Library MSS, 59.4.245, quoted in G. F. Nuttall, *Visible Saints* (Oxford, 1957), p. 136.

James Garth complained about the irreligious behaviour of his congregation in Hilperton, where the number who refused to take communion far exceeded the number who were nonconformists.[25] Corresponding members of the Society for Promoting Christian Knowledge bemoaned the ignorance of the people. In 1708 Francis Fox of Boscombe found 'people in that Country under a wretched Ignorance of the Principles of Religion'. John Jackson, minister of Hullavington, agreed in 1712 that he had found 'the country people of grown age very ignorant too in Religion'.[26] A Dorset correspondent observed 'that concubinage is openly maintained particularly in ye Diocess of Wilts'. '[F]or want of pious application to Catechizing,' he said, 'ye Deists, &c, undermine our flocks.'[27] The clergy's inability to tolerate any form of worship that fell short of complete conformity made it impossible for them to understand or appreciate lay religious practice.

One of the most extensive complaints about popular religious ignorance came from the parish of Pewsey, on the edge of the downs in eastern Wiltshire. In 1668 the rector Richard Watson submitted an eight-page presentment of the 'Enormities & Defects presentable' in his parish.[28] These offences cannot be attributed to nonconformity, for the rector reported that he knew of 'no parishioner that pretends to the name of Papist, Familiast, Anabaptist, Quaker, or other sectarie, unless any will answer to that of Presbyterian'. It is possible that some people retained a sympathy for Presbyterianism, because the parish had been served during the Interregnum by the prominent Presbyterian cleric Humphrey Chambers.[29] Nonetheless, no conventicles or separatists were reported in 1669 or 1676. Watson's testimony cannot necessarily be trusted to provide an accurate picture of popular religious practice. The rector was a strong-minded and irascible man who was unwilling to put up with independence and insubordination from his congregation.[30] Like his colleagues, John Tounson of Bremhill and Gervase Bland of Knooke,[31] he had suffered during the Interregnum, and this experience had hardly improved his temper. After the Restoration, he became one of the most litigious clerics in Wiltshire, bringing suits for non-payment of tithes against over thirty defendants. His unpopularity was established early in his incumbency, when he was embroiled in a long dispute with his labourers over wages. As one bitterly commented, 'what a good

[25] D1/41/4/43.   [26] SPCK, AL 1366; OL 3027.
[27] W. O. B. Allen and E. McClure, *Two Hundred Years: The History of the Society for Promoting Christian Knowledge, 1698–1898* (London: SPCK, 1898), p. 69.
[28] D1/54/3/1 (1668, C&M), ff. 4a–5d. Unless otherwise stated, all references to Watson's presentments come from this document.
[29] Chambers, who served from 1646 until his deprivation in 1662, had been a member of Westminster Assembly in 1643, campaigned against Pewsey alehouses in 1646, and headed the list of fifty-four Wiltshire ministers who wrote to Charles II in May 1660. Matthews, *Calamy Revised,* p. 107.
[30] Anthony Wood described Watson as 'vain and conceited'. Anthony Wood, *Athenae Oxoniensis*, 2nd edn (London, 1721), vol. II, f. 149.   [31] See chapters 4 and 5.

Samaritan the said great Doctor is that would turn the joy of harvest into a bitter lamentacon by detaining from his said labourers our most deserved hire'.[32] Relations between the rector and his congregation were poor, in consequence. The rector's isolation was increased by the blinkered view of popular religious practice which, as a learned author and divine, he shared with many of his fellow clerics.[33]

Watson submitted a comprehensive catalogue of the irreligion and immorality of his parish, where 'so many there are addicted to debaucherie & loosenes, if not inclin'd to Aitheisme that the publike service of God is too much neglected'. Fewer than half of his parishioners came to church on Sunday. Few heeded his admonitions to catechism, so that most of those who had recently reached the age of sixteen could not 'give any account at all of Christian religion; so that I have been faine to advise them to forbear the H[oly] comunion till better fitted for it'. Of the four hundred adults in the parish, only four received communion on any occasion but Easter, and half never received the sacrament at all. Despite frequent warnings, most of the parish continued their ordinary labour on holy days. Watson found himself opposed by all levels of society on the issue of holy days, commenting that 'I scarcely know any one from the highest to ye lowest excusable in this particular'. The churchwardens neglected to present those who worked on holy days and committed the offence themselves.[34] Ralph Smith, one of the wealthiest men of the parish,[35] whom parishioners called 'theire Master', was personally 'engaged in the most dirty part of it himself' on Midsummer day, and he laughed when Watson reproved him. Smith doubtless had economic reasons for encouraging labourers to work, but it is clear nevertheless that all levels of society shared his wish to work on holy days. Even Watson's own servant, Robert King, complained when the rector would not let him work on holy days, declaring: 'Let the Bishop & Church order what they please, I will worke upon all weeke dayes as well as other filke [*sic*].'

Watson's account suggests that the ministry of Humphrey Chambers had an impact upon popular religious practices, leaving a legacy of uncertainty about Anglican ceremonies which persisted during the 1660s. The disregard for holy days was consistent with puritan attempts to suppress them. Several parishioners assured the rector that 'but fower holy dayes were to be observed, & that from the civile authority of . . . ye Justices, who . . . declared it upon the Bench'. Presumably they were recalling an order issued by secular authorities during the

---

[32] A1/110, H1664/5, f. 149. See also A1/160/2, M1664, H1664/5; A1/110, M1664, f. 149, M1665, f. 180.

[33] Watson was author of several controversial publications. *Dictionary of National Biography*, q.v. 'Richard Watson'; Wood, *Athenae Oxoniensis*, vol. II, f. 149.

[34] D1/41/1/17 (24 May 1673); WRO 493/49, ff. 25v–57.

[35] Assuming that Ralph Smith inherited the estate of his father (also called Ralph) in 1664, he must have paid tax on six hearths; only three houses, including the parsonage, had more. PRO, E179/259/29, ff. 20–20v; WRO 493/3.

Interregnum.[36] Watson also reported widespread disregard of the ritual gestures to which the puritans had objected. Some failed to stand when the Creed and Gospel were read, few kneeled at prayers, and no one made signs of reverence at the name of Jesus. Many people rushed out before the beginning of the second service (the ante-communion), 'as [if] apprehending some superstition in it'. If Watson's biased account is to be trusted, it appears that the Interregnum had influenced the religious beliefs, not only of nonconformists but of many of those who remained within the Church. Yet puritanism cannot provide a full explanation for the pattern of non-observance in Pewsey, for the rector also complained about popular recreations. A local alehouse allowed tippling on Sundays and at other times, so that there was 'much disorder at other times, & that by persons of both sexes, unseasonably late in the night'. The observance of communion in Pewsey and Somerford Magna reflected general attitudes to the sacrament among the laity, which can in part be traced to the practice and liturgy of the Church of England.

After the Restoration, country churches quickly returned to the practice of administering communion three or four times a year at the great feasts of the religious calendar – Christmas, Easter, Whitsunday, and sometimes Palm Sunday or Michaelmas. This pattern, which can be documented from the purchases of bread and wine recorded in churchwardens' accounts, persisted throughout the eighteenth century.[37] Some ecclesiastics would have preferred the sacrament to have been administered more often. After all, in addition to gaining new importance as a test of political conformity, communion also came to represent the deepest form of Anglican piety.[38] Canon 13 encouraged parishioners to communicate 'often times', and in 1716 the newly enthroned bishop of Salisbury charged his clergy to 'bring your people frequently to the Sacraments'.[39] Bishop Henchman of Salisbury charged his clergy in 1662 to perform communion once a month, following the advice George Herbert had given in his widely read guide, the *Country Parson*, although Herbert had accepted that five or six times a year might be sufficient.[40] Yet the canons required parishioners to communicate only three times a year, including once at Easter. In Wiltshire the laity failed to fulfil even this minimal duty. Although it would be easy to interpret their 'neglect' as

---

[36] No formal order survives in either Quarter Sessions or Assize records. A1/160/1; A1/160/2; PRO, ASSI 24/22.

[37] See, for example, Grittleton, Churchwardens' Accounts, 1677–1799, WRO 1620/17; Alton Barnes, Parish Register, 1592–1747, WRO 496/1; Calstone Wellington, Churchwardens' Accounts, 1715–41, WRO 807/18. Cf. Broad Hinton, where the sacrament was administered six times a year in the middle of the eighteenth century. WRO 1505/2.

[38] J. Spurr, *The Restoration Church of England, 1646–1689* (New Haven and London, 1991), p. 344.

[39] William Talbot, *The Bishop of Sarum's Charge to the Clergy of his Diocese, at his Primary Visitation Anno. 1716* (London, 1717).

[40] 'Articles . . . 1662', title 10, query 10; George Herbert, *A Priest to the Temple, or the Country Parson his Character, &c* (London, 1632), reprinted in F. E. Hutchinson, ed., *Works* (Oxford, 1941), p. 259.

evidence of low commitment to the Church, this would misrepresent the complexity of lay views. Parishioners took communion rarely because they held the ceremony in awe, and believed that they should not participate lightly. Their reluctance to receive the sacrament from the hands of an unfit minister was consistent with their beliefs more generally.

Lay people rarely received the sacrament more than once a year, and over half received it even less often than that. The number who participated in the canonical three times a year was very small, as churchwardens and ministers occasionally testified in their presentments. In Wokingham in Berkshire, for example, it was reported in 1669 that 'those that doth come are very few in comparison of those which doth not come'. The Chicklade wardens and minister reported in 1689 that 'too many, too much neclect the Sacrament'. This had nothing to do with the toleration of dissent, they added three years later, because 'all our parishioners live in ye unitie of ye same professio[n]'.[41] Lists of communicants which would allow us to document this behaviour in more detail are very rare, but do survive for Pewsey in 1709–10 and Holt in 1719–20. The churchwardens' account book from Pewsey suggests that communion rates were even lower than Richard Watson had reported. The book records the names of eighty-four people who participated on either Christmas Day 1709 or Easter 1710. Only one in five adults took communion on these two most important feasts of the year.[42] Although it is possible that others received at Whitsunday or Michaelmas, for which no lists survive, it is clear that less than half of the adult population took communion in that year. A similar pattern prevailed in Holt, despite the curate's plan to administer the Lord's Supper six times a year, 'viz thrice at the 3 great festivals Christmas, Easter, & Whitsontide, as has been usual, & once in the Interval between Christmas & Easter; viz about ye middle of February, or the beginning of Lent and twice in the Interval between Whitsontide & Christmas viz about ye beginning of Aug & the middle of October'. Although he failed to fulfil his ambitious programme, his diary includes the names of those who received the sacrament on four occasions when it was administered in 1719 and 1720.[43] Only 20 per cent of adults participated at least once in a single year in Holt, around the same proportion as are named in Pewsey. Scattered evidence from other parishes suggests that an annual rate of around 20 to 25 per cent was typical.[44] These records also confirm that it was unusual to take communion

41 Wokingham: D5/28, 1669, f. 36; Chicklade: D1/54/12/3 (1689, A&C), D1/54/13/4 (1692, A&C).
42 Pewsey, General Entry Book, 1608–1855, WRO 493/49. The adult population figure is taken from D1/54/3/1 (1668, C&M), f. 5d.
43 Bodleian Library, MS Eng Misc f. 10, Diary 1718–60 (Phillipps 13531 and 13424).
44 In Chardstock 120 to 140 of its 500 to 600 adults received communion on occasion. D5/28, 1668, f. 41. Cf. Avebury, where 40 of 181 adults were prepared to receive communion on Christmas Day 1667. D1/42/58, f. 180v. The figure of 20 per cent is lower than the proportions of one-third to one-half found elsewhere. W. M. Jacob, *Lay People and Religion in the Early Eighteenth Century* (Cambridge, 1996), pp. 58–9; P. Laslett, *The World We Have Lost*, 2nd edn (New York, 1971), p. 74; P. Laslett and J. Harrison, 'Clayworth and Cogenhoe', in H. E. Bell and R. L. Ollard, eds.,

three times a year. In Holt less than half of communicants did so. In Pewsey, only eight of eighty-four people were named twice. The figures from Donhead St Andrew, where there were forty-five regular and twenty-five irregular communicants in 1743, are comparable.[45]

The deposition books of the bishop of Salisbury show that villagers often went years without receiving communion. Joyce Wordly of Downton admitted that she had not received for three years because 'her employment . . . [had] not permitted her to do it'. Even those who received the sacrament every year were unlikely to participate three times, as stipulated by the canons. A Downton brazier testified that 'for many years past he hath constantly received the sacrament . . . every Xtmas'.[46] This testimony must be treated with caution, since it came in response to questions the defendant asked to discredit those who testified. Yet witnesses freely admitted behaviour which fell short of canonical requirements, suggesting that ordinary people were neither aware of nor especially troubled by their apparent laxity. Lay depositions are confirmed by other evidence, such as the presentment of the churchwardens of Landford that no parishioners 'refuse to receive once a year but scarce any receive thrice'.[47] They also made little special effort to receive at Easter, the one time at which everyone was supposed to communicate. In Pewsey more people participated at Christmas 1709 than at Easter 1710.[48] Churchwardens purchased only slightly more bread and wine at Easter than at other feasts, and often the amounts were the same.[49] The inhabitants of Somerford Magna who missed successive communions at Easter and Whitsuntide were behaving normally. It was their rector who in their view was being unreasonable in expecting them to be present at every administration of the sacrament.

The refusal of lay people to take communion from unfit ministers was consistent with the care they took not to participate if they thought they themselves were not fit to receive. In Imber some villagers failed to take the sacrament in 1674 because they were waiting 'till they are better & fitter prepared'.[50] Other evidence suggests that they believed that it was dangerous to take communion unless one was properly prepared. The curate of Caddington (Beds.) reported to the bishop of Lincoln in 1692 that a man had told him that communion 'did nothing but damn people; [because] it was impossible to

Historical Essays, 1600–1750, Presented to David Ogg (1963), pp. 162–71; and J. Boulton, 'The limits of formal religion: the administration of holy communion in late Elizabethan and early Stuart England', *London Journal* 10 (Winter 1984): 145–6.

[45] Donhead St Andrew, Tithe Composition Survey Book, 1743, WRO 1732/15. The parish had 456 inhabitants in 1676, which suggests an adult population of around 270 and a communion rate of around 25 per cent.   [46] D1/42/61, ff. 61, 77.   [47] D1/54/3/2 (1668, C&A), ff. 3, 11.

[48] WRO 493/49.

[49] Based on the examination of several sets of churchwardens' accounts, including those for Grittleton, 1672–83 (WRO 1620/17), Calstone Wellington, 1716–30 (807/18), and Alton Barnes, 1677–84 (496/1).   [50] D1/54/6/3 (1674, A&P).

receive it worthily & those that received it otherwise did damn themselves'. Another said 'that those were damned, that so much as laughed after they had received it'.[51] Such beliefs persisted for a long time. A century later the vicar of Winterbourne Monkton reported to the bishop of Salisbury that many were 'deterred from communicating under a notion that they thereby bind themselves to lead a better and more Christian life than they are otherwise obliged to do under a heavier and more severe punishment hereafter'. The incumbent of Sutton Benger observed a similar 'misgrounded apprehension of the danger of attending communion' in his parish.[52] Parishioners appear to have believed that the sacrament of communion represented a promise that the recipient had repented past offences and would henceforth commit no more. Violation of this promise might lead to eternal damnation. It was therefore better to go without communion than to receive it and face the risk of being punished for failing to live a sufficiently virtuous life thereafter. The safest time to receive the sacrament was when one was old and thus unlikely to sin again. Thus several older men from Caddington said that there 'was time enough' to receive communion; they would do so 'when they saw it convenient'. As Archbishop Secker observed in 1741, 'Some imagine the sacrament belongs only to persons of advanced years or great leisure or high attainment in religion, and is a very dangerous thing for common persons to venture on.'[53] It was natural for clergymen to conclude that such behaviour demonstrated the ignorance and irreligion of the people.[54]

The religious regime during the Civil Wars and Interregnum provides one possible explanation for this 'misgrounded misapprehension'. The godly had been particularly concerned to prevent promiscuous communion. The enforcement of discipline, including examination to assess fitness to participate in the sacrament, was an important function of the Presbyterian classis. Parliamentary legislation established county committees in Wiltshire and other counties to lay down the rules according to which people might be excluded. There is little doubt that this practice increased the unpopularity of the puritan church. Continued support for Anglican communion can be seen in the survival and rapid revival of festal communion and in individual examples, such as that of Gervase Bland who in 1645 was able to attract worshippers from Salisbury to his

---

[51] Inhabitants also suggested that the sacrament was for the gentry and scholars. Lambeth Palace Library, MS 933, f. 9 (item folios 12–13).

[52] M. Ransome, ed., *Wiltshire Returns to the Bishop's Visitation Queries of 1783* (Wiltshire Record Society 27, 1971), p. 238.

[53] B. Porteus and G. Stinton, *Eight Charges . . . by Thomas Secker* (London, 1771), p. 60, quoted by A. Russell, *The Clerical Profession* (London, 1980), p. 102. See also Jacob, *Lay People and Religion*, p. 59; M. Smith, *Religion in Industrial Society: Oldham and Saddleworth 1740–1865* (Oxford, 1994), p. 52.

[54] The curate compared the inhabitants of Caddington with 'wild men of America'. Lambeth Palace Library, MS 933, f. 9 (item folio 2).

'promiscuous' communions in Knooke.[55] Puritan practices may nevertheless have increased the sense that the Lord's Supper was a dangerous ceremony not to be participated in lightly. In the case of Dulcibella Pinnock, the Civil Wars marked her final reception of communion, which she still had not received by the 1680s when she attempted to excuse her absence with her age and infirmities.[56]

The persistence of puritan views may have affected even those who remained within the Church, but it does not fully explain the low rates of participation in communion. Popular reluctance to receive the sacrament was also reinforced strongly by the wording of the communion service in the Prayer Book, which placed great stress upon the preparation of the recipient.[57] On the Sunday or holy day which immediately preceded the administration of communion, the minister announced the service and warned the congregation to prepare themselves to receive the sacrament. He read an exhortation from the liturgy which instructed his hearers how to prepare themselves and described the dangers of receiving unworthily. Although the sacrament was spiritual food for those who received it worthily, it was 'so dangerous for them that will presume to receive it unworthily'. Those planning to participate were to examine their consciences, to bewail their sins, and to confess their sinfulness to God 'with full purpose of amendment of life'. Without repentance, the promise of amendment, and reconciliation with enemies, they were warned, 'the receiving of the holy Communion doth nothing else but increase your damnation'. The devil would enter their bodies and bring them 'to destruction both of body and soul'. This exhortation was not meant to deter people from taking communion, but only to make them think before they did so. Protestant reformers had wished to discredit the frequent repetition of the mass and the superstitious uses to which it had been put, which they felt degraded the sacrament. Communion was to be taken seriously, and careful self-examination replaced auricular confession. Potential communicants were 'to consider the dignity of that holy mystery' and to search their consciences so that they 'may come holy and clean to such a heavenly feast', according to the communion service.

The Church was aware of the danger that this text might encourage too many in the congregation to neglect their duty. The Prayer Book provided the cleric with a less frightening alternative exhortation which stated that there was no excuse for not taking communion: 'If any man say, I am a grievous sinner, and therefore am afraid to come: wherefore do ye not repent and amend?' Yet although it asked absenters to consider 'how sore punishment hangeth over your heads', the second exhortation lacked the power and specificity of the first with

[55] W. A. Shaw, *A History of the English Church during the Civil Wars and under the Commonwealth 1640–1660* (London, 1900), vol. I, pp. 260–90, vol. II, pp. 142–51; BL, Add. MS 22,084, f. 10.
[56] D1/42/60, ff. 120–119v.
[57] The quotations in this and subsequent paragraphs are taken from the communion service in the Book of Common Prayer (1662).

its mention of destruction by the devil. Instead, it compared the failure to receive communion with the bad manners of someone who had been invited to dinner but refused to eat. Evidence from the Oxfordshire parish of Caversham indicates that the second exhortation was likely to be read only when the minister was under pressure to increase popular observance. The curate reported in 1682 that, in obedience to commands from the bishop, he had given notice before Whitsun communion 'and to stir them up to their duty, I did read the second exhortation as is appointed in case of the people's negligence'. This tactic, combined with his decision to administer communion three times in the Easter season, had, he thought, increased the total number of communicants that year.[58]

Even if the minister read the gentler second exhortation the week before he administered the sacrament, the communion service itself may have cancelled its good work. Before the Confession, which came just before the congregation were to communicate, they were reminded of the dangers of receiving unworthily. When we receive communion unworthily, they were told, 'we eat and drink our own damnation', provoking God's wrath so that he will 'plague us with diverse diseases, and sundry kinds of death'. 'Judge therefore yourselves, brethren,' the minister thundered, 'that ye be not judged of the Lord.' It is not surprising that this powerful warning frightened its hearers. The villagers from Caddington and Winterbourne Monkton echoed the words and tone of the Prayer Book. When villagers said that communion bound them to live a better life 'under a heavier and more severe punishment', they repeated the communion service's threat of increased damnation for those who received without 'full purpose of amendment of life'. A literal reading of the wording of the Prayer Book suggested that men and women had the power to damn themselves. Some of the punishments described in the communion service would be suffered in this world; unworthy reception provoked God to plague men with diseases and even death. Yet punishment might come in the next world as well. Anyone who received unworthily ate and drank his own damnation, bringing 'destruction both of body and soul'. Unworthy reception did 'nothing else but increase . . . damnation'.[59]

Villagers' anxieties about their salvation are far removed from the Pelagian confidence expressed by Asenetius in the popular tract, *The Plaine Mans Pathway to Heaven*: 'Tush, tush; what needs all this a doe? If a man . . . say no body no harme, and doe as he would be done to, have a good faith to God-ward, and be a man of Gods beleife, no doubt he shall be saved.'[60] Villagers were anxious

---

[58] M. Clapinson, ed., *Bishop Fell and Nonconformity: Visitation Documents from the Oxford Diocese, 1682–83* (Oxfordshire Record Society 52, 1980), pp. 7–8. I am grateful to Sue Wright for bringing this to my attention.

[59] See also Spurr, *The Restoration Church*, pp. 344–53, for a discussion of preparation and of the Church's less literal interpretation of the liturgy.

[60] Arthur Dent, *The Plaine Mans Path-way to Heaven* (London, 1607), p. 25.

about their salvation because they believed that they could jeopardise it by their own actions. A Salisbury woman testified to the strength of lay anxieties when she confessed on her death-bed her fear that she had 'damne[d] her body & soule' by perjuring herself, in violation of an oath.[61] The laity do not seem to have believed, however, that they could earn salvation through good works; only God had the power to save them. Their beliefs appear similar to the Arminian doctrine of resistible grace.[62] The connection between communion and damnation is particularly significant. People understood that communion represented a covenant with God, although they did not use the term explicitly. By participating in the sacrament, they were making a promise to live a godly life in future, a promise which many were not prepared to make. As a late seventeenth-century communion manual noted, 'Receiving the Sacrament is sealing the new Covenant made by God with mankind in his Son . . . the condicon of which is an entire obedience of all Gods comands on our part & the mercies promised on God's part are . . . title to everlasting life.'[63] Parishioners did not have to look any further than the Anglican liturgy to find the terms of this contract. The confusion in their theological views can be attributed in part to an overly literal interpretation of what they heard and in part to the hybrid character of the doctrines and liturgy of the Church, which themselves represented a series of compromises between conservative and reformed views of worship.

Communion was a matter of concern not only for the individual but for the whole community. An unfit communicant might make the sacrament dangerous for the entire congregation, just as might an unfit minister. This was the reason the vicar of Ramsbury asked the dean of Salisbury to explain why the husband in an incestuous marriage had been absolved and was to be readmitted to communion. He wrote that since the sinner still lived in incest parishioners would 'be much offended if they saw [him] be admitted to the sacrament before he be reformed'. If they came to receive at the same time as he did, the vicar reported, 'they will depart and not comunicate with him and indeed some have expressed no lesse'.[64] Villagers might feel unfit to receive the sacrament for other reasons, too, for example because they did not know their catechism or were too poor to afford 'cloathes fit for them to appear in, at the Worship of God'. In Pewsey, the leading inhabitants were three times as likely to receive communion in 1709–10 as were their impoverished neighbours. Villagers might also be prevented from

---

[61] D1/39/57, ff. 141–141v (1681).

[62] For the debate over Arminianism, see K. Fincham, ed., *The Early Stuart Church 1603–1642* (London, 1993), esp. chs. 7, 9; P. White, 'The rise of Arminianism reconsidered', *Past and Present* 101 (Nov. 1983): 33–54; P. G. Lake, 'Calvinism and the English Church 1570–1635', *Past and Present* 114 (Feb. 1987): 32–76.

[63] 'A Manual for the Sacrament Containing the Duties before, at & after it', Lambeth Palace Library, MS 1516, f. 1. *The Whole Duty of Man* (London, 1674) also uses covenant language.

[64] D5/28, 1670.

receiving by sickness, business or, of course, indifference.[65] Yet anxiety about the danger of receiving communion unworthily explains the apparent 'neglect' of the sacrament by many people.[66] Lay attitudes to communion were clearly complex. Despite their infrequent reception, many villagers vested great significance in the sacrament, regarding it with a mixture of fear and respect. For this reason, they were reluctant to receive it if they felt that either they, the minister, or fellow members of the congregation were unfit. The frequency of lay reception of communion cannot be used as an index of religiosity.

POPULAR PARTICIPATION IN WORSHIP

Attendance at divine service, which might be performed up to two hundred times each year in every parish church in England, was the form of worship in which the laity participated most often.[67] The canons directed all parishioners to celebrate the days on which it was administered, not least by 'hearing the word of God' in church and by abstaining from ordinary labour. However, although the Church expected everyone to attend every performance of divine service, little attempt was made to enforce this. Even the most stringent anti-recusant legislation required only one attendance per week, and churchwardens' presentments suggest lay people generally satisfied, but did not exceed, this minimum requirement.[68] Most went to divine service once a week and abstained from labour on Sundays when possible, although there were naturally some who stayed away, preferring the alehouse or the churchyard to the church.[69] But they were unlikely to attend more than once on Sunday or to take much notice of all but the most important holy days. The churchwardens of Market Lavington reported in 1686, for example, that 'Parishioners for bear their ordinary labour and come tolerably well to Church on Sundays but upon Holydayes . . . the most of our parish follow their bodyly imployments & but few come to church'.[70] The exceptions, as in Pewsey, were the four great holy days on which communion was normally administered, two of which fell on Sundays. The importance of Sunday service can be

[65] For examples of other excuses, see Alton Pancras, D5/28, 1676; Winterbourne Bassett, D1/41/1/41. For Pewsey, the leading parishioners are defined as those who were in the top quartile of ratepayers in 1710 or served as churchwardens or overseers for the poor in 1700–10, the poor as those on a list of alms recipients in 1705. WRO 493/49.
[66] For confirmatory evidence, see F. C. Mather, 'Georgian churchmanship reconsidered: some variations in Anglican public worship 1714–1830', *Journal of Ecclesiastical History* 36 (April 1985): 273, n. 89.
[67] The Book of Common Prayer of 1662 listed thirty feast and holy days and three solemn days on which service would be read twice, plus sixteen eves of holy days on which service might also be read. Another nine holy days fell on Sundays.
[68] Namely the Act of Uniformity, 1 Elizabeth c. 2.
[69] Prosecutions of such offenders were numerous. For examples, see Calne, D5/28, 1676 and 1685 (tippling); Collingbourne Kingston, D1/54/21/2 (1708, C&M, youths playing games).
[70] D1/54/11/3 (1686, A&P), f. 20.

seen from the frequency with which churchwardens complained against clergy-men 'for not letting us have prayer twice every Lords day', due to pluralism and the difficulties of serving parishes with chapelries.[71] Despite such complaints parishioners were unlikely to attend church more than once each Sunday. The decision about which service to attend might be based on practical or liturgical factors. As the rector of Lydiard Millicent explained to the bishop of Salisbury in 1747, people attended whichever service fitted best into their work schedule. On short winter days, people had to spend their afternoons 'about their worldly business in fothering & looking to their cattle'. As a result, 'he had a full congre-gation in the morning but in the Afternoon few or rather none at all'. On the longer days of the summer, people were 'more at liberty in the Afternoon', so that he had 'twice the number of people to what I had in the morning'.[72]

Clearly, some 'ordinary labour' did continue on Sundays. The rector of Lydiard Millicent was shocked by the practical considerations that determined his congregation's attendance patterns, and he apologised to the bishop that 'such severe general reflections (with a great deal of labor of mind) are sug-gested'. Yet the Anglican liturgy did not forbid all Sunday labour. Although the Prayer Book and canons acknowledged no exceptions, earlier church documents were more forgiving. The Elizabethan Injunctions of 1559 echoed those of Edward VI twelve years earlier in advising ministers to teach their parishioners 'that they may with a safe and quiet conscience, in the time of harvest, labour upon the holy and festival days, and save that thing which God has sent'.[73] Without saying so explicitly, this effectively sanctioned essential labour of all sorts. The 1676 Act for the Better Observation of the Lord's Day also exempted 'Works of Necessity' from its general ban on ordinary labour on Sundays.[74] Whether in harvest time or out, animals must be fed and cows milked, especially in a dairying parish like Lydiard Millicent.

Liturgical considerations also contributed to thinking about which service to attend. Whereas morning worship invariably included a sermon, afternoon worship usually replaced this with the catechism of the young. Congregations liked sermons but were unenthusiastic about catechism. They expected regular sermons and complained when they did not get them, as in Laverstock, whose wardens presented that they had only one sermon every three weeks.[75] With the exception of chapelries and parishes served by pluralists, most villagers got the regular sermons they desired, for over 90 per cent of incumbents had a licence to preach.[76] Wardens were thus able to present, as did those of Chicklade in 1662,

[71] For example, South Marston, D5/28, 1671, f. 12.
[72] D1/61/1/46. For a similar report from Oxfordshire, see Clapinson, *Bishop Fell and Non-conformity*, pp. 8–9.
[73] E. Cardwell, *Documentary Annals of the Reformed Church of England . . . from the year 1546 to the year 1716* (Oxford, 1844), vol. I, pp. 15–16, 24.   [74] 27 Charles II c. 7.
[75] D1/54/12/3 (1689, A&C).   [76] D1/48/1; D1/48/2.

that they did not need a copy of the Homilies because their parish was 'seldom destitute of a preaching minister'.[77] Laymen wanted not just a sermon but a good sermon, and they had their own opinion of what that meant. The parishioners of Downton, for example, reported in 1662 that their curate 'preached to the great content[ment] of many well affected people'. On the other hand, the inhabitants of West Harnham found their minister 'insufishent for preaching'. They complained 'that his sermons are only for sport for the rude people of Sarum the hole week following', so that they sometimes went into nearby Salisbury to hear better sermons. In addition to attending their own church, the inhabitants of Allington also went to hear sermons in other parishes when they were given on Sunday afternoons.[78]

The rubric directed the minister to instruct children in the catechism for half an hour each Sunday, and told householders to send their children and servants to be catechised. Lay obedience to these instructions was patchy, at best. Churchwardens sometimes complained when a cleric's illness or non-residence meant that he did not perform catechism, often because he had to officiate in another church in the afternoon. In Polshot the wardens reported that children had been catechised and were ready to be confirmed.[79] But it was far more common for wardens to present, as those of Salisbury St Martins did in 1686, a general neglect in sending children and servants to be catechised. In Minety, as in Pewsey, parents refused to send their children despite the minister's attempts to explain the catechism each Sunday and his exhortations to the parents. In Hilperton the minister tried setting aside a different time on Friday for catechism, but to no avail. Discouraged by the lack of popular response, the clergy sometimes discontinued catechism entirely.[80] The failure of youths to be catechised meant that they were not prepared to be confirmed and thus were ineligible to receive communion. We do not know how many ministers followed the example of Richard Watson of Pewsey in enforcing the exclusion of those who had not been catechised, but it was an unpopular step.[81] Parents still expected their children to be confirmed, and during Bishop Ward's illness in the 1680s, when few were confirmed, it was said that 'the people cry out for confirmation'.[82] The most likely explanation for the unpopularity of catechism lies once again in the legacy of the Civil Wars and Interregnum. As the Trowbridge wardens observed in 1662, immediately after the Restoration, 'The church catechisme hathe (of late yeares) been had in so small esteeme that Householders (for the

[77] D1/54/1/3 (1662, A&C), f. 22.

[78] D1/54/1/4 (1662, W&W), ff. 39b, 41b (Downton); D5/28, 1668, f. 16 (West Harnham); D1/54/1/3 (1662, A&C), f. 51 (Allington).

[79] D1/54/16/3 (1698, A&P, Charleton); D1/54/17/3 (1701, A&P, Charleton); D1/54/11/3 (1686, A&P), f. 26 (Polshot). See also Chicklade, D1/54/13/4 (1692, A&C), among other examples.

[80] D1/54/11/4 (1686, A&C&Subd, Salisbury); D1/54/1/1 (1662, M), f. 56 (Minety); D1/54/3/1 (1668, C&M), f. 5b (Pewsey); D1/41/4/43 (Hilperton).

[81] As the minister of Landford did. D1/54/3/2 (1668, C&A), f. 3.   [82] Tanner MS 28, f. 41.

most part) account it a needlis thing, either to teach it theyr familys at home, or to bring them to church to be taught it.'[83] The formation of voluntary societies such as the SPCK and the Society for Parochial Libraries showed the awareness of those within the Church that new measures needed to be taken to promote religious instruction.[84]

Popular observance of divine service shows that there was a delicate balance between liturgical requirements and practicalities. A compromise was possible on the fifty-two Sundays a year, according to which villagers forbore all but essential labour. No such compromise was possible on the other thirty-plus holy days each year, which took too large a chunk out of the working year. It is no coincidence that the only holy days lay people recognised were those on which communion was likely to be administered. Popular observance of these days makes it clear that the explanation for lay failure to take communion is not absence from church. On the contrary, villagers might attend church for years without receiving the sacrament. William Edom of Downton, his neighbours reported, 'seldom misses to go to his parish church on Sundayes & holydayes', but received the sacrament only once a year. When a fight broke out over the mayor's seat in Devizes church in 1707, three witnesses reported that they had never taken communion, although the eldest was 40 years old.[85] The low rate of reception meant that communion was a very different ceremony from the one it would become after Victorian reforms. In the modern Church, communion is administered frequently and virtually every adult who is present in the church receives the sacrament. In the late seventeenth and eighteenth centuries, only a minority of those in church did so. The majority of the congregation observed a ceremony involving others. This does not mean that they did not participate, but they did so vicariously as witnesses of a rite in which they chosen voluntarily not to take a more active role. The reluctance of most people to receive more than once a year explains why clergymen made few attempts to increase the number of communions from three or four times a year.

Attendance at divine service once a week was enforceable by law, at least until 1689, and this raises doubts about its value as evidence of commitment to the Church. Available information about how people behaved in church and what they thought about the service is unfortunately even sparser than it is about communion and church attendance. Divine service was long, repetitive, and left little room for lay participation or spontaneity, with the important exception of the singing of psalms. In the morning three services were usually read back to back: morning service itself, the litany and the ante-communion service, which included a sermon. The Lord's Prayer may have been said as many as five times, two different creeds were used, and there were four readings from the Bible.

[83] D1/54/1/2 (1662, A&P), f. 62.
[84] For the reforms that Burnet advocated, see Foxcroft, pp. 329–30, 499; Burnet, *Pastoral Care*, pp. 186–7. See also chapter 10.   [85] D1/42/61, f. 77; D1/42/66 (1708).

Evening prayer was shorter, for the litany and sermon were usually omitted. The
role of the laity was rigidly predetermined and ritualistic. This did not necessarily prevent the liturgy from gaining popular support, as the Latin mass had done
before the Reformation, although it was in a language which everyone understood.[86] The congregation participated by reciting prayers along with the officiant, by giving the responses in the Prayer Book – especially important in the
litany and the communion service – and by bowing, kneeling, or standing at
specified times. It has been estimated that morning prayer, including communion but excluding notices, banns and the sermon, gave the celebrant 3,500 words
to say, leaving the congregation with only 700.[87] Thus it would be no surprise if
much of the congregation did not pay attention and either fell asleep or behaved
in a disorderly manner, as some clerics complained.[88] That such misbehaviour
occasionally occurred is made clear by a presentment from Allington in 1689 in
which the curate complained about an 'offencive pew . . . which overtops all the
rest of the seats . . . serving onely for the more secure sleeping of those that sitt
in it'.[89] Congregations seriously disrupted worship in other churches. In
Hilperton, for example, parishioners apparently disturbed service regularly by
talking in church and playing games in the churchyard, and on one occasion they
rioted in the church. Such cases were unusual, however, and can normally be
explained by pre-existing tensions between clergy and laity. Even the rector of
Pewsey, who complained at length about the atheism of his congregation, had to
admit that 'the misbehaviour or disorder is not such as to cause disturbance'.[90]

It was more common for parishioners to resort to church, 'abiding quietly in
good order', as those of Codford St Mary did in 1674. There is evidence that
people paid attention to the service. Great Bedwyn's wardens, for example, complained in 1692 that their elderly vicar's voice was 'soe much decayed, that few
. . . of the congregacon can hear what hee reads or sayes'.[91] Literate villagers
clearly followed along in their Bible when the minister read the Lessons, Epistle
and Gospel, for West Grimstead's wardens presented in 1668 that the church
windows did not 'let in sufficient light for the Congregation to make use of their
Bibles'. Several parishes charged their minister with failing to read sections of
divine service. The most detailed of these presentments, from West Harnham,
reported that their minister omitted the beginning of morning prayer and all of
the ante-communion service except for a sermon and the Epistle and Gospel,
which he read in place of the biblical Lessons prescribed for the day. These details

---

[86] E. Duffy, *The Stripping of the Altars* (New Haven and London, 1992), ch. 2.
[87] J. G. Davies, 'The 1662 Book of Common Prayer: its virtues and vices', *Studia Liturgica* 1 (Sept.
    1962), p. 173, cited in H. Davies, *Worship and Theology in England*, vol. II, *From Andrewes to
    Baxter, 1603–1690* (Princeton, 1975), p. 388.
[88] K. Wrightson, *English Society, 1580–1680* (New Brunswick, N.J., 1982), p. 213.
[89] D1/54/12/3 (1689, A&C).
[90] D1/41/4/43 (Hilperton); D1/54/3/1 (1668, C&M), ff. 5b, 5d (Pewsey).
[91] D1/54/6/5 (1674, W&W), f. 27 (Codford); D5/28, 1692, f. 31 (Great Bedwyn).

show that villagers knew the liturgy well and had no wish to see the service short-ened by the omission of portions of it.[92] They accepted the use of set prayers, which the puritans had disliked, and expected the common prayer to be used in full.

The laity's view of Anglican worship nevertheless owed as much to the Interregnum as to the Prayer Book. The legacy of puritanism can be seen not only in the laity's liking of sermons and their neglect of catechism but also in their lack of commitment to ritualistic elements of the service, although the evi-dence is mixed. All persons were to kneel during General Confession and Absolution, the litany, prayers and collects, as well as when they received com-munion; they were to stand during the reading of the Creed and the Gospel; and they were to show reverence for Jesus by bowing each time his name was read during the service. Rejection of such superstitious gestures was an important part of the nonconformist critique of the liturgy. As we have seen, few people observed them in Pewsey, where no one made reverence at the name of Jesus. In other parishes, it appears that parishioners made the required gestures without much enthusiasm. The wardens of Cricklade St Mary reported in 1668, for example, that although no one refused to show reverence when Christ's name was read, they could 'not make an exact presentment' of those who did not 'because those who through forgetfulnesse as we suppose omit it sometimes with all reverence doe it other times'. Clearly, popular observance was far from com-plete and the wardens did not wish to name offenders.[93] Yet the parishioners of Somerford Magna, whom the rector accused of nonconformity, said that they wanted to perform these controversial gestures. They complained that the rector did 'not att all speake out when he reades the comon prayer soe that wee know not in what posture to demeane ourselves either to stand or to kneele'. In Compton Chamberlayne, the minister reported that parishioners generally made reverence when the name of Jesus was pronounced.[94]

In sum, parishioners conformed and yet did not conform. They remained committed to the Church, and to the community which it represented, without accepting every aspect of the Anglican liturgy. It would be an exaggeration to describe them as pious. Yet the opinion, widely shared by the clergy, that the laity were irreligious and sectarian is equally inaccurate. The inability of the clergy, distracted by the peril of nonconformity and overly dogmatic, to understand and accept popular patterns of worship was one of the failings of the Church in this period. Lay practices showed affinities with the puritan and nonconformist cri-tique of the liturgy. Parishioners preferred sermons to catechism, and many dis-liked the ritual gestures to which the puritans had objected. They chose to celebrate few of the holy days which the Church sought to reintroduce. The

[92] D1/54/3/2 (1668, C&A, West Grimstead); D5/28, 1668, f. 16 (West Harnham).
[93] D1/54/3/1 (1668, C&M), ff. 4, 5b.
[94] D1/41/4/39 (Somerford); D1/54/6/4 (1674, A&C), f. 11 (Compton Chamberlayne).

puritan campaign against promiscuous communion made many reluctant to receive the sacrament long after the Restoration. It proved easier to restore the structures of the Church than to erase the legacy of the Interregnum. Yet parishioners were not puritans. Their reasons for neglecting holy days were generally economic rather than theological. The general reluctance to receive the sacrament of communion shows how puritan and Anglican practices became knitted together in a new formulation which neither nonconformists nor churchmen would have accepted. The Prayer Book mattered to village Anglicans. They worshipped as they had learned to worship from their frequent hearing of the liturgy as it was read to them in church, week after week, year after year. The liturgy helped to form lay beliefs, just as the Latin offices had done before the Reformation. The frequent repetition of the Anglican liturgy built upon a strong sense of religious tradition established before the wars and disrupted by the enforcement of the Directory for Public Worship. No wonder that the Prayer Book continued to find support during the Interregnum and that its return was greeted with enthusiasm in 1660.[95] More importantly, most parishioners were not dissenters. They wished to remain within the community of the Church, rather than to separate from it. In challenging parsons like Nathaniel Aske, the laity demonstrated that they were not simply passive conformists, sitting in church because they were obliged to, and that they thought about what they heard. Their independence exhibited the vitality which established religion still possessed at the local level.

[95] J. Morrill, 'The Church in England, 1642–9', in J. Morrill, ed., *Reactions to the English Civil War* (London and Basingstoke, 1982), pp. 104–14.

9

Matters of life and death

Through its liturgy and its clergy the Church of England controlled the major rites of passage: birth, marriage and death.[1] In addition to representing these key stages in the life-cycle of each individual, the ceremonies of baptism, marriage and burial were also important to the broader society. The state insisted that they be recorded in parish registers, and in its search to raise revenue in the 1690s it even taxed them.[2] They were also central to the transmission of property. Participation in the church ceremonies prescribed by the liturgy and in associated secular occasions, such as christening and funeral dinners, served to integrate the community, whose members witnessed the transition of their neighbours through the life-cycle.[3] The use of the liturgical offices was, of course, not voluntary, but they nevertheless played an essential part in popular definitions of the rites of passage. The cleric's role was accepted as indispensable, even in the case of illegal ceremonies such as clandestine marriages. But the clerical role was closely circumscribed, and did not extend beyond liturgical functions.

THE INDISPENSABLE CELEBRANT

Churchwardens' presentments at visitations provided the laity with a means of complaining about clerical neglect. Relatively few ministers were presented for their failure to perform baptisms, marriages and funerals or to visit the sick, particularly when compared to the much larger number who were accused of providing inadequate divine service.[4] This statistic indicates that most clergymen

---

[1] For a valuable recent survey, see D. Cressy, *Birth, Marriage, and Death: Ritual, Religion, and the Life-Cycle in Tudor and Stuart England* (Oxford, 1997).

[2] 6&7 William III c.6.

[3] The classic study of death as a socially integrative transition is R. Hertz, 'A contribution to the study of the collective representation of death', in *Death and the Right Hand* (Aberdeen, 1960, originally pub. 1907), pp. 27-86. See also G. Gorer, *Death, Grief, and Mourning in Contemporary Britain* (London, 1965).

[4] The seven presentments relating to burials, baptisms and churchings after 1662 compared to thirty-eight for insufficient divine service. These figures do not include presentments against three nonconformist ministers in 1662, before their ejection later in the year. D1/54, 1662–1750; D5/28, 1662–1750. See chapter 5.

celebrated the key rites of passage satisfactorily. If they had failed to do so, then they would have been presented, because the laity accepted the essential role of the clergy as celebrants. Complaints about the failure of a minister to bury or baptise almost always occurred as part of a serious episode of lay–clerical conflict, often resulting in a consistory court suit. Gervase Bland of Knook, John White of Avebury, Nathaniel Aske of Somerford Magna, and Richard Lewis of Netheravon, each of whom was involved in serious conflict with their congregations, all had disagreements with parishioners over burials.[5] The ceremony might itself be the source of dispute, for example if the minister demanded a fee to perform the funeral, preach a sermon, or make an entry in the parish register. Although burial was in theory not to be denied for want of a fee, in practice this principle was overruled by local custom in many parishes.[6] Ministers could effectively hold families to ransom, refusing even to permit the body to be carried into the churchyard until they had received their fee.[7]

Pluralism and chapelries were the most common explanation for inadequate performance of divine service.[8] They were less serious obstacles to the due performance of baptisms, marriages and funerals, because these ceremonies were required only occasionally. Problems might nevertheless arise when a death occurred unexpectedly or a child needed to be baptised urgently. It was customary for burials to take place within a few days of death, so that a minister might need to be found quickly, particularly if the weather was hot. If the minister could not be found, then the minister of the neighbouring parish might be hired. When the rector of Tockenham Wick (who was absent in Worcestershire for most of the week) could not be found to bury two children in the 1680s, the vicar of Clyffe Pypard buried one and the vicar of Wootton Bassett buried the other.[9] Parishioners were reluctant to bury anyone without a minister being present to officiate, and they did so only in emergencies. As inhabitants of Winterbourne Stoke explained succinctly, a 'child was buried with out anie menester the menester not being at home the child stanke'.[10] The parishioners of Westport St Mary encountered the same problem in 1673 when they could not get news to their minister in time, so that they had to bury George Davis without 'any service performed according to the Book of Comon Prayer'. As they explained when the curate John Clarke complained that he had not received advance notice of the burial, 'the body . . . being an aged diseased person, was soe offensive . . . that it could not be kept any longer from buriall, being kept from about midnight 'till sunne sett'.[11] A large parish near Malmesbury which was divided into three

---

[5] See pp. 109–12, 134–41, 148, 174–6.   [6] R. Burn, *Ecclesiastical Law* (3rd edn, 1775), vol. I, p. 246.
[7] It was alleged in 1669 that William Meaden of Horningsham refused to enter marriages, christenings and burials into the register without payment of a fee of 4*d*. D5/28, 1669, f. 42. Nathaniel Aske would not permit the corpse into the churchyard without payment of a fee. D1/41/4/39.
[8] See chapter 5.   [9] D1/41/4/35, Smith c. Durston.
[10] D1/41/1/21. The inhabitants also had to hire a minister to church two women.
[11] D1/41/1/17, 23 Sept. 1673 and 11 Oct. 1673. Clarke alleged that the offence was repeated on two occasions.

distinct settlements – Charlton, Brokenborough and Westport – Westport St Mary was a difficult parish to serve.

An incident in Plaitford chapelry in the early eighteenth century demonstrates the difficulties parishioners might encounter in scheduling a funeral, when a minister insisted for reasons of personal convenience upon performing the burial service on the same day that he came to the parish or chapelry to read divine service. The resulting misunderstandings offended both lay and clerical proprieties and might lead to the worsening of relations between them. William Richman of Plaitford died one Saturday in October 1713, and his friends and relatives planned his funeral for the following Tuesday, to give them enough time to get a coffin and to make other arrangements. When the parish clerk notified the rector of West Grimstead, John Foot, of the funeral at prayers on the following day, Foot expressed his displeasure at these plans. He refused to come on Tuesday to perform the funeral, telling the parish clerk 'that since they had no[t] brought him to be buried on that day being Sunday, they might get some body Else to bury the sd corpse'. On Tuesday Richman's body was nevertheless 'carried to the chapple yard of Plaitford to be there interred', accompanied by 'the greatest part of the parishioners'. Foot was 'not there to do his duty', and since the parishioners had not found anyone to replace him the body had to be left in the chapel for two days until the minister next visited Plaitford. When he finally came, the minister performed the funeral quickly, instructing that the body be carried to the grave without first reading the church service. Only six people, including the widow and the parish clerk, were able to attend the funeral. Foot's behaviour offended lay sensibilities in several respects. His absence meant that the body had to be left for two nights in the chapel, after neighbours would have ensured that the deceased was attended during his final sickness and after his death. His unexpected arrival meant that most of the parish were unable to attend the hastily arranged funeral, violating the social nature of the ceremony. Foot's omission of sections of the funeral service also did not escape the notice of the parish clerk.[12]

These examples leave little doubt that the laity considered the minister's ceremonial role at funerals to be indispensable, and this was equally true of baptisms. The high rate of infant mortality meant that a baptism might be needed quickly if a new-born child was sickly and likely to die. The churchwardens of Horningsham noted that their minister, 'being resident in another parish & many times not at home, the Neighbours are greatly troubled to get a ministr to baptize a weake nere-born-babe'.[13] There was confusion in both popular and clerical minds about whether infants who died before they had been baptised would receive the benefits of Christ's sacrifice.[14] The reformed view was that baptism was not essential to save the soul of a weak new-born child, a stance which Baptists took to its logical consequence by delaying baptism until later in life. This meant that there was no need to perform emergency baptisms in

---

[12] D1/42/67, Flower c. Foot. [13] D5/28, 1669, f. 42.
[14] Cressy, *Birth, Marriage, and Death*, pp. 114–23.

midweek. The Church of England preferred to have the ceremony conducted during service on Sunday 'when the most number of people come together', so that they could witness the admission of a new member into their ranks and, at the same time, be reminded of their 'own profession made to God in their Baptism'.[15] Yet the liturgy nevertheless made provision for the ceremony to be performed on a weekday, and it barred those who had not been baptised from Christian burial. When illness required urgent baptism in the infant's home, then if the child recovered it was to be brought into church and shown to the assembled congregation on some later Sunday. The Prayer Book also made provision for the performance of baptism by members of the laity in cases of emergency. The issue of whether those who were not episcopally ordained could baptise had broader theological and political implications, however, which made the Anglican clergy reluctant to accept lay baptism. If lay baptisms were valid, then so also were those of dissenting ministers. The issue acquired additional political significance in 1708 when the doctrine that lay baptisms were invalid appeared to present a challenge to the Hanoverian succession.[16]

The clergy's insistence upon the importance of the social functions of baptism can be seen in their resistance to the practice of baptism in the family home, which had become more common during the Interregnum. In practice, there is relatively little evidence of private baptism in Wiltshire, although in 1661 the Dinton gentleman John North was still able to have his child christened at home by the vicar.[17] The avoidance of private baptism nevertheless contributed to clerical reluctance to perform emergency baptisms. In the 1680s William Gale, the vicar of Downton, refused to christen John Bampton's new-born child at his house, 'saying if the Child be ill I'le goe to them, but otherwise lett them bring it to Church'. The family conceded that the baby was healthy, but they still 'desiered it might be don at home'. Even private baptisms required a minister to officiate at the ceremony, and to Gale's irritation the vicar of Alderbury was prepared to perform the ceremony, no doubt in return for a fee. On this occasion, the social aspect of the christening was preserved by the presence of godparents and several neighbours as witnesses and by the holding of a christening dinner.[18]

The almost superstitious belief of the people in quick baptism made the behaviour of Matthew Whittley, vicar of Westport St Mary in the 1660s, particularly worrying to its inhabitants. In 1668 the churchwardens prosecuted Whittley, not only for his failure to perform baptisms and funerals but also for his scandalous

---

[15] The quotations are from the office of baptism in the Book of Common Prayer.

[16] G. V. Bennett, *The Tory Crisis in Church and State 1688–1730* (Oxford, 1975), pp. 151–5.

[17] D1/54/1/3 (1662, A&C), ff. 2–5. Cf. Exeter diocese, whose bishop complained in 1686 about the performance of private christenings for the richer sort. Tanner MS 30, f. 50.

[18] D1/39/1/57, ff. 120–2. Nicolas Noble of Calne also managed to procure a 'strange' minister 'to baptize his last borne child with Godfather and Godmothers' in 1668, although it is not clear whether this was a nonconformist or the Anglican incumbent of a nearby parish. D5/28, 1668, f. 62.

behaviour, which included the drunken performance of divine service and communion. On one occasion 'Hanna Foskett with some of her women neighbours came on a weekeday to Mr Whittlyes house (being in their way to the church of Charleton . . .) and desired him to baptize her child then wth her'. Whittley refused because it was a weekday, and he told the women that 'if they would bringe the saide child uppon the next Sunday followinge he would baptize itt'. On another occasion, a baby died unbaptised after Whittley refused to go to its parents' house to christen the sick infant. Whittley's refusal to perform emergency baptisms is unlikely to have been due to puritanism, even though he had been appointed during the Interregnum and remained after Black St Bartholomew's Day. In 1649 he had been charged with stirring up his flock against Parliament and had suffered ejection from a living.[19] Nor would puritanism have been consistent with his subsequent refusal to bury the unbaptised child, an act that can only have increased the laity's anxiety, while confirming their belief in the importance of speedy baptism.[20] Whittley was stubbornly insistent upon following the liturgy to the letter.

The puritans had sought to de-emphasise funeral rites,[21] but after the Restoration the Prayer Book restored the ceremonies in which the clergy naturally had a central role. The officiant managed the service and read the liturgy. A death in the parish was marked by the tolling of a church bell, and the bell was rung again before and after the funeral.[22] The funeral began when the body, covered by a black hearse cloth, was carried in procession from the home of the deceased to the churchyard. The minister met the coffin at the churchyard gate and conducted it to the church, reading the text 'I am the resurrection and the life' and other scriptural texts.[23] Once in the church, he read the first part of the burial service, including a prose psalm and the lesson, 'Now is Christ risen from the dead . . .' (from 1 Corinthians 15). The body was then carried into the churchyard for burial where the minister finished the office at the side of the grave: 'Man that is born of a woman, hath but a short time to live, and is full of misery.' The service finished with the collect to 'The Father of our Lord Jesus Christ, who is the resurrection and the life; in whom whosoever believeth, shall live, though he die', reminding the congregation of the promise of eternal life implicit in Christ's crucifixion and resurrection.

In Charlton this ceremony led to conflict when Whittley objected to what he perceived as violation of the liturgy and the diminution of his ceremonial role. One Sunday afternoon early in 1668 Thomas Hanckes and his neighbours

---

[19] Matthews, *Walker Revised*, p. 353.

[20] D1/42/62, witness 13; D1/41/4/35, Libel in Lane & Knight c. Whittley.

[21] C. Gittings, *Death, Burial and the Individual in Early Modern England* (London and Sydney, 1984), p. 48; Cressy, *Birth, Marriage, and Death*, pp. 403–9.

[22] Canon 67. A comprehensive presentment from Cricklade St Mary confirms that the parish clerk tolled the bell. D1/54/3/1 (1668, C&M), f. 14.

[23] The liturgy also allowed the body to be taken straight to the grave.

carried the body of Hanckes's son to Charlton church for burial, waiting at the churchyard gate for the vicar to conduct them into the church. When he did not turn up, they sent the parish clerk to fetch him. Whittley arrived fifteen minutes later and attempted to sneak into the church by another door. But the mourners saw him, and fearful that he might start the service without them, they quickly brought the body into the church and set it down. Their actions displeased the vicar, who insisted that they take the coffin back outside to the gate so that he could meet the procession. He managed to persuade the reluctant parishioners to take the body out to the grave, only then to tell them to return it to the church. Subsequent events suggest that the parishioners refused to co-operate. The minister returned to church and read evening prayers, and he then left without performing the burial despite pleas from Hanckes and others.[24]

Whittley may have been naturally cautious to avoid even the hint of nonconformity. Yet the explanation for his behaviour is more likely to be that the liturgy was increasingly coming to define Anglicanism itself and the clergy's role within it.[25] Many clergymen were unwilling to allow any deviation from the letter of the liturgy or any challenge to their role in and control over ceremonies. Disagreement over the timing of the burial or the performance of the ceremony could lead to open disputes at funerals and to bodies being left unburied. The clergy resisted lay attempts to tamper with the liturgy, for example by preventing the choir from singing a metrical psalm in place of the prose psalm which was to be read or sung by the minister. As church music grew in popularity in the first half of the eighteenth century, it became common for choirs to introduce a psalm into natural breaks in the service. For example, in 1742, the Boyton singers sang a psalm in church before the body was carried out into the churchyard.[26] This custom was already well established in some parishes, for twenty or so years earlier the parishioners of Somerford Keynes had shocked their new curate by singing at a funeral 'as they allways doe on such occasions'. In each instance, the minister refused to continue with the service and, when the singers persisted, left the church leaving the body unburied, despite lay attempts to detain him. A petition from the inhabitants testifies to the unpopularity of such clerical inflexibility, which disrupted popular understandings of the liturgy and their own place in it, as well as their sense of propriety. The signatories reported that 'some women Interrupted him by Laying hold of his Surplace and desireing him to be Quiet', but the curate nevertheless 'highly disobliged the whole parish' by walking out in a 'great passion' leaving the body unburied.[27]

Christenings and funerals had an important social aspect, and neighbours often celebrated them with a feast or dinner in addition to the formal ceremony.[28]

---

[24] D1/42/62, witnesses 13–15.
[25] J. Spurr, *The Restoration Church of England, 1646-1689* (London and New Haven, 1991), ch. 7.
[26] D1/36/2/13.   [27] D1/41/4/36, temp. Thomas Sherlock.
[28] Gittings, *Death, Burial and the Individual*, pp. 158–59; W. M. Jacob, *Lay People and Religion in the Early Eighteenth Century* (Cambridge, 1996), p. 73.

There was some tension in lay minds between the urge to baptise babies as quickly as possible and the social aspects of a christening. The social imperative prevailed in the decision of the parents in Winterbourne Bassett in 1662 that the baptism of their child should be 'deferred a weeke longer in expectation of the company of friends & the greater strength of the child'.[29] A funeral dinner affirmed the involvement of the entire community in the commemoration of a death, while confirming the social status of the deceased.[30] In 1673 Michal Lawson of Broad Chalke spent over £14 for a funeral dinner, for her late husband, 'a man of very good fassion & well beloved required the same'. Deponents 'observed a greate multitude of people neighbours . . . & others of his kin'red & friends from other places', perhaps two or three hundred of them. They were well fed and much was left, 'wch was disposed of to the poore'.[31] The social functions of funerals bridged religious differences. Thus, although William Hinwood absented himself from church and frequented a conventicle in Porton, 'sometyme he would com to church to the buriall of a friend'.[32] Similarly, although Rebecca Mayo of Somerford Magna was feuding with the rector and rarely came to divine service or took communion, she was 'sure to come to church if there be a funerall or Christning feast'.[33] Because the social functions of funerals surpassed religious differences, inhabitants were shocked when their minister refused to bury their nonconformist neighbours.

Nonconformists were legally required to seek burial in the churchyard by the Anglican minister, although Quakers used their own graveyards since they rejected both church ceremonies and the use of consecrated ground. The clergy were obliged to officiate at the burial of all but excommunicates (as well as suicides and the unbaptised). Yet the vicar of Avebury, John White, refused to bury Richard Bayly in 1710, after the Act of Toleration, because he was a Presbyterian, an offence for which he was later to be reprimanded.[34] White also took measures to prevent a funeral from being performed according to the liturgy by instructing the parish clerk to lock up the parish's copy of the Prayer Book. John Brinsden, minister of the neighbouring parish of Winterbourne Monkton, was present and would have been prepared to officiate if the Prayer Book had been available, but in the end the body had to be buried without ceremony. On another occasion White took malicious pleasure when, after he had refused to perform the funeral, villagers buried Walter Alexander incorrectly, with his head pointing in the wrong direction.[35] Parishioners nevertheless tolled the church bell at

---

[29] D1/54/1/2 (1662, A&P), f. 12.

[30] Processions might have a similar role in an urban setting. J. Whaley, 'Symbolism for the survivors: the disposal of the dead in Hamburg in the late seventeenth and eighteenth centuries', in J. Whaley, ed., *Mirrors of Mortality: Studies in the Social History of Death* (London, 1981), pp. 80-105.

[31] D2/6/2, ff. 35–45.   [32] D1/42/61, f. 9v.   [33] D1/41/1/17 (6 Oct. 1673).

[34] D1/42/68, Ponting & Caswell c. White. White also refused to bury Ruth Mills, because 'she had been formerly a lewd woman'. See chapter 6 for the context of this dispute.

[35] 'The grave was traditionally dug, at a depth of six feet, from east to west, the head lying to the west, in the words of Thomas Browne, "that he may rise with his face to the east".' Gittings, *Death, Burial and the Individual*, p. 139.

Alexander's burial, just as they did after the death and at the funeral in the 1670s of Mary Sympson, an excommunicate widow who was buried in Chisledon churchyard, much to the anger of the vicar.[36]

A degree of flexibility in the performance of baptisms or funerals did the clergy no harm, and as eighteenth-century parsons learned, could be necessary to retain the cooperation of congregations. The pluralist John Lewis was willing to christen on any day of the week, although this sometimes required him to walk from his home in Holt to his other cures in nearby Great Chalfield or Atworth.[37] The diarist William Cole of Blecheley (Bucks.) observed 'there is no parlying with your Parishioners on any Point of Doctrine or Discipline: for if you are rigid, they will either abstain from all Ordinances, or go over to the Dissenters'. This policy led him to actions which he considered absurd, including christening a child and churching its mother on the same day in his parlour.[38] Clerical inflexibility did the Established Church considerable harm, provoking hostility and widening the gap between the clergy and an uncomprehending laity, as can be seen in a dispute which took place in Turners Puddle (Dorset) church in 1682. When Elizabeth Compton brought her child to be baptised, the minister William Bradford refused to perform the ceremony because the godparents had never taken communion, claiming that 'it was against the Canons of the Church'. Bradford's offer to perform his office if friends or neighbours who had received the sacrament would stand as godparents was unacceptable. Compton 'fell out into a great rage' and told the minister, 'doe you chuse whet[her] you will baptize the said child or noe, for I will mainteyne it, that Children are better unbaptized than to be baptized and away she ran out of the church raylinge at the said Mr Bradford'.[39] Elizabeth Compton's words suggest that Bradford may have missed an opportunity to return Baptists to the Church, although it is also possible that they were conformists. As we have seen, it was common for adults to go many years without receiving communion. In any case, his rebuff did the Church little good. Compton is unlikely to have been the only person to prefigure the words of Thomas Hardy's Tess of the d'Urbervilles when a minister refused to give a Christian burial to her unbaptised baby: 'Then I don't like you! . . . and I'll never come to your church no more!'[40] The laity accepted the clerical monopoly over baptisms and burials and were outraged when clerical inflexibility prevented a minister from fulfilling his indispensable role. In the localities, the laity experienced the same clerical dogmatism and insistence upon forms and ceremonies that were the targets of an anticlerical critique on the national scene.

[36] D1/41/1/17, 15 Jan. 1673/4 and 8 Feb. 1673/4. See also D1/41/1/41, 24 May 1665 (Horningsham), for another nonconformist funeral.   [37] WRO 1981/1; Bodleian Library, MS Eng Misc f. 10.
[38] *The Blecheley Diary of the Rev. William Cole, 1765–67*, ed. F. G. Stokes (London, 1931), pp. 8–9. The couple had just been married in the church before signing the register in his parlour.
[39] D5/22/19, ff. 1–3.
[40] T. Hardy, *Tess of the d'Urbervilles* (London, 1975, originally publ. 1891), pp. 121–5. Tess had baptised the child herself.

CLANDESTINE MARRIAGE

The clergy were theoretically less crucial to marriages than they were to christenings and funerals. Marriages were often the result of long planning and extended negotiation, and normally were not urgent matters. Binding matrimony could in theory be agreed between the man and woman in private through spousals, although the Church had a role in solemnising unions.[41] Yet by 1640, it has been argued, the need for marriages to be performed by clergy in church was 'widely accepted at all levels', so that 'the wedding service of the Church of England had been absorbed as part of popular culture'.[42] The minister had become indispensable to marriages, in the same way as he was to baptisms and burials. One unintended consequence was to stimulate the growth of clandestine unions, for the late seventeenth century witnessed an explosion in the number of couples who married unlawfully. As many as one in four unions may have been clandestine in this period, although this figure is inflated by the number of Fleet marriages; the phenomenon appears to have declined again in the early eighteenth century.[43] Far from representing a rejection of the Church, clandestine marriage exhibited the success of clerical marriage as the mark of binding matrimony. Such marriages, which often were performed in churches, provided couples with a means of forming unions quickly, privately, and away from the eyes of their families.[44] Besides legal changes, a more general relaxation in sexual regulation, manifested in corresponding rises in bastardy and prenuptial pregnancy and a decline in the age of female marriage, may also have contributed to the rising numbers of unlawful marriages.[45]

The canons sought to guarantee that marriages were performed in public in the face of the community in which the couple lived in order to ensure that the families approved and that there were no other impediments to the alliance. Clandestine marriages were by definition conducted in secret, most likely in order to avoid risking family disapproval. Usually performed in church, they nevertheless failed to meet canonical requirements which would have made them

---

[41] Henry Swinburne, *Treatise of Spousal or Matrimonial Contracts* (London, 1686).

[42] M. Ingram, 'Reform', p. 143; Martin Ingram, *Church Courts, Sex and Marriage in England, 1570–1640* (Cambridge, 1987); M. Ingram, 'Spousals litigation in the English ecclesiastical courts, c.1350–c.1640', in R. B. Outhwaite, ed., *Marriage and Society: Studies in the Social History of Marriage* (New York, 1981), pp. 35–57.

[43] R. B. Outhwaite, *Clandestine Marriage in England, 1500–1850* (London and Rio Grande, 1995); E. A. Wrigley, 'Clandestine marriage in Tetbury in the late 17th century', *Local Population Studies* 10 (1973): 15-21; E. A. Wrigley and R. S. Schofield, *The Population History of England 1541-1871* (London, 1981), p. 263; Outhwaite, *Marriage and Society*.

[44] For this reason, the increased number of defective registers do not necessarily cast doubt on the centrality of the church ceremony. Cf. R. M. Smith, 'Marriage processes in the English past: some continuities', in L. Bonfield et al., eds., *The World We Have Gained* (Oxford, 1986), p. 99.

[45] E. A. Wrigley 'Marriage, fertility and population growth in eighteenth-century England', in Outhwaite, *Marriage and Society*, pp. 137–85.

public, either because banns were not read, a lawful licence was not purchased, or the rite was celebrated in the wrong church or at the wrong time.[46] The fact that, in the countryside at least, most clandestine marriages were performed by clergymen within church had religious significance. However unlawful they were, such marriages were among the services which clergy offered to lay people, alongside christenings, burials and, of course, lawful marriages. After almost a century of attempts at reform, the practice of clandestine marriage was finally outlawed by Hardwicke's Marriage Act in 1753.[47] By removing one of the Church's most popular services (at least with couples), this legislation may ironically have made the clergy even more remote.

The antiquarian John Aubrey documented the phenomenon of clandestine marriage in Wiltshire. Aubrey noticed that relatively few marriages were performed in Donhead St Mary and Broad Chalke, and he alleged that this was because villagers preferred to be married in the nearby parish of Ansty. He supported this observation with statistics from the Donhead parish register which showed that, given the number of baptisms, there were surprisingly few marriages in the parish church. Between 1680 and 1684 there were ninety-two baptisms in the parish but only eleven marriages, a ratio of 8.4 baptisms per marriage.[48] Effective fertility in early modern England was reduced by the relatively late age at which women married and the risk of mortality in childbirth. Between three and five births would normally be expected per marriage.[49] The higher rate apparently found in Donhead suggests that many couples who subsequently dwelled in the parish went elsewhere to marry. Unfortunately, the Donhead St Mary register for these years has not survived, perhaps because the friend of Aubrey's who supplied the statistics carelessly failed to return it to the parish. The next register indicates that by 1695–9 the ratio of baptisms to marriages had returned to a more normal 4.5 to 1. Even then, the minister (who was nervous of being prosecuted under the 1695 Marriage Duty Act) recorded five alleged marriages that he had not performed himself but suspected had been celebrated clandestinely outside the parish.[50] In Broad Chalke, another parish named by Aubrey as a net supplier of couples, there were no fewer than 9.5 baptisms per marriage, leaving little doubt that couples were going elsewhere to marry.[51]

The evidence for clandestine marriage in Wiltshire is inevitably piecemeal. The non-survival for most of the period of the act books for the bishop's correctional court where prosecutions would have been heard makes it difficult to carry

[46] Canon 62.   [47] Outhwaite, *Clandestine Marriage*, pp. 67–97; Tanner MS 447, ff. 39–41.
[48] Bodleian Library, MS Aubrey 1, f. 162.
[49] E. A. Wrigley, 'Baptism/marriage ratios in late 17c England', *Local Population Studies* 3 (1969): 15-17.
[50] WRO 980/2. A copy of the 1695 act is bound into the register, which also includes a parish census.
[51] C. G. Moore, ed., *Registers of Broad Chalke from 1538 to 1780* (London, 1881).

out a systematic survey. Bishop Seth Ward clearly took the offence seriously and sought to bring it under control. In around 1668, not long after his translation to the diocese, Ward received instructions from the archbishop of Canterbury to proceed against marriages that were performed without banns or licence.[52] This seems to have sparked an episcopal campaign, for citations and surviving act book references document a dramatic rise in the number of cases over the next three years.[53] Couples were the most common sufferers, but a few ministers were also cited. If effective action was to be taken against the practice, the clerics who illegally solemnised such unions needed to be disciplined. At about the same time, Ward began to note down the names of clerics who were unlawful marriers, some of whom he subsequently suspended.[54] In 1677 his court took correctional action against fifteen clerics, most likely for clandestine marriage.[55] Because the officiant and the couple were rarely prosecuted at the same time, it is difficult to study the context in which clandestine marriages occurred. Around thirty ministers are known to have married unlawfully in the late seventeenth century. Details of their names and parishes help to establish the centres of the trade, so long as it is remembered that the list is unlikely to be complete. The names and parishes of couples charged with clandestine marriage are uninformative on their own, without information on where they were married and by whom. Couples often ignored the citation against them and were excommunicated for their contumacy, so that no details are available. In a minority of cases, however, the couple appeared and confessed their offences, providing the identity of the officiant or location of the ceremony. Further details about clandestine marriage can be gleaned from depositions in suits brought to reform scandalous clerics and from parish registers. From these sources it is possible to determine the context of over forty marriages, and these unsystematic data will provide the main source for the analysis that follows. Although the information is regrettably sparse, particularly when compared to the rich case studies which Lawrence Stone has been able to construct, it is nevertheless valuable for the insight it provides into the behaviour of those lower down in society, most of whom would have been too poor to appeal their cases to the Court of Arches.[56]

Ward's approach to clandestine marriage involved a stern determination to enforce the law to the full extent of his authority, balanced by a degree of mercy, as can be seen from surviving correspondence with Lambeth Palace. The canons

---

[52] Tanner MS 44, f. 129.   [53] D1/41/1/11–14; D1/39/1/58.

[54] D1/27/1/1, ff. 71, 79, 86, 88, 90, 94, 97, 99; D1/39/1/58, f. 15 (16/5/1671).

[55] D1/39/2/13, 20 Nov. and 4 Dec. 1677. The act book does not record the offences of the clerics, although one, William Kiften, was also on Ward's list of unlawful marriers. D1/27/1/1, f. 71.

[56] L. Stone, *Uncertain Lives and Broken Lives: Marriage and Divorce in England 1660–1857* (Oxford, 1995). It was rare for clandestine marriage suits to be appealed to the Court of Arches. Only 24 of the 1,308 matrimonial cases in Stone's sample were for clandestine marriage. L. Stone, *Road to Divorce: England 1530–1987* (Oxford, 1995), p. 425. Clandestine marriage was often involved in appeals over other issues.

stipulated that clerical offenders should be suspended for three years, and Ward
felt that he had no authority to adjust this. So after Jonathan Heskins of
Marlborough St Peters had been suspended for performing marriages without
banns or licences, the bishop refused to restore the minister despite the attempts
at persuasion made by borough magistrates. Ward only agreed to Heskins's restoration by the archbishop after the minister had acknowledged his fault and the
magistrates had promised to use their best endeavours to execute the ecclesiastical laws, and he declared his determination to do his duty if they violated these
promises. On the other hand, he counselled mercy in the case of a Berkshire minister in the light of his otherwise faultless behaviour and the needs of his family.
The bishop took a harder line against Anthony Sadler of Berwick St James,
whose generally scandalous life left little room for forgiveness. Sadler was instituted at Berwick in 1671, after a chequered career which led to his expulsion from
the London and Winchester dioceses. When the bishop learned not long afterwards that Sadler was performing marriages without banns or licences, he
instructed his chancellor to take action against him, and the minister was
suspended and excommunicated in 1675. Sadler denied the bishop's authority
and the case was still lingering in 1681 when the churchwarden tried literally to
drag him from his pulpit.[57]

Sadler claimed that as a royal manor Berwick St James was exempt from diocesan jurisdiction. Although this was patently untrue, it nevertheless directs our
attention to the 'lawless churches' which are thought to have been the most
popular venues for clandestine marriages. Also known as peculiars, these were
'any place[s] pretending to be exempt from the Visitation of the Bishop of the
Diocese' in which they were located.[58] Such anomalies were a feature of English
secular and ecclesiastical administration. The county of Wiltshire included parishes in Gloucestershire and Berkshire, and its hundreds often included non-con-
tiguous areas. Around forty-five Wiltshire parishes lay within ecclesiastical
peculiars, which ranged in size from the single parish in the peculiar of
Trowbridge to the large deanery of Salisbury, with seventy parishes scattered
across four different counties. Yet the fact that these parishes lay outside the correctional machinery of the bishop did not mean that they were free from ecclesiastical supervision. As Richard Burn explained, 'Exempt jurisdictions are so
called, not because they are under no ordinary; but because they are not under
the ordinary of the diocese', namely the bishop.[59] Almost all peculiars in
Wiltshire lay under the jurisdiction of the dean of Salisbury. Various prebendaries of Salisbury cathedral had primary jurisdiction over most of these parishes
and visited them annually, but the dean visited them every three years and used
his court to correct offenders. Other parishes were under his primary jurisdiction

[57] Tanner MS 44, f. 129; 38, f. 108; 143, ff. 119–20; 290, f. 180; D1/39/2/13, 16 Nov. 1675.
[58] The phrase is taken from 6&7 William III c.6.
[59] R. Burn, *Ecclesiastical Law*, 2nd edn (London, 1767), vol. II, p. 69.

and were visited annually. These ecclesiastical peculiars were therefore not lawless at all, for each not only had its own court and visitations, presided over by the prebend himself or by his surrogate, but also was subject to the dean's court. Prebendal visitations seem often to have been more important for such administrative functions as swearing in the new wardens than for correction. Yet if, as was often the case, the prebend was also the incumbent of a parish within the peculiar, he might take a particular interest in that peculiar. By and large peculiars left matrimonial matters to the dean.[60] Although the bishop of Exeter claimed that the Dorsetshire peculiars were factious because Dean Thomas Pierce never visited them, the visitation records themselves indicate that the dean's visitations were just as rigorous as those of the bishop.[61]

The authorities took measures in the late seventeenth century to close the loophole which exempt jurisdictions seemed to provide. The High Commission order in November 1686 against Trinity Minories and other exempt parishes in London had broader implications in theory, for the court forbade all ministers to celebrate marriages without banns or a lawful licence and ordered diocesan chancellors to publish the order in all churches, whether or not they were exempt.[62] In practice, the order appears to have had little immediate effect in the provinces. But a decade later Parliament tightened the screw in the Marriage Duty Act, specifying a penalty of £100 against clerics who performed marriages in exempt jurisdictions without banns or licence.[63] In Wiltshire the majority of clandestine marriages whose context we know about were performed in peculiars. As Aubrey stated, the most popular venue was the parish of Ansty in the south-west corner of the county, only twelve miles from the city of Salisbury. As a royal peculiar, Ansty was the only parish in Wiltshire which was truly exempt from ecclesiastical jurisdiction.[64] The parish was served by a curate who received the modest stipend of only £10 which he might supplement by solemnising illegal marriages.[65] The parish's exempt status failed to give either the couples or the officiant complete protection from prosecution. Couples were liable to prosecution in the parish in which they lived after the marriage, which of course was unlikely to be Ansty. The paradox of clandestine marriage was that even if the ceremony itself was secret the existence of the marriage was bound to come out when the woman became pregnant or the couple cohabited. At this point the couple became vulnerable not only to family and community disapproval but

[60] Only one Wiltshire peculiar has left any trace of matrimonial administration. P. Stewart, *Diocese of Salisbury Guide to the Records of the Bishop* . . . ([Trowbridge,] 1973).

[61] Tanner MS 30, ff. 51–51v. Pierce was embroiled in a bitter dispute with Bishop Ward over prebendal patronage.   [62] D1/41/4/1.   [63] 6&7 William III c.6, 7&8 William III c.35.

[64] Other parishes where the Crown had the advowson lay within the bishop's jurisdiction.

[65] WRO 869/1. Although Ansty lay in the region of Wiltshire where many of the county's recusants lived (and the stipend was paid by the Catholic Lord Arundell of Wardour), none of the couples known to have married in Ansty and the ministers known to have officiated were Catholic. J. A. Williams, *Catholic Recusancy in Wiltshire, 1660–1791* (Catholic Record Society, 1968), esp. Appendix F.

also to prosecution. The officiating cleric might also be prosecuted if, like Edward Worley, he was also a curate or incumbent in another parish. Worley got into trouble with the dean of Salisbury in 1668 for solemnising clandestine marriages, and he was threatened with removal from the curacy of Swallowcliffe. He was saved by a testimonial in his favour from the villagers of Swallowcliffe and by his promise to reform, which he supported by signing a bond. Three years later, however, he sought to recover his bond, presumably to enable him to continue in the trade. Indeed, Worley celebrated at least four illegal marriages in 1670–1 and was still performing them towards the end of the decade, despite his excommunication by the bishop.[66] Another cleric, William Anderson, continued the trade in the 1690s when he was named by several couples who were prosecuted in the bishop's court.[67] These marriages cannot be verified in the parish register, in which no marriages were recorded between 1655 and 1694. The register was then carelessly kept until 1712, recording only one or two marriages per year, mostly from Ansty itself. Even this inadequate record, which is unlikely to be complete, has questionable features. Five of the marriages were technically illegal because both bride and groom came from outside the parish.[68] Clearly, Ansty was a logical destination for couples who wished to marry in secret. When William Sweet and Elinor Bull discussed marriage they planned to go to Ansty, although ultimately their plans came to nothing. The Ansty and Donhead St Mary registers both confirm that some inhabitants of the latter parish went to the former to get married.[69]

The parish of Great Bedwyn had a tradition of illegal marriage that was almost as strong as Ansty's. Three vicars were accused of celebrating clandestine marriages in the half century or so after the Restoration. Robert Billings married a Marlborough man and his bride in 1662. In 1678 the succeeding vicar Robert Randall faced charges of drunkenness and clandestine marriage, and William Meaden faced similar charges in 1713. Although they were beneficed, the vicars of Great Bedwyn shared the poverty of the curates of Ansty, since they were guaranteed an annual stipend of only £12. The churchwardens confirmed 'ye smallnesse of o[u]r vicarage as being too small a competency to maintaine a minister'. In this desperate situation, each incumbent grasped at any expedient, including clandestine marriage, that might supplement his modest income.[70] Depositions taken in the consistory court case against Robert Randall provide unusually full details of the context in which clandestine marriages occurred. Thomas Morie, an agricultural labourer, and his wife-to-be, 'being minded to bee married privately and not to have their Banns published openly in the parish church of

---

[66] D5/28, 1668, f. 13; D5/31/1 (1670); D5/29/3, ff. 3v–4; D1/39/2/13 (16 Nov. 1675); D1/41/1/21.
[67] D1/39/1/64, 1 Jan. 1693/4, 30 April 1694, 15 May 1694.   [68] WRO 869/2.
[69] D1/42/59, f. 59; WRO 869/2; WRO 980/2.
[70] In the 1660s the vicar's stipend was sometimes supplemented by a gift of £5 from the duke of Somerset. For more on the poverty of Great Bedwyn, see chapter 2.

North Tidworth where they dwelt', went together to the vicar and asked him to marry them. Randall 'very kindly accepted' the arrangement and performed the ceremony that morning. The parish clerk and a friend from North Tidworth, Thomas Noyse, acted as witnesses. When Noyse himself decided to marry a woman from Figheldean, he knew where to go.[71] Once a couple decided to get married, they acted quickly, although they often later repented at leisure. James Edwards and Katharine Newman met in a field where she was milking a cow, and they decided to get married. Edwards then went to nearby Bramshaw to make arrangements with the minister. To his disappointment, the disapproval of family and friends led her to withdraw from the match.[72] John Marchant was compelled to marry by the friends of his potential bride. Tired of his delaying tactics, they dragged the couple to Caleb Bevan, the curate of Westwood two miles away. Marchant later claimed that he would have preferred to wait for banns to be read, but that the friends forced an immediate marriage because they were afraid that he would slip through their fingers. Marchant and Bevan each later paid the price for the marriage in the consistory court.[73]

It was rare for couples to seek a clandestine marriage in their parish of residence, most likely because they wished to avoid embarrassing questions from a minister who knew them. The minister might also be fearful of the wrath of family and friends. It is significant that Robert Randall behaved with particular care when he married a man from the same parish, even though he came from the separate settlement of Wilton. First, he encouraged Thomas Strange to go home to get his father's approval. He finally agreed to perform the marriage, but only if it could be done quickly, and unusually the ceremony was performed in great secrecy, after midnight and in the vicar's own house.[74] Although couples avoided their own parish, they tended to stay relatively close to home. Most marriages were performed within ten miles of the residences of the bride and groom, and often closer, despite John Aubrey's claim that couples came from thirty or more miles away to marry in Ansty. In practice, although Ansty attracted couples from no fewer than fifteen parishes, most of these were within five miles of the village. Couples from further afield most often came from the nearest urban centre, the city of Salisbury, twelve miles away. Great Bedwyn attracted couples from nine parishes. These two peculiars were not the only options available to young couples. At least twenty parishes were each the venue of at least one clandestine marriage in the period. Frustratingly, the sources often provide details of a single marriage while mentioning that the minister performed many more. Ansty and Great Bedwyn may, if anything, have had wider catchment areas than other places because of their notoriety. Most marriages occurred within six to ten miles of home, roughly the same area, it has been suggested, as that within

[71] D5/22/17, ff. 12–30.   [72] D1/42/59, f. 47.   [73] D1/39/1/58, ff. 15, 83.
[74] D5/22/17, ff. 12–30.

which most people would have spent a large part of their lives.[75] This was as far as couples needed to travel to maximise their chances of remaining anonymous. This point should not be exaggerated, since the short life histories which church court deponents supplied demonstrate that it was common for people from different parishes to know one another. Servants were particularly mobile,[76] and their youth, independence from parents, and unmarried employment made them more susceptible to the attractions of secret marriage.

No part of Wiltshire was far from a church where a clandestine marriage could be arranged quickly. Indeed, the range of ten miles had no respect for county or diocesan borders. The minister of Horningsham did a roaring trade in marriage on the Wiltshire–Somerset border, marrying couples not only from Dilton Marsh in Wiltshire but also from Marston Biggott, Trudoxhill and Witham Friary just across the border. Since these parishes were within the diocese of Bath and Wells, such marriages were heterodox and required a special licence.[77] Nor was the trade all in a single direction. Witham Friary hosted the marriage of a couple from Mere, and further south couples from Donhead St Mary also went to Somerset to marry. On the other side of the county, similar exchanges occurred with Berkshire and Hampshire.[78]

Clandestine marriage was closely linked to marriage by licence. The common complaint against weddings in exempt jurisdictions was that they were performed without banns or licence. This was true of most of the marriages in Ansty, although Edward Worley seemed to believe that a certificate that the marriage had been performed in what he carefully called 'the King's chapel at Ansty' would be sufficient to protect couples from the attention of the courts. Robert Billings claimed that because Great Bedwyn lay in a peculiar the vicar could provide marriage licences under his authority, although there is reason to doubt that he believed it. He used the claim as a defence in a case of clandestine marriage in which he had failed to supply any licence at all, and couched it as part of a more general refutation of the right of either the dean or the bishop to hold visitations.[79] This suggests deeper opposition to the restored Church of England and its discipline, although angry bluster of this sort was also an understandable (if inadvisable) reaction to prosecution. Anthony Sadler also denied the right of the bishop to question his marriages, while insisting upon his loyalty to Church and King.[80] Yet neither man was correct. The bishop and dean could license marriages, but neither archdeacons nor other lesser jurisdictions were permitted to do so. Billings's successor, Robert Randall, made no claim to be able to grant licences under his own authority. Instead he used licences which came to hand. He married Morie with

[75] M. Spufford, *Contrasting Communities* (Cambridge, 1974).
[76] A. Kussmaul, *Servants in Husbandry in Early Modern England* (Cambridge, 1981).
[77] D5/28, 1668, f. 35.   [78] D5/29/7, f. 37v; WRO 980/2; D1/41/1/27; D1/39/1/58; D1/39/1/64.
[79] D5/22/15, ff. 43–47v.   [80] Tanner MS 143, f. 121.

a licence from the archbishop of Canterbury, for which he charged 25 shillings, including his own fee. In Noyse's case, he used a licence from the dean of Salisbury for 20 shillings.[81] It is not clear from where he obtained these licences. They may have been blanks which he purchased for the purpose or licences left by other couples.

Marriage by licence became more popular during the seventeenth century. The numbers of licences supplied by Salisbury diocese rose from 90 in 1616 to 144 in 1665 and 121 in 1676, and a similar rise in the number of licences has been detected elsewhere.[82] The growing popularity of licences demonstrates that privacy was becoming more attractive to couples, so it is not surprising that the social status of licensees also rose during the century, although the gentry still accounted for only a quarter of licences in 1675. If a couple decided to marry by licence, they went to the bishop's officers in Salisbury or on visitations, swore a bond that there were no impediments to the marriage, and paid the fee, which was 11 shillings in the late seventeenth century.[83] Only bishops, diocesan chancellors and their officers were specifically entitled to grant licences, although in practice deans had the same authority.[84] If residents of different dioceses wished to marry, they required a licence from the archbishop of Canterbury. A licence was valid only in the parish church it specified, which in theory was to be where either the bride or groom dwelled. Yet it was common for licences to name several parishes where the marriage might take place, including some outside the couple's residences.

Licences were already being abused in the sixteenth century. In 1597 Convocation defended licences against criticisms from Parliament. Yet the canons of 1597 and 1604 included new clauses intended to shore up the undermined system, and it was then that the requirement that those applying for licences were to swear out a bond was added. In 1602 Archbishop Whitgift reiterated that archdeacons and their officials were not to grant licences.[85] The canons confirmed that deputies and surrogates were not empowered to do so.[86] The repetition of these concerns suggests that abuse was rife, and it continued to be so after the Restoration. In 1671 the registrar of Salisbury diocese ordered that oaths of two persons were to be taken before any licence was granted, an order that was already being ignored in the following year.[87] Couples who requested a licence often did not even collect it in person. The files are filled with letters requesting licences, which were brought by a friend, gentleman, cleric, or apparitor, indeed by anyone who

[81] D5/22/17, ff. 12–30.
[82] E. Nevill, 'Marriage licences of Salisbury', *The Genealogist*, n.s., vols. 24–38.
[83] D1/27/1/1, ff. 173–172v.   [84] Canon 101.
[85] P. McGrath, 'Notes on the history of marriage licences', in B. Frith, ed., *Gloucestershire Marriage Allegations 1637–1680*, Bristol and Gloucestershire Archaeological Society Records Section, 2 (1954), pp. xx–xxvi.
[86] Canon 101. Nonetheless, the appointment of surrogates for the issue of marriage licences was common practice in the eighteenth century, e.g. in Salisbury diocese. D1/64.   [87] D1/62/1/12.

might have business in the city.[88] One request was brought by a Quaker. Episcopal officers often no longer even made personal contact with the people to whom they awarded licences. This practice had the benefit of making licences easier to obtain, but the system was also wide open to abuse. It was only a small step to the distribution of multiple licences and to blank licences, a matter of concern to Convocation in 1702.[89] It is not clear how widespread these abuses were in Salisbury, although it should be noted that the requests that survive on file were made directly to the registrar in Salisbury and were for individual marriages. There is no evidence of the bulk purchase of blank licences in the late seventeenth century, and given Ward's concern about clandestine marriage it would be surprising if he had sanctioned such practices.[90] Not until 1739 would an account book recording the dispatch of licences and payment of fees (and conveniently organised by minister) leave evidence that Salisbury diocese had institutionalised the bulk distribution of licences.[91] It is possible that Randall's use of a licence from the dean points to provision of blank licences by his surrogates, but the dean's reaction suggests that this was not the case. Dean Thomas Pierce, quick to anger when he detected any challenge to his authority, took special measures to assist the prosecution against the vicar. The fact that the couples came from his son's rectory of North Tidworth gave him additional reasons for action.[92]

The motives for a licence were often similar to those for a clandestine marriage, in particular speed and privacy. By obtaining a licence a couple did not need to wait three weeks for banns to be read. Of course, procuring the licence itself took time, particularly for those who lived some distance from Salisbury and sent their request by letter. Arthur Adye specifically asked that a licence be returned speedily, within the week if possible, but he had to wait ten days. The dividing line between a licence and a clandestine marriage was often thin. John Brinsden of Winterbourne Monkton served as bondsman for a licence for a couple from Wootton Bassett. Aged 26 and 25 respectively, the pair were formally old enough to marry without parental consent, and their reasons for wishing to be married in another parish are unclear. A licence allowed the marriage itself to be conducted in private and sometimes in another parish. Yet privacy did not necessarily mean secrecy, and in this respect licences and clandestine marriages often differed from one another. Whereas an unlawful marriage allowed the couple to evade family disapproval, at least temporarily, licence allegations were often supported by parents or local ministers. Some

---

[88] D1/62/4; Nevill, 'Marriage licences of Salisbury', *The Genealogist*, n.s., 33 (1916–17): 46, 121–2.
[89] McGrath, 'Notes on the history of marriage licences', p. xxix.
[90] For evidence of bulk distribution in Gloucestershire in the 1690s, see B. Frith, ed., *Gloucestershire Marriage Allegations, 1681–1700*, Publications of the Bristol and Gloucestershire Archaeological Society Records Section, 9 (1970), pp. 180, 184.   [91] D1/62/2.
[92] J. W. Packer, *The Transformation of Anglicanism, 1643-1660* (Manchester, 1989), p. 54.

couples wished to be married by a particular minister. Thomas Eston of Bristol requested a licence to marry Frances Gape of Amesbury 'at Dr Addeson's church at Milston', although neither resided there. As author of the *Primitive Institution* and dean of Lichfield, Addison was of sufficient dignity to marry this Bristol merchant who was able to endow his bride with a jointure of £200 a year.[93]

Clerics must have known that they were violating the law when they celebrated clandestine marriages. Although the exempt status of some parishes provided a handy, if often ineffectual, defence, the motives of such ministers were almost certainly pecuniary. The common stereotype is of the unbeneficed curate, but, as we have seen, clandestine marriage also provided a valuable means for incumbents with poor livings to earn additional fees, even if it meant breaking the law.[94] Although they knew that they risked suspension for three years, such ministers often yielded to the temptation to respond to lay demand for clandestine marriages. The Revd Christopher Symons refused to marry a couple without banns in the 1660s, although he was present when Matthew Whittley pronounced them man and wife. Yet thirty years later he was himself suspended for marrying a couple clandestinely, and in order to be released from his suspension he promised the bride's father that he would never repeat his offence.[95] The similarities between licensed and clandestine marriage may have created some confusion in the minds of many couples.[96] It is possible that some had no idea that they were violating the law, although the case of Christopher Symons serves to remind us that couples also welcomed the opportunity to marry in secrecy, often against family wishes. The claims of ministers to be able to supply licences increased confusion. A Marlborough man named Mudge, whom Billings married unlawfully in Great Bedwyn, was so disappointed by the vicar's deception that he prosecuted him in the consistory court for the offence.[97] Clandestine marriage was the natural extension of marriage by licence. Indeed, many marriages by licence were themselves technically clandestine since they violated the requirement that the marriage be conducted in the parish of one or the other partner. The system of licences was itself riddled with abuses. The layman can have seen little difference between buying a licence at visitations or through correspondence and buying one directly from the minister on the day of the wedding. For humbler members of the population, such as the agricultural labourers who were married by the vicar of Great Bedwyn, it was easiest to travel to the next parish to marry clandestinely. Most likely illiterate, they were unable to write to Salisbury for a licence, and if the minister did

---

[93] Nevill, 'Marriage licences of Salisbury', *The Genealogist*, n.s. 37 (1921): 218.
[94] Cressy, *Birth, Marriage, and Death*, p. 325.
[95] D1/42/62, ff. 17v–18; D1/29/1/64, 9 Oct. 1694.
[96] Lawrence Stone stresses the complexities, ambiguities and contradictions of marriage law. *Uncertain Lives and Broken Lives.*   [97] D5/22/15, 43–47v.

not see the need to do so why should they? During the seventeenth century, the rich made more use of licences, whereas the poor increasingly resorted to clandestine marriage.[98]

Most clandestine marriages were performed by a minister, a fact which was clearly of great importance to the couples. There were good legal reasons for this, of course, since it ensured that the marriage was recognised as valid. Men and women adapted to the decline in contract unions in favour of church unions by exploiting private means of marriage. It was the minister rather than the church who was important. Couples turned to the ministers of neighbouring parishes to marry them, just as in extreme cases they arranged for them to baptise, church and bury. It might be argued that this devalued the spiritual role of the minister, turning him into little more than a functionary. Yet by choosing to be married by a minister, villagers also reaffirmed the importance they attributed to the church ceremony and to the cleric's role as indispensable celebrant.

VISITING THE SICK AND DYING

On 10 January 1720 Thomas Smith of Shaw became concerned about the serious illness of his wife, and he spent the day with her.[99] When the doctor visited he advised the gentleman that 'her time is very short', and Mrs Smith died two days later in the company of the vicar Bohun Fox and several other people. Five hours before she died, she had 'received the Holy Sacrament much to her comfort having been very desirous of it'. Fox, who remained at her bedside from the morning until her death, also read the liturgy for the sick, which included prayers for those who were seriously ill, 'recommending her soul into the Hands of her Creator'. The funeral was held four days later, and Smith noted that 'the ceremony [was] perform'd with Pomp at least sufficient for my state'. This must at the very least have included giving gloves, scarves, hatbands and rings to mourners and the display of escutcheons, as was done in the funeral of Fox's own wife in 1747.[100] Smith's diary does not record a funeral banquet or the gift of money to the poor, although such events were customary. Despite his love for his wife, Smith felt uncomfortable with his grief. The day after her death he confessed that he had 'been too much afflicted really'. The household now began a period of mourning. For two weeks the family stayed away from church services, where they were represented by a solitary servant. Even this brief mourning was too long for Smith, who recorded in his diary that on the second Sunday they had

[98] The proportion of licensees who were husbandmen fell from 15 per cent in 1616 (N=61) to only 7 per cent in 1675 (N=113), while the proportion of gentlemen rose from 15 per cent to 27 per cent. Licensees whose occupation or degree was unrecorded are not included in this calculation. The fall in their number (29 of 90 in 1616, but only 8 of 121 in 1675) is another indication of rising status. Nevill, 'Marriage licences of Salisbury', *The Genealogist*, n.s., vols. 24, 36.
[99] Diary of Thomas Smith of Shaw, Melksham, 1715–22, WRO 161/70.
[100] Bodleian Library, MS Eng Misc f. 10, Diary 1718–60 (Phillipps 13531 and 13424).

been 'advis'd to be absent out of a certain ceremony . . . perfectly contrary to my inclination'. He returned to church on Saturday, 30 January, a day of great spiritual and political importance to him as a Tory, commemorating the execution of Charles I, martyr to the cause of the Church of England.

Mistress Smith died a good death, attended by the parson, who ensured that she died on good terms with God and the Anglican Church. The minister managed the deathbed. The doctor, whose profession was, it has been argued, to gain importance at the deathbed later in the century, played only a subordinate role, retiring from the scene two days earlier.[101] Family and friends were present as supporting players. Because this was the death of a gentlewoman, it may not have been typical of those of the common people. Politics and personal links combined to give the clergy a more central role than may have been typical. As a Tory defender of the Church (who was also an active supporter of the SPCK), Smith was likely to turn to the Anglican clergy and liturgy during this crisis. Bohun Fox, the vicar of Melksham, was also a close friend, so he had personal as well as professional reasons for his close attendance at the side of the sick woman.[102] Mrs Smith's death represented a more intense variant of a pattern that prevailed widely. In the homes of ordinary villagers, friends and neighbours managed deathbeds. Yet, although the role of the clergy was circumscribed, they nevertheless had an important role to play.

The Reformation had reduced the role of the minister at the deathbed. For Catholics the priest's presence at the deathbed was essential. He managed the deathbed, hearing final confession, giving absolution and administering the viaticum and extreme unction. The last hour of life was of crucial importance for a Catholic, for death without confession and absolution seriously imperilled one's salvation. Failure to receive final absolution might have practical consequences as well, for the Catholic Church might refuse to bury an unabsolved sinner.[103] A Catholic feared a sudden death more than any other. The Church of England had, of course, abandoned these doctrines as part of a shift in emphasis from the dead to the living, but it was nevertheless important to be well prepared for death and to make one's peace with family, neighbours and God.[104] The minister remained an important visitor to the beds of the sick and dying. The Anglican liturgy expected the clergy to visit the sick, although it carefully avoided popish

---

[101] R. Porter, 'Death and the doctors in Georgian England', in R. Houlbrooke, ed., *Death, Ritual, and Bereavement* (London and New York, 1989), pp. 77-94.

[102] Thomas Smith also recorded the close attendance of the vicar at other deaths, such as that of Captain Selfe, to whom Fox read the prayer for the sick.

[103] E. Duffy, *The Stripping of the Altars* (New Haven and London, 1992), pp. 312–27; J. McManners, *Death and the Enlightenment: Changing Attitudes to Death among Christians and Unbelievers in Eighteenth-Century France* (Oxford, 1981), chs. 7–8. On the significance of death and the dead before the Reformation, see Cressy, *Birth, Marriage, and Death*, chs. 9, 10; A. D. Brown, *Popular Piety in Late Medieval England* (Oxford, 1995), ch. 4.

[104] L. M. Beier, 'The good death in seventeenth-century England', in Houlbrooke, *Death, Ritual, and Bereavement*, pp. 43-61; Cressy, *Birth, Marriage, and Death*, pp. 389–93.

rituals. Canon 67 required the parish minister to visit the dangerously sick and to comfort them in their distress, and the Prayer Book provided a service for visiting the sick, in which the patient received communion, and prayers were provided for the minister to read over the very sick. Bishops and deans checked in their visitation queries that their clergy performed this duty, which was also reaffirmed in the Injunctions of 1694. The canons also allowed the minister to administer communion to the dangerously ill in their own houses (Canon 71). By requiring that at least two or three people received communion with the patient, Canon 21 placed some distance between this sacrament and the Catholic viaticum, while stressing the social nature of the sacrament. The only exception was contagious disease such as plague, when the patient might be unattended. Communion at home was designed simply to provide the sacrament to someone unable because of illness to receive in church, and was not intended as essential preparation for imminent death. The minister had to be given notice, to ensure that he had sufficient sacralised bread and wine. Yet it was easy for superstitious views of the deathbed to creep back in. In his description of the life of the ideal country parson, George Herbert reaffirmed and elaborated on the importance of visiting the sick. The parson was to visit the sick and persuade them to confess. Herbert commented on the almost magical ability of such communions to heal the sick, both physically and spiritually, treading dangerously close to the popular beliefs which the canons shunned.[105]

The visitation of the sick was the only formal clerical function which was normally performed in private homes, so it provided a unique opportunity for pastoral care. This was one reason why George Herbert encouraged this duty. Indeed, Bishop Gilbert Burnet advocated regular visits to parishioners whether or not they were ill.[106] Churchwardens' presentments, allegations and depositions show that the families of the sick valued clerical visits and were disappointed in the rare cases when ministers neglected this function.[107] Walter Kelloe of Winterbourne Stoke complained in 1678 when the vicar Benjamin Culme refused to visit his sick wife. 'My vife was sick', he reported, 'and I desiered the m[ini]ster to com and adminester the sacrament to her and he told me he was not provided for et.'[108] It appears that Culme was claiming that he had not received sufficient notice to ensure that he had communion bread and wine. In the 1730s thirty-five parishioners of Somerford Keynes complained that their curate 'hath Refused severall tymes to visitt the Sick tho he hath been earnestly Intreated soe to doe'. These were the same petitioners who clashed with the curate over singing at funerals.[109] The excuses supplied by neglectful ministers

---

[105] George Herbert, *A Priest to the Temple, or the Country Parson* (London, 1632), ch. 14. For popular superstitions about the mass before the Reformation, see K. V. Thomas, *Religion and the Decline of Magic* (London, 1971), ch. 6.

[106] Gilbert Burnet, *A Discourse of the Pastoral Care* (London, 1692), pp. 205–8.

[107] There were only four presentments for failure to visit the sick.   [108] D1/41/1/21, c. 1678.

[109] D1/41/4/36, temp. Thomas Sherlock.

were often less satisfactory than Culme's. Mr Dockwray, the curate of Aldermaston (Berkshire), asked to be excused until the next day when William Wordon asked him 'to pray with or adm[ini]ster the Sacrament to his . . . mother who then lay sick and near unto death' because the minister had been drinking.[110] When William Willis of Anderston (Dorset) was asked 'to come and pray wth one Eliz Little who then lay very ill', he refused saying 'He would not for she's damned already'.[111] In 1763 John Hall was unable to convince the vicar of Blewberry (Berkshire) to 'come and pray by [his sick wife] and give her such Ghostly comfort and advice as the exigency of her case required'.[112] Family and friends regarded the minister's visit to the sickbed as an important part of the process by which the dying prepared themselves for death. By his presence, the minister could comfort the dying man or woman, giving strength through his prayers and administration of the sacrament.

Most Wiltshire ministers were more conscientious than the few who were charged with neglect.[113] The Revd John Lewis recorded his regular visits to the sick in the diary he kept for several years in the 1720s.[114] Lewis took his pastoral responsibilities seriously despite his pluralism. He read George Herbert's *Country Parson* and the *Parson's Councillor*, and he prepared a sermon on the importance of visiting the sick. These visits were not particularly onerous since his cures were small and close together, although they often required him to walk to another parish. He may not have visited every person who was seriously ill, for his diary records a handful of funerals for people whom he made no record of visiting. But few months passed without a visit to at least one sick villager, and in some months he visited five or more, sometimes going to see the same person several times. August 1719 was a particularly busy month. Lewis visited Jonathan Sartain in his sickness on the 5th and again on the 11th and 12th when Sartain was very ill. Sadly, the illness was fatal, and Lewis performed Sartain's funeral on the 19th. The minister visited five more sick people on 20 and 21 August. Lewis provided few details about the visits he made; he sometimes even failed to record the patient's name. His notes reveal that he administered communion on some, but not all, occasions. On 23 March 1722, for example, only two of the three people he visited received communion, although whether this should be attributed to their personal preferences or to the progress of their illnesses is unclear. Lewis visited both those with acute illnesses, some of whom died shortly thereafter, and those with chronic diseases such as gout. Both types of patient would have been in need of comfort, and this pattern of visiting was consistent with the Church's de-emphasis of the deathbed. He had a close

---

[110] D1/42/68, Dockwray c. Wordon.   [111] D1/42/69, Tregonwell c. Willis.   [112] D5/28, 1763.

[113] The small number of presentments does not confirm the sad picture in Exeter diocese, whose bishop complained in 1686 of the disuse of visiting the sick in their homes and of ministers' habit of reading the office for the visitation of the sick in church instead. Tanner MS 30, f. 50.

[114] The following paragraphs are based on WRO 1981/1; Bodleian Library, MS Eng Misc f. 10.

relationship with several of those whom he visited, testifying to his sympathetic bedside manner. In some cases his friendship with the patient dated from before the patient's final illness. Some patients asked him to preach a funeral sermon for them and specified the text that he should use, evidence that there was a bond of trust and understanding between them. He did not give a special sermon for every funeral, and he received an extra fee when he did.

Yet John Lewis did not manage the deaths of his parishioners in the way that his friend and colleague, Bohun Fox, did for Thomas Smith's wife. In this, he reflected the subtle liturgical shift from the visitation of the dying to the visitation of the sick. He was rarely present at a death, but normally visited one or more days before. Communion for the sick did not of course have the great significance that the viaticum had for Catholics, so it was not essential to receive the sacrament close to death as Mistress Smith did. Lewis administered the sacrament to one local gentleman three days before he died. If the cleric was not expected to manage the illness, it made sense for him to visit as soon as he learned that someone was seriously ill, when he was best able to provide comfort and to help the patient to settle his or her affairs. Death was unpredictable and might come at any time, or the patient might become confused or lose consciousness in the final stages of their illness. Patients might be ill for a long time before they died, and in such cases the minister might visit several times, as occurred in the case of Jonathan Sartain. Mrs Slade, whom Lewis visited on 20 August 1719, did not die until the following February, when he preached her funeral sermon. The minister fulfilled his pastoral duties conscientiously and sympathetically, and patients and their families valued the comfort he brought to the sick and dying, preparing them for a Christian death.

Lewis played a supporting role at sickbeds that were managed by family and neighbours. This picture is confirmed by the evidence of depositions for testamentary cases, which were brought when there was a disagreement over the estate of the deceased. References to the presence of clergymen at the sickbed are rare in these sources. Ministers are mentioned in only two of forty cases heard in the bishop's and dean's courts between 1660 and 1740, including one case in which the cleric was required to act merely as a scribe. In March 1673 when William Nash 'lay very weak' he sent for William Rawlins of Whaddon. Rawlins went immediately, 'supposing it had been to performe some ministeriall offices wth him'. On his arrival, however, Nash cleared the room and asked Rawlins to write his will for him. Unfortunately, Nash became increasingly weak so that he was unable to assent to the will. His scribal duties finished, Rawlins left the room, apparently without having read the liturgy or provided any spiritual comfort to the dying man. Soon afterwards news was brought to him that Nash had died.[115] We know about Nash's death only because those who survived

---

[115] D1/42/61, ff. 96–8.

him brought a case in the bishop's consistory court when they were unable to agree about the disposition of his estate, a not infrequent event. In such cases, the parties called witnesses to tell whether the deceased had made a will, and if so how. If they disliked the will, parties tried to discredit it with testimony that the will was forged or that the testator had not been capable of making a will. Since most wills were drawn up in the last sickness of the testator, these depositions provide useful information about the way common people died and about popular attitudes towards death, information which otherwise cannot be gleaned from either gentry or clerical diaries.[116]

Depositions in testamentary cases do not, of course, provide complete descriptions of the last moments of testators, and they are likely to be the most detailed about the time when the will was made. The failure to mention the minister does not prove that he did not visit. He may have attended the patient at another time before or after the will was made and was neither expected nor permitted to control the sickbed. The minister was one of several visitors, and his visits were usually brief. Family and neighbours might stay for hours, attending to and reading to the patient, as happened in the case of William Webb of Pitton. One Sunday in the summer of 1670, Mary Mannings of Pitton, a small village in north Wiltshire, went to visit William Webb, having heard that he was ill. She found the wives of Richard Palmer and William Hinwood, also of Pitton, were attending Webb, who was 'verie weak and feeble nor likely long to live in this world'. Goodie Mannings asked Webb how he was and offered to read to him, and he assented 'wth all his hart'. She 'read to him in a certeyne book wch was then lyinge in the sick mans chamber some certeyne sentences or lynes fitt to read to a sick person'. Webb thanked her for reading to him and told her that 'Christ dyed for synners and that he hoped he had made his peace with the Almightie & soe prayed to God to forgiue him all his synnes'. Mary left the sick man, but at least one attendant would have remained through the night. Early the following morning, at about 5 or 6 o'clock, a local squire sent a maidservant with cordial water. When Mary Manning visited Webb later in the morning, she found Christian Blake was already with him. Webb died the following Sunday.[117] Like Mistress Smith of Shaw, he had been fortunate in dying a good death in the company of his neighbours, who provided both physical and spiritual comfort. Despite the clergy's indispensable liturgical role, they did not have a monopoly on providing spiritual comfort. When Thomas Witt wished to confess to relieve his conscience so that he could die in peace, he sent for a local gentleman.[118]

William Webb's death sounds idyllic. Surrounded by concerned friends who read spiritual passages to him, he passed away after expressing his faith in the

---

[116] See also K. Wrightson and D. Levine, 'Death in Whickham', in J. Walter and R. Schofield, eds., *Famine, Disease and the Social Order in Early Modern Society* (Cambridge, 1989), pp. 129-66.
[117] D1/42/61, ff. 2–19v.   [118] D1/42/59, ff. 165–71.

efficacy of Christ's sacrifice and in God's mercy. Death remained, above all, a
public act in which the entire community, and not just the family, continued to
be concerned.[119] The ringing of a church bell when someone was dying and after
they had died informed the entire parish of the progress of an illness. The importance of neighbours stands out in depositions, for they ensured that no one died
alone. The dangerously ill were kept company by family, friends and neighbours,
who helped to prepare the dying for their final moments. Women, the wives of
other householders, took particular responsibility for attending the dangerously
sick. Webb was attended by the wives of four of his neighbours, as well as by
several male friends. Others were attended in the same manner. Joane Davis happened to visit Thomas Marten of Swindon to fetch water and found him ill. So
she sent for neighbours, made him a posset and stayed with him through
morning prayer until others could arrive to sit with him. Another woman, on
hearing Marten was sick, went to visit him after morning prayer.[120] William
Nash died in the presence of Elizabeth Rawlins, his wife, his sister and several
other relatives.[121] No fewer than eight people were present at Edward Kellow's
sickbed: his wife, three sons and two other relatives, as well as two servants.[122]
In addition to family and neighbours, if the dying person wished to make a will,
a scribe and witnesses would be sent for, in theory ensuring that the will was
drawn up by people who had nothing to gain from it. The dying person was not
left alone at night, either. When John Major was ill, Margaret Parsons and John
Paule watched over him all night.[123]

How did people greet sickness and possible death? Their first reaction when
they felt death coming was to settle their affairs so that they could die in peace.
Many gained peace of mind by disposing of their worldly goods through a
formal will and testament or an informal statement of their wishes to those
attending them. People could not die comfortably with the thought that their
heirs would squabble over their estate after their death. After Edward Kellow
had made his will, he asked his son Robert to make sure 'that there may be noe
controversies arise betwixt him & his brothers about' the will.[124] Despite his
concern, the will was challenged in court, although not by his sons. Margaret
Parsons 'thanked God her mynd was setled for that she had made her will'.[125]
Wills were often made in the testator's final illness, although the liturgy
advised clergymen to encourage their congregations to settle such matters
earlier if possible. Of a sample of forty wills written in the village of Pewsey,
15 per cent were made less than a week before the testator's burial and thus
only a few days at most before death. Another 30 per cent were made within
a month of burial. These figures are confirmed by a sample of wills written

---

[119] Cf. Gittings, *Death, Burial and the Individual*, p. 14; McManners, *Death and the Enlightenment*,
pp. 462–3. See also Duffy, *The Stripping of the Altars*, p. 322.   [120] D5/22/15, ff. 73–6.
[121] D1/42/61, ff. 96–8.   [122] D1/42/60, ff. 68–87.   [123] D2/6/2, ff. 20–4.
[124] D1/42/60, f. 63.   [125] D1/42/59, f. 126v.

throughout Wiltshire. Almost half (49 per cent) of the wills examined included a statement in the preamble that the testator was sick, very weak, or aged and infirm.[126]

Illness often gave people enough time to prepare for death. Alice Blake, a Devizes widow, was well enough to be able to walk to the house of William Stevens to ask for his help in preparing her will. As she explained to him, 'by reason of age & infirmityes she was not like to live long, & was therefore willing to settle that little she had by will'. Widow Blake invited Stevens and several others to come to her house that evening in order to draw up and witness the will.[127] The same pattern can be found in case after case, as imminent death reminded the sick of their responsibilities to survivors. Most testators were already unable to leave their bed when they called for a scribe.[128] If anyone forgot, neighbours were there to remind them of their responsibilities. Thomas Marten was encouraged to call a local gentleman to draw up his will because he was growing increasingly weak. When Marten resisted the call of death, replying that 'he hoped he might be well the tomorrow', Joane Davis reminded him of his duty: 'what if you should not live till tomorrow, you should doe well to declare who shall have yor estate'.[129] Such intervention was not always appreciated by the sick person. Two days before Robert Jordan died, William Story visited him and asked whether he 'had or would make his will or not at wch the said Robert seemed somewhat angrie and bidd him . . . hold his peace and meddle . . . wth his owne busines'.[130] Death came too quickly for some people. Joane Davis had been right to advise Thomas Marten to settle his affairs quickly. He delayed preparing his will too long, so that there was not enough time to write it down. Instead of calling a scribe such people had to be satisfied with stating their wishes to those who attended them. Marten told Joane Davis that he wished 'that his daughter Margery should have all that he had'.[131] While Margaret Parsons and John Paule watched over John Major one night, Major asked for a woman named Eleanor, telling his hearers, 'if please God I live to recover this sicknesse . . . I intend to be married unto her, but if I dye I give unto her all that I have'.[132] Parishioners might also settle their affairs by reconciling themselves with enemies or with the Church. In an illness several months before his death, William Webb had asked William Reeves to reconcile his differences

---

[126] The Pewsey sample included forty out of seventy-five wills proved before the archdeacon of Wiltshire in 1660–1750 (those whose surnames began with the letters A–C, H, P and S). Another eight wills were sampled but were undated. The date on the will was then compared with the date of burial given in the parish register (WRO 493/3, 5). The county-wide sample was taken by reading all wills written by testators whose surnames began with the letter A in 1660–80, 1700–10, and 1740–50. In the archdeaconry of Wiltshire, thirty-five of eighty-eight wills (40 per cent) mentioned illness, while forty-nine out of eighty-two (60 per cent) did so in the archdeaconry of Salisbury. [127] D1/42/61, f. 106.
[128] For example, Thomas Bushell of Fittleton. D1/42/61, ff. 36–7. [129] D5/22/15, ff. 73–6.
[130] D2/6/2, ff. 46–51. Story's intervention may have been resented because he was a Quaker.
[131] D5/22/15, f. 74v. [132] D2/6/2, ff. 20–4.

with William Hinwood, even though he claimed that Hinwood had cheated him, so that 'he might dye in peace'. Unfortunately, Hinwood would not agree and called Webb a hypocritical knave. The disappointed Webb did not make a second attempt at reconciliation when he fell sick again later that summer.[133] Death was also a time to make peace with the Church. Richard Amor of Pewsey, 'being weak in body', sought absolution from the bishop of Salisbury for his excommunication, and in this way cleared the way for his burial by the parson in the churchyard.[134]

Wiltshire men and women faced the prospect of death with equanimity unless they had particular crimes to confess. In post-Reformation England the hour of death was no longer the struggle of good and evil for the soul of the dying person represented in earlier centuries by the *ars moriendi*.[135] Most of those who died showed no signs of any anxiety about their salvation. As we have seen, William Webb died mindful that 'Christ dyed for synners' and hopeful that 'he had made his peace with the Almightie'. His was a classic Protestant 'good' death. Webb had no reason to doubt that God would be merciful and bestow on him the salvation which Christ had made possible. The curate of Dauntsey, John Stump, noted in the parish register that Sarah Bishop, who died in January 1724 at the age of 16 or 17, was 'a very godly maid much addicted to reading'. Before she died, she said 'pray . . . father . . . let us goe home, meaning to heaven'.[136] Sarah showed no fear of death, and apparently had no doubt that heaven, not hell, was to be her destination. Her identification of heaven with home made death something to welcome rather than to fear, expressing the romantic vision of death which was becoming popular in the eighteenth century.

Others expressed anxiety about their salvation, revealing a belief that individuals had sufficient free will to lose their opportunity for salvation. Thomas Witt and Mary Bannister were concerned because they knew that they had committed specific crimes, rather than out of a general sense of sinfulness, and they both felt the need to relieve their minds by confessing before they died. Witt sent for a local gentleman, John Gastrell, to hear his confession. He said 'That there was something that troubled his conscience & that he could not die in peace till he had revealed it'. He had 'not done righteous things', because he had forged the will of Margaret Parsons, and he directed Gastrell to record his confession in writing. By confessing his crime, Witt had relieved his mind, just as did those who settled their affairs by making a will or by reconciling themselves with an enemy. 'I am glad I have now spoken wth you to declare my conscience unto you', he said, 'for I could not die in quyet till I had done it.' He expressed the hope that

---

[133] D1/42/61, ff. 2–19v.
[134] D1/41/1/21, 3 Jan. 1678/9. Amor had originally been prosecuted for his failure to pay tithes, but had apparently paid them by this time. He was absolved at the recommendation of the churchwardens and the rector on 13 Jan. 1678/9.
[135] Duffy, *The Stripping of the Altars*, pp. 316–17; P. Ariès, *The Hour of Our Death* (New York, 1981), esp. ch. 3.   [136] WRO 1070/4.

'God forgive me for 't'.[137] The case of Mary Bannister was similar. When she was 'lying very sick of a violent feavour past recovery in the judgment of all people, [she] was taken wth remorse, & a sense of her former crime'. Four years earlier she had wrongly named the father of her bastard child. Bannister sent for Thomas Henchman, the curate of Salisbury St Edmund's parish, to confess her sin 'in private confession', and thereafter 'publiquely & frequently . . . confesst & passionately & sorrowfully declared' that she had perjured herself by falsely swearing that Dr Davenant was father to her bastard child. She feared she 'had highly offended God . . . by her perjury, wch she said she was tempted to by . . . Francis Pistle . . . who had made her damne her body & soule'.[138]

These descriptions of sickbed scenes show that villagers' attitudes towards death and salvation were complicated. Both William Webb and Sarah Bishop placed their trust in a merciful God. Webb explicitly accepted the Protestant doctrine that salvation was by God-given faith rather than works, because of Christ's sacrifice on the cross. His trust may, of course, have expressed his confidence that he had lived a good life. Witt and Bannister were anxious that they might have harmed their chances for salvation by their actions, and that any sins they had committed would weigh against them. Thus Bannister feared that her perjury had damned her soul and she cursed Francis Pistle for tempting her. It is not possible to say for certain whether they were rejecting predestinarianism in favour of an Arminian-like belief in lapsed grace, revealing the survival of remnants of traditional religion, or alternatively were expressing a Pelagian belief that those who did not harm or speak badly of others would be saved. The label matters less than the evidence these deathbed scenes provide of popular beliefs. People reasoned, whatever their doctrinal justification, that those who had lived a good life would be saved, while those who had not would be damned. This was consistent with the reluctance of many to receive communion regularly for fear that they might damn their souls unless they reformed their lives. Confession at death was reminiscent of Catholic last rites, through which one might counterbalance one's sins through repentance, although the Protestant version was only a pale imitation. Having made his confession, Thomas Witt felt much relieved, and hoped that God would forgive him for his sin. Mary Bannister had no such confidence, but she clearly confessed in hopes of saving herself. While some Wiltshire villagers were able to trust in a merciful God, others were troubled by anxieties that their behaviour might jeopardise their state of grace.

These deathbed scenes show some continuities with those before the Reformation. The hour of death ceased to be the occasion for the final struggle for the soul, but it remained a crucial time of preparation. Death remained a communal act, in which the clergy, family and neighbours facilitated the

---

[137] D1/42/59, ff. 165–71.   [138] D1/39/1/57, ff. 141–141v.

transition from life to death, and helped to ease fears and anxiety by providing practical and spiritual support. The spirit of individualism had not triumphed. The effect of theological changes was to shift the balance of power from the clergy to the neighbours and family. The clergy's role remained important, but it was no longer critical, as it changed from the administration of last rites to the visitation of the sick. The reduced importance of the clergy at death is the clearest example of the way in which their functions were circumscribed, and defined more narrowly by the offices which they administered. Yet the laity nevertheless accepted the clergy's indispensable role as celebrants at the offices of baptism, burial and marriage. The church ceremony was an accepted element of popular definitions of these rites. Clandestine marriages, which by definition were held in secret, may appear to be part of a more general trend towards privacy. Yet the social function of lawful ceremonies marking stages in the life-cycle remained important. The social impulse expressed itself, not only in church, but also in secular celebrations, held outside the church and so outside the control of the clergy. Clerical insistence upon maintaining control within the church created tensions, nevertheless, which would manifest themselves even more clearly in the issue of church music.

10

Singing and religious revival

'Tis hardly possible for me to express what a fondness the generality of my People, both old and young, now have for this Divine Ordinance, of Singing Psalms . . . 'Tis to the great Joy of my Soul, that by this little Labour, and the Blessing of God upon it . . . I have brought the greater Number of my Congregation to Joyne in the Singing of Psalms.[1]

In 1717 George Millard rejoiced in the success of his efforts to promote psalmody in the parish of Box, near Bath. Inducted into the vicarage in 1707, Millard was to serve the parish for over thirty years. Although he was a pluralist, his other two benefices in Wiltshire were small and did not prevent him from fulfilling his pastoral duties with enthusiasm.[2] After his death in 1740, one of Millard's clerical friends described him as 'a Clergyman of great Piety, Zeal, Integrity, & Charity'.[3] Although his years as vicar were not entirely free from conflict, he was a model clergyman. In his long incumbency he embarked on a series of religious and social initiatives which did much to reinvigorate worship in Box and nearby parishes. Millard exhibited pastoral qualities not normally attributed to the parish clergy in the years before the evangelical movement and he demonstrated the vitality that the worship of the Church of England was capable of possessing in country parishes. A corresponding member of the Society for Promoting Christian Knowledge (SPCK), which provided the focus for much of the activity that contributed to the religious revival of the early eighteenth century, Millard was a member of a network of Wiltshire clergymen.

George Millard began charity schools in Box and in another of his parishes, Calstone Wellington, not long after his induction. He was eager to become a corresponding member of the SPCK, and in 1711 he was admitted on the recommendation of the Revd Todhunter of Somerset. Over the next ten years, Millard used several reforms to bring about a substantial improvement in the religious

---

[1] SPCK, L 5213. The originals of this and other letters at the WRO were reprinted as 'Four letters written by the Rev. George Millard, A.D. 1712–18', WAM 31 (June 1900): 33–41, quoting p. 38.

[2] Haselbury had neither church nor parsonage and was traditionally served by the vicar of Box. Calstone Wellington had only four families in 1716, so that Millard sometimes had to fill some of the six places in its charity school with poor children from the neighbouring town of Calne. SPCK, L 4805; WAM 31: 36.   [3] Bodleian Library, MS Eng Misc f. 10.

knowledge and observance of his parishioners, especially in Box. Not content to limit his attentions to the education of the children, he also encouraged adults to learn to read, showing some imagination in the manner in which he rewarded those who made progress. When an adult scholar learned to read a chapter in the Bible, the scholar and teacher each received a reward of five shillings. Millard distributed hundreds of moral pamphlets against swearing, drunkenness and Sabbath-breaking, and he rejoiced 'in the good effects they have had'.[4] His SPCK book orders reveal that he also gave out religious pamphlets. In February 1720, for example, he ordered 50 copies of the church catechism, another 25 catechisms in question format, plus 25 copies each of the *Christian Monitor*, *The Communicant Instructed at Easter*, and *The Sacrament of the Lord's Supper Explained*.[5] Millard set up a library in the charity school room, next to the chancel, placing in it two copies of every book sent to him by the Society, and he encouraged parishioners to browse through the library before Sunday service instead of lounging in the churchyard.[6] His concern for the poor led to his involvement in the founding of a workhouse in Box.

Millard's greatest enthusiasm was reserved for the reinvigoration of singing in church. He was troubled to find that only a few members of the congregation placed in the gallery joined in singing psalms during services while the rest remained silent. Determined 'to redress this Grievance', Millard gave 'several Discourses from the Pulpit, setting forth the necessity, usefullness, and Advantage of the Duty'. He used the basic SPCK technique of increasing religious knowledge: first teach the children, who are at the most impressionable age, and their parents will follow their example. In February 1717, he began 'to teach all o[u]r Charity Children . . . to sing Psalms by Notes'. After only just over a week of practice, two hours a day, 'they became perfect in 4 Tunes', which they sang in church the following Sunday 'to the Admiration of the whole Congregation then present'. Impressed at the 'Speedy Improvement' of the charity children, now 'most of the young men & maidens, and little Children of the Parish, (to the number of 160 and odd) [were] very desirous to be admitted to the same Instruction'. Millard gave each youth a small psalm book and he met with them 'every Tuesday, Thursday, & Saturday at night in the church; where we usually sang about an hour and a half'. In addition, he chose two or three psalms to be sung before and after Sunday afternoon service.

Millard's efforts met with great success. He rejoiced that the majority of his congregation now joined in the singing of psalms and hoped that soon the entire congregation 'will have skill enough to bear a part in this Heavenly Exercise'. The improvement of congregational singing was rewarding not only for its impact on the service but also for its positive effects on attendance. Millard told the SPCK that 'the Church is now so fill'd that we have scarce Room enough to

[4] SPCK, AL 2732.   [5] SPCK, Packets, f. 26; Bodleian Library, Rawlinson MS C844, f. 83v.
[6] SPCK, AL 2589, 2732, 3994, 4805, 5213, 6056; *WAM* 31: 33, 36–7.

contain the People', although they had added an aisle holding over 100 persons just four years earlier, and he attributed the increase to the popularity of singing.[7] A year later he reported that his labours had far surpassed his expectations: 'The Number of Singers do still continue increasing; and the greatest part of 'em are become Masters of 30 Tunes.' Many of the younger sort had memorised the psalms, so 'that upon naming only the 1st Line in every verse they are able to goe through the rest without the help of a Book'.[8] Millard continued to exhibit his powers of innovation in promoting psalmody. In February 1718 he held a psalm recitation contest for 40 children of the parish, to which he succeeded in attracting an audience of 200 or more, many of whom were from distant parishes.[9] As Millard had found, church singing could be an important part of popular religious culture, for it provided one of the few opportunities for personal expression and participation within divine service.

THE SOCIETY FOR PROMOTING CHRISTIAN KNOWLEDGE

George Millard was one of seventeen clerical corresponding members of the Society for Promoting Christian Knowledge who resided in Wiltshire. Four other clerics, a succession of bishops of Salisbury, and an archdeacon of Wiltshire were subscribing (or resident) members.[10] The SPCK was one of several religious societies whose formation in the late seventeenth and early eighteenth centuries represented a flowering of religiosity. These societies sought to combat the impiety, immorality and disorder which seemed to many contemporaries to be overwhelming England. Devotional societies of clergy and laity were formed in London and Westminster as early as 1678. The 1690s saw the establishment of societies for the reformation of manners in London and provincial cities such as Bristol which, with the help of sympathetic magistrates, combated immorality by prosecuting offenders of the laws against prostitution, profane swearing and Sabbath-breaking, among other offences.[11] The decade saw an explosion in the number of religious societies in London, from 14 in 1694 to 39 in 1699.[12]

---

[7] SPCK, L 5213; *WAM* 31: 38. [8] SPCK, L 5618; *WAM* 31: 40.
[9] SPCK, L 5213, 5618; *WAM* 31: 38, 40; AL 2604.
[10] SPCK Minutes, vols. 1–21; Misc. Abstracts, 1709–33; E. McClure, ed., *A Chapter in English Church History: Being the Minutes of the Society for Promoting Christian Knowledge for the Years 1698–1704* (London, 1888), pp. 4–13.
[11] R. B. Shoemaker, *Prosecution and Punishment: Petty Crime and the Law in London and Rural Middlesex, c. 1660–1725* (Cambridge, 1991), ch. 9; D. W. R. Bahlman, *The Moral Revolution of 1688* (New Haven, 1957); T. C. Curtis and W. A. Speck, 'The societies for the reformation of manners: a case study in the theory and practice of moral reform', *Literature and History* 3 (1976): 45–64; A. G. Craig, 'The movement for the reformation of manners' (Ph.D. thesis, Edinburgh University, 1980); T. Isaacs, 'The Anglican hierarchy and the reformation of manners 1688-1738', *Journal of Ecclesiastical History* 33 (1982): 391-411.
[12] J. Spurr, 'The Church, the societies and the moral revolution of 1688', in J. Walsh, C. Hayden and S. Taylor, eds., *The Church of England, c.1689–c.1833: From Toleration to Tractarianism* (Cambridge, 1993), pp. 127-42.

Three other religious societies were formed at around the same time, under the co-ordination of Dr Thomas Bray, with the intention of bringing people to religion through education rather than punishment.[13] The Society for the Promotion of the Gospel was primarily concerned with missionary work. The Society for Parochial Libraries aimed to stimulate the creation of libraries of religious works. Although it established no libraries in Wiltshire, some parishes such as Box created them under their own initiative.[14] The Society for Promoting Christian Knowledge, initially formed in 1699 as a small discussion society, encouraged the establishment of charity schools to teach poor children reading and the fundamentals of Christianity. The SPCK intended to deal with ungodliness by getting at the root of the problem. According to its Preamble, 'the growth of vice and immorality is greatly owing to gross ignorance of the principles of the Christian religion'.[15] Such London-based activities of the Society as the processions of uniformed children to hear the annual charity school sermon attracted particular attention. Yet the Society also created a large network of corresponding members from country and urban parishes all over the country. The SPCK sent each of its correspondents circular letters containing advice and a standard packet of religious and moral books. It also sold books published by its printer Joseph Downing to correspondents at reduced rates. In return, correspondents sent reports of their success to London. By 1730 the Society had received 10,000 letters, whose contents they summarised in abstract books. These letters provide an unparalleled record of the activities of members and of the nature of parish religion.

The SPCK's records naturally emphasise the central role of its London headquarters, where the committee met to review correspondence, agree circulars and plan publications. It is easy to visualise its network of correspondents as a star, with the Society at the centre and each member at the end of a different point. This model is unsatisfactory, however, because it fails to represent the relationships which existed, both formal and informal, among correspondents and between members and non-members. The abstract letters testify to the existence of informal contacts among clerics, who recommended colleagues for membership, reported their activities and ordered books on their behalf. The SPCK encouraged its members to form religious societies which would extend its influence more widely. Initially, the Society anticipated having relatively few correspondents. In November 1699 it resolved to 'establish a correspondence with one or more of the Clergy in each County . . . in order to erect societies'. Each

[13] For an early plan of the work of all three societies, see W. O. B. Allen and E. McClure, *Two Hundred Years: The History of the Society for Promoting Christian Knowledge, 1698–1898* (London: SPCK, 1898), pp. 22–3. See also M. G. Jones, *The Charity School Movement: A Study of Eighteenth Century Puritanism in Action* (Cambridge, 1938).
[14] Other parishes already had libraries, such as Marlborough St Mary (begun 1678) and Steeple Ashton (begun 1569). T. Kelley, *Early Public Libraries* (London, 1966), p. 255.
[15] Allen and McClure, *Two Hundred Years*, p. 29; also Shoemaker, *Prosecution and Punishment*.

correspondent would report monthly. The following February the Society resolved to instruct correspondents 'to gett as many of the Clergy & Laity as they can to joyn in Societys', and this instruction was issued in the Second Circular Letter to Correspondents.[16] Sir George Wheeler of Durham suggested that these societies be organised into a hierarchy of rural deaneries, archdeaconries, dioceses and archdioceses, and he compared these to the apostolic *presbouterion*, avoiding the obvious comparisons to the synods and voluntary associations of the 1650s.[17] In 1710, the Society's secretary Henry Newman expressed his reluctance to accept recommendations for additional correspondents in Berkshire and Wiltshire, where the committee thought they had 'a competent number'. It was feared that the additional members would increase the Society's administrative load with little 'advantage to the good cause'.[18] This policy was quickly to change in response to the enthusiasm of clergymen to join. The number of Wiltshire clerics who were corresponding members rose from four in 1710 to thirteen in 1720.[19]

The Society was able to point to the success of a religious society formed in Bedfordshire, which was described in a letter that the Society placed in the standard packet they sent to all new correspondents from February 1700 onwards. The campaign to promote local religious societies often did not meet with immediate success. The archdeacon of Wiltshire, Cornelius Yeate, reported in 1700 that he had not found his clergy 'very forward to fellow the example' of Bedfordshire, and in 1718 John Smith of Little Hinton reported little more enthusiasm.[20] Yet some clerical societies began to form in the diocese. A Berkshire correspondent reported in 1700 that thirteen clergymen had subscribed to an association to assist in the education of poor children and the promotion of the gospel in the plantations. It was acknowledged that this society had already accomplished more than Bishop Burnet, an enthusiastic supporter, had been able to achieve in eleven years in the diocese.[21] By 1706 the city of Salisbury had its own religious society.[22] In the following decade, a vigorous clerical society formed in northern Wiltshire. This society, known as the Clergy Club of Melksham, included George Millard of Box among its ten members. From 1718 to 1724 the Clergy Club met at least once a month during the summer. Club members were bound by their clerical status, politics and friendship. In addition to their formal meetings, they dined and visited one another frequently and provided one another with practical assistance. Several members also had in

---

[16] Allen and McClure, *Two Hundred Years*, pp. 40–2.   [17] Ibid., pp. 76–7.
[18] SPCK, CS3/2/33.
[19] SPCK, Minutes, vols. 1–8; AL 2; McClure, *A Chapter in English Church History*, p. 86. Both figures include Francis Fox, initially a residing member, but who became parson of Boscombe in 1708 and moved to Potterne in 1726.   [20] SPCK, AL 53, 5487.
[21] Allen and McClure, *Two Hundred Years*, pp. 63–4. For Burnet's support of societies for the reformation of manners, see Craig, 'The Movement for the Reformation of Manners', p. 103; SPCK, AL 53.   [22] SPCK, Minutes, 1, 403.

common their membership, as correspondents, of the SPCK.[23] The decision of Daniel Fettiplace of Yatesbury to join the Society was most likely stimulated by his fellow members in the club. Through the club, the SPCK was embedded in a network which spread its influence more widely and linked members with other Society members such as the Revd Francis Fox of Potterne.[24]

When John Foster became a correspondent of the SPCK in 1701, he reported that he had been promoting meetings among fellow clergymen for twelve years. The purpose of their association was to spread Foster's pastoral work in Longbridge Deverell, where he had started a small school and had formed two lay societies. One was 'of Elderly People, Zealous & Able' who sought to promote piety among themselves, reform manners and provide a godly education to the young. The second society consisted of younger people and was intended to prepare them for confirmation and communion.[25] While the SPCK stimulated new activity, it also provided a convenient umbrella for much work that was already under way. In 1704 an anonymous donor gave the parish of Rodbourne Cheney books on the sacrament and against drunkenness, swearing and uncleanness for distribution to the poor. These were targeted at the particular needs of each recipient, and are unlikely to have been gratefully received. The donor, although he was not an SPCK correspondent, ordered the books from the Society's printer Joseph Downing.[26] William Itchener of Christian Malford, with the help of a gift of money from a relative, had kept a charity school for several years before he became a correspondent in 1722. He claimed 'a large acquaintance with the Clergy in the Northern parts of Wiltshire' and offered 'to give them easy and cheap opportunities of displaying good Books among the people'.[27] George Millard also arranged for a library of books worth £30 to be sent to the parish of Colerne.[28] The reduced prices available to Society members would have been attractive to others such as Mr Arnold of Nettleton, who was giving away many books in 1723.[29] One of the strengths of the SPCK was that it provided a ready distribution network through which successes in one parish could be broadcast throughout the country, both to members and through religious societies to others. The reinvigoration of religion spread beyond the parishes with corresponding members. By 1724 thirty Wiltshire villages had charity schools, of which only fourteen had an SPCK correspondent.[30]

Several corresponding members besides Millard encouraged church singing. In Devizes Robert Townsend taught his charity children to sing psalms and noted

[23] George Millard of Box, Bohun Fox of Melksham and John Rogers of Bradford-on-Avon.
[24] WRO, 1981/1; Bodleian Library, MS Eng Misc f. 10. Lewis drew up a rate for Fox, a subscribing member of the SPCK, at Millard's request. For further details of the club and the diarist John Lewis, see chapter 2.   [25] SPCK History, 100–1; SPCK, Minutes 1698–1704, 349–50; AL 335.
[26] WRO 680/8.   [27] SPCK, AL 11, 7158.   [28] SPCK, AL 15, 10857.
[29] SPCK, AL 12, 7354.
[30] Based upon list of parishes in Jones, *The Charity School Movement*, p. 371.

the admiration of those that heard them.[31] Thomas Frampton of Broad Hinton held public catechisms on Wednesdays, Fridays and Sundays, and always concluded with the singing of a psalm and prayers.[32] He encouraged parents to attend by tolling a bell. William Itchener contributed to the cost of the seats the parish of Christian Malford built for the singers in 1719.[33] Frampton and John Smyth of Bishopston desired editions of the divine hymns and anthems 'to promote piety and virtue'.[34] The ministers of Bradford-on-Avon and Little Hinton also ordered psalters from the SPCK, as did Millard himself.[35] These correspondents encountered the same positive reaction to singing as Millard did. As Frampton noted, 'the young people in those parts very much delight in Ch[urc]h music'. In 1718 Millard began to teach psalmody to charity children and young people in his other parish of Calstone Wellington, as well as at Marshfield, a nearby town in Gloucestershire. He reported that 'The Children and young People of both these Places have already made a very good Progress in their Singing'. Millard was 'in good hopes that the Influence of these our Examples will soon extend to a great many other Parishes', and had 'been lately inform'd that 2 or 3 more at a small distance from me are going upon it'.[36]

The SPCK was very pleased with Millard's success in bringing his 'Parishioners to the knowledge & devout use of Psalmody, a thing lamentably neglected in most parts of the Kingdom'. It viewed psalmody as both a good technique of religious education and an important means of religious expression. In June 1717 Henry Newman wrote to Millard to express the Society's approval: 'I believe it may be truly said that wherever [Psalmody] is neglected all the other parts of Divine Worship are perform'd in a cold & lifeless manner, and the sense of Religion in most places may in good measure be estimated, by the reverent or irreverent use of Psalmody.'[37] Millard's description of his method of encouraging psalmody was copied into the Abstract Book in full, further evidence of its impact. The Society never distributed a pamphlet describing Millard's work in Box to other correspondents, but other success stories were circulated. SPCK packets included the third edition of Josiah Woodward's *Account of the Rise and Progress of the Religious Societies*, which contained a letter from Old Romney in Kent describing how many youths sought instruction after three or four had been taught psalmody. This example in turn inspired Samuel Wesley's *Account of the Religious Society begun in Epworth . . . Lincolnshire'*, where the father of the Methodist John Wesley had formed a religious society with the help of 'some of the most sensible and well dispos'd persons among my singers'.[38] The SPCK recommended the Prayer Book with Singing Psalms and

---

[31] SPCK, AL 2604 (6 June 1711).   [32] SPCK, AL 5987 (1719).   [33] WRO 1710/32.
[34] SPCK, AL 10523 (1729), 10466 (1729).
[35] SPCK, Packets, pp. 108, 50, 149, 26, 34, 79, 125, 164.   [36] SPCK, L 5618. WAM 31: 40–1.
[37] SPCK, Society Letter 6.
[38] Josiah Woodward, *An Account of the Rise and Progress of the Religious Societies* (3rd edn, London, 1701); Allen and McClure, *Two Hundred Years*, pp. 89, 167.

'some book of psalmody' to charity school masters, and in 1718 it published Archbishop Wake's collection of psalms. To its embarrassment the Society was forced to withdraw the collection after finding that the Arian Samuel Clark had tampered with its contents, but another volume was being planned in 1724.[39]

GALLERIES AND SOCIETIES OF SINGERS

The SPCK and its correspondents contributed to a general reinvigoration of religion in early eighteenth-century Wiltshire in which music played a central role. Society members erected galleries for charity children – as in Box, Wroughton and Salisbury St Thomas – and they taught psalmody to these children first.[40] Yet their goal was to encourage everyone, young and old, to sing. The children were not expected to serve as a choir, leaving the congregation as silent auditors of their performance. Even in Box, Millard did not succeed in bringing everyone to sing. As we have seen, his drive to promote congregational music was prompted by his concern that church music had been taken over by choirs sitting separately in their own gallery or seats in the church. The dominance of west gallery choirs was itself the result of an earlier attempt to encourage lay participation in parish music. The Restoration ushered in a campaign to form singing societies, and these were encouraged by the erection of galleries or the allocation of particular pews to seat them. Although their tactics differed, both the charity school movement and the gallery movement were part of the same drive to encourage the congregational performance of church music in country parishes, a drive which evoked an enthusiastic popular response.

In 1674 the leading parishioners of Corsham petitioned the bishop of Salisbury for permission to refit and enlarge the gallery for their newly formed group of singers. The bishop Seth Ward was delighted to grant their request, writing that 'we . . . can't but thinck ourselves obleidged so farre as in us lyes to promote so good a work'. In doing so he was reviving a tradition of promoting church music that went back to before the Civil War. The minister of Bishop's Cannings was said by John Aubrey to have 'made several of his parishioners good muscians, both for vocal and instrumentall musick; they sung the Psalmes in consort to the organ, which Mr. Ferraby procured to be erected'.[41] Now Bishop Ward saw the Corsham society as an excellent means for 'traineing and Nurseing

[39] Allen and McClure, *Two Hundred Years*, p. 186; C. Rose, 'The origins and ideals of the SPCK 1699-1716', in *The Church of England, c.1689–c.1833*, p. 186; SPCK, AL 9, 5822; Bodleian Library, Rawlinson MS D839, f. 93. For earlier plans to publish psalms, see W. Weber, *The Rise of Musical Classics in Eighteenth-Century England* (Oxford, 1992), pp. 50–1.

[40] SPCK, AL 3783; D1/61/1a, pp. 103–4, 66–7.

[41] Aubrey relates how Ferraby entertained James I with four-part bucolics of his own composition sung by his parishioners, organ playing, bell ringing and football, for which he was rewarded by being made a chaplain in ordinary. John Aubrey, *Natural History of Wiltshire* (New York, 1969), p. 108.

up of Youth for the attaineing of good skill and knowledge in Church Musick'
and hoped that this might prepare them to sing in cathedrals and collegiate
chapels.[42] The story of the gallery in Corsham church in the seventeenth and
eighteenth centuries was that of music in many provincial towns. The gallery had
been built in 1637 to hold organs, as well as pews seating twelve people. The
organs were gone by 1648 when the gallery was used entirely for seating, and
during the Interregnum people bought seats 'in the littell Gallery where the
organs one time stood'. With the bishop's support, after the Restoration the
parishioners 'fitted & enlarged [the gallery] for the more convenient recepcon &
use of the sd young person's . . . where in they may sitt together for the more
decent harmonious and ordrly singing of the publique psalms'. There was still a
separate gallery known as 'the singers' gallery' in 1741.[43]

In 1679 the leading parishioners of Highworth also built a gallery for their
singers, subscribing 9 shillings each to the cost.[44] As in Corsham, the impetus to
form a singing society came from below, although it had the support of the minister and substantial inhabitants. The parishioners reported 'That in our parrish
there are very lately many persons that have by great industry Learned to glorifie
god in his publique Wo[rshi]pp by singing of Psalmes'. So the parish decided to
build a gallery 'for the convenient placeing of that singing party', and they hoped
that as a result the congregation would 'bee exceedinglie increased & incouraged
to appeare there and to ioyne wth them in that everlasting dutie'. The new gallery
would also enable more of the parish to participate in divine service, by re-
seating some auditors whose old seats were so far from the reading desk and
pulpit 'that they are deprived thereby not only of heareing the word butt ioyne-
ing with [the minister] in that great Wo[rshi]pp'.[45] Unfortunately, they had built
the new gallery without first gaining official permission in the form of a faculty,
or licence, from the dean of Salisbury. Although 'an excellent musician' himself,
Dean Thomas Pierce was intolerant of violations of his authority. In May 1679
he ordered 'that the Gallery be forthwith pulled downe'.[46]

Parishioners were supposed to request a faculty from their ordinary (bishop,
dean, or archdeacon) before beginning any major construction work on church
or churchyard such as building a gallery, moving the pulpit, erecting a monu-
ment, or rebuilding the tower. In theory, the granting of a faculty proceeded
through several clearly demarcated stages. First, the churchwardens, with the
consent of the major landholders perhaps gained at a vestry, petitioned the

[42] D1/61/2/1; WRO 1285/11.
[43] WRO 1157/1, 4; D1/61/2/1. The Warminster organs were hidden under the floor of the tower. A.
D. Dodge, 'The rise and fall of the west gallery musicians in Wiltshire', *Wiltshire Folklife* 33 (1996):
3. I am grateful to Dr Dodge for sending me a copy of this article.
[44] By March 1680 ten parishioners had subscribed 9s. each, leaving the parish short of the total cost
of £7 10s. WRO 1184/19.   [45] D5/17/1/1.
[46] D5/29/6, f. 17. Evelyn is the source of information about Pierce's musicianship. *DNB*, q.v. 'Thomas
Pierce'.

ordinary for his approval. The ordinary then issued a citation to be read in the parish church, specifying a date on which anyone with objections to the proposal was to appear before him. If no one appeared, he would authorise the construction and have his order enrolled in his register of faculties. These steps can be clearly seen in a faculty for a gallery in Wantage (Berks.) 'for the more comodious reception of the parishioners'. After the churchwardens petitioned for permission to build a gallery, the dean ordered objectors (naming three) to appear on 28 September 1714. When none appeared he issued his faculty three days later.[47] This three-stage process – petition, citation and faculty – allowed the ordinary to make sure that the construction would damage neither the church nor the interests of any parishioners. If anyone had objected, the dean might have sent his surrogate to the parish to examine witnesses and inspect the church, as he did in faculties for singing galleries in Leigh and Ramsbury.

At least fifteen faculties for Wiltshire galleries were approved between 1710 and 1740, of which only two were for singers. Faculties were more common for galleries to provide more seats to hold growing congregations or for the personal use of gentlemen who felt that elevated seating was more appropriate to their position in the community.[48] One gentleman's gallery even had a separate entrance accessed by a staircase built up the outside wall of the church. Galleries were also licensed for organs, in the urban parish of Salisbury St Edmunds and the rural parish of Potterne, and charity children, in Wroughton. A comprehensive study of galleries is not possible before 1710–12, when the bishop began a register of faculties, but at least two singing galleries were licensed, for Corsham and Burbage. In 1702 the dean licensed a gallery at the west end of the Burbage church 'built for the use of the young men and other parishioners being singers . . . to hear divine service & sermon and to sing the spalmes [*sic*]'.[49]

Although most singers' galleries were built before official permission was sought, only Highworth had the misfortune of having its illegal construction pulled down. Edward Foyle of Somerford Keynes erected 'a decent and commodious Gallery . . . for the use of the [sin]gers [of] the Ps[al]mes' in 1713, at the same time building a new stone tower in place of the dilapidated and dangerous old timber belfry. Foyle claimed that this work had the support 'of the major part of the inhabitants and landholders', and the bishop confirmed the new belfry and gallery although he had not been asked for permission beforehand.[50] The chapel of Leigh in Ashton Keynes built a new singing gallery in 1717 at the expense of the minister and two others and 'with the advice and consent of the whole Parish assembled in a vestry Nemine Contradicente'. The gallery was 'put to the use for which it was intended and no other namely for the incoureigment and convenience of the singers of Psalms', although those who wished to sit

---

[47] D5/33/1, ff. 4–5.   [48] There were five faculties each for growing congregations and for gentlemen.
[49] D5/33/2.   [50] D1/61/1a, pp. 42–5.

there also paid for their seats. The new gallery increased the capacity of the chapel and the wardens noted that 'without the sd gallery we have not room in our chapel for our Congregation'. Despite the objections of John Bisse and others that now they could neither read nor hear the service, the bishop confirmed the construction in 1719.[51] A record of these galleries survives only because the parishes realised after the fact that they needed a faculty.

Other galleries never received an official licence, and a record of these only survives through incidental mentions in presentments or parish records. The churchwardens of Berwick St James admitted in their presentment of 1703 to the bishop that a gallery had recently been built in the west end of the church next to the belfry for 'the conveniency of the young & other people of the sd parishe to stand sett & kneele in, to hear divine service and sermon there; & to sing Psalmes'. Although they had 'ignorantly omitted to aske leave' of the bishop, he apparently allowed them to keep the construction, for a year later the wardens presented two people for intruding into the gallery erected for singers.[52] No faculty appears to have been obtained for the pews which Christian Malford agreed to build for singers in 1719 or for the gallery which the vestry approved for the use of singers in Cricklade St Sampsons in 1726, although the same parish sought a faculty for another gallery two years later.[53]

It was not always necessary to build a gallery to hold a new group of singers. The parish might move the singers into a pre-existing gallery or assign them particular pews. Although a faculty was not strictly necessary in this case, a few parishes sought one anyway, either to gain authority for extensive modifications or simply to err on the side of caution. In 1725 the dean confirmed the exclusive use by singers of part of the gallery in Ramsbury church. Several parishioners had reported that the south part of the west gallery was 'very commodious and useful for persons who shall sing psalmes', noting that no one had any property rights to these seats, which were used only by children. In June the congregation assembled for the dean's surrogate to view the church, and two weeks later the dean directed that these seats were 'for the sole use of such persons as shall sing psalmes'. He authorised the three petitioners and vicar to dispose of vacancies as they saw fit.[54] This was probably the same gallery whose construction in 1698 had forced the removal of pews used by singers in the north-western corner of the church.[55] Many other parishes used galleries or pews for singers without seeking official permission. Lacock was using its gallery for singers in 1700 when the vestry agreed to exclude boys and others who were disturbing the singing.[56] We only know that the Pewsey gallery was used for singers because in May 1710 'the Singers, Possessours, and Owners of the Gallery in Pewsey Church' signed

[51] D1/61/1/28; D1/61/1a, pp. 71–4.   [52] D1/54/18; D1/54/19/5 (1704, W&W).
[53] WRO 1710/32; WRO 1632/18; D1/61/1/32–3. Galleries were also erected in Marden (1699), Mere (1705) and East Knoyle (1714). Dodge, 'The rise and fall of the west gallery musicians', p. 4.
[54] D5/33/1, ff. 25–6.   [55] D5/33/8; D5/33/2.   [56] WRO 173/1.

a seating chart and agreed each to pay the parish clerk 2*d*. a year to clean their seats.[57] Singers sat in a gallery in Box church when George Millard arrived in 1707. Millard himself did not request a faculty for the gallery which he built for charity children in 1713.[58] As we have seen, there were separate pews for singers in Ramsbury church until 1698, and Fisherton Anger singers also had their own pews, although these were falling into disrepair in 1747.[59]

The widespread erection of unlicensed galleries for singers indicates a popular movement to improve church music by forming societies of singers. There must have been many parishes where singing societies went unrecorded. Indeed, the Church's attempts to control singers in the 1730s uncovered other parishes with choirs, some with their own galleries, whose existence would otherwise have remained hidden. The new choirs initially had the full support of the authorities. Ministers and other parish leaders agreed to build galleries to hold the singers and subscribed the amounts necessary to fund their construction. In some cases, such as Somerford Keynes, a local gentleman stepped in to subsidise the work. Subscribers to the petition requesting a gallery for Corsham included the minister, churchwardens and four gentleman. William Eyres and William Duckett were among the leading gentry of the county; both were justices of the peace and Eyres was a member of the quorum, the inner circle of the magistracy. The Highworth inhabitants who petitioned the dean to allow them to keep their new gallery included the vicar, and nineteen of the twenty-four other signatories were churchwardens at some time in their lives.[60] Some parishes became carried away by their zeal to encourage church music. The Highworth petitioners had no doubt that the dean would approve of 'such a worke that tended soe much to the promoting of pietie'. Although they were proved wrong, other parishes were more fortunate. Ecclesiastical support for choirs can be seen in an almost universal willingness to permit illegally built galleries to remain standing and to license them after the fact. Ordinaries confirmed new galleries even when other parishioners objected to them, as happened in Burbage in 1702 and Leigh in 1718. In the latter case opponents complained that the new gallery blocked their view, darkened the church so that they could not read, and threatened the stability of the church.[61] Ecclesiastics upheld the interests of singers against those of other parishioners. They also took steps to ensure that singing societies had exclusive use of the new galleries.

By 1730 ecclesiastical and parochial authorities had been encouraging singing in Wiltshire churches for sixty years. Psalmody thrived elsewhere in England as well. A correspondent from east Devon reported in 1699 that, with the support of a local gentleman, Mr Joseph Harris, 'most of ye . . . well disposed persons in ye parishes round about me, have been promoting a laudable designe of making ye Psalmody in or Churches something more regular . . . [as] an ornament to or

[57] WRO 493/49, f. 40v.   [58] SPCK, L 5213, AL 3783.   [59] D5/33/2; D5/33/8; D1/54/40.
[60] D5/17/1/1; WRO 1184/19.   [61] D5/33/2; D1/61/1/28, and D1/61/1a, pp. 71–4.

Divine Service'.[62] Hambledon (Hants.) had a singers' gallery in 1723 when the churchwarden found himself in trouble for removing a stained glass window to make more light for it.[63] There was a spontaneous movement in many parishes to form singing societies and to erect galleries or reserve pews to hold the new choirs. In the early eighteenth century the SPCK taught psalmody to charity children and encouraged the rest of the congregation to sing. Societies of singers received musical training and learned to sing increasingly complex settings, as art music was introduced into parish churches. The societies of singers took their music seriously. By the 1730s the Church was receiving reports that 'persons of all ages and sexes meet together in the parish churches' after Sunday afternoon services and on weekday evenings to hold rehearsals.[64] Psalmody also promoted cultural exchanges between parishes. George Millard held psalm-recitation contests and he rejoiced in their popularity and in his success in attracting people from outside the parish of Box. In the 1730s it was said that singing societies 'make a practice of going in companies from their own churches to sing in other churches'. The Church of England had succeeded in nurturing a vibrant popular religious and musical culture and had seen congregations grow as a result. Yet it greeted the independent choirs which it had created with horror. Bishop Thomas Sherlock was dismayed at the reports that persons were meeting 'at unseasonable times under pretence of learning to sing psalms . . . which meetings give scandal and just offence to sober . . . persons' and that 'persons conceited of their own singing' were singing in other churches, 'a very disorderly practice, and frequently attended with ill consequences'. The Church now performed a complete *volte face*. Official support for choirs abruptly stopped, as the parochial authorities embarked on a concerted campaign to suppress lay choirs.

ANGLICAN REACTION

The last faculty for a singing gallery was approved in 1725, and Wiltshire correspondents made no further reference to parish singing in their letters to the SPCK after 1729. The years that followed witnessed a series of disputes over music in parish churches. The Church sought to suppress choirs and to protect plain music against art music. Although their justification was their wish to promote congregational singing, their attempts to suppress choirs had as much to do with anxiety over the loss of control over church services. The first clear evidence of a campaign against choir singers in Wiltshire came not long after the translation of Thomas Sherlock to the see of Salisbury in 1734.[65] Sherlock disliked the

---

[62] Devon RO, Basket D/17/102. J. H. Bettey, *Church and Parish* (London, 1987), pp. 118–20, quotes a 1731 faculty from Sussex for a gallery to promote psalm singing.
[63] Hampshire RO, 21 M 65/C9/53 (Winchester Diocesan Records). I am grateful for this reference to Professor David Underdown.   [64] D1/61/1b, p. 69.
[65] Sherlock's translation from Bangor was confirmed in November 1734. J. Le Neve, *Fasti Ecclesiae Anglicanae* (Oxford, 1854), vol. II, p. 610.

growing practice of singing anthems in parish churches. Anthems were multi-part choral settings of psalms or other texts which had become popular in cathedral churches during the Restoration and which during the eighteenth century spread to some country churches.[66] Sherlock instructed his archdeacons to assist their clergy in suppressing anthem singers and in 1737 he ordered them to 'give a strict charge' at their next visitations to churchwardens to stop evening meetings and to present 'disorderly strollers'.[67] The dean of Salisbury, John Clarke, shared Sherlock's concerns about singers, and in the previous year he had responded to complaints of 'Irregularities and Innovations' in Calne church by ordering the minister and churchwardens to place restrictions on psalmody and organ playing. Only two psalms set to plain tunes were to be sung in each service, and the organist was also permitted to play a grave voluntary. No one but the organist was to be permitted to play the organ during divine service.[68] Ministers and churchwardens also took action against singers in other churches, such as Mere.

When in 1737 the minister of Gillingham (Dorset) tried to expel 'Anthemists' from the gallery, Bishop Sherlock's policy led him into direct confrontation with the subdean Thomas Naish. The son of a chorister in Salisbury Cathedral, Naish had been subdean of Salisbury for over forty years and his views on church music were those of the previous generation. In 1700 he had expressed his own love of music in a sermon to the Society of Lovers of Music, and he also taught singing and the spinet.[69] Gillingham lay in the subdean's jurisdiction, although the bishop was the patron of the benefice. Naish took the singers' side against the minister Mr Prince and issued a mandate in their favour. The choir was further strengthened by the arrival of singers who had been expelled from Mere church, and when conflict resulted from Prince's continued efforts to suppress them Naish went to Gillingham himself to see that his orders were followed. At this point, Prince turned for help to Bishop Sherlock and succeeded in gaining his support. The subdean was forced to back down and to assign the disposition of gallery seats to the minister and churchwardens, giving them the power they needed to expel the singers.[70]

The Gillingham singers disturbed church services on three successive Sundays in August 1737 before Naish conceded defeat. On one occasion they 'broke out into an Anthem . . . and made such a noise and disturbance that Mr. Prince cou'd not perform the remaining part of the service'. Wiltshire churches were the scenes of several disruptive quarrels in the 1730s and the decades that followed.

[66] On anthems, see N. Temperley, 'Music in churches', in H. D. Johnson and Roger Fiske, eds., *Music in Britain: The Eighteenth Century* (Oxford, 1990), pp. 363–6, 384–5.
[67] D1/61/1b, p. 69.   [68] D5/33/1, f. 33v; and draft version in D5/17/1/3.
[69] D. Slatter, ed., *The Diary of Thomas Naish*, WANHS RB 20 (Devizes, 1961), pp. 4, 42, 48, 70. Naish had also clashed with Bishop Burnet over politics thirty years earlier. Ibid., pp. 44–55.
[70] Lambeth Palace Library, MS 1741, ff. 134–5.

In 1739 Wokingham church was the site of direct confrontation between the singers and the churchwardens and parish clerk. The singers named and sang whatever psalms and anthems they pleased, ignoring the directions of the parish clerk. Matters came to a head on 29 April after the minister and churchwardens ordered the singers to follow the parish clerk's instructions. When the choir refused to sing, the congregation was not able to sing any psalms at all. The singers defiantly remained after the service to sing an anthem until a church-warden expelled them. The singers boycotted services for two weeks, but on 20 May they returned to mount a demonstration. Assembling in the chancel, they stood in front of the communion table (where they had laid their hats) facing the congregation and 'when the Clerk had named the psalm; began in a very loud . . . manner singing in their new way'.[71] At about the same time, the curate and parishioners of Somerford Keynes (where a singers' gallery had been built in 1713) clashed over whether the singers should be allowed to perform psalms during a funeral service. Several women asked the curate to remain but he angrily removed his surplice and refused to finish the service. In a petition to the bishop, parishioners threatened to 'turn dessenter' if the offending curate was not replaced.[72] In August 1742 the rector of Boyton, Thomas Clifton, suffered three disturbances by singers in eight days, forcing him to suspend services on two occasions.[73] A similar dispute occurred in Castle Combe in 1747 after the minis-ter finished his sermon one Sunday afternoon. The parish clerk named the psalm and he and other members of the congregation began to sing. But it was alleged that Daniel Wallop and others in the singers' gallery started to sing an entirely different tune.[74] The description of Wallop and his colleagues as 'the old singers' is significant. As far as parish authorities were concerned, the days of the inde-pendent choir were over.

The Church's campaign against singers was not limited to Wiltshire. In the diocese of Exeter, the bishop had already begun to take action against the new singing societies in the 1720s. In 1699 a correspondent had written to the chan-cellor Dr James to obtain the bishop's approval for making psalmody more regular in churches because James was a 'known patron of Art', and in the fol-lowing year the archdeacon of Exeter's surrogate supported new singers in South Tawton.[75] Yet tensions between the old and new singers were already present. Difficulties had arisen in South Tawton because the majority of parishioners objected to the new way of singing psalms, although the minister encouraged it. By 1724 the official policy had changed. The faculty for a new gallery in East Teignmouth specifically instructed that it was 'not [for] ye use of a New Singing Gallery or to place any new singers therein'.[76] This restriction had been requested by parishioners, perhaps because they realised how the atmosphere

[71] D5/17/1/3; D5/28, 1739.   [72] D1/41/4/36.   [73] D1/36/2/13.
[74] D1/41/4/3.   [75] DRO, Principal Registry, Basket D/17/102, 30.
[76] Ibid., Basket D/2/101, 102.

had changed. In the next decade no fewer than fourteen faculties for galleries included a standard clause which explicitly barred their use by new singers, although most parishes had not requested this condition.[77]

The change in official policy towards lay choirs resulted from several interrelated factors. First, ecclesiastical and parochial authorities objected to musical innovation in parish churches, and in the process they revealed tension between two very different visions of church music, the art music found in cathedrals and the plainer traditions of parish churches.[78] The authorities also wished to ensure that the whole congregation, and not just the choirs, participated in church music. Last, and most important, they were concerned about their loss of control over an increasingly vibrant culture of popular church music. Dislike of innovation is a theme which runs through virtually all of the complaints against what were described as the 'new singers'. The Wokingham wardens reported that the choir sang psalms 'according to their new and unintelligible way'. Exeter diocese faculties forbade 'ye least Innovation in our Church Service', including 'any new & unaccustomed way of singing'. Innovation might affect the text, tunes, harmonisations and place in the service of the music. Unlike the Congregationalists, who introduced hymns in 1719, the Church of England continued to use the psalms of David. The Wokingham singers were unusual in singing 'songs composed by themselves' that were 'no ways ordered . . . in the book of psalms'. The version of the psalms chosen for singing was itself subject to controversy. The psalm texts in the Prayer Book were difficult to set to music, and throughout the seventeenth century congregations sang the psalms in the metrical version of Sternhold and Hopkins, first published in 1562. Sternhold and Hopkins was much criticised for being poor poetry and an inexact translation of the original texts. Thomas Bray of the SPCK was one of many who argued 'that the Contempt into which Singing of Psalms is grown amongst us, is owing to the very ill and ridiculous Metre of *Hopkins* and *Sternhold*, and the equally bad singing of them in our Country Churches'.[79] The puritans had sought to replace Sternhold and Hopkins with a more literal versification. In 1696 a new metrification by Tate and Brady was introduced, but it was slow to catch on even though it received some official support. Sternhold and Hopkins remained popular. New metrifications not only meant new words to remember but also that a psalm might no longer be sung to the familiar tune. In 1700 the Lacock parish vestry agreed 'That the old tunes to the psalms of David which have always heretofore been used and sung in the parish church . . . be continued, And that noe other

---

[77] Ibid., Basket D/2/103–4, 111–13. Also Pelynt, 1728; Okehampton, 1729; Northam, 1730; St Germans, Callington, Bampton, 1731; Huxham, Clyst St George, St Mary, St Lawrence Exeter, 1732; Kinkerswell, 1733.

[78] N. Temperley, *The Music of the English Parish Church* (Cambridge, 1979), vol. I, p. 4; H. Davies, *Worship and Theology in England . . . 1603–1690* (Princeton, 1975), ch. 7.

[79] H. P. Thompson, *Thomas Bray* (London, 1954), p. 11. Bray was rector of Sheldon from 1690 to 1730.

new tunes be sung there for the future'.[80] The bishop of Exeter refused to license the use of Tate and Brady in 1717 despite a petition claiming that this would 'create a unity & conformity & silence the gainsayers'.[81] In order to make it easier for congregations to adopt the new version, a supplement to Tate and Brady published in 1702 stressed that it had the 'whole variety of metres' from the old version and that psalms were set to such familiar tunes as Windsor and St David's.[82] Yet Sternhold and Hopkins continued to outsell all competitors well into the eighteenth century; the nineteenth edition was being advertised in the *Salisbury Journal* in 1739.[83] In 1763 John Brown of Newcastle was still lamenting the state of music in parish churches 'where the cold, the meagre, the disgusting Dulness of Sternhold and his Companions, hath quenched all the poetic Fire and devout Majesty of the royal Psalmist'.[84]

The authorities objected to the spread of art music into parish churches. Their views represented the latest stage in the struggle between contrasting styles of music as worship, art music and plain music, which dated back to the Reformation. Elizabeth I's Injunctions of 1559 had authorised modest song so long as it was 'as plainly understood as if it were read without singing', while also allowing 'for comforting of such that delighted in music . . . an hymn, or such like song to the praise of Almighty God, in the best sort of melody and music that may be conveniently devised, having respect that the sentence of the hymn may be understanded and perceived'.[85] Supporters of the plain style stressed the scriptural content of singing and its role in the edification of worshippers. Only psalms were to be sung, and these were to be simple so that the whole congregation could participate and understand what they sang. The call for simplicity also reflected suspicion of secular music and determination that it should not pollute worship. Indeed, the ideal would be for psalmody to reach out into the streets and fields. Thus the incumbent of Old Romney rejoiced that 'Our shepherds, ploughmen and other labourers at their work perfume the air with their melodious singing of psalms'.[86]

The proponents of the art style of church music supported the idea of the beauty of holiness as the most respectful way of worshipping God. The historian of church music Nicholas Temperley draws a distinction between the music of

---

[80] WRO 173/1.   [81] DRO, Principal Registry, Basket D17/1/1.

[82] Nicholas Brady and Nahum Tate, *A Supplement to the New Version of Psalms* (3rd edn, London, 1702).

[83] *Salisbury Journal*, 10 July 1739. The same newspaper included advertisements for William Knapp's *Set of Psalm Tunes* (10 July 1739) and William Tans'ur's new volume, *Sacred Mirth . . . Being a Choice and Valuable Collection of Psalms, Hymns, Anthems and Canons on Various Divine Subjects* (22 May 1739).

[84] John Brown, *A Dissertation on . . . Poetry and Music* (London, 1763), p. 213, quoted in J. W. Legg, *English Church Life from the Reformation to the Tractarian Movement* (London, 1914), p. 187.

[85] E. Cardwell, *Documentary Annals of the Reformed Church of England . . . from the year 1546 to the year 1716* (Oxford, 1844), pp. 228–9.

[86] Woodward, *An Account of the Rise and Progress of the Religious Societies*.

cathedrals and choirs and that of parish churches.[87] Certainly, in the 1730s this was a distinction that ecclesiastical authorities sought to enforce. Bishop Sherlock and Mr. Prince shared 'a great dislike to what they call'd Anthems, as they are us'd in the parish churches'. The anthem was the only musical setting explicitly mentioned in the liturgy. According to the rubric, the anthem was to be sung 'In Quires and Places where they sing' immediately before the prayers which ended the first service. Although the reference to 'Quires' in the rubric suggests that the instruction was intended primarily for cathedral and college choirs, it might nevertheless be used to justify the introduction of anthems into parish churches. The character of the new music can be seen in the complaints against it. In Calne the organ played voluntaries in a manner that was 'highly improper and indecent to be used in the House of God', a reference to the ornamented and polyphonic music imported from cathedrals and concert halls. Sherlock was to some extent reacting against the increased ambition of country choirs.[88] But in emulating the music of cathedrals, these choirs were drawing upon a tradition of parish music that dated back to the Restoration. Support for music in country parishes had come from those who were involved with developments in art music and wished to re-establish the high traditions of church music in all places.

The introduction of harmonised forms of singing meant that the new choirs required musical training and therefore effectively excluded the rest of the congregation. After the Restoration musical training appeared to have many advantages. The contempt in which Sternhold and Hopkins was held was exacerbated by the system of 'lining-out' which the puritans had introduced during the Civil Wars in the Directory for Public Worship. The puritans removed organs from those churches that had them, leaving the parish clerk to lead the congregation in psalmody without accompaniment.[89] 'Lining-out', by which the parish clerk read or sang each line first and was then imitated by the congregation, allowed the entire congregation to sing without having to be able to read a psalter. The primary objection to 'lining-out' was aesthetic. The alternation between clerk and congregation had the effect of breaking the song up into discrete sections, eliminating musical, thematic and poetic unity, and meant that it was sung slowly. Where it has continued to develop, for example in the Western Isles of Scotland and in some Baptist churches in the American South, 'lining-out' has become an art form in its own right.[90]

'Lining-out' did not appeal to the ears of ecclesiastics like Seth Ward who were more familiar with the music of cathedral choirs and the Chapel Royal. They

[87] Temperley, 'Music in churches', p. 358.   [88] Ibid., pp. 384–5.
[89] P. A. Scholes, *The Puritans and Music in England and New England* (London, 1934), pp. 232–3.
[90] For an American example, see B. Sutton and P. Hartman, *Primitive Baptist Hymns of the Blue Ridge* (sound recording) (Chapel Hill, 1982), which includes a useful discussion. In black Primitive Baptist churches in North Carolina, the lining-out is itself melodic, and the lined-out phrase is never exactly the same as the phrase which is sung thereafter (p. 16). I am grateful to Professor Jonathan Chu for bringing this recording to my attention.

believed that as a form of worship music should be beautiful, whether performed in cathedrals or parish churches. Ward had the art music of cathedrals clearly in mind when he approved the faculty for Corsham in 1674.[91] He expected that its establishment 'maybe of good purpose and benefitt by traineing and nurseing upp of youth for the attaineing of good skills and knowledge in the science of harmony and singing who as occasion shall offr may qualify and make them profitable for the glorious service of god in Cath[edra]ll and Colleg[ia]te Ch[urche]s'. There was already a school (of medieval foundation) for choristers in Preshute church.[92] Ward sought to create a petty Chapel Royal, a professional choir in which a select few would 'sing according to Art'. The bishop's hopes foreshadowed those of early eighteenth-century High Churchmen like Thomas Bisse, chancellor of Hereford Cathedral and one of the founders of the Three Choirs festival. Bisse believed that worship should be holy and beautiful in both cathedrals and parish churches, and in 1716 he preached that 'parish-churches should as much as possible, conform to the customs of the cathedral churches'.[93]

In the aftermath of the cessation of cathedral music during the Civil War, Ward wished to restore the quality of music. When he visited Salisbury Cathedral in 1671 he asked whether 'ye choristers [were] instructed carefully in the Art of Musicke'.[94] He must have been saddened in 1686 when his dispute with Dean Pierce led him into conflict with the singing-men and organist who in consequence neglected the performance of church music.[95] The gentry supporters of the Corsham petition had the improvement of worship at the forefront of their minds, but their support for the choir also reflected a well-developed interest in art music. The daughter-in-law of William Duckett, one of the petitioners, left the makings of a chamber ensemble when she died in 1695: two lutes, three violins, a bass and a bandora, two flutes, and even an hautboy, an instrument which had only recently been developed. William Duckett's grandson appointed George Millard to his first living at Calstone Wellington.[96] There is no evidence of the form of musical training which the Corsham singers received, although Ward hoped that they would be educated in 'the science of harmony'. In Box Millard provided musical instruction himself, holding special music rehearsals for the purpose. From the SPCK he ordered copies of *The Devout Singer's Guide* and of John Playford's *Introduction to the Skill of Music*. The former included

---

[91] WRO 1285/11.

[92] D1/36/2/7. The school had apparently been at Preshute church since 1320, when it was appropriated by an earlier bishop.

[93] Thomas Bisse, *The Beauty of Holiness in the Common Prayer (Four Lectures)* (London, 1716), pp. 6, 48–9, 95n. See also Thomas Bisse, *Musick the Delight of the Sons of Men* (London, 1726); Weber, *The Rise of Musical Classics*, pp. 114–15.   [94] D1/57/3/1.

[95] Bodleian Library, Tanner MS 30, f. 50; *DNB*, q.v. 'Thomas Pierce'.

[96] WRO, Archdeaconry of Wilts., Will and inventory of Martha Duckett, proved 6 March 1694/5. The bandora was a stringed instrument similar to the cittern, an ancestor of the guitar; *WAM* 31: 33.

brief instruction in reading music, including the gamut (or scale), the appearance
of the notes and the 'sol fa' system, with a mnemonic verse to help the reader
remember in which order to sing the notes. Each psalm was set to a familiar tunes
such as Coleshil, Cambridge or York, and a subject index advised parish clerks
on the choice of psalms which were appropriate to the topic of the sermon.[97]
Millard also sent regular orders for Common Prayer Books with psalms, specifically requesting that the printer 'bind up 8 leaves of writing paper rul'd for
Tunes at ye End of the Singing Psalms'. Millard's singers learned to read music.
The vicar taught his charity children 'to say Psalms by Notes', and he gave each
child a small psalm book, 'pricking down the Tunes for them'. The scale of the
instruction he provided can be seen in the fact that he ordered at least 104 Prayer
Books with psalms between 1720 and 1726.[98] Under the tutelage of SPCK ministers and schoolmasters and later of itinerant singing teachers, the standard of
parish choirs improved, as they learned new tunes and techniques of counter-
point and harmony.[99]

There were strong connections between the drive to promote music in parish
churches and developments in art music, particularly the renewed interest in
musical classics during the period from 1690 to 1730. Members of the SPCK
and of other religious societies, such as Arthur Bedford, and Tories actively
supported the ancient music movement. Bedford believed 'that church music
could provide the central thrust in Anglican revival', and he sought to bring
the music of cathedral and parish churches closer together, although it is likely
that many of his colleagues in the ancient music movement would not have
agreed. He called both for clergymen and parish clerks to educate their congregations to sing psalms and for the revival of the high traditions of church
music.[100] John Smyth of Bishopton wrote to the Society in 1729 to encourage
it to distribute anthems and hymns 'to promote piety and virtue'.[101] The
Gillingham singers were called 'gamutters', referring to the scale they learned
in order to read music. In Wokingham the choir sang 'sal: fa:', evidence that a
singing teacher had been active there also.[102] Parishioners were receiving
musical instruction in South Tawton (Devon) as early as 1700, when the parish

---

[97] John Playford, *An Introduction to the Skill of Music* (London, 1674); S. S., *The Devout Singer's Guide* (London, n.d.).
[98] SPCK, Packets, 26, 29, 34, 79, 125, 164; Bodleian Library, Rawlinson MS, C844, f. 83v.
[99] Temperley, *Music*, ch. 6.
[100] Weber, *The Rise of Musical Classics*, pp. 12, 13, 50–2, 63, 67; J. Barry, 'Cultural patronage and the Anglican crisis: Bristol c.1689-1775', in Walsh, Haydon and Taylor, *The Church of England*, p. 203.   [101] SPCK, AL 10466.
[102] 'Sol-fa' was a method of teaching singing in which each note of the scale was assigned a syllable, depending on the interval between it and the base note, making it easier to learn and remember melodic intervals. Although the method was to be given its modern form by John Curwen in the mid-nineteenth century under the name 'tonic sol-fa', it was first recorded early in the eleventh century. *The New Grove Dictionary of Music and Musicians* (London, 1980), q.v. 'Solfeggio', 'Solmization', 'Tonic Sol-fa'.

was ordered 'to take a skillful master of musick to teach' the new way of singing.[103] Without musical instruction no choir would have been able to sing anthems. The description of church singers provided by Elias Hall may no longer have been accurate in many parishes. In a description well calculated to sell his *Psalm-singer's Compleat Companion*, Hall described how in recent years in Lancashire: '. . . the People yawl an hundred parts / Some roar, some whine, some creak like Wheels of Carts: / Such Notes the Gam-ut yet did never know'. The printers of Sternhold and Hopkins responded to the demand for popular instruction by adding 'a new Gamut, or Introduction to Psalmody, in a clear and easy Method, for the use of young Beginners', taken from Playford.[104]

A choir needed to sit together if it was to sing together, and this could be ensured by providing a gallery or specific set of seats for its members. Ecclesiastical and parochial authorities jealously protected the rights of these new choirs to sit in galleries against the intrusions of others, even though there was the potential for tension with the custom of selling or renting pews.[105] Thus, in his faculty enabling Corsham to refit its gallery for singers, Bishop Seth Ward ordered that 'noe other person or persons whatsoevr be permitted or prsume to sitt in the Gallery so appointed . . . but those of the prsent Quire or select company of singers', and he directed how the members were to be chosen.[106] The dean of Salisbury included a similar requirement in his faculty of 1725 to Ramsbury, where the seats were to be 'for the sole use of such persons as shall sing psalmes'.[107] Ward's faculty reserved the Corsham gallery for singers at the request of parishioners, and other parishes also took steps to exclude non-singers. In 1704 the churchwardens of Berwick St James presented Mary Frapwell and her 5-year-old daughter to the bishop 'for intrudeing . . . into a Gallery erected wthin our parish church for the use & service of the singers of Divine Hymnes & Psalm[es]'.[108] In 1700 the Lacock parish vestry agreed to forbid 'boyes or others to sitt in the Gallery who have not properly seats there, or come with designe to disturbe the usuall manner of singing'.[109] Although parish leaders carefully separated 'the singers', they still expected the rest of the congregation to sing following the lead of the choir. Hence, the builders of the Highworth gallery hoped that the congregation 'will bee . . . incouraged . . . to ioyne wth them in that everlasting dutie'.[110]

The expectation that choirs would improve the standard of music sung by the

---

[103] DRO, Moger Basket D/17/30.

[104] Elias Hall, *The Psalm-Singer's Compleat Companion* (London, 1706), p. 2; T. Sternhold and J. Hopkins, *The Whole Book of Psalms* (19th edn, London, 1738), as advertised in *Salisbury Journal*, 10 July 1739.

[105] W. M. Jacob, *Lay People and Religion in the Early Eighteenth Century* (Cambridge, 1996), p. 219.

[106] D1/61/2/1.   [107] D5/33/1, ff. 25–6.   [108] D1/54/19 (1704, W&W).

[109] WRO 131/1. Curiously, offenders were to be reported to a JP, rather than to the consistory court.

[110] D5/17/1/1.

entire congregation ultimately went unfulfilled. Choirs left the congregation as silent auditors of their musical performances. This was the situation George Millard found in Box and other parishes. He reported that for some years he had 'to my sorrow observ'd that the Pious Exercise of Singing Psalms in the Publick-worship of God is confin'd in my own Church . . . only to a few Select Persons in the Congregation, and these for the most part plac'd in a Gallery by themselves, or some other apartment in the church'.[111] The remainder of the congregation were 'Silent, & seem no way concern'd in that part of Divine Worship'. Millard claimed that the same was true 'in most of our Countery-Churches', and he directed his efforts to bringing the rest of the congregation to sing. Yet the problem remained in many parishes. The SPCK used choirs of charity children to promote congregational singing, and the musical training which Millard and others gave only increased the separation of the choir from the rest of the congregation. Even in Box, the entire congregation did not join in singing, despite the popularity of psalmody.

Musical innovation contributed to the exclusion of congregations from church singing. As the Wokingham wardens observed in 1739, the choir sang psalms 'according to their new and unintelligible way to the general part of the Congregation, whereby they cannot Join in singing as they were usualy wont'.[112] In 1729 Wiltshire members of the SPCK requested copies of anthems. In the 1730s the Salisbury diocesan authorities took direct action to stamp out anthem singers and allow the participation of the entire congregation in church music. This included a rejection of the traditions of art music encouraged by Seth Ward and his successors. Ward had hoped that Corsham would train young singers in harmony, so that they eventually might be able to sing anthems and hymns in cathedral churches. As early as 1724, Bishop Gibson of London was advising clerics against 'the inviting or encouraging those Idle instructors' of music who taught new and difficult tunes. Gibson even suggested that ministers reintroduce lining-out 'by directing the clerk to *read* the Psalm, Line by Line as they [i.e., the congregation] go on'.[113] In Wokingham it appears that the congregation followed Gibson's advice. In the choir's absence 'the Clerk named and *read* the psalms, And the same were set and sung by the Congregation in general as antiently Customary *in the old way*'.[114]

Ecclesiastical and parochial authorities were genuinely worried that the growth of choirs had excluded congregations from participation in church music. At the same time, they were also concerned about the dangers of an increasingly independent choral tradition. Millard had kept the Box singers firmly under control. He had personally taught the children and appointed the psalms to be sung on Sunday and had attended the evening practices and given

---

[111] SPCK, L 5213; reprinted in *WAM* 31: 38.   [112] D5/17/1/3.
[113] Edmund Gibson, *Directions Given to the Clergy of the Diocese of London in the Year 1724 . . .* (London, 1749), pp. 17–18.   [114] My emphasis. D5/17/1/3; D5/28, 1739.

out the psalms himself. To make it easy for the congregation to participate, he obliged the singers 'to keep only to a few tunes, and those the oldest, and most Grave'. And he made sure that parishioners showed proper reverence when singing, requiring 'them to perform it always STANDING, as the most becoming posture for it; which is now observed throughout the whole Church, as well by those that doe not, as by those that doe sing'.[115] The SPCK must have been pleased by Millard's maintenance of control, for the Society stressed the predominance of the clergy. As Thomas Bray observed, 'The laity should know its place.'[116] Yet by the 1730s the new singers were increasingly independent of clerical control. Ecclesiastical authorities disliked and feared independent religious meetings, whether they were the 'prophesyings' of the early seventeenth century or the conventicles of the post-Restoration years, for religious meetings might serve as a disguise for political conspiracy. This was even more so in the anxious years between the Jacobite rebellions. The Whig rector of Potterne, Francis Fox, an early residing member of the SPCK, perceived potential dangers in singing meetings in 1718 at a time when the Society was concerned to rebut accusations of Jacobitism. Fox advised the Society that 'much Disaffection to the King [had been] sowed among young people under the Pretence of meeting together to learn to sing Psalms'.[117] Private meetings were still viewed as politically dangerous twenty years later, when the Wokingham wardens were concerned that the singers not only sang in church after service 'but even in the Evenings of the week days and then and their used to make and appoint their private meetings & Caballs as is conceived [are] to the great prejudice & destruction of many of them'.[118] Their use of the politically loaded word 'cabal' to describe these meetings underlines the nature of their concerns.

The control of the church service was itself at issue. Fox recommended that the Society obtain an Act of Parliament empowering bishops to prepare and publish 'a select number of Psalms wch shall be sung and none else in all parish churches & chapels in England'. This 'would hinder every ordinary parish clerk from singing such Psalms as he himself shal choose or be influenced by any person of note in the Neighbourhood'.[119] This was still a matter of concern in 1724, when the Society was planning a book of psalms and occasional hymns. Bishop Gibson was concerned that the minister direct the choice of proper psalms and he provided a schedule of psalms to be sung every six months. George Wheeler agreed that it was important that 'as little as possible may be left to the Discretion of County-Clarks, since most Ministers, either for Want of some Skill in Musick, or of a due Concern for ye Decency of this Part of divine worship, commonly leave ye whole Affair to their Conduct, as a thing (it seems) beneath their care'.[120] The justice of Wheeler's concern about ministerial indifference was

[115] SPCK, L 5213; *WAM* 31: 38.   [116] Rose, 'The origins and ideals of the SPCK', pp. 178, 180.
[117] SPCK, AL 5822.   [118] D5/17/1/3.   [119] SPCK, AL 5822.
[120] Gibson, *Directions*; Bodleian Library, Rawlinson MS D839, f. 93.

to be confirmed by testimony that in 1740 the minister of Lydiard Millicent fell asleep during the service when the people were singing the psalm.[121]

The performance of psalms did sometimes lead to disagreements between minister and parish clerk, as in Tockenham Wick in 1691 where the minister found fault with the psalm and tried to remove the clerk from the chancel forcibly.[122] Yet most church quarrels over singing that reached the courts saw an alliance of the minister, churchwardens and parish clerk against the new choirs, who insisted upon singing what and when they chose. When the minister decided to take charge of the service and to tell the clerk what psalm to sing, confrontation was inevitable. In Boyton the singers insisted upon singing the sixth psalm, rather than the 100th psalm that the parish clerk had named at the minister's instruction, and they sang so loudly that Clifton was prevented from preaching his sermon. The singers' choice of text was deliberate and pleaded their case: 'O Lord, rebuke me not in thine indignation; neither chasten me in thy displeasure.' In Castle Combe the singers insisted on singing a different tune. The Wokingham singers were equally defiant, as we have seen. The choir's members initially reacted to the attempts of the minister and parish officials to regulate their singing by boycotting services. When they returned after two weeks they occupied the chancel and sang as they wished.[123] Tension between generations sometimes contributed to disputes between the choir and parish authorities, for singers were often described as youths and girls. In Wokingham the young singers persuaded the ancient parish clerk's son to take their side against his father.

In addition to disagreements over who should set the psalm and the tune to be sung, singers and parish authorities also quarrelled over the place of music in the service. The authorities disliked the expanding role of music in the service. The only specific mention of music in the liturgy came near the end of the first service, between the collects and prayers, when the anthem might be sung. Psalms might also be introduced into other pauses in services, although placement varied from church to church.[124] Bishop Gibson of London advised his clergy to sing psalms in the gaps between the different services – morning prayers, the litany and communion – so 'that the Transitions from one service to another may not be too sudden and abrupt'.[125] *The Clergy-man's Vade Mecum*, a contemporary handbook, agreed that this practice was more agreeable than reading the offices one after another. The announcements before the sermon provided another natural pause when a psalm might be introduced. This is clearly when the psalm was sung in Boyton in 1742, and in 1736 it was ordered that two psalms be sung in Calne 'in the morning service (that is to say) one after the Litany the other before the Sermon'. Parish musicians attempted to introduce music elsewhere. In Calne the dean acted against those who sang 'Anthems *and Services* instead of plain Psalm Tunes which the congregation hath been

---

[121] The defendants were charged with vilifying the minister for saying that he fell asleep because he was drunk. D1/41/4/6.   [122] D1/41/4/35.   [123] D5/17/1/3.
[124] Temperley, *Music*, pp. 46–8.   [125] Gibson, *Directions*, p. 15.

customarily used to have sung'. This suggests that the choir also sang musical settings of the canticles, hymns and psalms, such as the Te Deum, which were built into the service, a practice which would be introduced more widely in the nineteenth century. The dean conceded that the organ might play a plain voluntary after the reading of psalms, allowing another musical innovation in the service. Choirs also introduced psalms into baptismal and funeral services, despite the objections of the minister. Again, it made most sense to introduce a psalm in a pause in the service. Thus in Boyton the choir tried to sing a psalm after a baptism and when obstructed declared their intention: 'we will sing for all you'. They also introduced a psalm into the funeral service in the pause between the end of the church service and the carrying of the body into the churchyard.[126]

Although the authorities sought to suppress these innovations, the choirs often had the support of the congregations. By objecting to singing at a funeral, the curate of Somerford Keynes offended the entire congregation, and no less than thirty-three people, including two churchwardens, supported a petition requesting his removal.[127] In the absence of an effective parish clerk, the inhabitants of Wokingham were dependent upon their choir to lead them in singing. When the choir refused to sing, no psalm was sung at all, because the congregation was not prepared to sing. There is little evidence that the congregation itself objected, beyond general statements by the wardens that the singing of the choir was 'greatly to the disquietude of the whole church'. In Gillingham, the choir seems to have had considerable popular support, although it was suggested that this was only from 'idle Fellows and their Encouragers' and not the best people. The arrival of the subdean Thomas Naish to officiate in support of the singers was welcomed by 'the bells ringing and great rejoyceings'. The musical performances of choirs continued to enjoy considerable support despite the disapproval of the Church.

CHURCH MUSIC AFTER 1740

The attempt to suppress singing societies in the 1730s failed. Choirs continued to occupy galleries for the rest of the century,[128] sometimes introducing musical instruments, and a number of parishes witnessed disputes over singing. In 1770 members of the Warminster choir were prosecuted for brawling in church because they insisted on singing a different psalm and a different tune from the rest of the congregation.[129] The diarist James Woodforde had problems with the gallery singers in Castle Cary (Somerset) church on more than one occasion in 1769. In November they insisted on singing the responses in the communion service despite Woodforde's order not to do so. Two weeks later they stayed away from church because, the cleric thought, they were highly affronted. In December the cleric and singers again disagreed over the choice of psalm. The dispute

---

[126] D5/33/1, f. 33v; D1/36/2/13.   [127] D1/41/4/36.
[128] For example, in Trowbridge, where there was still a gallery for singers in 1771. D1/61/3/3.
[129] D1/41/4/3.

ended only on Christmas eve when Woodforde gave the singers a lecture and two shillings and they promised to amend their behaviour.[130] Although the Church failed to suppress choirs, some clerics still had doubts about their role in church music. John Brown, the vicar of Newcastle, criticised the mean performance of psalms 'when a Company of illiterate People form themselves into a Choir distinct from the Congregation. Here devotion is lost, between the impotent Vanity of those who sing, and the ignorant Wonder of those who listen'.[131]

Yet, despite ecclesiastical objections, the singing societies continued to develop in the second half of the eighteenth century.[132] Musical instruments returned to churches after a long absence, and some parishes began to pay their singers. The health of parish music can be seen in the success of three volumes of psalm, service and anthem tunes intended 'for country choirs' which were published by John Smith of Market Lavington from 1748 to 1755.[133] Smith's inclusion of services and anthems suggests that art music continued its spread into parish churches, although plain multi-part psalm settings were also provided for less advanced choirs. Few country choirs would have been able to sing the service and anthem tunes without musical instruction. They were often complex settings, calling for singers to enter at different points and including long melisma. Many of the subscribers to the first volume came from the immediate area. Each of the subsequent volumes was more popular than the last and reached a wider area. At least forty-five parishes in Wiltshire were represented in the lists of subscribers, and since booksellers from Bath, Salisbury and Devizes also bought multiple copies, this understates the circulation of the volumes. Most subscribers were gentlemen, who most likely purchased the volumes for family use. Yet ten parish choirs, including four from Wiltshire, subscribed to the third volume in 1755. One of these was the Warminster choir whose independence would lead to conflict in church in 1770. The incumbents of nine Wiltshire parishes, a pair of churchwardens, two schoolmasters and five singing masters also purchased at least one volume.[134] Most singing masters lived in such towns as Marlborough, Devizes and Salisbury, where they probably earned much of their living giving

---

[130] James Woodforde, *The Diary of a Country Parson 1758–1802*, ed. J. Beresford (Oxford, 1978).

[131] Brown, *Dissertation*, p. 213, quoted in Legg, *English Church Life*, p. 187. Cf. M. Smith, *Religion in Industrial Society: Oldham and Saddleworth 1740–1865* (Oxford, 1994), p. 56.

[132] At least twenty-five parishes offer evidence of choral or instrumental music in the late eighteenth century.

[133] John Smith, of Market Lavington, *A Set of Services, Anthems & Psalm Tunes for Country Choirs* [1748]; *Book the Second Containing Twelve Anthems and Twelve Psalm Tunes for Country Choirs all intirely new Composed* (Lavington, [1751]); *Book the Third . . .* (Lavington, 1755).

[134] The following were subscribers: the choirs of Bishop's Cannings, Chilmark, Shalbourn and Warminster; the ministers of Little Cheverell, Edington, Market Lavington, West Lavington, Rushall, Trowbridge, Upavon, Wilcot and Wilsford; the churchwardens of Little Cheverell; schoolmasters in Great Bedwyn and Devizes; and singing masters in Bromham, Devizes, Dinton, Marlborough and Salisbury.

music lessons to the children of the gentry and merchants. Some may also have been involved in training choirs. An entry in the Melksham churchwardens' accounts suggests money was paid to a singing master.[135]

The purchase of Smith's volumes by parish ministers and churchwardens suggests that the authorities continued to support the development of music in some places. None of the fifteen parishes concerned had previously been recorded as having a choir. Churchwardens' accounts document musical purchases, although such evidence is inevitably patchy. Detailed accounts do not survive for many parishes, and even where they do church music did not necessarily lead to parish expense. Ministers and others purchased books themselves, and musicians brought their own instruments to the church. Nonetheless, the accounts suggest a slight expansion of church music in the second half of the eighteenth century, as the choirs were supplemented by instruments and became professionalised. The addition of instruments was itself significant. The Civil War had seen the removal of organs from many cathedrals and churches. It was long feared that the addition of instruments to church music would lead to the introduction of inappropriate secular music. Yet in 1709 the annual festival of the Corporation of the Sons of Clergy added instruments to the church music it performed, and the place of instruments in church music began to be accepted.[136] Organs were the first instruments returned to churches, although they were slow to be reintroduced. Many may have agreed with John Brown when he wrote in praise of the music in town churches where 'the Union of this Instrument with the Voices of a well-instructed Congregation, forms one of the grandest Scenes of unaffected Piety that human Nature can afford'.[137] Only a few parishes had an organ, although these were certainly not restricted to towns. Two parishes received faculties for organ galleries in the first half of the eighteenth century, the urban parish of Salisbury St Edmunds and the rural parish of Potterne. The dean's intervention documents the presence of an organ in the small town of Calne in 1736. His order strengthened the position of Calne's organist by giving him a monopoly over the use of the instrument and guaranteeing his role in the service. The parish's organist subscribed to all three volumes of Smith's psalm tunes, presumably for use in church services. The number of organs rose slowly in the late eighteenth and early nineteenth centuries, but it is impossible to say whether these were used to support or replace choirs. Bradford-on-Avon had an organ gallery by 1794, Horningsham added one by 1798, and Bishop's Cannings received a faculty for an organ gallery in 1810.[138]

Country parishes were more likely to add smaller instruments, such as the bass viol, at a time when members of the violin family were replacing the viol in the concert hall. Initially, expenditure often amounted to little more than the

---

[135] WRO 1368/56.   [136] Weber, *The Rise of Musical Classics*, p. 111.
[137] Brown, *Dissertation*, p. 213, quoted in Legg, *English Church Life*, p. 187.
[138] D1/61/3/14; WRO 182/14; D1/61/3/17.

purchase of an occasional viol string or bow. Donhead St Mary purchased a set of viol strings in 1753, presumably for an instrument that was privately owned or donated. The parish had to spend a shilling or more for a new string each year into the 1790s when it bought its own viol; the church was still maintaining a viol in the 1820s.[139] The parish of Melksham was already buying bass violin strings in 1778 when it purchased a violoncello, case and bow. Shortly thereafter the vestry decided that the singers should be paid and these payments rose from £1 1s. a half year in 1779 to a 'salary' of £2 12s. in 1793. Bell ringers had long been rewarded by many parishes, but this was usually through the purchase of ale rather than direct payments. In Melksham they began to be paid a salary at about the same time. Melksham also set aside a gallery for the singers, purchased books for them, and paid for them to be taught.[140] The small rural parish of Horningsham was a focus for musical activity, perhaps helped by support from Longleat nearby. Simon Hinton of Horningsham published two editions of his *Collection of Church Musick* in the 1750s, at about the same time as John Smith of Market Lavington was producing his volumes.[141] The parish purchased strings, a bow and a bag for a bass viol in the 1760s, as well as books for the singers, and strings were an ongoing expense during the 1770s and 1780s. By 1798 Horningsham had an organ and paid an organist £5 5s. a year for playing it.[142] The purchase of wind and stringed instruments testifies to the popularity of music in many parishes in the century after 1740.[143] Developments in Wiltshire paralleled those elsewhere in England, for example in West Sussex, where the churchwardens of Selsey purchased a bassoon and an oboe in the 1770s.[144] These payments show that there continued to be support for choirs and bands at the local level in some parishes, at least from churchwardens. But the independence of such choirs, now supported by instruments, still sometimes led to conflict, not least on grounds of musical taste. As the vicar of Bremhill, William Bowles, observed in 1828, 'Singing to the praise of and glory of God in general is little better than singing to the annoyance of all who have any ear for harmony.'[145]

The late seventeenth and early eighteenth centuries witnessed a dramatic shift in official attitudes towards church music. Whereas in the 1670s choir members were

---

[139] Donhead St Mary, Book of Church Accounts, 1730–1831, WRO 980/19.

[140] Melksham, Churchwardens' Accounts, 1749–95, WRO 1368/56.

[141] Nicholas Temperley identifies Simon Hinton as of Horningsham and dates the two editions in about 1751 and 1755. *The Hymn Tune Index* (Oxford, 1997), p. 255.

[142] Horningsham, Churchwardens' Accounts, 1688–1817, WRO 182/14.

[143] The instruments purchased by the Codford St Mary, Cherhill, Corsley, Seend and Westwood parishes included clarinets, flutes and a bugle, as well as strings. Dodge, 'The rise and fall of the west gallery musicians', pp. 4–5.

[144] West Sussex RO, PAR 166/8/1, ff. 17v, 18v (Selsey Churchwardens' Accounts). I am grateful to Professor David Underdown for providing me with this reference.

[145] W. L. Bowles, *The Parochial History of Bremhill* (London, 1828), quoted in Dodge, 'The rise and fall of the west gallery musicians', p. 7. See, for example, the episode described by A. D. Dodge, 'West gallery music and musicians in Wessex', in C. Turner, ed., *Georgian Psalmody 2* (Corby Glen, 1999), p. 10.

described as persons 'of sober & honest life', sixty years later their meetings were seen as scandalous. By encouraging church singing, ecclesiastical and parochial authorities had stimulated the blossoming of a vibrant and popular religious culture. In their enthusiasm to join singing societies or to flock to services to hear their performances, the laity expressed their desire to participate more actively in religious worship. Yet the encouragement of music bred in the increasingly sophisticated choirs a degree of independence, which the Church viewed with concern. Singing societies stretched the parochial system to its limits, violating the principle that people should worship only in their own parish churches by performing in those of neighbouring parishes. They met outside the framework of the services, taking charge of the church for their meetings. They challenged the liturgy itself and the authority of the minister and churchwardens. The Church could not countenance such apparently dangerous behaviour, and in the 1730s, after decades of support, it sought to suppress the threat to its authority. However heartfelt the call for a return to plainer music in which the whole congregation could participate may have been, the wish to reassert control was the primary reason for the clergy's reaction against choirs. Yet in this, as in so much else, the Church and its clergy showed how out of touch with popular worship they had become. Whether or not they sang themselves, the laity loved the music that their choirs were performing. Although John Wesley shared the Anglican clergy's dislike of the manner in which choirs and bands performed music in parish churches, the Methodists understood the importance of singing.[146] George Whitefield praised religious societies in 1737 for 'the commendable, pious zeal you exert by providing and encouraging Divine Psalmody',[147] to which Charles Wesley would add his hymns. The Methodists found that singing was a popular and emotionally powerful form of worship. As Bishop Beilby Porteus observed in 1790, 'many of those who separate from our communion understand perfectly well the use and force of this commanding instrument, and apply it with success'.[148] The Anglican clergy, having in the short term lost the battle to suppress choirs, were unable to prevent church music from continuing to develop through the addition of instrumentalists in the second half of the eighteenth century. In encouraging his clergy to promote singing, Porteus's charge marked a renewal of the Church's attempts to establish control over church music, but this campaign did not succeed until well into the nineteenth century.[149]

[146] Temperley, *Music*, pp. 208–13.
[147] G. Rupp, *Religion in England 1688–1791* (Oxford, 1986), p. 328.
[148] Beilby Porteus, *A Charge Delivered to the Clergy of the Diocese of London . . . in 1790*, in *Works* (London, 1808–11), vol. VI, p. 244. See also D. Hempton, *The Religion of the People: Methodism and Popular Religion c. 1750–1900* (London and New York, 1996), pp. 56, 67.
[149] V. Gammon, '"Babylonian performances": the rise and suppression of popular church music, 1660–1870', in E. Yeo and S. Yeo, eds., *Popular Culture and Class Conflict 1590–1914: Explorations in the History of Labour and Leisure* (Sussex, 1981), pp. 62–84; J. Obelkevich, *Religion and Rural Society: South Lindsey, 1825–1875* (Oxford, 1976), pp. 146–50; Dodge, 'The rise and fall of the west gallery musicians', p. 8.

❦ 11 ❧

Conclusion

There was much that was positive about the Church of England in the late seventeenth and early eighteenth centuries. Anglican worship was able to command considerable popular support. It was not merely imposed upon unwilling congregations by a partnership of squire and parson. The laity accepted the Church's standing as the institutional focus of religious worship. They also accepted the clergy's professional and intellectual position, and valued their pastoral role. Parishioners insisted that the role which the liturgy defined for parsons as officiants at divine service and communion and at key rites of passage was vital to the spiritual welfare of the community. The radical sects had contributed to Interregnum concerns about disorder, and most people greeted the return of the Church at the Restoration with relief. Anglicanism was reinvigorated in the early eighteenth century, both at the grass roots and nationally. The Society for Promoting Christian Knowledge reached out to parishes through its extensive network of correspondents, and its successes were made possible by the support and enthusiasm of these local ministers, who were already committed to the cure of souls of their parishioners. These men showed imagination and energy in promoting religious education and singing, and their pastoral efforts bore fruit. In Salisbury diocese, Bishop Gilbert Burnet embarked on an ambitious programme of reform intended to raise clerical standards, improve pastoral care and reawaken the spirit of religion among the people.

This study has paid particular attention to the disputes which regularly broke out between clergymen and members of their congregations. These episodes of conflict might have serious implications for worship and for popular participation in church offices. In some parishes, disagreements between laity and clergy blighted religious life for many years. Clergymen were well aware of the hazards of disputes, for their involvement did not fit comfortably with their pastoral role. At best, they might find court action distracting; in the worst cases, they lived in fear of parishioners and sought to escape their responsibilities. Yet the prevalence of conflict is not in itself evidence that the Church was in danger. Lay criticisms, despite clerical claims, were most often directed at specific offenders and did not represent attacks upon the clerical estate or the Church more generally.

Indeed, where clerical neglect was involved, parishioners used the courts to uphold standards of worship within their churches. Such episodes document the importance which members of the laity vested in their own participation in established religion. On this point a broad spectrum of society, including squires, the parish elite and the meaner sort of people, could agree. Whatever differences there may have been between the cultures of different groups in society, there was plenty of scope for co-operation. The sharp fall in court activity in the closing years of the seventeenth century, continuing into the eighteenth century, was, if anything, a worrying indication that neither the laity nor the clergy any longer found that the Church's courts were sufficiently authoritative or effective to provide a suitable venue in which to resolve their grievances.

At the same time, episodes of lay–clerical conflict exposed the stresses and strains that weakened the Church and divided clergymen from their congregations. Many of these problems were not new. Although lay complaints reveal popular concern about pluralism and non-residence, these problems, along with chapelries, were a function of long-standing economic and structural weaknesses in the Church. There were many poor livings, even in the relatively prosperous diocese of Salisbury, and pluralism helped some incumbents to eke out an appropriate standard of living. Pluralism would become more serious later in the eighteenth century. Yet a pluralist was not necessarily an inferior pastor, as the case studies of such ministers as John Lewis of Holt and George Millard of Box have shown. These pluralists were able to fulfil their pastoral duties conscientiously. Indeed, their pluralism actually had the positive effect of enabling them to spread their cure of souls more widely. Not all clergymen deserve the accepted stereotype, repeated by Burnet, of the eighteenth-century incumbent as grasping after preferment, more interested in maintaining the comfortable life style of a gentleman than in matters of spirituality or pastoral care, although no doubt some did. The prevalence of this stereotype demonstrates nevertheless the damaging effects of pluralism and non-residence on the reputations of the Church and of individual clergymen.

Tithes had long been unpopular, and they would continue to be so until they were commuted in the nineteenth century. Dislike of tithes came to the surface when the Church came under broader attack, as in the 1730s. More damaging, however, was the corrosive effect on lay–clerical relations in numerous parishes of disagreements over the collection of tithes. Although the principle of their payment was rarely at stake, the clergy's reliance upon such a varied and complicated set of rights for their income made it more difficult for them to fulfil their pastoral duties as shepherds to their congregations, and might have have direct and negative effects upon worship. Political issues reinforced the clergy's separation from the laity. By imposing a narrow definition of uniformity the Restoration church settlement helped to create nonconformity, with far-reaching consequences. The persecution of dissent weakened the Church nationally and

locally. Its association with intolerance and dogmatism undermined its disciplinary machinery. In the localities, parishioners had little sympathy with clerical
efforts to persecute those of their neighbours who chose to attend conventicles,
and this contributed to clerical unpopularity. The Restoration settlement also
elevated liturgical uniformity and episcopal ordination, so that they were of
central importance in defining both Anglican practice and the status of the
Anglican clergy. To resist the challenge of nonconformity, the clergy placed
greater emphasis upon the sacerdotal control over the liturgy and sacraments to
which ordination entitled them. Determined to defend their clerical monopoly,
the clergy were in a poor position either to hear or to respond to lay desire for
greater participation in worship. The emphasis upon uniformity therefore had
the effect of distancing parsons further from their parishioners. Concerned
about nonconformity, the clergy found it difficult to distinguish between dissent
and other unorthodox forms of worship and were reluctant to permit the laity
too much responsibility for church worship.

The social and professional position of the clergy confirmed their separation
from the laity. Although the clergy were not a profession in the modern sense of
the word,[1] it is clear that they represented a distinct and cohesive social group.
Their education and occupation of the study set them apart from the laity.
Through sociability in societies like the Clergy Club of Melksham, and through
the extension of clerical dynasties, the clergy expressed their sense of fellowship
with one another. Social and political factors were as important as, if not more
so than, vocational factors in these societies. It is significant that the laity themselves understood and accepted the clergy's separateness from the rest of society,
represented by their unique status as scholars. The emerging alliance between
clergy and gentry, assisted by the addition of clergymen to commissions of the
peace and consolidated in the late eighteenth century by the growing prosperity
of incumbents, would widen the gap further.

The 1730s were to expose the limitations of the Church, and these proved to
be more psychological than structural. It is unlikely to be a coincidence that the
reaction against choirs came at a time when the Church felt itself to be under
attack from all sides. Bishops Thomas Sherlock and Edmund Gibson, who led
resistance to the Quakers' Tithe Bill, were also concerned about the independence of lay singers, although they were not alone.[2] Defensive and inflexible,
churchmen proved reluctant to relinquish their grip over religious worship. In
part a consequence of the legacy of dissent left by the Civil Wars, clerical

---

[1] Compare R. O'Day, *The English Clergy: The Emergence and Consolidation of a Profession
1558–1642* (Leicester, 1979); G. Holmes, *Augustan England: Professions, State and Society,
1680–1750* (London, 1982); P. J. Corfield, *Power and the Professions in Britain 1700–1850*
(London, 1995); and B. Heeney, *A Different Kind of Gentleman: Parish Clergy as Professional Men
in Early and Mid-Victorian England* (London, 1976).
[2] N. Sykes, *Edmund Gibson* (Oxford, 1926), pp. 161–6; E. Carpenter, *Thomas Sherlock 1678–1761*
(London, 1936), pp. 104–27.

defensiveness was also a product of the supercharged political and intellectual atmosphere, in which the clergy felt themselves to be in danger. The Church turned inwards, defining any deviation from its own vision of worship as heterodox, and in the process alienating supporters. Ironically, in stressing clericalism and in enforcing a narrow definition of conformity, the Church confirmed the charges of dogmatic and intolerant 'priestcraft' brought by its enemies. The clergy proved unable to understand popular forms of religiosity and reluctant to give them scope for expression within the framework of the liturgy.

On 17 July 1739 John Wesley preached for the first time in Wiltshire, at Bearfields in Bradford-on-Avon. During the next three months, John and his brother Charles returned several times and preached to thousands of hearers.[3] Northern Wiltshire also witnessed an awakening led by John Cennick, a follower of George Whitefield, in 1740–1. The progress of Methodism in the county was slow before 1780 and, although generally well received, preachers were sometimes greeted with hostility.[4] It spread rapidly afterwards, so that by 1829 over half of the communities in Wiltshire had at least one dissenting meeting-house, attracting roughly one-third of the population.[5] The development of Methodism was a complex phenomenon, and has been the subject of much historical debate.[6] The weakness of the Church of England is not in itself a sufficient explanation for the dramatic expansion of evangelical nonconformity in the century after 1740 and particular after 1790, although the movement was initially strongest where the Church was weakest.[7] Furthermore, it is important to recognise the continuities between established religion and evangelical nonconformity. Methodism, which did not break formally with the Church until late in the eighteenth century, grew out of the same movement for religious revival that had stimulated the formation of the SPCK. Indeed, some charity schools were seen as 'Nurseries of Methodists'.[8] The experience of the High Churchman Samuel Wesley, father to John and Charles, who formed a local religious society

[3] *The Journal of the Rev. John Wesley, A.M.* (London, 1909–16), vol. II, pp. 243, 248, 255; VCH *Wilts*, III (1956), pp. 127–8.
[4] As in June 1741, when John Cennick was met near Stratton St Margaret by water, mud, and the rough music of guns and cowbells, and later was burned in effigy. William Horne to Mr Francis Blandy, 28 June 1741, WRO 116/20.
[5] G. C. Smith, '"The *knowing* multitude": popular culture and the evangelical revival in Wiltshire, 1739–1850' (unpublished Ph.D. thesis, University of Toronto, 1992), pp. 275–8, 326.
[6] For recent contributions, see D. Hempton, *The Religion of the People: Methodism and Popular Religion c. 1750–1900* (London and New York, 1996); K. Hylson-Smith, *The Churches in England from Elizabeth I to Elizabeth II*, vol. II: *1689-1833* (London, 1997), ch. 4; G. Rupp, *Religion in England 1688–1791* (Oxford, 1986), chs. 20, 21.
[7] A. D. Gilbert, *Religion and Society in Industrial England* (London and New York, 1976), pp. 94–110; Smith, 'Knowing multitude', *passim*.
[8] W. M. Jacob, *Lay People and Religion in the Early Eighteenth Century* (Cambridge, 1996), pp. 91, 172. See Smith, *Religion in Industrial Society*, p. 60, for potential for co-operation between the parish church and Methodists.

and promoted singing in Epworth in Lincolnshire, was publicised to clergymen all over England. The evangelical revival also had its supporters within the Established Church.[9]

The Church's attempt to suppress singing societies exemplified its disregard for popular religious culture. It is no coincidence that Methodism exploited features of worship in which the Church of England had failed, enabling it to tap popular patterns of religiosity. The involvement of worshippers in singing was a powerful attraction of Methodism. William Vincent estimated in 1790 that 'for one who has been drawn away from the Established Church by preaching, ten have been induced by music'.[10] The conversion experience that lay at the heart of the evangelical revival also tapped a deeply seated need among the laity to believe that they had personal responsibility for their own salvation, which, as we have seen, they expressed in their attitudes towards communion and preparation for death. The Methodists' most significant innovation, however, was to break away from traditional Anglican structures, allowing spontaneity and participation to an extent that was impossible within the parish church. Itinerant ministers and lay people preached at open air meetings, while small groups held informal religious meetings in their own homes, practices which significantly were condemned by churchmen such as Bishop Gibson for leading people to believe that regular attendance at church services was not sufficient.[11] The ultimate failure of the Church, including of its evangelicals, was its inability to understand or accept lay views of worshop or to permit the laity's involvement in any but a passive way. James Obelkevich's study of religion in nineteenth-century Lincolnshire found the same phenomenon: 'excessive reliance upon the clergy was symptomatic of the Anglican campaign against Methodism and helps to explain its limited success'.[12] Evangelical nonconformists, who relied heavily upon lay participation and leadership, did not make the same mistake.[13] In breaking from the framework of liturgical services and the rigid control of the clergy, the Methodists provoked the fears and hostility of the clerical establishment. Anglican incumbents discouraged the activities of itinerant preachers and even organised violence against them, as they had done against Quakers a century

---

[9] Hylson-Smith, *The Churches in England*, ch. 5.

[10] W. Vincent, *Considerations on Parochial Music* (2nd edn, London, 1790), quoted by N. Temperley, 'Music in churches', in H. D. Johnson and Roger Fiske, eds., *Music in Britain* (Oxford, 1990), p. 389. See also M. Smith, *Religion in Industrial Society: Oldham and Saddleworth 1740–1865* (Oxford, 1994), p. 213.

[11] Rupp, *Religion in England*, pp. 391–5, and p. 381, citing Edmund Gibson, *Against Lukewarmness on the one hand and Enthusiasm on the other* (1739).

[12] J. Obelkevich, *Religion and Society: South Lindsey, 1825–1875* (Oxford, 1976), pp. 168–73, quoting p. 173.

[13] Gilbert, *Religion and Society*, pp. 57–8; Hylson-Smith, *The Churches in England*, pp. 161, 169–70; Smith, *Religion in Industrial Society*, ch. 5, esp. pp. 186, 215, 225; D. M. Valenze, *Prophetic Sons and Daughters: Female Preaching and Popular Religion in Industrial England* (Princeton, 1985).

earlier.[14] Clerical incumbents condemned the very aspects of Methodism, such as its 'disorderly preaching', that were the keys to its success. In the years after 1740, the quickening forces of social and economic change would make flexibility particularly important. The defensiveness and mental rigidity of the Church of England and its clergy did not bode well for the future. As Bishop Gilbert Burnet had perceived, the main danger to the Church came from within.

[14] In Devizes, the curate Mr Innys stirred up the crowd against Methodists. Rupp, *Religion in England*, p. 376. Compare how the Revd William Gunn led a mob against Marden Quakers in 1660. Friends' House Library, Great Books of Sufferings, vol. II, Wilts., p. 7. See also B. Reay, 'Popular hostility towards Quakers in mid-seventeenth-century England', *Social History* 5 (Oct. 1980): 387–407; J. Walsh, 'Methodism and the mob in the eighteenth century', in G. J. Cuming and D. Baker, eds., *Popular Belief in Practice*, Studies in Church History 8 (1972), pp. 213–27; Hempton, *The Religion of the People*, ch. 8.

SELECTED BIBLIOGRAPHY

MANUSCRIPT SOURCES

WILTSHIRE RECORD OFFICE, TROWBRIDGE

Bishop of Salisbury

D1/2	Bishops' Registers
D1/3/5/1	Benefice Papers, Valuations, Return of Livings, *c*.1707
D1/14	Ordination Papers
D1/22	Subscription Books
D1/24	Glebe Terriers
D1/27/1	Bishops' Private Papers, Seth Ward
D1/36/2/7	Miscellaneous Papers
D1/39/1	Act Books, Instance
D1/39/2	Act Books, Office
D1/39/3	Act Books, Miscellaneous
D1/41/1	Court Papers (Citations)
D1/41/4	Court Papers (Miscellaneous)
D1/42	Deposition Books
D1/48	Diocese Books
D1/54	Churchwardens' Presentments
D1/61	Faculties
D1/62	Matrimonial Records

Dean of Salisbury

D5/1/2	Register of Institutions, 1549–1846
D5/17	Miscellaneous Papers
D5/19	Act Books
D5/21/1	Court Papers (Citations)
D5/21/4	Court Papers (Transmissions of Process)
D5/22	Deposition Books
D5/28	Churchwardens' Presentments
D5/29	Visitation Books
D5/31	Miscellaneous Visitation Papers
D5/33	Faculties

Other Jurisdictions

D2/6/2	Archdeacon of Salisbury, Deposition Book
D3/12	Archdeacon of Wiltshire, Churchwardens' Presentments
D21/2	Peculiar of the Lord Warden of Savernake Forest, Churchwardens' Presentments
D25/12	Peculiar of the Precentor, Churchwardens' Presentments
	Archdeacon of Salisbury, Wills and Inventories
	Archdeacon of Wiltshire, Wills and Inventories

Quarter Sessions

A1/100	Commissions of the Peace
A1/110	Great Rolls
A1/160	Order Books
A1/250	Certificates of Dissenters' Places of Worship from 1695
A1/260	Certificates of Summary Convictions

Other Records

84/43, 44	Correspondence relating to Alderton
116/20	Correspondence from William Horne to Francis Blandy
118/149	Langley Burrell, Poor Rate, 1705
131/1	Lacock, Summary Accounts, 1701–36
161/70	Diary of Thomas Smith of Shaw, Melksham, 1715–22
173/1	Lacock, Churchwardens' Accounts, 1583–1821
182/14	Horningsham, Churchwardens' Accounts, 1688–1817
184/1, 2, 4	Holford correspondence
184/8	Journals of Sir Richard Holford's visits to Avebury
212A/34	Box, Poor Rate, 1695
493/3, 5	Pewsey, Parish Registers, 1654–1759
493/49	Pewsey, General Entry Book, 1608–1855
496/1	Alton Barnes, Parish Register, 1592–1747
539/11	Combe Bissett, Churchwardens' Miscellaneous Papers, 1704–1922
680/8	Rodbourne Cheney, Vestry Book, 1676–1747
807/18	Calstone Wellington, Churchwardens' and Overseers' Accounts, 1715–41
869/2	Ansty, Parish Register, 1694–1712
895/30	Clyffe Pypard, Churchwardens' and Overseers' Accounts, 1652–1820
980/2	Donhead St Mary, Parish Register, 1695–1702
980/19	Donhead St Mary, Book of Church Accounts, 1730–1831
1176/1	Avebury, Parish Register, 1679–1765
1184/19	Highworth, Churchwardens' Accounts, 1620–1705
1259/83	'A description of the reverend Mr. Goldney's journey to Horfield to preach a gift Sermon on the 23 February 1730'
1285/11	Corsham, Licence for Gallery
1368/56	Melksham, Churchwardens' Accounts, 1749–95
1505/2	Broad Hinton, Parish Register, 1682–1773
1620/17	Grittleton, Churchwardens' Accounts, 1677–1799
1632/18	Cricklade St Sampson, Churchwardens' Accounts, 1670–1730
1699/18	Book of Quaker Sufferings in Wiltshire, 1653–1756
1710/32	Christian Malford, Churchwardens' Accounts, 1666–1761
1732/15	Donhead St Andrew, Tithe Composition Survey Book, 1743
1762/1	Sermons of Thomas Hochkis of Stanton Fitzwarren

1981/1   Diary of John Lewis of Holt, 1720
1981/2   Sermons of John Lewis of Holt

PUBLIC RECORD OFFICE, KEW

C5   Chancery, Pleadings, Six Clerks Series, Bridges
C33   Chancery, Entry Books of Decrees and Orders
C104   Chancery, Masters' Exhibits, Tinney (Papers of the Revd Francis
          Henry Carey, boxes 63, 109, 135, 137, 269)
E112   Exchequer Bills and Answers
E126   Exchequer, Entry Books of Decrees and Orders
E134   Exchequer Depositions taken by Commission
E179/259/29, 26B   Subsidy Rolls (Hearth tax returns, 1662)
IND 1/16827–16841 Exchequer Bill Books
IND 1/17050   Wood's Index
PROB 11   Prerogative Court of Canterbury, Wills and Administrations

BODLEIAN LIBRARY, OXFORD

MS Eng Misc f. 10   Diary of John Lewis, 1718–60
MS Tanner   Tanner Manuscripts (esp. 28, 30, 44, 80, 143)

SOCIETY FOR PROMOTING CHRISTIAN KNOWLEDGE, LONDON

Abstract Letter Books (CR), nos. 1–23
Minute Books, vols. 1–21
Miscellaneous Abstracts, 1709–33
Original Letters
Society Letters (CS2)
Society Packets
Special Letters to Correspondents (CS3/2)

References to other manuscripts from the Bodleian Library, the British Library, the Devon Record Office, Dr Williams's Library, the Friends' House Library, Lambeth Palace Library and the Wiltshire Archaeological and Natural History Museum are given in the footnotes.

PRINTED SOURCES

Addison, Launcelot. *A Modest Plea for the Clergy*. London, 1677.
Bodington, E. J. 'The church survey in Wilts, 1649–50', WAM 40: 253–72, 297–317, 392–416; 41: 1–39, 105–28.
Burnet, Gilbert. *A Discourse of the Pastoral Care*. London, 1692.
Bushnell, Walter. *A Narrative of the Proceedings of the Commissioners . . . for Ejecting Scandalous and Malignant Ministers*. London, 1660.
Cardwell, Edward. *Documentary Annals of the Reformed Church of England . . . from the year 1546 to the year 1716*. Oxford, 1844.
The Case of Peoples Duty in Living Under a Scandalous Minister Stated and Resolved. London, 1684.
Chambers, Humphrey. *An Answer of Humphrey Chambers . . . to the Charges of Walter Bushnel*. London, 1660.

Chandler, John, ed. *Wiltshire Dissenters' Meeting House Certificates and Registrations, 1689–1852*, Wiltshire Record Series 40. Devizes, 1985.

Clark, John. *A Sermon Preached at the Funerall of Mr. Nathaniel Aske, Late Rector of Somerford-Magna in North-Wilts*. London, 1676.

Consett, Henry. *The Practice of the Spiritual or Ecclesiastical Courts*. London, 1685.

Cunnington, B. H., ed. *Records of the County of Wilts, being Extracts from the Quarter Sessions Great Rolls of the Seventeenth Century*. Devizes, 1932.

Duckett, George, ed. *Penal Laws and Test Act*. London, 1882.

Eachard, John. *The Grounds & Occasions of the Contempt of the Clergy and Religion enquired into*. London, 1670.

Eagle, F. K. and Younge, E. *A Collection of the Reports of Cases, the Statutes and Ecclesiastical Laws relating to Tithes*. London, 1826.

Ecton, J. *Liber valorum et decimarum*. London, 1711.

Firth, H. and Rait, R. S. *Acts and Ordinances of the Interregnum, 1642–1660*. London, 1911.

Foster, J. *Alumni Oxoniensis, Part I*. Oxford and London, 1888–91.

'Four Letters written by the Rev. George Millard, A.D. 1712–18', *WAM* 31 (June 1900)

Fowler, D. B. *The Practice of the Court of Exchequer upon Proceedings in Equity*. London, 1795.

Foxcroft, H. C., ed. *A Supplement to Burnet's History of My Own Time*. Oxford, 1902.

Freeman, Jane, ed. *The Commonplace Book of Sir Edward Bayntun of Bromham*, Wiltshire Record Society 43. Devizes, 1988.

Gibson, Edmund. *Directions Given to the Clergy of the Diocese of London in the Year 1724 . . .* London, 1749.

Hannah, Gavin, ed. *The Deserted Village: The Diary of an Oxfordshire Rector, James Newton, of Nuneham Courtenay 1736–86*. Stroud, 1992.

Herbert, George. *A Priest to the Temple, or, The Country Parson his Character*. London, 1632.

Legg, J. Wickham. *English Church Life from the Reformation to the Tractarian Movement*. London, 1914.

McClure, Edmund, ed. *A Chapter in English Church History: Being the Minutes of the Society for Promoting Christian Knowledge for the years 1698–1704*. London, 1888.

Matthews, A. G. *Calamy Revised*. Oxford, 1934.

   Walker Revised. Oxford, 1948.

'Netheravon petition against the vicar, 1681', transcr. C. R. Everitt, *WAM* 45 (June 1930): 84–6.

Nevill, Edmund. 'Marriage licences of Salisbury', *The Genealogist*, n.s., vols. 24–38.

Penny, Norman. 'Quakerism in Wiltshire', *Wiltshire Notes and Queries*, vols. 2–6.

A Poll for the Wiltshire Election of 1705. London, 1705.

Ransome, Mary, ed. *Wiltshire Returns to the Bishop's Visitation Queries of 1783*, Wiltshire Record Society 27. Devizes, 1971.

Salisbury Journal.

Second Report of the Commissioners . . . into the . . . Conduct of Public Worship . . ., House of Commons Parliamentary Papers, 1867–8.

Slatter, Doreen, ed. *The Diary of Thomas Naish*, Wiltshire Archaeological and Natural History Society Records Branch 20. Devizes, 1961.

Smith, John, of Market Lavington. *A Set of Services, Anthems & Psalm Tunes for Country Choirs*. London, [1748].

   Book the Second Containing Twelve Anthems and Twelve Psalm Tunes for Country Choirs all intirely new Composed. Lavington, [1751].

   Book the Third . . . . Lavington, 1755.

'The Society's MSS – Chiseldon and Draycot', *WAM* 30 (1898): 51–4.

The Spectator. Edited by Donald F. Bond. Oxford, 1965.

Talbot, William. *The Bishop of Sarum's Charge to the Clergy of his Diocese, at his Primary Visitation Anno. 1716.* London, 1717.

Turner, G. Lyon, ed. *Original Records of Early Nonconformity.* London, 1911–14.

Wesley, John. *The Journal of the Revd John Wesley, A.M.* London, 1909–16.

Whiteman, Anne, ed. *The Compton Census of 1676: A Critical Edition.* London, 1986.

Willis, Browne. *A Survey of the Cathedrals. . .* London, 1742.

Woodforde, James. *The Diary of a Country Parson 1758–1802.* Selected and edited by John Beresford. Oxford, 1978.

Woodward, Josiah. *An Account of the Rise and Progress of the Religious Societies.* 3rd edn, London, 1701.

SECONDARY SOURCES

Addy, J. *Sin and Society in the Seventeenth Century.* London and New York, 1989.

Allen, W. O. B. and McClure, Edmund. *Two Hundred Years: The History of the Society for Promoting Christian Knowledge, 1698–1898.* London, 1898.

Bahlman, Dudley W. R. *The Moral Revolution of 1688.* New Haven, 1957.

Ball, R. M. 'Tobias Eden, change and conflict in the Exchequer Office, 1672–1698'. *Journal of Legal History* 11 (1990): 70–89.

Beier, A. L., Cannadine, D. and Rosenheim, James M., eds. *The First Modern Society.* Cambridge, 1989.

Bennett, G. V. *The Tory Crisis in Church and State 1688–1730.* Oxford, 1975.

Best, G. F. A. *Temporal Pillars: Queen Anne's Bounty, the Ecclesiastical Commissioners, and the Church of England.* Cambridge, 1964.

Boulton, Jeremy. 'The limits of formal religion: administration of Holy Communion in late Elizabethan and early Stuart England'. *London Journal* 10 (1984): 135–54.

Brewer, John. *The Sinews of Power.* Cambridge, Mass., 1990.

Brooks, C. W. *Pettyfoggers and Vipers of the Commonwealth: The 'Lower Branch' of the Legal Profession in Early Modern England.* Cambridge, 1986.

Brown, Andrew D. *Popular Piety in Late Medieval England: The Diocese of Salisbury 1250–1550.* Oxford, 1995.

Brown, Callum G. 'Did urbanization secularize Britain?'. *Urban History Yearbook* (1988): 1–14.

Burke, Peter. *Popular Culture in Early Modern Europe.* New York, 1978.

Champion, J. A. I. *The Pillars of Priestcraft Shaken: The Church of England and its Enemies, 1660–1730.* Cambridge, 1992.

Chapman, Colin R. *Ecclesiastical Courts, their Officials and their Records.* Dursley, 1992.

Clark, J. C. D. 'England's ancien regime as a confessional state'. *Albion* 21 (1989): 450–74.

English Society 1688–1832: Ideology, Social Structure and Political Practice during the Ancient Regime. Cambridge, 1985.

Clay, Christopher. '"The Greed of Whig bishops"?: church landlords and their lessees 1660–1760'. *Past and Present* 87 (May 1980): 128–57.

Collinson, Patrick. 'The English conventicle'. In *Voluntary Religion*, pp. 223–59. Edited by W. J. Sheils and Diana Wood. Studies in Church History 23. Oxford, 1986.

Corfield, Penelope J. *Power and the Professions in Britain 1700–1850.* London and New York, 1995.

Craig, A. G. 'The movement for the reformation of manners'. Unpublished Ph.D. thesis, Edinburgh University, 1980.

Cressy, David. *Birth, Marriage, and Death: Ritual, Religion, and the Life-Cycle in Tudor and Stuart England*. Oxford, 1997.

Currie, R., Gilbert, A. and Horsley, L. *Churches and Churchgoers: Patterns of Church Growth in the British Isles since 1700*. Oxford, 1977.

Davies, Horton. *Worship and Theology in England*, vol. II, *From Andrews to Baxter and Fox, 1603–1690*. Princeton, 1975.

Duffy, E. *The Stripping of the Altars*. New Haven and London, 1992.

Durston, C. and Eales, J., eds. *The Culture of English Puritanism, 1560–1700*. London, 1996.

Evans, E. J. '"Our faithful testimony": the Society of Friends and tithe payments, 1690–1730'. *Journal of the Friends' Historical Society* 52 (1969): 106–21.

  'A history of the tithe system in England, 1690–1850, with special reference to Staffordshire'. Unpublished Ph.D. thesis, Warwick University, 1970.

  'Tithing customs and disputes: the evidence of glebe terriers, 1698–1850'. *Agricultural History Review* 18 (1970): 17–35.

  'Some reasons for the growth of English rural anti-clericalism *c*.1750–*c*.1830'. *Past and Present* 66 (February 1975): 84–109.

  The Contentious Tithe: The Tithe Problem and English Agriculture, 1750–1850. London, 1976.

  'The Anglican clergy of northern England'. In *Britain in the First Age of Party 1680–1750*, pp. 221–40. Edited by C. Jones. London and Ronceverte, 1987.

Every, George. *The High Church Party 1688–1718*. London, 1956.

Fincham, Kenneth, ed. *The Early Stuart Church, 1603–1642*. London, 1993.

Finlayson, M. G. *Historians, Puritanism and the English Revolution: The Religious Factor in English Politics before and after the Interregnum*. Toronto and London, 1983.

Gammon, Vic. '"Babylonian performances": the rise and suppression of popular church music, 1660–1870'. In *Popular Culture and Class Conflict 1590–1914: Explorations in the History of Labour and Leisure*, pp. 62–88. Edited by Eileen Yeo and Stephen Yeo. Brighton, Sussex, 1981.

Gilbert, Alan D. *Religion and Society in Industrial England: Church, Chapel and Social Change, 1740–1914*. London and New York, 1976.

Ginter, Donald E. 'Measuring the decline of the small landowner'. In *Land, Labour and Agriculture, 1700–1920*, pp. 27–47. Edited by B. A. Holderness and M. Turner. London and Rio Grande, 1991.

Gittings, Clare. *Death, Burial and the Individual in Early Modern England*. London and Sydney, 1984.

Goldie, Mark. 'Priestcraft and the birth of Whiggism'. In *Political Discourse in Early Modern Britain*, pp. 209–31. Edited by Nicholas Phillipson and Quentin Skinner. Cambridge, 1993.

Green, I. M. *The Re-establishment of the Church of England 1660–1663*. Oxford, 1978.

  'The persecution of "scandalous" and "malignant" parish clergy during the English Civil War'. *English Historical Review* 94 (July 1979): 507–31.

Griffiths, Paul, Fox, Adam, and Hindle, Steve, eds. *The Experience of Authority in Early Modern England*. Houndmills, 1996.

Haigh, Christopher, ed. *The English Reformation Revised*. Cambridge, 1987.

Harris, Tim, ed. *Popular Culture in England, c. 1500–1850*. London, 1995.

Harris, Tim, Seaward, Paul and Goldie, Mark, eds. *The Politics of Religion in Restoration England*. Oxford, 1990.

Hay, Douglas et al. *Albion's Fatal Tree: Crime and Society in Eighteenth-Century England*. New York, 1975.

Heath, P. *The English Clergy on the Eve of the Reformation*. London and Toronto, 1969.

Heeney, B. *A Different Kind of Gentleman: Parish Clergy as Professional Men in Early and Mid-Victorian England*. Hamden, Conn., 1976.

Hempton, David. *The Religion of the People: Methodism and Popular Religion c. 1750–1900*. London and New York, 1996.

Henning, Basil D., ed. *House of Commons 1660–1690*. London, 1983.

Hill, Christopher. *Economic Problems of the Church from Archbishop Whitgift to the Long Parliament*. Oxford, 1956.

Society and Puritanism in Pre-Revolutionary England. 2nd edn. New York, 1967.

Hirschberg, D. R. 'The government and church patronage in England, 1660–1760'. *Journal of British Studies* 20 (1980): 109–39.

Holmes, G. *Augustan England: Professions, State and Society, 1680–1730*. London, 1982.

Horle, Craig W. *The Quakers and the English Legal System 1660–1688*. Philadelphia, 1988.

Horwitz, Henry. *Chancery Equity Records and Proceedings, 1600–1800*. PRO Handbook 27, 1995.

Horwitz, Henry and Moreton, Charles. *Samples of Chancery Pleadings and Suits: 1627, 1685, 1735, and 1785*. List and Index Society, 1995.

Horwitz, Henry and Polden, Patrick. 'Continuity or change in the Court of Chancery in the seventeenth and eighteenth centuries?'. *Journal of British Studies* 35 (1996): 24–57.

Houlbrooke, Ralph. *Church Courts and the People during the English Reformation*. Oxford, 1979.

ed. *Death, Ritual, and Bereavement*. London and New York, 1989.

Hunt, Norman C. *Two Early Political Associations: The Quakers and the Dissenting Deputies in the Age of Sir Robert Walpole*. Oxford, 1961.

Hutton, Ronald. *The Rise and Fall of Merry England: The Ritual Year 1400–1700*. Oxford, 1994.

Hylson-Smith, Kenneth. *The Churches in England from Elizabeth I to Elizabeth II*, vol. II, *1689–1833*. London, 1997.

Ingram, Martin. 'Religion, communities and moral discipline in late sixteenth and early seventeenth century England: case studies'. In *Religion and Society in Early Modern Europe, 1500–1800*, pp. 177–93. Edited by Kaspar von Greyerz. London, 1984.

Church Courts, Sex and Marriage in England, 1570–1640. Cambridge, 1987.

Isaacs, Tina. 'The Anglican hierarchy and the reformation of manners 1688–1738'. *Journal of Ecclesiastical History* 33 (1982): 391–411.

Jacob, W. M. *Lay People and Religion in the Early Eighteenth Century*. Cambridge, 1996.

James, Margaret. 'The political importance of the tithes controversy in the English Revolution, 1640–60'. *History* 26 (June 1941): 1–18.

Johnson, H. Diack and Fiske, Roger. *Music in Britain: The Eighteenth Century*. Oxford, 1990.

Jones, M. G. *The Charity School Movement: A Study of Eighteenth Century Puritanism in Action*. Cambridge, 1938.

Kinnear, Mary. 'The correction court in the diocese of Carlisle, 1704–1756'. *Church History* 59 (1990): 191–206.

Lancaster, Henry. 'Nonconformity and Anglican dissent in Restoration Wiltshire, 1660–1689'. Unpublished Ph.D. thesis, Bristol University, 1995.

Landau, Norma. *The Justices of the Peace, 1679–1760*. Berkeley, 1984.

Langford, Paul. *Public Life and the Propertied Englishman 1689–1798*. Oxford, 1991.

McClatchey, Diana. *Oxfordshire Clergy, 1777–1869: A Study of the Established Church and of the Role of its Clergy in Local Society*. Oxford, 1960.

McManners, John. *Death and the Enlightenment: Changing Attitudes to Death among Christians and Unbelievers in Eighteenth-Century France.* Oxford, 1981.

Maltby, Judith. '"By this book": parishioners, the Prayer Book and the Established Church'. In *The Early Stuart Church, 1603–1642*, pp. 115–37. Edited by Kenneth Fincham. Houndmills, 1993.

Prayer Book and People in Elizabethan and Early Stuart England. Cambridge, 1998.

Marchant, Roland A. *The Church under the Law: Justice, Administration and Discipline in the Diocese of York 1560–1640.* Cambridge, 1969.

Mather, F. C. 'Georgian churchmanship reconsidered: some variations in Anglican public worship 1714–1830'. *Journal of Ecclesiastical History* 36 (April 1985).

Meldrum, Tim. 'A women's court in London: defamation at the bishop of London's consistory court, 1700–1745'. *London Journal* 19 (1994): 1–20.

Miller, John. *Religion in the Popular Prints, 1600–1832.* Cambridge, 1985.

Morgan, Nicholas. *Lancashire Quakers and the Establishment 1660–1730.* Halifax, 1993.

Morrill, John. 'The Church in England 1642–9'. In *Reactions to the English Civil War*, pp. 89–114. Edited by John Morrill. London and Basingstoke, 1982.

Munsche, P. B. 'The game laws in Wiltshire 1750–1800'. In *Crime in England, 1550–1800*, pp. 210–28. Edited by J. S. Cockburn. Princeton, 1977.

Newby, Howard. 'The deferential dialectic'. *Comparative Studies in Society and History* 17 (1975): 139–64.

O'Day, Rosemary. *The English Clergy: The Emergence and Consolidation of a Profession 1558–1642.* Leicester, 1979.

Education and Society, 1500–1800: The Social Foundations of Education in Early Modern Britain. London and New York, 1982.

Obelkevich, James. *Religion and Rural Society: South Lindsey, 1825–1875.* Oxford, 1976.

Outhwaite, R. B., ed. *Marriage and Society: Studies in the Social History of Marriage.* New York, 1981.

Clandestine Marriage in England, 1500–1850. London, 1995.

Packer, John W. *The Transformation of Anglicanism, 1643–1660.* Manchester, 1989.

Perkin, Harold. *The Origins of Modern English Society 1780–1880.* London, 1969.

Phillips, John A. 'The social calculus: deference and defiance in later Georgian England'. *Albion* 21 (1989): 426–49.

Pocock, J. G. A. 'The classical theory of deference'. *American Historical Review* 81 (1976): 516–23.

Prest, Wilfred R. *The Inns of Court under Elizabeth I and the Early Stuarts, 1590–1640.* London, 1972.

Pruett, John H. *The Parish Clergy under the Later Stuarts: The Leicestershire Experience.* Urbana, 1978.

Ramsbottom, John D. 'Presbyterians and "partial conformity" in the Restoration Church of England'. *Journal of Ecclesiastical History* 43 (1992): 249–70.

Reay, Barry. 'Popular hostility towards Quakers in mid-seventeenth-century England'. *Social History* 5 (October 1980): 387–407.

Popular Cultures in England 1550–1750. London and New York, 1998.

Rollinson, David. 'Property, ideology and popular culture in a Gloucestershire village 1660–1740'. *Past and Present* 93 (1981): 70–97.

Rule, John. 'Methodism, popular beliefs and village culture in Cornwall, 1800–50'. In *Popular Culture and Custom in Nineteenth-Century England*, pp. 48–70. Edited by Robert D. Storch. London, 1982.

Albion's People: English Society, 1714–1815. London, 1992.

Rupp, Gordon. *Religion in England 1688–1791.* Oxford, 1986.

Salter, J. L. 'Warwickshire clergy, 1660–1714'. Unpublished Ph.D. thesis, University of Birmingham, 1975.

Sedgwick, Romney, ed. *The House of Commons, 1715–1754.* London, 1970.

Sharpe, J. A. *Crime in Early Modern England, 1550–1750.* London, 1984.

  'Scandalous and malignant priests in Essex: the impact of grassroots puritanism'. In *Politics and People in Revolutionary England*, pp. 253–73. Edited by C. Jones, M. Newitt and Stephen Roberts. Oxford, 1986.

Shaw, W. A. *A History of the English Church during the Civil Wars and under the Commonwealth 1640–1660.* London, 1900.

Shoemaker, R. B. *Prosecution and Punishment: Petty Crime and the Law in London and Rural Middlesex.* Cambridge, 1991.

Smith, Gregory Charles. '"The knowing multitude": popular culture and the evangelical revival in Wiltshire, 1739–1850'. Unpublished Ph.D. thesis, University of Toronto, 1992.

Smith, M. G. *Pastoral Discipline and the Church Courts: The Hexham Court 1680–1730.* Borthwick Papers 62. York, 1982.

Smith, Mark. *Religion in Industrial Society: Oldham and Saddleworth 1740–1865.* Oxford, 1994.

Snell, K. D. M. 'Deferential bitterness: the social outlook of the rural proletariat in eighteenth- and nineteenth-century England and Wales'. In *Social Orders and Social Classes in Europe since 1500: Studies in Social Stratification*, pp. 158–84. Edited by M. L. Bush. London, 1992.

Sommerville, C. John. 'The destruction of religious culture in pre-industrial England'. *Journal of Religious History* 15 (June 1988): 76–93.

  The Secularization of Early Modern England: From Religious Culture to Religious Faith. New York and Oxford, 1992.

Spaeth, Donald Arragon. 'Parsons and parishioners: lay-clerical conflict and popular piety in Wiltshire villages, 1660–1740'. Unpublished Ph.D. thesis, Brown University, 1985.

Spufford, Margaret. *Contrasting Communities: English Villagers in the Sixteenth and Seventeenth Centuries.* London and New York, 1974.

  'Puritanism and social control?'. In *Order and Disorder in Early Modern England*, pp. 41–57. Edited by A. J. Fletcher and J. Stevenson. Cambridge, 1985.

Spurr, John. *The Restoration Church of England, 1646–1689.* New Haven and London, 1991.

Stevenson, Janet H. 'Will a man rob God? . . . Some aspects of disputed tithe payment in Draycot Foliat, 1664–1702'. *Wiltshire Archaeological and Natural History Society Magazine* 72/3 (1980): 149–52.

Stewart, P. *Diocese of Salisbury: Guide to the Records of the Bishop . . .* n.p., 1973.

Stone, Lawrence. *Uncertain Lives and Broken Lives: Marriage and Divorce in England, 1660–1857.* Oxford and New York, 1995.

Sutherland, L. S. and Mitchell, L. G. *History of the University of Oxford*, vol. V, *The Eighteenth-Century.* Oxford, 1986.

Sykes, Norman. *Church and State in England in the XVIIIth Century.* Cambridge, 1934.

  From Sheldon to Secker: Aspects of English Church History, 1660–1768. Cambridge, 1959.

Taylor, Stephen. 'Sir Robert Walpole, the Church of England, and the Quakers Tithe Bill of 1736'. *Historical Journal* 28 (1985): 51–77.

  'Church and state in England in the mid-eighteenth century: the Newcastle years 1742–1762'. Unpublished Ph.D. thesis, Cambridge University, 1987.

Temperley, Nicholas. *The Music of the English Parish Church*. 2 vols. Cambridge, 1979.

Thirsk, Joan. 'Seventeenth-century agriculture and social change'. In *Seventeenth Century England: Society in an Age of Revolution*, pp. 72–109. Edited by Paul S. Seaver. New York, 1976.

ed. *Agrarian History of England and Wales*, vol. V.2. Cambridge, 1985.

Thomas, Keith V. *Religion and the Decline of Magic*. New York, 1971.

Thompson, E. P. 'Patrician society, plebeian culture'. *Journal of Social History* 7 (Summer 1974): 382–405.

Customs in Common. London, 1991.

Underdown, D. E. *Revel, Riot, and Rebellion: Popular Politics and Culture in England 1603–1660*. Oxford, 1985.

Valenze, Deborah M. *Prophetic Sons and Daughters: Female Preaching and Popular Religion in Industrial England*. Princeton, 1985.

Victoria County History of the Counties of England: *A History of Wiltshire*.

Virgin, Peter. *The Church in an Age of Negligence: Ecclesiastical Structure and Problems of Church Reform 1700–1840*. Cambridge, 1989.

Walsh, J. 'Methodism and the mob in the eighteenth century'. In *Popular Belief and Practice*, pp. 213–27. Edited by G. J. Cuming and D. Baker. Studies in Church History 8. Cambridge, 1972.

'Religious societies: Methodist and evangelical 1738–1800'. In *Voluntary Religion*, pp. 279–302. Edited by W. J. Sheils and Diana Wood. Studies in Church History 23. Oxford, 1986.

Walsh, J., Haydon, C. and Taylor, S., eds. *The Church of England, c.1689–c.1833: From Toleration to Tractarianism*. Cambridge, 1993.

Watt, Tessa. *Cheap Print and Popular Piety 1550–1640*. Cambridge, 1991.

Watts, Michael R. *The Dissenters*, vol. 1, *From the Reformation to the French Revolution*. Oxford, 1978.

Weber, William. *The Rise of Musical Classics in Eighteenth-Century England*. Oxford, 1992.

Whiteman, Anne. 'The re-establishment of the Church of England, 1660–3'. *Transactions of the Royal Historical Society* 5th ser., 5 (1955): 111–37.

Whiteman, E. A. O. 'The episcopate of Dr. Seth Ward, bishop of Exeter (1662 to 1667) and Salisbury (1667–1688/9) with special reference to the ecclesiastical problems of his time'. Unpublished D.Phil. thesis, Oxford University, 1951.

Williams, J. Anthony. *Catholic Recusancy in Wiltshire, 1660–1791*. Catholic Record Society, 1968.

Wrightson, Keith. 'The puritan reformation of manners with special reference to the counties of Lancashire and Essex 1640–1660'. Unpublished Ph.D. dissertation, Cambridge University, 1973.

English Society 1580–1680. New Brunswick, N.J., 1982.

Wrightson, Keith and Levine, David. *Poverty and Piety in an English Village: Terling, 1525–1700*. New York, 1979.

Wunderli, R. M. *London Church Courts and Society on the Eve of the Reformation*. Cambridge, Mass., 1981.

INDEX

Cambridge Studies in Early Modern British History

Titles in the series

* *Also published as a paperback*

Gender

Consumption & world of goods?

Narrative & history / micro histories

Violence & Civility 1500-1800
• violent crime < homicide / assault
• domestic violence
• w-craft
• military violence + warfare
• colonial expansn
• ritual & violence
    (NZD - rites of violence)
• dueling
• bloodsports / sport
• riot & rebellion
• executⁿ & punishment

• courtesy & civility
• politeness
• honour